# Public Relations Cases

07

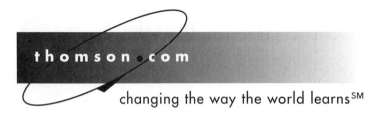

# Public Relations Cases

## FOURTH EDITION

**Jerry A. Hendrix**

American University

Wadsworth Publishing Company

I(T)P® An International Thomson Publishing Company

Belmont, CA • Albany, NY • Bonn • Boston • Cincinnati • Detroit • Johannesburg
London • Madrid • Melbourne • Mexico City • New York • Paris • Singapore
Tokyo • Toronto • Washington

Communications Editor: Randall Adams
Assistant Editor: Michael Gillespie
Editorial Assistant: Megan Gilbert
Project Editor: Dianne Jensis
Senior Print Buyer: Barbara Britton
Marketing Manager: Mike Dew
Production Editor: Hal Lockwood, Penmarin Books
Interior and Cover Designer: Juan Vargas, Vargas Williams Design
Cover Image: Nick Gunderson. © Tony Stone Images, Inc.
Copy Editor: Hal Lockwood
Compositor: G&S Typesetters
Printer: Malloy Lithographing, Inc.

Printed in the United States of America

2  3  4  5  6  7  8  9  10—03  02  01  00  99  98

For more information, contact Wadsworth Publishing Company, 10 Davis Drive, Belmont, CA 94002, or electronically at http://www.thomson.com/wadsworth.html

International Thomson Publishing Europe
Berkshire House 168-173
High Holborn
London, WC1V 7AA, England

International Thomson Editores
Campos Eliseos 385, Piso 7
Col. Polanco
11560 México D.F. México

Thomas Nelson Australia
102 Dodds Street
South Melbourne 3205
Victoria, Australia

International Thomson Publishing Asia
221 Henderson Road
#05-10 Henderson Building
Singapore 0315

Nelson Canada
1120 Birchmount Road
Scarborough, Ontario
Canada M1K 5G4

International Thomson Publishing Japan
Hirakawacho Kyowa Building, 3F
2-2-1 Hirakawacho
Chiyoda-ku, Tokyo 102, Japan

International Thomson Publishing GmbH
Königswinterer Strasse 418
53227 Bonn, Germany

International Thomson Publishing Southern Africa
Building 18, Constantia Park
240 Old Pretoria Road
Halfway House, 1685 South Africa

**Library of Congress Cataloging-in-Publication Data**

Hendrix, Jerry A.
    Public relations cases / Jerry A. Hendrix.—4th ed.
        p.  cm.
    Includes bibliographical references and index.
    ISBN 0-534-52236-X
    1. Public relations—United States—Case studies.   2. Publicity—
Case studies.   I. Title.
HM263.H437   1997
659.2—dc21                                                        97-19270

# CONTENTS

**Chapter 4**

# Internal Communications   113

**Chapter 5**

# Community Relations   170

## Chapter 6

# Public Affairs and Government Relations   215

## Chapter 7

# Investor and Financial Relations   259

## Chapter 8

# Consumer Relations   289

# Appendixes   411

# PREFACE

This fourth edition is the most extensively revised of all the editions of this book. It includes a completely new chapter on international public relations, an important area for contemporary practitioners. Of the 27 cases in the book, 25 are completely new. One of the two carryovers from the previous edition, the U.S. Chamber of Commerce case, was revised by its author and includes new display material. The other carryover is the classic ACX Technologies investor relations case.

In preparing this edition, I continue to believe that readers should encounter a clear set of guiding public relations principles accompanied by cases that generally illustrate those principles in a positive light and thus serve as models of effective management and practice. To add some balance, however, two of the cases illustrate spectacular public relations failures. The first is the monumental Clinton health care plan, which died a humiliating death in the U.S. Congress. The other chronicles the struggle between a modern-day Goliath, the Walt Disney Company, and a victorious contemporary David, the Piedmont Environmental Council, a determined citizens group that waged a Third Battle of Manassas (also known as Bull Run) in the rolling hills of northern Virginia to keep out an unwanted theme park.

The book is divided into three sections. In Part I, I begin the introductory chapter with a philosophy I have held for a long time—that the best public relations is characterized by interaction, or better still, interactive participation between or among sources and receivers of communication. This, in turn, is based on the underlying premise that public relations is mostly persuasion. Some years ago communication researchers discovered that the most effective means of persuasion is *self*-persuasion. Audience involvement thus becomes a crucial ingredient of successful public relations.

The opening chapter also includes a new section on ethics in public relations. As in previous editions, I have included the PRSA Code of Professional Standards in Appendix III, but I also include some additional dimensions of ethics in Chapter 1.

In Chapter 2 I retain my process model, which involves initial research, the setting of objectives, programming, and evaluation. (The elements of this process model form a convenient mnemonic device, the acronym ROPE.) This model focuses special attention on the significance of objectives and their arrangement in a hierarchical order of output and impact functions. Another feature of this process model, reflecting my own training and background in speech communication, is special emphasis on the role of interpersonal communication, including speeches, speakers bureaus, small-group and one-on-one formats, and nonverbal aspects of communication. In a word, my process model is interactive.

Part II consists of audience-centered applications of the process, with accompanying illustrative cases. The audience-centered forms of public relations included are media relations, employee and member relations, community relations, public affairs and government relations, investor relations, consumer relations, international public relations (a new chapter), and relations with special publics. Most of the cases were winners in the prestigious Silver Anvil Awards contest, conducted annually by the Public Relations Society of America. They therefore constitute some of the finest examples of public relations practices available. They also follow the prescribed Silver Anvil entry format, which is somewhat different from the format of my ROPE model. The major difference is that I set objectives apart as a separate category, and the Silver Anvil format does not. My programming phase includes planning and communication (execution), and both Silver Anvil and ROPE begin and end with research and evaluation. Thus, the two models have a difference only in format, not substance.

Part III includes both theory and illustrative cases for emergency or crisis public relations. This field of PR is not oriented to a particular audience, so I have set it apart in a separate section of the book.

Finally, the appendixes contain questions for class discussion and analysis of the cases, exercises, or case problems for each form of public relations presented, and the PRSA Code of Professional Standards, guidelines for the ethical practice of public relations.

Since more than 90 percent of the cases in this fourth edition are new, there are many public relations practitioners who helped me and granted permission to use their cases. I hope they will accept my gratitude and understand that space does not permit a list of their names.

I want to thank former American University graduate fellows Ahu Lotifoglu, Maria Krouskal, Tanya Accone, and Catherine Daley for their assistance with exercises and information in the *Instructor's Manual*.

I am especially grateful to my colleague in the American University School of Communication, Leonard Steinhorn, who contributed the important essays on the Clinton health care plan and the Disney efforts to build a new theme park in northern Virginia. Professor Steinhorn also authored the new *Instructor's Manual* and produced the video to accompany the fourth edition. Instructors who adopt the book can obtain both the *Instructor's Manual* and the videocassette on request from the publisher.

As with previous editions, I am indebted to Sanford Ungar, Dean of the American University School of Communication, for his support in reducing my teaching load and for financial assistance.

Finally, I gratefully acknowledge the following reviewers, whose constructive comments helped in the development of this fourth edition: E. Joseph Broussard, Nicholls State University; E. W. Brody, University of Memphis; David W. Guth, University of Kansas; Tracey M. Harrison, Mississippi College; Barbara J. DeSanto, Texas Tech University; and Ronda Beaman, Northern Arizona University.

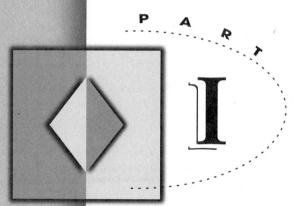

# Solving Public Relations Problems

# 1

# Public Relations in Action

ONE OF THE BEST WAYS TO LEARN ABOUT PUBLIC relations is through the study of contemporary examples of its practice. Such case studies can bring public relations to life in a way that theoretical textbooks and classroom lectures cannot. Here we will first examine the nature of public relations through its definition and a process model. Then we will look at various forms of public relations along with several cases to illustrate each form.

One way of defining public relations has been simply to invert the term so it becomes "relations with publics." An improved modification of this definition is "*interrelationships* with publics." This better reflects the nature of contemporary public relations as an *interactive* form of communication in which the

targeted audiences yield information to the organization through its research efforts and often *participate*
in the public relations programming itself. This interactive or mutual dimension of public relations is seen
in the comprehensive description adopted by the Public Relations Society of America in 1982:

| | |
|---|---|
| Exhibit 1-a | PRSA's Official Statement on Public Relations* |

Public relations helps our complex, pluralistic society to reach decisions
and function more effectively by contributing to mutual understanding
among groups and institutions. It serves to bring private and public
policies into harmony.

Public relations serves a wide variety of institutions in society such
as businesses, trade unions, government agencies, voluntary associations, foundations, hospitals, and educational and religious institutions.
To achieve their goals, these institutions must develop effective relationships with many different audiences or publics such as employees, members, customers, local communities, shareholders, and other institutions, and with society at large.

The managements of institutions need to understand the attitudes
and values of their publics in order to achieve institutional goals. The
goals themselves are shaped by the external environment. The public
relations practitioner acts as a counselor to management, and as a me-
diator, helping to translate private aims into reasonable, publicly acceptable policy and action.

As a management function, public relations encompasses the
following:

- Anticipating, analyzing, and interpreting public opinion, attitudes
  and issues that might impact, for good or ill, the operations and
  plans of the organization.
- Counseling management at all levels in the organization with regard to policy decisions, courses of action and communication, taking into account their public ramifications and the organization's
  social or citizenship responsibilities.
- Researching, conducting, and evaluating, on a continuing basis,
  programs of action and communication to achieve informed public

*Formally adopted by the PRSA Assembly on November 6, 1982. Reprinted
courtesy PRSA.

understanding necessary to the success of an organization's aims. These may include marketing, financial, fund raising, employee, community or government relations, and other programs.

- Planning and implementing the organization's efforts to influence or change public policy.
- Setting objectives, planning, budgeting, recruiting and training staff, developing facilities—in short, *managing* the resources needed to perform all of the above.
- Examples of the knowledge that may be required in the professional practice of public relations include communication arts, psychology, social psychology, sociology, political science, economics, and the principles of management and ethics. Technical knowledge and skills are required for opinion research, public issues analysis, media relations, direct mail, institutional advertising, publications, film/video productions, special events, speeches, and presentations.

In helping to define and implement policy, the public relations practitioner utilizes a variety of professional communication skills and plays an integrative role both within the organization and between the organization and the external environment.

# PROCESS

The public relations process is a method for solving problems. It has four phases: research, objectives, programming, and evaluation. Each element may be modified by the demands of different audiences or publics, including employees, members, customers, local communities, shareholders, and, usually, the news media.

The *research* phase of the process involves identifying and learning about three key elements: (1) a *client* or institution that has (2) a *problem* or potential problem to be solved, which involves (3) one or more of its *audiences,* or publics.

The second phase of the public relations process involves the setting of *objectives* for a program to solve the problem. These objectives may include the kind of influence the client hopes to exert with the audiences, such as informing them or modifying their attitudes or behaviors. The objectives may also include statements about the program itself, such as its composition or how it will operate.

The third phase of the process consists of planning and executing a *program* to accomplish the objectives. The program comprises a central theme, messages, and various forms of communication aimed at reaching the audiences.

Finally, *evaluation,* as defined in this process, consists of two parts. First, it includes an ongoing procedure of program monitoring and adjustment. Second, evaluation refers back specifically to the objectives that were set in the second phase of the process and examines the practitioner's degree of success in achieving them.

# CASES

The illustrations of this process in action—the cases—are grouped in this text according to the various audiences that public relations practitioners reach. Each audience calls for some modifications in the overall four-step process, and the cases illustrate the modified process in action.

Cases are presented to illustrate relations with the media, with internal audiences, with the community, with the government, with investors, with consumers, with international audiences, and with special groups.

Effective public relations cases serve as models for students and practitioners alike. They enhance public relations theory, making it come alive with illustrations and examples of the PR process in action. Moreover, audience-centered cases exemplify the constraints involved in conducting research, setting objectives, designing and executing a program, and evaluating what has been done. In sum, cases, especially audience-centered cases, effectively illustrate public relations principles and management and test theoretical applications in real situations and environments.

# ETHICS

The Code of Professional Standards for the Practice of Public Relations, adopted by the Public Relations Society of America Assembly in 1988, pledges that PRSA members will conduct themselves "professionally, with truth, accuracy, fairness, and responsibility to the public."

This commitment to ethical practices is intended to counter the image of public relations practitioners as "hired guns" who will say or do whatever it takes to accomplish the goals of their clients. There is some basis for this negative public perception of the profession. The following is a discussion of some of the practices that have earned public relations a sometimes-less-than-savory reputation.

On a continuum going from bad to worse we might begin with the relatively innocuous practice of *lowballing*. This consists of downplaying expectations for a program or project that may not be especially successful in its outcome. The mass media frequently accuse the White House of "lowballing" a presidential visit abroad, a peace initiative in some part of the world, or some other effort that may not yield much tangible results.

Closely related to lowballing is the ubiquitous *spin* that is used by governmental and corporate public relations practitioners to make their programs look good. The "spin" actually consists of the one-sided use of facts or data to create a desired impression. These practitioners are often referred to by the mass media as *spin doctors*. By selectively using only positive aspects of a program or a political campaign, practitioners can portray their clients' activities in a favorable light. Conversely, the endeavors of an opponent may be selectively portrayed only in the negative.

Next we might examine six types of *distortion* sometimes found in the practice of public relations. The first of these is commonly called *hype*. Hype is the use of hyperbole or magnification, sometimes referred to as the "blowing out of proportion" of the attributes of a person, event, or product. The mass media are fond of portraying various criminal acts as "the crime of the century." Advertising constantly uses hype in its exaggerated claims for products and services, and public relations practitioners have been known to "stretch the truth" about clients and their programs.

A second type of distortion is *minimizing,* the exact opposite of hype. Sometimes practitioners will play down the seriousness of a failure or the negative aspects of a product or other problems experienced by a client.

A third type of frequently used distortion is *overgeneralization,* or drawing sweeping conclusions based on one isolated case or example. If a candidate for the presidential nomination of a political party loses the New Hampshire primary, for example, the mass media, along with the candidate's opposition, usually conclude that the nomination is lost, based on the results of that one primary election. Similarly, singular successes have been used to draw sweeping positive conclusions. One case study should never be the sole basis for such generalizations.

*Categorization* is a fourth type of distortion sometimes found in the practice of public relations. An example of categorization may involve the portrayal of a person, event, or product as "good" or "bad" with no middle ground or shades of gray. Other frequently used categories include "successful," "unsuccessful," "useful," "useless," and the like.

Closely related to categorization is the practice of *labeling*. An individual or program may be labeled either a "winner" or a "loser," often on the basis of sketchy or nonexistent evidence. History is replete with the use of such labels as "witch," "communist," "limousine liberal," and "right wing conservative." The list could go on endlessly.

A final form of distortion may be called *image transfer*. This involves the deliberate shifting of image from one person, event, or product to another, but dissimilar, person, event, or product. Such advertising techniques as the identification of a product with an attractive or sexy model is perhaps the most frequent use of image transfer. Public relations practitioners also seek to transfer the high-credibility images of popular paid spokespersons to low-credibility or unknown programs, causes, or events.

In addition to lowballing, spinning, and a variety of distortions, we should consider the even more offensive practices of using outright *lies* and *coverups*. One example of these practices is the manufacturer that knows its product is defective and potentially dangerous. Instead of making this information public, the company blames accidents on improper consumer use and handles resulting litigation on a case-by-case basis. These case-by-case settlements are usually substantially less expensive than staging a product recall. Meanwhile, the company's public relations office is busy denying product fault, issuing statements blaming the consumer. In regard to coverups the defining event *that has become generic* in its field was the Watergate affair, a major turning point in American political history and the coverup by which all subsequent coverups have been measured.

This is by no means and exhaustive list of unethical public relations practices. The PRSA Code of Professional Standards cites other activities such as corruption of communication channels, guaranteeing results beyond the practitioner's control, and the like. For an understanding of the ethical practice of public relations, the student of public relations should carefully study the Code of Professional Standards in Appendix III, along with the unethical practices discussed here.

In the public relations workplace, the best argument for ethical practices is that they are "good business." The positive side is that the company or organization can point with pride to its ethical practices. The negative side is that, if an organization or client is caught by the ubiquitous mass media in an unethical practice, this will become a headline news story and perhaps blot out all previous positive accomplishments. This study of applied ethics should therefore become an overriding concern in the education of public relations practitioners.

# THE OVERALL PLAN
# OF THIS BOOK

Part I introduces you to public relations, with special emphasis on the process outlined above. The elements of this process are eclectic, but the arrangement of those elements form the acronym ROPE (research, objectives, programming, evaluation). A major feature is a new emphasis on and a new way of classifying public relations objectives. Objectives are viewed as the central and guiding element in the process, and they are arranged in a hierarchical order.

Another feature of this public relations process, consistent with its interactive nature, is a heightened emphasis on interpersonal interaction as a form of controlled communication. The importance of speeches and speakers bureaus as methods of public relations communication is recognized, but this book also advocates the extensive use of small-group and dyadic (one-on-one) interpersonal formats, along with a treatment of nonverbal communication. A recurring theme is that in truly effective communication there can be no substitute for direct interaction.

Part II explores how public relations reaches major audiences. It looks at media relations; internal communication, including employee and member relations; community relations; public affairs, or government relations; investor and financial relations; consumer relations; international public relations; and relations with special publics. Following a conceptual treatment of each form of relations are several example cases. Most of these illustrative cases have won Silver Anvil Awards from the PRSA. As such, they represent the very best among models of public relations.

Part III concentrates on emergency public relations, an important area in contemporary practice. Both students and professionals need to be reminded of the need to study crisis PR procedures. Unlike such audience-centered forms as media relations or community relations, emergency PR is an area in which no one specializes. Yet all practitioners need to be prepared for it.

Finally, the appendixes include the most recent PRSA Code of Professional Standards and its various interpretations, along with exercises for each form of public relations discussed.

# GENERAL PUBLIC RELATIONS READINGS

Aronoff, Craig, and Otis W. Baskin. *Public Relations: Profession and Practice,* 3rd ed. Dubuque, IA: Wm. C. Brown, 1992.

Brody, E. W., ed. *New Technology and Public Relations.* Sarasota, FL: Institute for Public Relations Research and Education, 1991.

Center, Allen H., and Patrick Jackson. *Public Relations Practice: Managerial Case Studies and Practice,* 5th ed. Englewood Cliffs, NJ: Prentice-Hall, 1995.

Cutlip, Scott M., Allen H. Center, and Glen M. Broom. *Effective Public Relations,* 7th ed. Englewood Cliffs, NJ: Prentice-Hall, 1994.

Grunig, James E., ed. *Excellence in Public Relations and Communication Management.* Hillsdale, NJ: Erlbaum, 1992.

Hiebert, Ray Eldon, ed. *Precision Public Relations.* New York: Longman, 1988.

Hunt, Todd, and James E. Grunig. *Public Relations Techniques.* Fort Worth, TX: Harcourt Brace, 1994.

Lesly, Philip, ed. *Lesly's Handbook of Public Relations and Communications,* 4th ed. New York: Amacom, 1991.

Marlow, Eugene. *Electronic Public Relations*. Belmont, CA: Wadsworth, 1996.

Nager, Norman R., and Richard H. Truitt. *Strategic Public Relations Counseling: Models from the Counselors Academy*. New York: Longman, 1987.

Newsom, Doug, Judy VanSlyke Turk, and Dean Kruckeberg. *This Is PR: The Realities of Public Relations*, 6th ed. Belmont, CA: Wadsworth, 1996.

Seitel, Fraser P. *The Practice of Public Relations*, 6th ed. Englewood Cliffs, NJ: Prentice-Hall, 1995.

Simon, Raymond, and Frank W. Wylie. *Cases in Public Relations Management*, 4th ed. Lincolnwood, IL: NTC Business Books, 1994.

Wilcox, Dennis L., Phillip H. Ault, and Warren K. Agee. *Public Relations: Strategies and Tactics*, 4th ed. New York: HarperCollins, 1995.

———, and Lawrence W. Nolte. *Public Relations Writing and Media Techniques*, 2nd ed. New York: HarperCollins, 1994.

# 2

# A Public Relations Process

As we saw in Chapter 1, the public relations problem-solving process involves four procedures. First, initial research is performed to establish the basic elements of the communication transaction. Second, objectives for the transaction are established. Third, programming, including all the methods of communication used, is planned and executed to carry out the objectives. Finally, ongoing and follow-up evaluation is conducted both to monitor and to measure how well the program accomplished its objectives.

Now for a detailed look at each of the elements in this process.

# RESEARCH

Research consists of investigating three aspects of the overall public relations procedure: the client or organization for whom the program is being prepared, the opportunity or problem that accounts for the program at this time, and all audiences to be targeted for communication in the PR program.

## Client Research

First, public relations practitioners must be thoroughly familiar with their clients. If the practitioner is working in an in-house PR department, the client will be the organization housing the department. An employee of a PR firm will obviously be independent of the client. In either case, background data about the client or organization—its financial status, reputation, past and present public relations practices, and public relations strengths, weaknesses, and opportunities—are an essential starting point for any program.

If the organization is a business, the practitioner needs to be familiar with its products and services as well as the overall competitive environment. The practitioner should also know about the marketing, legal, and financial functions of the organization in order to coordinate them with the public relations efforts. Interviews with key management personnel and documents such as annual and quarterly reports can provide this information. The location of the organization, whether in a single city or in multiple branches, the delivery system for the products or services (such as the use of a dealer network), the organization's major suppliers, and, of course, the identity and demographics of the customers are all necessary to understand the client.

If the organization is nonprofit, the practitioner must become acquainted with the services provided and the organization's clientele, including major donors.

Other important background information includes the precise mission of the organization, its management's goals, priorities, and problems, and how this proposed public relations program might help accomplish these overall objectives.

Along with this background information the practitioner needs a good working knowledge of the organization's personnel—its total work force, both management and nonmanagement. Special attention must be given to key management people, not just the director of public relations, if there is one. How does top management view the role of public relations? Are PR people regarded as problem solvers and decision makers, or are they simply "hired guns"?

The financial status of a publicly owned corporation is easy to determine. Financial data for such organizations must be reported to the U.S. Securities and Exchange Commission (SEC), and this information is always available in the company's annual report or other financial publications.

Finally, the practitioner needs to raise questions that directly relate to public relations. What is the client's reputation in its field and with its customers or clientele? The answers to these questions constitute the organization's public image, an area of primary concern to PR practitioners. What image liabilities or assets does the organization possess? What are its present and past public relations practices? Does the organization have particular PR strengths, that is, practices or programs that would enhance its public image? What are its PR weaknesses, the practices or programs that might create an unfavorable image or negative public opinion? What opportunities exist for promoting favorable public opinion or behavior toward the organization?

Thus, the first requisite for effective research in the public relations process is an in-depth understanding of the client for whom the program is preppared.

## Opportunity or Problem Research

The second aspect of research, a logical outgrowth of knowledge of the client, consists of clearly determining why the organization should conduct a particular PR program at a particular time. Is it because of a unique opportunity to favorably influence public opinion or behavior toward the client, or is it in response to the development of unfavorable opinion or behavior toward the client? If it is the latter, extensive research must be done on the source of the problem, whether it be an individual or an organization.

Public relations programs that arise out of opportunities are called *proactive* programs. In the short run, effective proactive programming may seem extravagantly expensive to management, but these programs often head off the need to respond to problems with even more expensive *reactive* programs. The proactive program is like preventive medicine, or the concept of "wellness" now being widely promoted by health maintenance organizations. Preventive medicine is far more desirable than surgery in response to a severe illness. Similarly, an organization should keep close tabs on its ongoing relations with its constituent audiences to avoid PR problems.

This is not to argue that proactive programs are good and reactive programs are bad. In spite of all efforts to avert them, problems may develop. The reactive program then becomes necessary and perhaps beneficial. When a fire breaks out, we must call the fire department. Public relations practitioners must be ready to extinguish "fires," but they should also be skilled in "fire prevention."

Because they are preventive, proactive programs are generally long-range in nature. The organization cannot afford to let its guard down in maintaining good relations with important audiences. Reactive programs, on the other hand, are usually short-range, often ending as soon as the immediate problem is cleared up. But a good, ongoing, proactive program with the same audience may prevent the recurrence of similar problems.

Thus, an investigation of why a public relations program is necessary, whether it should be proactive or reactive, and whether it should be ongoing or short-range is the second aspect of research in the public relations process.

## Audience Research

The third aspect of research in the public relations process involves investigating the target audiences, or "publics." This part of the research process includes identifying the particular groups that should be targeted, determining appropriate research data that will be useful in communicating with these publics, and compiling or processing the data using appropriate research procedures.

**Audience Identification.** All organizations have long-range, and sometimes short-term, "relations," or communications, with certain "standard" publics. The publics of principal concern to most organizations include the media, internal employees or members, the organization's home community, and the national, state, and local governments. A business that provides a product or service for customers is concerned with consumers as an important public. A publicly owned business has the additional, significant audience of its shareowners and the financial community. Finally, all organizations have unique groups of constituent audiences, or special publics. Nonprofit organizations are concerned with donors as a special public. Schools are interested in maintaining communications with parents. Large corporations may need to communicate regularly with their dealers and suppliers.

To address publics most effectively, we should segment each public into its diverse components, so each component may become a separate public to be targeted for special messages. The media, for example, should be segmented into mass and specialized groups. Of the two internal publics, employees should be segmented into management and nonmanagement, and members should be divided into organization employees, officers, members, prospective members, state or local chapters, and related or allied organizations (see Chapter 4). The organization's home community should be segmented into community media, community leaders, and community organizations. Government publics should be subdivided into federal, state, county, and city levels; then each of these levels should be further segmented into legislative and executive branches. Consumer publics can be subdivided into groupings that include company employees, customers, activist consumer groups, consumer publications, community media, and community leaders and organizations (see Chapter 8). Investor publics for financial relations should be segmented into shareowners and potential shareowners, security analysts and investment counselors, the financial press, and the SEC. (See Exhibit 2-a for suggested segmentation of these major publics.)

**Targeting.**  Once the publics have been identified and segmented into their components, the practitioner is ready for the more difficult task of targeting the most important publics on a priority basis. This *prioritizing* calls for a situational assessment of the significance to the client or organization of each potential public. The importance of a potential public is determined by its degree of influence, prestige, power, or perhaps need, and by its level of involvement with the client or organization. Four key questions to consider in targeting and prioritizing publics are:

- Who is this public (demographics, psychographics, and so on)?
- Why is it important to us?
- How active or involved is this public, relative to our interests?
- Which publics are most important to us, in priority rank order?

**Desired Data.**  Once target publics have been segmented into their key components, the practitioner is ready to assess informational needs for each public. Typically, the practitioner will want to know each targeted public's level of information about the organization; the image and other relevant attitudes held about the organization and its product or service; and past and present audience behaviors relevant to the client or organization. Researching the demographics, media habits, and levels of media use of each targeted audience will tell the practitioner how best to reach it. All these data are used to formulate objectives for the public relations program.

## Research Methods

With this general framework of informational needs in mind, the practitioner must next decide which research procedures will yield the necessary data. Public relations people use two general methods of research: *nonquantitative* and *quantitative*.

**Nonquantitative Research.**  One source of nonquantitative data is organization or client *records* (business reports, statistics, financial reports, past public relations records) and communications (speeches by executives, newsletters, news releases, memorandums, pamphlets, brochures).

Exhibit 2-a

Major Publics

# Media Publics

Mass media
- Local
  - Print publications
    - Newspapers
    - Magazines
  - TV stations
  - Radio stations
- National
  - Print publications
  - Broadcast networks
  - Wire services

Specialized media
- Local
  - Trade, industry, and association publications
  - Organizational house and membership publications
  - Ethnic publications
  - Publications of special groups
  - Specialized broadcast programs and stations
- National
  - General business publications
  - National trade, industry, and association publications
  - National organizational house and membership publications
  - National ethnic publications
  - Publications of national special groups
  - National specialized broadcast programs and networks

# Employee Publics

Management
- Upper-level administrators
- Midlevel administrators
- Lower-level administrators

Nonmanagement (staff)
- Specialists
- Clerical personnel
- Secretarial personnel

Uniformed personnel
    Equipment operators
    Drivers
    Security personnel
    Other uniformed personnel
Union representatives
Other nonmanagement personnel

## Member Publics

Organization employees
    Headquarters management
    Headquarters nonmanagement (staff)
    Other headquarters personnel
Organization officers
    Elected officers
    Appointed officers
    Legislative groups
    Boards, committees
Organization members
    Regular members
    Members in special categories—sustaining, emeritus, student members
    Honorary members or groups
Prospective organization members
State or local chapters
    Organization employees
    Organization officers
    Organization members
    Prospective organization members
Related or other allied organizations

## Community Publics

Community media
    Mass
    Specialized
Community leaders
    Public officials
    Educators
    Religious leaders

Exhibit 2-A
(continued)

Professionals

Executives

Bankers

Union leaders

Ethnic leaders

Neighborhood leaders

Community organizations

Civic

Service

Social

Business

Cultural

Religious

Youth

Political

Special interest groups

Other

## Government Publics

Federal

Legislative branch

Representatives, staff, committee personnel

Senators, staff, committee personnel

Executive branch

President

White House staff, advisers, committees

Cabinet officers, departments, agencies, commissions

State

Legislative branch

Representatives, delegates, staff, committee personnel

Senators, staff, committee personnel

Executive branch

Governor

Governor's staff, advisers, committees

Cabinet officers, departments, agencies, commissions

County

County executive

Other county officials, commissions, departments

City
    Mayor or city manager
    City council
    Other city officials, commissions, departments

## Investor Publics

Shareowners and potential shareowners

Security analysts and investment counselors

Financial press

    Major wire services: Dow Jones & Co., Reuters Economic Service, AP, UPI

    Major business magazines: *Business Week, Fortune,* and the like—mass circulation and specialized

    Major newspapers: *New York Times, Wall Street Journal*

    Statistical services: Standard and Poor's Corp., Moody's Investor Service, and the like

    Private wire services: PR News Wire, Business Wire

Securities and Exchange Commission (SEC), for publicly owned companies

## Consumer Publics

Company employees

Customers

    Professionals

    Middle class

    Working class

    Minorities

    Other

Activist consumer groups

Consumer publications

Community media, mass and specialized

Community leaders and organizations

## International Publics

Host country media

    Mass

    Specialized

Host country leaders

    Public officials

Exhibit 2-a
(continued)

Educators

Social leaders

Cultural leaders

Religious leaders

Political leaders

Professionals

Executives

Host country organizations

Business

Service

Social

Cultural

Religious

Political

Special interests

Other

## Special Publics

Media consumed by this public

Mass

Specialized

Leaders of this public

Public officials

Professional leaders

Ethnic leaders

Neighborhood leaders

Organizations composing this public

Civic

Political

Service

Business

Cultural

Religious

Youth

Other

A second source of nonquantitative data is *published materials*. These include news articles from mass media and trade publications, published surveys or polls, library references, government documents, directories, and published trade association data.

Third, nonquantitative research can be conducted through interviews or conversations with *key members of targeted publics*. Important civic leaders, elected officials, business leaders, religious leaders, educators, influential editors, reporters, and other key individuals in the community can provide invaluable background information for a public relations program.

Fourth, feedback from the client's *customers* or *clientele* can be helpful as a means of nonquantitative research. Customer responses may come via telephone, mail, or face-to-face interactions.

Fifth, talking with *organized groups* with an interest in the client can be useful. These groups may include the organization's formal advisory boards, committees, commissions, or panels from inside or outside the organization.

Sixth, on-line databases have become an essential source of information for public relations practitioners. The most widely used on-line database service is Nexis, providing access to a vast array of information sources. Other on-line services include DataTimes, Dialog, Dow Jones News/Retrieval, CompuServe, and NewsNet.

Finally, groups created especially for research purposes can provide valuable insight. The most popular form of this procedure is the *focus group,* usually consisting of 8 to 12 people who are representative of the audience the client wishes to reach. A moderator who is skilled in interviewing and group-process management encourages the participants of the focus group to consider the client's image, products, services, and communication proposals or other issues affecting the client. The focus-group meetings are usually videotaped and carefully studied to identify and analyze participants' reactions and comments.

It should be emphasized that although these seven methods of nonquantitative research may yield useful data regarding all areas of concern in the research process, the data will not be scientifically reliable. For a scientific level of reliability, statistical research methods must be used.

**Quantitative Research.** Three methods of quantitative research are widely used in public relations: sample surveys, experiments, and content analysis. The key to each is the use of statistical methods.

The *sample survey* is the most frequently used quantitative research method in the public relations process. It is most useful in determining audience information levels, attitudes, behaviors, and media habits. Surveys can be conducted by mail, by telephone, or in person, with cost increasing in that order.

Mail questionnaires are the least expensive survey method because of lower staffing requirements. They can yield more data because length is no problem and respondents can give thorough answers. The major problem with such questionnaires is the low response rate. Unless the intended respondents have a high level of interest in the subject, mail questionnaires can be a big waste of the researcher's time and money.

Telephone interviews have become the most popular means of conducting surveys. Sampling can be done using the random digit dialing technique and an ordinary telephone directory. Although more expensive than mail questionnaires, telephone interviews provide a more economical use of staff time. The limitations of communicating by voice alone may hamper the rapport between interviewer and respondent since the interviewer cannot make judgments about accuracy and sincerity based on nonverbal cues. Nonetheless, telephone interviewing has become the first choice in the conduct of sample surveys.

Personal interviews remain an important, though expensive and time-consuming, survey method. The interviewer can make judgments based on the respondent's nonverbal as well as verbal cues, so no survey method is more accurate. Getting a good sample, however, is much more difficult than with the random digit dialing technique used for telephone interviews. Many people are reluctant to consent to a personal interview because of the time and inconvenience involved. As with mail questionnaires, personal interviews are most effective with respondents who are truly interested in the subject and willing to sacrifice their time.

With all their limitations, and with the onus of being considered "quick and dirty" by most social and behavioral scientists, surveys remain the most popular of quantitative research methods used in public relations.

*Controlled experiments* have been gaining in popularity in recent years, however. Conducted either in laboratory settings or in the field, experiments are the most accurate indicator of causality in the behavioral sciences. Experiments are often used in advertising or public relations to determine which forms of communication or messages may be most effective with selected audiences. In the experimental method, two groups of subjects are randomly chosen. One group is exposed to the communication media, and the other is not. Both groups are tested before and after the communication exposure. If the responses of the exposed group change significantly after the communication, then these responses can be attributed causally to the messages.

A third quantitative method of research often used in public relations is *content analysis.* This systematic procedure is used in analyzing themes or trends in the message content of selected media. Content analysis can be used to learn how the media are treating clients—their public image as reflected in the media, negative or positive coverage, and the like. This research procedure is also useful in issues management, in which practitioners identify and analyze the impact of public issues on a client's corporate or organizational interests. Thus, content analysis can be helpful in the evaluation of media treatment in the publicity process and in tracking social, economic, or political trends or issues that may affect clients.

Quantitative research should be conducted only by professional firms with good reputations in their field or by staff members who are trained and experienced researchers. Public relations staff members who have not received formal training in research techniques will waste the client's time and money. Worse, their work will probably be inaccurate and misleading.

With the public relations program's informational needs satisfied through nonquantitative or quantitative research methods, the practitioner is ready to attend to the second phase of the process—that of formulating objectives.

# OBJECTIVES

Objectives are the single most important element in this public relations process. They represent the practitioner's desired outcomes in communicating with the targeted publics. They are the raison d'être for PR programs. Some writers draw a distinction between "goals" as more general outcomes and "objectives" as specific, immediate results. Here we avoid that confusion by consistently using one term to signify desired program outcomes, and that term is *objectives*. Whether they are to be broad or narrow, long-range or short-range, should be stipulated in the statement of the objective itself. Before we discuss the types of objectives used in public relations, we should examine the method used in formulating such objectives.

Many organizations are now using management by objectives (MBO) to determine both general organizational objectives and those for individual work units, such as the public relations department. MBO is a well-established procedure that involves cooperative goal setting by groups of superiors and subordinates in the employee hierarchy. For example, the director of public relations and the assistant director may represent management, and various writers, graphics specialists, and other staff members may represent the "subordinates" in the MBO process. Together they devise short-term and long-range objectives and evaluation procedures for the work unit and for its particular programs. Then, using these procedures, both groups cooperatively evaluate their work at agreed-on times. They also periodically review and revise their objectives and evaluation procedures.

Our concern here is with objectives for individual PR programs. Regardless of whether such objectives are determined using MBO or more traditional authoritarian means, two criteria apply to all program objectives.

First, objectives should be stated in the form of infinitive phrases, each containing one infinitive and each being a specific and separately measurable desired outcome. An infinitive phrase consists of *to* plus a verb plus the complement, or receiver of the verb's action. For example, a practitioner may hope that, after the PR program is executed, the audience will be informed that a special event is taking place and will attend the event. The phrasing of the objectives in infinitive form could be:

- To publicize special event X
- To stimulate attendance at special event X

These objectives could be combined—to publicize and stimulate attendance at special event X—but this compound phrasing would complicate the measurement or evaluation of both objectives.

Second, public relations objectives should be verifiable. To be verifiable, the desired outcome should be stated in quantified, measurable terms, and a time frame or target date should be set for its accomplishment. Although the objectives just stated meet our infinitive test, they are not stated specifically in quantitative or chronological terms. Thus, they can be reworded:

- To publicize special event X through the community's daily newspaper, its TV station, and its three radio stations during the month of October
- To stimulate an attendance of at least 1,500 persons at special event X on May 15

We can measure the first objective by determining, through the use of a clipping service and a broadcast media monitoring service, how many media outlets actually used the announcement of the special event. We can measure the second objective by checking actual attendance figures or ticket sales at the event itself.

Two basic types of objectives are used in public relations programs: *impact objectives* and *output objectives*. Together, they can be viewed as a hierarchy in ascending order of importance (see Exhibit 2-b). Within each category, however, there is no performance hierarchy or order of importance. For example, informational objectives need not be completed before attitudinal or behavioral objectives, and the importance of each of these subsets of impact objectives is purely situational.

| Exhibit 2-b | A Hierarchy of Public Relations Objectives |

## Impact Objectives

Informational objectives
> Message exposure
> Message comprehension
> Message retention

Attitudinal objectives
> Attitude creation
> Attitude reinforcement
> Attitude change

Behavioral objectives
> Behavior creation
> Behavior reinforcement
> Behavior change

## Output Objectives

Distribution of uncontrolled media
Distribution or execution of controlled media

### Output Objectives

Output objectives, the lower category in the hierarchy, represent the work to be produced, that is, the distribution or execution of program materials. Some writers refer to these activities as "process objectives," "support objectives," or "program effort." Whatever the terminology, these activities should not be confused with desired program impacts. Output objectives, as discussed here, refer to stated intentions regarding program production and effort (or output). They are classified as a form of objective because they describe a type of desired outcome often stated in public relations programs. In fact, the PRSA's Silver Anvil Winners use a much higher percentage of output objectives than impact objectives. In the best of all possible worlds, PR directors would use only impact objectives. But here it seems appropriate to deal with PR objectives as they actually exist in the real world. Such objectives can easily be made specific and quantitative. For example:

- To send one news release to each of the community's major media outlets: its daily newspaper, its TV station, and its three radio stations by May 10

- To make an oral presentation to an important conference of security analysts in each of the following five cities: New York, Los Angeles, Chicago, Houston, and Denver, before December 15

These objectives can then be measured easily by counting the number of news releases actually sent to the media outlets and the number of oral presentations actually made to security analysts. Time frames can be added if desired.

Some practitioners use only output objectives in their public relations programs. The advantage of such usage is that output objectives set definite, specific, and attainable goals, which can be measured quantitatively. Once these goals have been met, the practitioner can claim success. Unfortunately, output objectives are unrelated to the actual impact the program may have on its intended audiences, and for this we must move to the top, and more significant, category in our hierarchy of public relations objectives.

## Impact Objectives

There are three kinds of impact objectives: informational, attitudinal, and behavioral. These are called impact objectives because they represent specific intended effects of public relations programs on their audiences.

**Informational Objectives.** Informational objectives include message exposure to, message comprehension by, and/or message retention by the target public. Such objectives are appropriate when the practitioner wishes to publicize an action or event; seeks to communicate instructions, operating procedures, or other forms of information; or wants to educate an audience about a noncontroversial subject. Two examples of informational objectives are:

- To increase awareness of the company's open house (by 10 percent) among all segments of the community (during the month of May)
- To increase employee awareness of new plant safety procedures (by 50 percent during our three-month safety campaign)

**Attitudinal Objectives.** Attitudinal objectives aim at modifying the way an audience feels about the client or organization and its work, products, or services. Attitude modification may consist of forming new attitudes where none exist, reinforcing existing attitudes, or changing existing attitudes.

There will probably be no public attitudes toward a completely new organization. The task of public relations, then, will be the creation of favorable attitudes toward the organization. Two examples of such objectives are:

- To create favorable public attitudes toward a new department store (among 25 percent of mall shoppers during the grand opening celebration)
- To promote favorable attitudes toward a company's new retirement policy (among 80 percent of current employees during the current fiscal year)

It should be stressed that this type of attitudinal objective (forming new attitudes) applies only to organizations and actions that are not controversial and therefore have not generated prior audience attitudes. Some new organizations or actions immediately create reactions among affected groups. In these cases, objectives that seek to reinforce or change existing attitudes are more appropriate.

The second form of attitudinal objective has as its goal the reinforcement, enhancement, or intensification of existing attitudes. A given audience may have moderately favorable, but weak, attitudes toward an organization. In this case, public relations may seek to strengthen these attitudes through a variety of actions, events, or communications. An example of this might be:

- To reinforce favorable public opinion toward a nonprofit organization (among 80 percent of its past donors during March and April)

The final form of attitudinal objective is the changing, or reversing, of (usually negative) existing attitudes. In this case, the practitioner must be careful not to take on a "Mission Impossible." The reversal of attitudes is, of course, the most difficult of all tasks in public relations, so the old military adage "Don't fight a losing battle" may serve as a useful guideline here. Attitude or behavior reversal takes time and, as a rule, it cannot be accomplished with one short-range PR campaign. When Ivy Lee attempted to reverse the public image of John D. Rockefeller, Sr., the task took years. Little by little, Lee was successful in converting Rockefeller's image from that of the ogre responsible for the deaths of Colorado miners and their families to the image of a beloved philanthropist. Many practitioners would rightly have regarded such an enormous task as a "losing battle," given the resources of most individuals or organizations. But with unlimited Rockefeller money, the task was finally accomplished.

Sometimes the practitioner will seek to reverse existing positive attitudes. For example, some Republicans in Congress (and in the White House) have attempted to portray many of the government's social programs in a negative light, although most of these programs have enjoyed great popularity since their inception during President Franklin D. Roosevelt's New Deal era.

Two examples of objectives that seek attitude change are:

- To reverse (within a period of one year) the negative attitudes and ill will now being expressed toward the manufacturer of a defective product (among 20 percent of the manufacturer's former and current customers)

- To change the favorable attitudes that exist regarding the proposed program (among 10 percent of the members of the U.S. Congress before the vote on the bill)

Attitudinal objectives, then, may involve any of three goals: formation of new attitudes where none exist, reinforcement of existing attitudes, or change in existing attitudes.

**Behavioral Objectives.**   Behavioral objectives involve the modification of behavior toward the client or organization. Like attitude modification, behavior modification may consist of the creation or stimulation of new behavior, the enhancement or intensification of existing favorable behavior, or the reversal of negative behavior on the part of an audience toward the practitioner's client or organization.

Examples of the creation of new behavior might include:

- To accomplish adoption of new safety procedures (among 75 percent of the organization's employees by September 15)

- To persuade (60 percent of) persons over the age of 50 to regularly take a colon cancer test (during the next two years)

- To stimulate new diet procedures (among 70 percent) of children in the city school system (during the current school year)

Enhancement or intensification of existing positive behaviors might involve such objectives as:

- To encourage (30 percent) greater usage of seat belts in automobiles (this year)

- To stimulate (50 percent) higher attendance at meetings by association members (during the next national convention)

The reversal of negative behaviors could include:

- To discourage defacement of public monuments (by 20 percent) in a city park (over a period of eight months)

- To discourage smoking (by 80 percent) in the east wing of the restaurant (during the next three months)

Objectives, as presented here, result from and are shaped by the findings revealed in the research phase. As mentioned earlier, research data should be sought in the area of audience information levels, attitudes, behaviors, and media habits. If information levels about the client or related matters are low, then informational objectives are called for in the public relations program. If audience attitudes toward the client are nonexistent, weak, or negative, then the practitioner will know the kinds of attitudinal objectives to formulate. Finally, if desired audience behaviors are nonexistent, weak, or negative, the practitioner will have a framework for developing appropriate behavioral objectives. Data regarding audience media habits may not contribute directly to the formulation of program objectives, but these findings are useful in determining appropriate media usage in the programming phase of the process.

In addition to impact objectives, the practitioner may devise output objectives for each PR program. These objectives are of less significance because they represent outcomes that have nothing to do with program effects on target audiences.

In the public relations process, objectives precede and govern programming decisions. The degree of influence these objectives exert can best be seen in the programming phase itself.

# PROGRAMMING

Public relations programming, as presented in this process, includes the following elements of planning and execution:

1. Stating a theme, if applicable, and the messages to be communicated to the audiences
2. Planning the action or special event(s) sponsored by the client
3. Planning the use of the media, either uncontrolled or controlled
4. Effectively communicating the program

## Theme and Messages

The first element of a program, its theme and messages, should encompass the program's entire scope and must be carefully planned in conjunction with the action or special event central to the program.

The program theme should be catchy and memorable. The best themes are in the form of short slogans consisting of no more than five words. Not all programs require themes or slogans, but a brief, creative theme can become the most memorable part of the entire public relations effort.

Most PR programs will have one central message epitomized in such a slogan or theme. In some cases, programs may have several messages, possibly one for each separate audience. The practitioner should work out as concisely as possible just what is to be communicated to each audience during the entire program.

## Action or Special Event(s)

A central action or a special event to be sponsored by the client should be considered along with the program's theme and message. The client's actions or events will usually be the focal point of the theme and messages, although some PR programs omit this element and concentrate on theme and messages alone. However, it is highly recommended that programs be action oriented. A central action or event can make most programs more newsworthy, interesting, and effective. To best advance the public image of the client, this action or event should be substantive, usually serious, and in the public interest. It will be most effective if the event involves large numbers of people and includes the presence of at least one celebrity. Shallow "pseudoevents" should be avoided; they sometimes do more harm than good by damaging the client's credibility. For the most part, gimmicks and stunts are best left to carnivals and circuses. There are exceptions, of course. Sometimes carnivals, circuses, beauty pageants, and similar activities can be presented as a means of raising funds for worthy causes. If these events can be seen as serving the public interest, they may enhance the client's credibility. Typical public relations actions and special events are included in Exhibit 2-c.

## Uncontrolled and Controlled Media

The two forms of communication used in public relations are usually classified as *uncontrolled* and *controlled media.*

The use of uncontrolled media involves the communication of news about the client or organization to the mass media and to specialized media outlets. Specifically, the decision-making editors of these outlets become the target audiences for uncontrolled media. The objective of this form of communication is favorable news coverage of the client's actions and events. The standard formats used to communicate client news to the media include news releases, feature stories, captioned photographs or photo opportunities, and news conferences. A more complete listing of these formats can be found in Exhibit 2-d. They are called uncontrolled media because the practitioner loses control of these materials at the media outlet itself. An editor may choose to use the practitioner's release or feature story in its entirety, partially, or not at all; or editors may send reporters who will write or videotape their own stories about the client, ignoring the practitioner's efforts. Because the client opractitioner does not pay the media outlet to use the story as advertising, the use of the material is at the complete discretion of the media outlet.

The use of controlled media, on the other hand, involves communication about the client that is paid for by the client. The wording of the material, its format, and its placement in the media are all at the

| Exhibit 2-c | Actions and Special Events |

Special days, nights, weeks, months

Displays and exhibits

Trade shows and exhibitions

Fairs, festivals, expositions

Meetings, conferences, conventions, congresses, rallies

Anniversaries, memorial events

Special awards, retirements, salutes

Open houses, plant tours

Town meetings, public debates, parties

Coffee hours, teas

Contests

Parades, pageants, beauty contests

Sponsoring community events

Sponsoring organizations (community youth organizations, Little League, Junior Achievement Organization)

Sponsoring scholarships, contributions

Creating charitable and educational foundations

Receptions

Concert tours, theatrical tours

Performing and graphic arts tours

Visits, pleasure tours for selected publics and groups

Picnics, outings, cookouts, barbecues

Nature trails, flower shows

Ground-breaking ceremonies, cornerstone layings, safety programs

Product demonstrations

Traveling demonstrations, home demonstrations

Visits by dignitaries, celebrities

Guest lectures, kickoffs, farewells, going-aways, welcome-backs, welcoming ceremonies

Elections of officers

Issuing reports or statistics

Announcing results of polls or surveys

Grand openings

Announcing an appointment

Announcing a new policy or policy change

Announcing a new program, product, or service

Exhibit 2-c
(continued)

Announcing important news about the client or organization

Public relations personalities (Miss America, Miss Universe, Maid of Cotton)

Dedications

School commencements, assemblies, events, convocations

Fetes, galas, proms, dances, balls, disco parties

Banquets, luncheons, breakfasts, dinners, buffets

Art shows, openings, exhibits

Concerts, plays, ballets

Film festivals, fashion shows

Animal shows (dogs, cats, birds)

Sporting events, ski trips, ocean cruises, pack trips, hikes, marathons, bike-a-thons, swim-a-thons, miscellaneous-a-thons, races

Celebrity sporting events, cruises

Museum tours, home tours

Embassy tours

Celebrity appearances, autograph-signing ceremonies

Car washes, neighborhood cleanups, services for the elderly

Health screening tests

Committee hearings

Training programs

Opinion-leader meetings and conferences

Special education programs: thrift education, health education, conservation education

Leadership programs

Participation in community events

Celebrations of national holidays

Theme events and celebrations: "Roaring Twenties," "Old New Orleans," "Colonial New England," "Ancient Greece"

Events honoring other nations or cultures

Events honoring the client or organization

Exhibit 2-d

## Uncontrolled Media

News releases—print and video news releases (VNRs)

Feature stories

Photographs with cutlines (captions) or photo opportunities

News conferences

Media kits

Radio/TV public service announcements (PSAs) (nonprofit organizations only)

Interviews

    Print media

    Broadcast media

Personal appearances on broadcast media

News tapes for radio

News slides and films for TV

Special programs for radio and TV

Recorded telephone news capsules and updates from an institution

Informing and influencing editors, broadcast news and public service directors, columnists, and reporters (phone calls, tip sheets, newsletters with story leads, media advisories)

Business feature articles

Financial publicity

Product publicity

Pictorial publicity

Background editorial material (backgrounders and fact sheets)

Letters to the editor

Op-ed pieces

## Controlled Media

Print communication methods

    House publications

    Brochures, information pieces

    Handbooks, manuals, books

    Letters, bulletins, memos

    Bulletin boards, posters, flyers

    Information racks

Exhibit 2-d
*(continued)*

External periodicals: opinion-leader periodicals, corporate general public periodicals, distributor-dealer periodicals, stockholder periodicals, supplier periodicals, periodicals for special publics

Annual reports

Commemorative stamps

Exhibits and displays

Mobile libraries, bookmobiles

Mobile displays

Attitude or information surveys

Suggestion boxes, systems

Instructions and orders

Pay inserts

Written reports

Billing inserts

Financial statement inserts

Training kits, aids, manuals

Consumer information kits

Legislative information kits

Teacher kits, student games

Teacher aids

Print window displays

Audiovisual communication methods

Institutional films

Slide shows

Filmstrips

Opaque projectors, flannel boards, easel pad presentations

Transparencies for overhead projectors

Telephone calls, phone banks, dial-a-something, recorded messages

Multimedia exhibits and displays

Audio tapes and cassettes

Videotapes and cassettes

Visual and multimedia window displays

Oral presentations with visuals

Multimedia training aids

Teacher aids, student games

Specially equipped vans, trains, buses, boats, airplanes, blimps

Interpersonal communication methods

Formal speeches, lectures, seminars

Roundtable conferences

Panel discussions

Question-and-answer discussions

Oral testimony

Employee counseling

Legal, medical, birth-control, miscellaneous counseling

Committee meetings

Staff meetings

Informal conversations

Demonstrations

Speakers bureaus: recruiting and training speakers, speech preparation, clearance of materials with management, list of subjects, speakers' guide, engagements and bookings, visual aids, follow-up correspondence

Training programs

Interviews

Personal instructions

Social affairs

Face-to-face reports

Public relations advertising (not designed to stimulate product sales)

Print and broadcast advertising

Institutional advertising—image building

Public affairs (advocacy) advertising: institutional or organizational statements on controversial issues

Direct mail institutional advertising

Outdoor advertising: billboards, signs

Yellow Pages institutional advertising

Transit advertising, skywriting, fly-by advertising

Specialty items: calendars, ash trays, pens, matchbooks, emery boards, memo pads discretion of the client. The formats for controlled media include print materials, such as brochures, newsletters, and reports; audiovisual materials, such as films, slide shows, and the like; and interpersonal communication, including speeches, meetings, and interviews. Also included in controlled media are institutional advertising, aimed at enhancing the client's image; advocacy advertising, communicating the client's stand on a controversial issue; and other forms of nonproduct advertising. Exhibit 2-d includes a more detailed listing of the forms of controlled media.

## Effective Communication

The final aspect of programming is the effective communication of the program. Thus, the factors of source, message, channel, receivers, and feedback will be useful in our examination of communication principles. That is, effective communication depends on:

1. Source credibility
2. Salient information (message)
3. Effective nonverbal cues (message)
4. Effective verbal cues (message)
5. Two-way communication (channel and feedback)
6. Opinion leaders (receivers)
7. Group influence (receivers)
8. Selective exposure (receivers)
9. Audience participation (feedback)

**Source Credibility.**  The success or failure of the entire public relations transaction can hinge on how the *source* of communication, the spokesperson for the client or organization, is perceived by the intended audience. Credibility involves a set of perceptions about sources held by receivers or audiences. The personal characteristics of believable sources that continually appear in communication research are trustworthiness, expertise, dynamism, physical attractiveness, and perceived similarities between the source and receivers.[1] These characteristics should serve the PR practitioner as guidelines for selecting individuals to represent the client or organization. Communication coming from high-credibility sources will clearly be in the best interests of the PR program.

**Salient Information.**  A second principle of effective communication involves the use of salient information in the client's messages addressed to target audiences. Members of audiences can be viewed as information processors whose attitudes and behaviors are influenced by their integration of significant new information into their preexisting beliefs.[2]

This is another way of saying that the message content must be motivational for the intended audiences—it must strike responsive chords in their minds. Information that is not salient to a given audience in a given context should be discarded.

**Nonverbal Cues.** A third principle of effective communication involves the use of appropriate nonverbal cues in the PR program's messages. Countless volumes have been published on a variety of aspects of nonverbal communication. But for purposes of effective programming, the PR practitioner should closely examine the nature of the client's actions or special events that are to serve as a basis for the overall effort. Choosing appropriate symbols to represent the client or the cause can be the most important aspect of nonverbal communication. Questions involving the mood, or atmosphere, desired at the event, the personnel to be used, the guests to be invited, the setting, the forms of interpersonal interaction, and the scheduling should be raised. These are essential details that can make the difference between success and failure for the client. Exhibit 2-e provides more details useful in planning effective nonverbal communication for the client.

---

| Exhibit 2-e | Nonverbal Communication |

Appropriate symbols

Mood or atmosphere desired: excitement, quiet dignity

Organizational personnel involved, including spokesperson(s) to be used

> Demographics of the audience: white/anglo, African American, Hispanic, Jewish, Asian, Arab (if applicable)
>
> Appearance, dress, actions/interactions expected

Guests: appearance and dress expected

Setting

> Buildings, rooms, or exterior environment desired
>
> Colors
>
> Background: banner, logo
>
> Lighting
>
> Sound system
>
> Nature and use of space
>
> Types and arrangement of furniture, seating arrangements
>
> Other artifacts to be used: paintings, wall tapestries, sports banners, colored balloons
>
> Nature of central presentation appropriate for setting (vice versa)

**Exhibit 2-e**
*(continued)*

Music: type, volume

Entertainment (if any)

Food, beverages, refreshments (if any)

Forms of interpersonal interaction: sit-down dinner, stand-up cocktail party, reception

Use of time: where will emphasis be placed; will activity build to climax?

**Verbal Cues.**   The use of effective verbal message cues, or the actual wording of the client's messages, is the fourth principle of communication considered here. The two most important characteristics of effective language usage are *clarity* and *appropriateness.*

To be clear, language must be accurate. The forms of communication used in a PR program should use words precisely, so the practitioner may need to consult a dictionary or thesaurus. Messages should be tested with a small audience to eliminate ambiguity before their actual use in a PR program. In addition to accuracy, simplicity of word choice contributes to language clarity. Why use big words when simple ones will do? Audiences will relate to such words as *try* better than *endeavor, help* better than *facilitate, explain* better than *explicate, tell* better than *indicate,* and *learn* better than *ascertain.* Finally, coherence is an important factor in clear language. The words in a message should be logically connected—they should hang together well. The use of simple sentences rather than compound or complex ones contributes to coherence. Clear transitions and summaries in messages also aid coherence. Accuracy, simplicity, and coherence, then, are the major factors in constructing clear messages.

Messages should also be appropriate to the client, the audience, and the occasion. If the client is the city's leading bank, some levels of language may be inappropriate. Language used by a fast-food chain is different from that used in the messages of a funeral home. Similarly, language must be appropriate to the demographic level of the audience. Teenagers will obviously respond to a different use of language than senior citizens. The occasion for the use of the message also influences the level and type of language to be used. A diplomatic function held in a Washington embassy requires a different level of language from that used at a locker room gathering of an athletic team. Thus, appropriateness and clarity are the two major requisites for effectiveness in the use of verbal message cues.

**Two-Way Communication.**   The fifth principle of effective communication involves two-way interaction. Communication was once considered a linear process involving the transmission of a message from a source through a channel to a receiver. On receipt of the message at its destination, the communication transaction was considered complete. Today, however, the PR practitioner must program two-way communication activities that permit audience response—or feedback—in brief, the interactive aspects discussed earlier.

A variety of print-oriented response mechanisms are available, such as the suggestion box for employee communication, response cards to be returned to the source of communication, and letters to the editors of publications. The most effective means of two-way interaction, however, is interpersonal communication activities: speeches with question-and-answer sessions, small-group meetings, and one-on-one communication. It is usually possible to divide target audiences into small groups that provide excellent opportunities for interpersonal communication. This is the most effective form of persuasion because of the high level of source-receiver engagement.

**Opinion Leaders.** The sixth principle of effective communication involves the identification and targeting of opinion leaders as receivers of communication. Sometimes communication operates efficiently in a direct, one-step flow from source to receiver. On many occasions, however, communication is more effective when staged in a two-step or multiple-step flow. In these cases, the practitioner should seek opinion leaders, or "influentials," who in turn will communicate with their followers or cohorts. One simple way to identify opinion leaders is to catalog the leadership of all important groups in a given community or institution. These may include elected political leaders and others who hold formal positions in the community. In some cases, opinion leaders may hold no formal positions, but their advice is nonetheless sought and respected within given groups, institutions, or communities. Practitioners should create a list of opinion-leader contacts, much like their media contacts list, including all relevant data about the leaders, their positions, their availability, and their influence on other audiences.

**Group Influence.** A seventh effective communication principle involves the use of group influence. People belong to a variety of formal and informal groups. The most valued groups, which exert the greatest influence on their members, are known as *reference groups*. Members feel a sense of cohesiveness, of belonging together; have mutual, face-to-face interactions and influence each other; and share a set of norms and roles that structure and enforce a degree of conformity by each member.

The practitioner's task is to identify and target for communication key groups that can be most useful to the client or organization. Special effort should go into the preparation of a group contacts list, similar to the media and opinion-leader lists. Groups should be reached through interpersonal communication (speeches or presentations) as well as other appropriate methods. It is especially important to contact a formal group's program chairperson to schedule a speech or other presentation on behalf of the client. Acceptance of the client's message or position by key group leaders will then effectively engage the essential nature of group influence: acceptance by all members because of the group's operative cohesiveness and conformity.

**Selective Exposure.**   An eighth principle of effective communication that should be observed by the public relations practitioner is selective exposure. Because the objectives of public relations include attitude and behavior modification, the temptation is always present to take on the most difficult of all tasks: changing existing attitudes or behaviors. Why is this the toughest task? The principle of selective exposure holds that people will accept and even seek out communication supporting their beliefs. However, communication researchers have also found that people will not necessarily avoid information incompatible with their views, as was once thought to be the case.[3] Moreover, other communication research indicates that when a persuasive message falls within the region (latitude) of personal acceptance, opinion or attitude will change in the direction of the advocated position. But when it falls within the region of rejection, attitudes will not change.[4] These communication research findings send a clear message to the PR practitioner— the easiest task in persuasion is reinforcement of existing attitudes or behaviors.

Clearly, trying to change attitudes or behavior is difficult and counterproductive, particularly in the face of strong resistance. Always avoid fighting a losing battle.

When controversial messages are necessary, audiences or individual receivers should always be categorized on the basis of their agreement or disagreement with the message in question. Using terms that coincide with the Likert scale often used in attitude surveys, audiences can be categorized as "positive" (those who strongly agree with the message); "somewhat positive" (those who agree with the message); "undecided"; "somewhat negative" (those who disagree with the message); and "negative" (those who strongly disagree with the message).

The principle of selective exposure dictates that the practitioner first target the "positives," then the "somewhat positives," next the "undecideds," and last, if at all, the "somewhat negatives." The pure "negatives," those strongly opposed or in disagreement with the program's message, should usually be written off. If their attitudes are hardened, and especially if they have publicly expressed their disagreement, they are highly unlikely to change their minds. Given a long period of time, along with perhaps unlimited funds, the hard-core negatives may be slowly changed; but for most practical and immediate situations requiring persuasion, conversion of the negatives is not worth the time, effort, or money.

**Audience Participation.** A final principle of effective communication, observed whenever possible, is the use of audience participation. This is the only means of communication that encourages audience self-persuasion through direct experience or involvement with the client's services or products. Communication researchers have found that self-persuasion is more effective, by far, than any other means of influence.[5] Therefore, the practitioner should constantly seek opportunities to include audience participation in PR programs.

In summary, public relations programming consists of planning, including attention to theme and message, the use of an action or special event, the use of uncontrolled and controlled media, and program execution following the principles of effective communication.

# EVALUATION

Evaluation as discussed here is an ongoing process of monitoring and, when appropriate, final assessment of the stated objectives of the PR program. It is usually inadvisable to wait until the execution of the program has been completed to begin the evaluation process. Instead, the practices described here should be engaged in at stipulated intervals during the execution, with program adjustments made as deemed appropriate.

## Evaluating Informational Objectives

The measurement of informational objectives includes three dimensions: message exposure, message comprehension, and message retention.

*Message exposure* is most commonly determined by publicity placement through national or local clipping and media monitoring services. It can also be measured through the circulation figures and audience-size data readily available for publications and broadcast media. Attendance figures for events or meetings also provide an index of message exposure. Finally, exposure is measured by computerized tracking systems that have been developed by some public relations firms for monitoring their effectiveness in delivering messages to audiences.

*Message comprehension,* or at least the potential for comprehension, is most frequently determined by the application of readability formulas to the messages used in PR programs. The most often used are the Flesch Reading Ease Formula, the Gunning Fog Index, the Dale-Chall Formula, the Fry Formula, and the Farr-Jenkins-Patterson Formula.[6] These predict ease of comprehension based on measuring the difficulty of the words and the length of the sentences used in messages, but surveys must be used to measure actual message comprehension.

*Message retention* is usually tested by asking appropriate questions designed to check target audiences' knowledge of the client's message. Although message retention can be measured by the nonquantitative research methods discussed earlier, retention questions are usually administered in the form of sample surveys.

Thus, the key to determining the effectiveness of informational objectives lies in the assessment of message exposure, comprehension, and retention. The more of these measurements used, the more accurate the evaluation of effectiveness is likely to be.

## Evaluating Attitudinal Objectives

Attitudinal objectives can be measured by several well-established survey research instruments, the most frequently used being Likert scales and the Semantic Differential.[7] Both of these instruments measure attitude intensity and direction; thus, they are useful in assessing whether new attitudes have been formed or whether existing attitudes have been reinforced or changed. These measurements require both pretesting and posttesting of target audiences to determine the degree of influence on attitudes attributable to the PR program. To be of any value at all, attitude measurement must be done by competent professionals well-schooled and experienced in quantitative research methods.

## Evaluating Behavioral Objectives

Finally, behavioral objectives can be measured in two ways. First, target audiences can be asked what their behaviors have been since exposure to the PR program. Like attitude measurement, assessment of audience behaviors requires testing before and after program exposure. However, the questions used will be different from those used in attitude research. Closed-end multiple-choice questions or checklists designed to determine audience behaviors are commonly used for this measurement.

A second means of assessing audience behavior is simply observing the behaviors of target audiences. In some cases, these can be counted, as in attendance at special events or numbers of telephone calls received. And in many situations, audiences may be small enough to observe before, during, and after exposure to the PR program.

Nonquantitative research methods can provide useful information both in asking audiences about their behaviors and in observing these behaviors. To obtain the most reliable evaluations of all three types of impact, however, competent professionals with established reputations in research should be retained.

## Evaluating Output Objectives

In addition to measuring impact objectives, the PR practitioner must be concerned with assessing the effectiveness of output objectives, which involve the distribution of uncontrolled and controlled media. This effectiveness can be evaluated by keeping records of the number of news releases sent to publications and broadcast stations, the number of contacts made with journalists, the number of speeches given to targeted audiences, the number of publications distributed to each public, and the number of meetings held with key audiences. In the realm of output objectives, practitioners accomplish their goals by distributing appropriate quantities of media according to their original plans. Although these are easily achievable objectives, it should be reiterated that they have no bearing whatever on the PR program's priority goal—audience impact.

Evaluation of the two general forms of program objectives—impact and output—constitutes an ongoing dimension of this public relations process model. The process will not be completed, however, when the program objectives are evaluated. These evaluative data are recycled as part of a continuing procedure. They are useful in adjusting ongoing relations with various audiences, and they can be helpful when planning the client's next short-term PR program with similar audiences.

## Summary

The public relations problem-solving process includes four parts: research, determination of objectives, programming, and evaluation. The following outline provides a useful summary and review of the whole process.

### Outline of the Public Relations Process

I. Research

    A. Client/organization: background data about your client or organization—its personnel, financial status, reputation, past and present PR practices, PR strengths and weaknesses, opportunities

    B. Opportunity/problem: proactive or reactive PR program; long-range or short-range campaign

    C. Audiences (publics): identification of key groups to be targeted for communication

        1. Desired research data: each targeted audience's level of information about your client/organization; image and other relevant attitudes held about your client/organization and its products or services; audience behaviors relevant to your client/organization; demographics, media habits, and media-use levels of each targeted audience

        2. Research procedures: nonquantitative and quantitative

II. Objectives

    A. Impact objectives

1. Informational objectives: message exposure, comprehension, retention

2. Attitudinal objectives: formation of new attitudes, reinforcement of existing attitudes, change in existing attitudes

3. Behavioral objectives: creation of new behavior; reinforcement of existing behavior; change in existing behavior

B. Output objectives: distribution or execution of uncontrolled and controlled media

III. Programming—planning and execution of:

A. Theme (if applicable) and message(s)

B. Action or special event(s)

C. Uncontrolled media: news releases, feature stories, photos; controlled media: print, audiovisual, interpersonal communication, PR advertising

D. Effective communication using principles of: source credibility, salient information, effective nonverbal and verbal cues, two-way communication, opinion leaders, group influence, selective exposure, and audience participation

IV. Evaluation—ongoing monitoring and final assessment of:

A. Impact objectives

1. Informational objectives: measured by publicity placement, surveys

2. Attitudinal objectives: measured by attitude surveys

3. Behavioral objectives: measured by surveys and observation of behaviors

B. Output objectives: measured quantitatively by simply counting the actual output

# NOTES

1. For a summary of this research, see Erwin P. Bettinghaus and Michael Cody, *Persuasive Communication,* 5th ed. (New York: Holt, Rinehart & Winston, 1994), and Mary John Smith, *Persuasion and Human Action* (Belmont, CA: Wadsworth, 1982), pp. 219ff, a classic in its field.

2. For a detailed discussion of the information integration approach to persuasion, see Smith, *Persuasion and Human Action,* pp. 243–261.

3. The best discussion of selective exposure is David O. Sears and Jonathan L. Freedman, "Selective Exposure to Information: A Critical Review," *Public Opinion Quarterly* 31 (1967): 194–213.

4. For a good explanation of this research, called *social judgment theory,* see Nan Lin, *The Study of Human Communication* (Indianapolis: Bobbs-Merrill,

1977), pp. 118–122. Also see Smith, *Persuasion and Human Action,* pp. 264–274.

5. For a review of this research, see Smith, *Persuasion and Human Action,* pp. 191–207.

6. For the Flesch Formula, see Rudolf Flesch, *How to Test Readability* (New York: Harper & Row, 1951); Gunning's Fog Index is found in Robert Gunning, *The Technique of Clear Writing,* rev. ed. (New York: McGraw-Hill, 1968); for the Dale-Chall Formula, see Edgar Dale and Jeanne Chall, "A Formula for Predicting Readability," *Educational Research Bulletin* 27 (January and February 1948); the Fry Formula is found in Edward Fry, "A Readability Formula that Saves Time," *Journal of Reading* 11 (1968): 513–516, 575–578; for a review of readability research, see Werner J. Severin and James W. Tankard, Jr., *Communication Theories: Origins, Methods, Uses* (New York: Hastings House, 1979), Chap. 6.

7. For a discussion of these and other research instruments used in attitude measurement, see Kathleen Kelley Reardon, *Persuasion: Theory and Context* (Beverly Hills, CA: Russell Sage Foundation, 1981), pp. 220–232.

# READINGS ON THE PUBLIC RELATIONS PROCESS

## Research

Alreck, Pamela L., and Robert B. Settle. *The Survey Research Handbook,* 2nd ed. Burr Ridge, IL: Irwin Professional Publishing, 1994.

Brody, E. W., ed. *New Technology and Public Relations: On to the Future.* Sarasota, FL: Institute for Public Relations Research and Education, 1991.

———, and Gerald C. Stone. *Public Relations Research.* New York: Praeger, 1989.

Broom, Glen M., and David M. Dozier. *Using Research in Public Relations: Applications to Program Management.* Englewood Cliffs, NJ: Prentice-Hall, 1990.

Grunig, James E., and Larissa A. Grunig, eds. *Public Relations Research Annual.* Hillsdale, NJ: Erlbaum (annual volumes since 1989).

Hamelink, Cees J. *Mass Communication Research: Problems and Policies.* Norwood, NJ: Ablex, 1993.

Hamilton, Seymour. *A Communication Audit Handbook: Helping Organizations Communicate.* New York: Longman, 1987.

Johnson, James M., and H. S. Pennypacker. *Strategies and Tactics in Behavioral Research,* 2nd ed. Hillsdale, NJ: Erlbaum, 1993.

Masterton, John. "Discovering Databases." *Public Relations Journal* 48 (November 1992): 12ff.

Nasser, David L. "How to Run a Focus Group." *Public Relations Journal* 44 (March 1988): 33–34.

Pavlik, John V. *Public Relations: What Research Tells Us,* Vol. 16. Newbury Park, CA: Sage CommText Series, 1987.

Simpson, Andrea L. "Ten Rules of Research." *Public Relations Quarterly* 37 (Summer 1992): 27ff.

"Using Research to Plan and Evaluate Public Relations" (special issue). *Public Relations Review* 16 (Summer 1990).

## Objectives

Broom, Glen M., and David M. Dozier. "Writing Program Goals and Objectives." In *Using Research in Public Relations: Applications to Program Management.* Englewood Cliffs, NJ: Prentice-Hall, 1990, pp. 39–44.

Cutlip, Scott M., Allen H. Center, and Glen M. Broom. "Step One: Defining Public Relations Problems." In *Effective Public Relations,* 7th ed. Englewood Cliffs, NJ: Prentice-Hall, 1994.

Frederico, Richard F. "What Are Your Core Communication Values?" *Communication World* 11 (October 1994): 14ff.

Grunig, James E., and Todd Hunt. "Defining and Choosing Goals and Objectives." In *Managing Public Relations.* New York: Holt, Rinehart & Winston, 1984, pp. 114–137.

Hauss, Deborah. "Setting Benchmarks Leads to Effective Programs." *Public Relations Journal* 49 (February 1993): 16ff.

Koestler, Frances A. *Planning and Setting Objectives.* New York: Foundation for Public Relations Research and Education, 1977.

Nager, Norman R., and T. Harrell Allen. *Public Relations Management by Objectives.* New York: Longman, 1984.

Shelby, Annette Neven. "Organization, Business, Management, Communication and Corporate Communication: An Analysis of Boundaries and Relationships." *Journal of Business Communication* 30 (1993): 241ff

Winokur, Dena, and Robert W. Kinkead. "How Public Relations Fits Into Corporate Strategy." *Public Relations Journal* 49 (May 1993): 16ff.

## Programming

Aronoff, Craig, and Otis W. Baskin. *Public Relations: Profession and Practice,* 3rd ed. Dubuque, IA: Wm. C. Brown, 1992.

Cutlip, Scott M., Allen H. Center, and Glen M. Broom. "Step Two: Planning and Programming." In *Effective Public Relations,* 7th ed. Englewood Cliffs, NJ: Prentice-Hall, 1994.

Grunig, James E., ed. *Excellence in Public Relations and Communication Management.* Hillsdale, NJ: Erlbaum, 1992.

Hunt, Todd, and James E. Grunig. *Public Relations Techniques.* Fort Worth, TX: Harcourt Brace, 1994.

Lesly, Philip, ed. *Lesly's Handbook of Public Relations and Communications,* 4th ed. New York: Amacom, 1991.

Newsom, Doug, Judy VanSlyke Turk, and Dean Kruckeberg. *This Is PR: The Realities of Public Relations,* 6th ed. Belmont, CA: Wadsworth, 1996.

Seitel, Fraser P. *The Practice of Public Relations,* 6th ed. Englewood Cliffs, NJ: Prentice-Hall, 1995.

Wilcox, Dennis L., Philip H. Ault, and Warren K. Agee. *Public Relations: Strategies and Tactics,* 4th ed. New York: HarperCollins, 1995.

## Evaluation

Broom, Glen M., and David M. Dozier. "Using Research to Evaluate Programs." In *Using Research in Public Relations: Applications to Program Management.* Englewood Cliffs, NJ: Prentice-Hall, 1990, pp. 71–88.

Cutlip, Scott M., Allen H. Center, and Glen M. Broom. "Step Four: Evaluating the Program." In *Effective Public Relations,* 7th ed. Englewood Cliffs, NJ: Prentice-Hall, 1994.

Grunig, James E. "Basic Research Provides Knowledge that Makes Evaluation Possible." *Public Relations Quarterly* (Fall 1983): 28ff.

Hauss, Deborah. "Measuring the Impact of Public Relations: Electronic Techniques Improve Campaign Evaluation." *Public Relations Journal* 49 (February 1993): 14–21.

Holloway, Deborah. "How to Select a Measurement System That's Right for You." *Public Relations Quarterly* 37 (Fall 1992): 15ff.

Lindemann, Walter K. "An 'Effectiveness Yardstick' to Measure Public Relations Success." *Public Relations Quarterly* 38 (Spring 1993): 7–9.

"Measuring Public Relations Impact" (special issue). *Public Relations Review* (Summer 1984).

Richter, Lisa, and Steve Drake. "Apply Measurement Mindset to Programs." *Public Relations Journal* 49 (January 1993): 32ff.

Rossi, Peter H., and Howard E. Freeman. *Evaluation: A Systematic Approach,* 3rd ed. Beverly Hills, CA: Russell Sage Foundation, 1985.

"Using Research to Plan and Evaluate Public Relations" (special issue). *Public Relations Review* 16 (Summer 1990).

Wiesendanger, Betsy. "Electronic Delivery and Feedback Systems Come of Age." *Public Relations Journal* 49 (January 1993): 10–14.

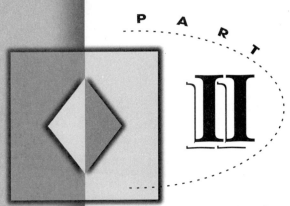

P A R T

# II

# Reaching Major Audiences

# Media Relations

JOURNALISTS REPRESENTING THE MASS AND SPECIAL-
ized media usually make up the external audience of
highest priority for public relations practitioners. Media relations consists essentially of obtaining appropriate publicity, or news coverage, for the activities of
the practitioner's client or organization. The field of
public relations began as publicity and for many
years was called that. Indeed, this process remains the
basis for the burgeoning disciplines of public relations, public affairs, and corporate communications.

Media relations involves targeting the "gatekeep-
ers" of the mass and specialized media for communication about the client or organization. However, the
media are actually intermediate audiences. The ultimate targeted audiences in media relations are the
*consumers* of the media.

# RESEARCH

The research process for media relations includes investigation of the practitioner's client or organization, of the opportunity or problem that accounts for communication with the media, and of the various audiences themselves to be targeted for the PR effort.

## Client Research

First, the practitioner should be familiar with background data about the client or organization, including its personnel, financial status, and reputation. Special attention must be given to past and present relations with media representatives. Has the client had negative or positive news coverage in the past? Has there been little or no coverage? Does the client have any particular media coverage strengths, such as unusual or glamorous products or a newsworthy chief executive officer? On the other hand, what are the client's publicity "negatives"? In what areas is the client vulnerable? Finally, the practitioner should assess the client's publicity opportunities. What special events can be most profitably staged for the client? What can be done to tie the client in with ongoing community or national special events? With information of this kind the practitioner will be better prepared to serve the client's publicity or media relations needs.

## Opportunity or Problem Research

The second aspect of research in preparation for media relations involves determining the reason for the program. Is it because an opportunity has presented itself for good news coverage, or has some problem arisen that will bring media representatives to the client's doorstep? This chapter is concerned more with the former situation, the publicity *opportunity*. For information on managing the media when a problem or crisis develops, see Chapter 11, "Emergency Public Relations."

## Audience Research

The final aspect of research for media relations is thought by most practitioners to be the most important—identifying the appropriate media and *their* audiences to target for communication. These media fall into two broad categories, mass and specialized, each of which can be further subdivided (see Exhibit 3-a).

With these media categories, the practitioner's task is to prepare a comprehensive list of media contacts. Appropriate *media directories*, such as those listed in the suggested readings in this chapter, should be consulted in preparing such a list. Practitioners may find that much of their work has already been done for them by these directories. The national, regional, state, and city directories are thorough, but in some cases more information must be gathered. To be of optimal use, the media contacts list should include:

1. The type and size of the audience reached by each media outlet
2. The type of material used by the media outlet—spot news, feature material, interviews, photos
3. The name and title of the appropriate editor, director, reporter, or staff writer who handles news of organizations such as the client's
4. The deadlines for that media contact—monthly, weekly, daily, morning, afternoon, evening, date, day, or hour

The best advice for the practitioner in media relations is simply to *know the media outlet*. Each outlet has its own unique set of departments and editorial staffing, with particular requirements for submitting material. If in doubt, call the media outlet to obtain the necessary guidelines, along with the name and address of the person who holds the editorial position. It is usually best not to ask to speak with journalists themselves. They may be very busy and resent intrusions for routine information. As a rule, news releases for newspapers should be addressed to the city editor if general in nature or to the appropriate section editor if they are of special interest. For broadcast stations, news releases should usually be addressed to the news director or, in some cases, to the public service director.

Practitioners should never feel that their media contacts lists are complete when they have compiled necessary information about the mass media alone. Each client or organization will be operating in a special field. Automobile manufacturers, fashion designers, dentists, rock music groups—all have their own organizations or associations. And all are served by their own specialized publications. Public relations practitioners must be aware of all such publications that serve their client's field. The process of compiling a list of specialized media contacts begins with consulting a media directory. Among the best of such publications for comprehensive listings in a great variety of fields are *Bacon's Publicity Checker* and *Working Press of the Nation*, both listed later in this chapter. Also listed are directories for medical, scientific, military, and minority media contacts.

Among the finished products of the practitioner's audience research, then, will be *two* media contacts lists: one for mass media and the other for specialized media. News releases, photos, and feature stories directed to and published in specialized publications can often be of greater value to the client than similar exposure in the mass media. It should be emphasized that the purpose of compiling these two media contacts lists is communication with the consumers of both the mass and specialized media—the client's ultimate intended audiences.

In the cases included later in this chapter, these audiences are sometimes specialized and sometimes mass in character.

---

Media Publics

# Mass media

Local

Print publications

Newspapers

Magazines

TV stations

Radio stations

National

Print publications

Broadcast networks

Wire services

# Specialized media

Local

Trade, industry, and association publications

Organizational house and membership publications

Ethnic publications

Publications of special groups

Specialized broadcast programs and stations

National

General business publications

National trade, industry, and association publications

National organizational house and membership publications

National ethnic publications

Publications of national special groups

National specialized broadcast programs and networks

Thus, the research process in media relations involves a thorough understanding of the practitioner's client or organization; the reason—opportunity or problem—for communicating with the media; and, most important, knowledge of the targeted media themselves—the nature of the media outlets, audiences reached, types of material used, specific names and titles of staff contacts, and their deadlines.

# OBJECTIVES

Media relations uses both impact and output objectives. Some typical examples of both types are examined here, along with a sampling of the objectives used in the media relations cases included in this chapter.

## Impact Objectives

Impact objectives represent the desired outcomes of modifying the attitudes and behaviors of target audiences. In media relations they usually include such statements as:

1. To increase knowledge of news about the client among community media representatives
2. To enhance the client's credibility among media people
3. To reinforce favorable attitudes toward the client on the part of media representatives
4. To increase favorable client news coverage

Note that in each of these statements, percentages and time frames can be added as desired. The first statement could be rephrased to read: to increase knowledge of news about the client by 30 percent among community media representatives during the period June 1–December 1. However, a majority of the award-winning cases in this book do *not* quantify their objectives or set time frames.

Almost invariably the objectives used in our sample cases targeted the client's ultimate audiences, rather than the media audiences, for desired impact. It is understood in each case, however, that the media must be the intermediate target audience. Perhaps the objectives would have been clearer and easier to measure if they had targeted *both* the desired media and the ultimate audiences.

## Output Objectives

Output objectives in media relations refer to the efforts made by the practitioner on behalf of the client. These statements have nothing to do with the client's desired influence on audiences. Output objectives may include:

1. To be of service to the media—both proactively and reactively
   a. Proactively, to provide *newsworthy* stories about the client or organization
   b. Reactively, to be available for responses to media inquiries
2. To coordinate media interviews with client or organizational officers and personnel

# PROGRAMMING

Programming for media relations includes the same planning and execution elements used in other forms of public relations: (1) theme and messages, (2) action or special event(s), (3) uncontrolled or controlled media, and (4) principles of effective communication.

## Theme and Messages

Program themes, especially in connection with special events, should be included in the messages sent to media outlets. In media relations, the messages themselves should always be governed by the requirements for newsworthiness applicable to the targeted media outlets. Since media relations essentially involves the communication of client news to media outlets or the stimulation of news coverage of the client, the practitioner must understand the nature of news and the criteria for newsworthiness.

Some practitioners believe there are two kinds of news: "hard" and "soft." It is more accurate, however, to think of *spot news* and *feature material* as the two kinds of news.

Spot news is temporal, or time-bound, in nature. Within the rubric of spot news are two subcategories: hard and soft. *Hard spot news* is normally found on prominent pages of major metropolitan dailies. It affects large numbers of people and is of great and immediate interest to the audiences of most mass media outlets. Unfortunately, most hard spot news handled by PR practitioners is *bad news* about the client, such as disasters, plant closings, or layoffs. *Good* news about clients can usually be classified as *soft spot news*. It may not be of much interest outside the organization itself, in which case it should be printed in a house publication and not sent to a mass media outlet. A major challenge to the practitioner is to create special events or *make* good news about the client that will receive favorable coverage in the media.

Feature material, on the other hand, is not time-bound but may be used as "filler" for print and broadcast media. Feature stories for both kinds of media usually focus on human interest topics. Types of feature stories include "a day in the life of . . ."; profiles of personalities; interviews; descriptions of events that emphasize human interest factors and the personalities involved; and sidebars, or feature stories designed to accompany spot news stories in newspapers.

Keeping in mind the differences between spot news and feature material, the practitioner should also be sensitive to the general criteria used by journalists to determine what is newsworthy. The usual characteristics of news include what is new or novel, involves famous persons, is important to large numbers of people, involves conflict or mystery, may be considered confidential, will have significant consequences, is funny, is romantic, or involves sex.

News has also been defined as anything a media outlet chooses to print, broadcast, or film as "news." Since the selection is always the outlet's choice, the public relations practitioner must become familiar with the criteria used by that particular group of editors. This is simply another way of saying, *Know the media outlet.*

Like other aspects of programming, theme and messages should be governed by the practitioner's understanding of what is news and both the general and particular newsworthiness criteria in use at individual media outlets.

## Action(s) or Special Event(s)

The use of actions on the part of the client and the staging of special events assumes special importance in media relations. They provide the basis for news coverage. They *are* the news about the client. Thus, the PR practitioner should review the list of actions and special events included in Exhibit 2-c. These can serve as methods of *making* news for the client. Each action or special event should be carefully planned and orchestrated for its maximum news value. If possible, celebrities should be present, and as many other news criteria should be incorporated as is feasible.

The cases in this chapter illustrate a broad range of special events, including an anniversary and the sponsorship of a major sporting event.

## Uncontrolled Media

Uncontrolled media are the major vehicles for reporting client news to media representatives. The most commonly used forms are:

1. News releases—print and video
2. Photographs and photo opportunities
3. News conferences
4. Media interviews

**News Releases.** Of these four frequently used formats, news releases are the most popular with public relations practitioners. News releases provide a quick, economical means of communicating client spot news or feature material to appropriate media outlets.

Unfortunately, news releases have become overused in major markets throughout the United States. Each morning, editors may be confronted with a stack of 70 to 100 or more releases from practitioners seeking news coverage for their clients or organizations. A prominent Washington bureau chief confided to one of my classes that, faced with his daily pile of news releases, he simply pulls a large, desk-top-high wastebasket over to the edge of the desk and "files" most of the morning mail.

How, then, can practitioners expect to break through the blizzard of news releases to call attention to their own client's news? The "secret" of successful news releases lies in the first word of the term itself—*news*. A really newsworthy story about a client can easily be telephoned to a city editor. The editor, if interested in the story, will assign a reporter to cover it. Major metropolitan editors or broadcast news directors rarely use news releases verbatim or even partially. If a story is there, the news release may alert them to it; but they invariably prefer to assign their own staff people to do the actual news gathering and writing.

Practitioners' news releases may be used verbatim in smaller markets, served by low-circulation dailies or weekly newspapers. Faced with staff and time limitations, these small-market media outlets rely heavily on the work of public relations people.

All media outlets, in markets large or small, depend on PR practitioners for *information* about news events in their market areas. News releases, despite their overuse, remain the major method of transmitting information from the client to the journalist.

An increasingly popular form of client news is the *video news release (VNR)*. Like their print counterparts, successful VNRs must focus on *news* rather than on promotional pap about the client. These news releases are used most frequently in medium or small, rather than major metropolitan, markets. They should be produced by a reputable firm specializing in VNRs and, ideally, the firm should be equipped to handle the entire task, including scripting, production, and distribution.

**Photographs and Photo Opportunities.** Photographs are a second widely used form of uncontrolled media. As with news releases, public relations photographs are seldom used by major metropolitan daily newspapers. But, like news releases, they may serve to attract the attention of major editors to client news that might otherwise be overlooked. Public relations photographs have a better chance of being used by smaller publications in smaller markets. They are important enough to warrant attention to the details of their proper composition and preparation for PR purposes.

Good public relations photographs should be creative and imaginative in composition, avoiding the clichés a client may request, such as a speaker standing at a podium, one person handing something to another, a group shot of ten or more people, or one person sitting at a desk. Photographs of this kind usually find their way into house publications. A good public relations photograph depicts something a newspaper photographer cannot duplicate or restage. Unique and interesting photographs may be used because of their creativity and news value.

A frequently used contemporary technique is the staging of a "photo opportunity," especially in markets where the major dailies or magazines are likely to assign their own photographers to a story. The photo opportunity should be carefully planned in advance and staged in a natural—not theatrical—way, so that it becomes an integral or necessary part of the news story and not something that can be missed by the assigned journalists and photographers.

**News Conferences.**  A third frequently used form of uncontrolled media is the news conference. News conferences should be used sparingly since they are usually inconvenient for journalists. A good one-word rule for holding news conferences is *don't*. Of course, all rules have exceptions, and news conferences should be staged under exceptional circumstances. If staged, the conference must live up to its descriptive adjective, *news*. Even on their very best days, metropolitan journalists are easily annoyed. They can resent being summoned to a news conference to hear a routine announcement that could have been faxed to the city desk or reported in a written release.

Many organizations use news conferences for significant announcements, such as major corporate changes, takeovers, mergers, introductions of new product lines, or responses to false accusations of wrongdoing. Other than for major government agencies, news conferences should never be routine. They should be reserved for truly newsworthy occasions that call for a personal presentation by the organization's chief executive officer or by a visiting celebrity or dignitary.

News conferences can be conducted profitably, but the practitioner should always keep the preceding reservations in mind and usually resist the urge to hold one.

**Media Interviews.**  Media interviews are a fourth frequently used form of uncontrolled media. Whether given to print or broadcast journalists, interviews provide the most direct contact between the client and the media. The practitioner's role in this situation is that of a link, or coordinator, and sometimes also that of a trainer or coach for the client.

In the case of print interviews, clients may have the options of declaring beforehand that their comments will be for background, not for attribution, or completely off the record. In these cases the client's name cannot be used; and in off-the-record interviews the content of the interview cannot be used in the media. Aside from interviews with high government officials in sensitive positions, however, most clients want to be both quoted and identified in the media as a means of promoting their organizations' interests.

Broadcast interviews do not permit the luxury of being off the record. If clients consent to broadcast interviews, they do so with the knowledge that while on camera (or microphone), they may be put through a "third degree" by an enterprising journalist. Moreover, the client loses control of the editing function. For this reason many organizations insist on bringing their own videotaping equipment and crew in order to have an independent record of the interview. Increasingly, organizations are paying specialized consultants for "media training" for their executives, who can then significantly influence favorable public opinion about their organizations.

Print and broadcast interviews, then, are one of the four most frequently used forms of uncontrolled media in the client's communication with journalists. In addition to news releases, photographs, news conferences, and interviews, the practitioner should consider the other communication vehicles listed in Exhibit 2-d.

## Controlled Media

A variety of forms of controlled media can be used to provide journalists with background information. For example, the typical *media kit* includes such printed materials as brochures, folders, annual reports, speeches, and backgrounders. In the true sense of the term, however, controlled media are not used in media relations. When journalists are given controlled communications, they make their own uses (or nonuses) of them. Thus, the client or practitioner has no control over how such materials will be used by journalists.

A case can be made that public relations advertising constitutes the use of controlled communications in media relations. The practitioner *does* deal with media outlets in such cases, but not with journalists. Advertising is purchased directly from the media outlet's advertising department.

The exhibits included with the cases in this chapter demonstrate the scope of both uncontrolled and controlled communications used in media relations.

## Effective Communication

In media relations, the communication process can be aptly described as a two-step flow. The traditional two-stage model depicts a stream of messages from a mass media source to opinion leaders and then to the colleagues of the opinion leaders. In media relations, this process is partially reversed. Communication flows from the practitioner's client to the media and then in turn to the media audience.

Because of the special nature of media relations, not all of the nine principles of effective communication discussed in Chapter 2 apply.

Source credibility clearly *is* applicable in the case of media relations. Media representatives must perceive the client or organization and its spokesperson as trustworthy and reliable. Salient information, on the other hand, must be redefined for media relations. Information that meets the criteria of newsworthiness constitutes the salience for journalists. Both nonverbal and verbal cues contribute to communication effectiveness in media relations, just as they do in other forms of public relations. The use of two-way communication, however, plays a less important role in media relations than in other forms. Journalists generally resent inquiries from practitioners to see if a client's news releases are going to be used. The feedback that practitioners really want in media relations is the use of their materials in the media.

The use of opinion leaders in the usual sense is not a part of media relations. In media relations, practitioners communicate directly with journalists. In some instances, journalists are regarded as community opinion leaders, but this principle applies more directly to community relations. The selective exposure principle may apply in some cases to media relations but, in general, journalists are more open-minded and often seek information that they may personally disagree with. Finally, the audience participation principle is valid and useful in media relations. When introducing new product lines, for example, many companies invite journalists to use the product on an introductory basis. Journalist participation at news conferences and other meetings arranged by PR practitioners provides other instances of effective audience participation in media relations.

Thus, most of the principles of effective communication apply to media relations to some degree. However, the group-influence principle is rarely used in media relations since journalists pride themselves on their independence of thought and action. But on the whole, principles of effective communication should be a priority concern of the public relations practitioner in media relations.

# EVALUATION

The evaluation process in all forms of public relations always refers to the program's stated objectives. In media relations, as in all of public relations, impact objectives are of the highest priority.

## Evaluating Impact Objectives

The impact objective of informing the media about the client is generally measured by assessing the exposure of the message in the media, or publicity placement. National or local clipping and media monitoring services are usually retained to take this measure of effectiveness. Message exposure can also be measured by the circulation figures and audience-size data available from the publications and broadcast media themselves. Additionally, some public firms use sophisticated computerized tracking systems to evaluate effectiveness in delivering messages to audiences. Publicity placement, however, remains the predominant method for evaluating the success of message exposure.

Attitude objectives in most forms of public relations are measured by conducting sample surveys of the target audiences, but this may not be feasible with journalists targeted for communication. Some might react negatively to such an intrusion from a PR practitioner. Content analyses of media placement, however, can yield the desired measurements. A scientific assessment of attitudes is therefore possible and relatively easily obtained.

This same procedure is also useful in measuring favorable client news coverage. This objective is the ultimate goal of all media relations.

## Evaluating Output Objectives

Along with the measurement of impact objectives, practitioners want to determine the effectiveness of their media relations output objectives. These consist essentially of distributing uncontrolled media to outlets, being responsive to media inquiries, and coordinating media interviews. They can be evaluated by keeping records of all such transactions. Although these objectives are easily accomplished, the practitioner should be reminded that these goals have no bearing on media relations impact.

Evaluation of media relations, then, is heavily concentrated on successful and favorable placement of the practitioner's uncontrolled media. Other objectives are useful, but successful media relations ultimately boils down to the matter of placement. This is clearly visible in the priority given to placement in the evaluations of the cases in this chapter.

# SUMMARY

With some modifications, the four-stage process is as useful in media relations as it is in other forms of public relations. Essentially, media relations involves establishing a favorable working relationship between PR practitioners and journalists representing appropriate mass and specialized media.

The most important aspect of research for media relations is the preparation of up-to-date lists of media contacts for both mass and specialized outlets. Objectives in media relations usually emphasize the desired behavioral impact of obtaining favorable news coverage for the client. An absolute essential for media relations programming is an understanding of the particular media outlets' audiences and the media's definitions of news for those audiences. This information should provide criteria for the development of newsworthy, client-centered special events, news releases, photographs, news conferences, interviews, and/or other forms of uncontrolled media used in reaching journalists.

Evaluation of media relations always refers back to the program's stated objectives. Impact objectives are generally measured through publicity placement, circulation and audience data, computer tracking of messages, or content analysis. The accomplishment of output objectives can be simply determined by counting or otherwise observing the desired outputs as they are set in motion. In essence, however, the effectiveness of media relations always comes down to media placement, that is, obtaining the desired publicity for the client.

# READINGS ON MEDIA RELATIONS

Bernstein, Gail. "Meet the Press." *Public Relations Journal* 44 (March 1989): 28–32.

Collins, David. "Ten Rules of Editorial Etiquette." *Public Relations Quarterly* 39 (Fall 1994): 8.

Detweiler, John S. "Source Power: New Leverage in Media Relations." *Public Relations Quarterly* 37 (Summer 1992): 19ff.

Dilenschneider, Robert L. "Use Ingenuity in Media Relations." *Public Relations Quarterly* 37 (Summer 1992): 13ff.

Goff, Christine F. *The Publicity Process,* 3rd ed. Ames, IA: Iowa State University Press, 1989.

Grabowski, Gene. "Seven Deadly Sins of Media Relations." *Public Relations Quarterly* 37 (Spring 1992): 37ff.

Graham, Barbara Florio. "Two Dozen Ways to Guarantee Failure in Media Relations." *Public Relations Quarterly* 37 (Summer 1992): 26ff.

Howard, Carole M., and Wilma K. Mathews. *On Deadline: Managing Media Relations,* 2nd ed. Prospect Heights, IL: Waveland, 1994.

Klein, T., and F. Danzig. *Publicity: How to Make the Media Work for You.* New York: Scribner's, 1985.

Marken, G. A. "Let's Do Away With Press Releases." *Public Relations Quarterly* 39 (Spring 1994): 46ff.

———. "Press Releases: When Nothing Else Will Do." *Public Relations Quarterly* 39 (Fall 1994): 9ff.

Martin, Dick. *Executive's Guide to Handling a Press Interview.* Babylon, NY: Pilot Books, 1990.

"Media Relations: What's News?" (special section). *Public Relations Journal* 45 (November 1989): 14–22.

Morton, Linda P. "Producing Publishable Press Releases: A Research Perspective." *Public Relations Quarterly* 37 (Winter 1992): 9ff.

———, and John Warren. "News Elements and Editors' Choices." *Public Relations Review* 18 (Spring 1992): 47–53.

Wester, Natalie. "Build Confidence With Media Training." *Public Relations Journal* 48 (February 1992): 26ff.

Winter, Grant. "Improving Broadcast News Conferences." *Public Relations Journal* 46 (July 1990): 25–26.

## Media Directories

*Bacon's Media Alerts.* Chicago: Bacon's Publishing Co., published annually with bimonthly updates. Publicity opportunities.

*Bacon's Publicity Checker.* Chicago: Bacon's Publishing Co., published annually with quarterly supplements.

*Bacon's Radio/TV Directory.* Chicago: Bacon's Publishing Co., published annually with quarterly supplements.

*Broadcasting/Cablecasting Yearbook.* Washington, DC: Broadcasting Publications, published annually.

*Burrelle's Media Directories.* Livingston, NJ: Burrelle's, published annually.

*Burrelle's Special Directories: Black Media: Hispanic Media: Women's Media.* Livingston, NJ: Burrelle's, published annually.

*Caduceus '94: The Health and Medical Media Directory.* Chicago: Caduceus Communications, updated three times annually.

*Editor and Publisher International Yearbook.* New York: Editor and Publisher Co., published annually.

*Gale Directory of Publications* (formerly *Ayer Directory of Publications*). Detroit: Gale Research, published annually.

*Guide to U.S. Business, Financial and Economic News Correspondents and Contacts.* New York: Larriston Communications, published annually.

*Guide to U.S. Medical and Science News Correspondents and Contacts.* New York: Larriston Communications, published annually.

*Hudson's Washington News Media Contacts Directory.* Rhinebeck, NY: Hudson's, published annually with quarterly updates.

*Military Publications.* New York: Richard Weiner, published annually.

*National Directory of Corporate Affairs.* Washington, DC: Columbia Books, 1994.

*National Directory of Magazines.* Detroit: Gale Research, 1994.

*Rolles Blue Book.* Bethesda, MD: Rolle Communications, published annually.

*TV Publicity Outlets Nationwide.* Washington Depot, CT: Public Relations Plus, published three times a year.

*Working Press of the Nation.* Chicago: National Research Bureau, published annually.

# Media Relations
# Cases

*An early commitment of the Clinton administration was the most extensive national health care reform since Medicare in the 1960s. The failure of the Clinton health care plan can be attributed to a failure in timing, failure to develop clear and consistent messages, failure to maintain an image of openness, a problem with the First Lady as spokesperson, and a lack of understanding of the imperatives of the news media.*

**CASE 3-1**

## The Clinton Health Care Plan: What Went Wrong?

Leonard Steinhorn, Assistant Professor, School of Communication, American University

### Background

It was to be the pivotal achievement of the Clinton presidency. It would improve the lives of millions and provide peace of mind for every American. It was long overdue. What Social Security was for Franklin Roosevelt, health care reform would be for Bill Clinton. And generations of Americans would thank him for it.

Expectations for health care reform were high when Bill Clinton took the oath of office in January 1993. Other presidents had failed in the past to change the health care system, but this time it was different. The cost of health care was skyrocketing beyond inflation, nearly 40 million citizens lacked insurance, and millions more feared they were only a pink slip away from having no coverage at all. Candidate Clinton made health care reform a major campaign issue in 1992, and by election day polls showed it to be a decisive concern among the voting public. One of his first initiatives as president was to create a White House health care task force, under the leadership of First Lady Hillary Rodham Clinton, that would be charged with drafting legislation. The president promised that he would present a plan to Congress 100 days after taking office.

Reform seemed so inevitable early on that much of the health care industry—including insurance and pharmaceutical companies as well as groups representing doctors—initially positioned themselves not to block it but merely to have a place at the table. When the president finally unveiled his plan in September 1993, polls were showing 60 to

70 percent support. At the time, even Senate Minority Leader Bob Dole endorsed a fundamental principle of the Clinton plan—universal coverage—and called the president's proposal "a good beginning" that would result in final passage of a bill. The question was not whether reform would pass, but what shape it would take.[1]

Just 20 months after the president's inauguration, in September 1994, health care reform was declared officially dead. Public support for Clinton's plan has plummeted. Neither house of Congress ever voted on a bill. Senator Dole, most Republican members of Congress, the health care industry, and the business community had become steadfast opponents of the president's initiative. The great expectations of January 1993 turned into dashed hopes by mid-1994. Reform's failure led to the historic election of 1994, when Republicans took over both houses of Congress for the first time in 40 years. "It's hard to remember the hope and optimism with which the Clinton health care plan was greeted," wrote one reporter in early 1995.[2] What happened to the Clinton health care plan in so short a time offers a compelling lesson in some of the pitfalls and mistakes to avoid—and some of the strategic decisions to anticipate—when attempting a major national communications campaign.

## What Went Wrong?

Health care reform failed for many reasons. Special interests, particularly the insurance industry and the small business lobby, seized on weaknesses in the Clinton plan and poured millions of dollars into advertising, public relations, and lobbying. Estimates of spending by opponents range from $100 million to $300 million. The Health Insurance Association of America (HIAA) alone spent $15 million on its famed "Harry and Louise" ads, which depicted a middle class couple expressing concern about "government-run" health care that would limit their choice of doctors and lower the quality of care.[3] The opposition to reform was "the most costly and intensively waged lobbying battle in U.S. history," write Haynes Johnson and David Broder, authors of *The System*, a book on the failure of Clinton's health care plan.[4]

Another cause of failure was the inability of the Democrats in Congress to unite behind a single plan. Because House Republicans unanimously opposed the Clinton proposal, there was little room for discord among Democrats. But discord is precisely what happened, in part because the lobbying barrage of reform opponents swayed some key Democratic members and in part because of tension between the White House and Capitol Hill. Asking Congress to reform a sector representing one-seventh of the economy was a large enough task without these problems.[5]

But even with these obstacles and opponents, health care reform still might have prevailed had the Clinton administration done a better job selling it to the public. Public support for the plan at first was very high, and the momentum for change seemed unstoppable. Even some of the most ardent reform opponents in the health care industry were initially hesitant to defy public opinion and challenge the president's plan directly.

What was needed was an effective communications strategy from the White House. "Clinton has the biggest public relations weapon at his hand—the presidency," one Washington operative told *USA Today* in January 1993.[6] "The President is going to have to sell [his plan] week by week. He's going to have to get out in the country because the whole effort will rise and fall on how successfully he is selling the American people on the plan's value," said a key Democratic senator.[7] Clinton himself acknowledged as much in an interview with ABC's Ted Koppel the day following his September 1993 health care speech to Congress. When asked if he could hold on to the speech momentum, Clinton answered that it in part "depends upon how good a line of communication you can maintain with the American public."[8]

On the surface, the White House implemented an aggressive campaign to win public approval. Their tactics combined the best of traditional public relations with the grassroots media outreach that has come to characterize political communication in the 1990s. From a nationally televised town meeting to briefings with influential Washington journalists to hosting 200 talk radio shows on the White House lawn, the administration actively sought to sell its program. As head of the health care task force, the First Lady traveled the country, met with senior citizens, testified before Congress, held teach-ins, and appeared on news and talk shows. Administration officials courted doctors, unions, and nonprofit groups. Understanding the power of images, the White House created a "health security card" that symbolically tied the president's initiative to Social Security. And lest anyone fear that the Clintons were going too far with their reform, the First Lady surrounded herself with two of the nation's most popular physicians—former Surgeon General C. Everett Koop and pediatrician T. Berry Brazelton—during the president's September 1993 speech to Congress. It was, as *Business Week* called it, a "publicity carpet bombing."[9]

So how did such an effort fail? It failed because the White House committed serious errors in judgment, strategy, and execution that undermined its communications campaign and gave its well-funded and well-organized opponents an opening to reshape the debate. It was an opening the opponents gladly seized. Instead of controlling the debate, the White House ended up on the defensive; instead of defining the message, the White House ceded it to reform opponents. Once the president lost his communications advantage, there was little hope of regaining it and winning over an increasingly skeptical public.

The administration's communications errors cut to the very core of what constitutes effective public relations strategy. The White House failed in timing the plan, in developing clear and consistent messages, in maintaining an image of openness, in choosing spokespersons, and in understanding the imperatives of the news media. Problems with any one of these could foil even the best public relations plan; in this case, problems with all of them did.

## Timing Is Everything

One of Bill Clinton's first promises as president was to submit a health care reform proposal to Congress 100 days after taking office. Five days after his inauguration, he appointed his health care task force and named the First Lady as its chair. The task force generated a flurry of activity, with more than 600 people toiling in "clusters" and "working groups." From all appearances, it seemed as if the White House would meet its self-imposed deadline.

But 100 days came and went, and there was no proposal. The president and his cabinet were preoccupied with the federal budget. A date early in May was pushed to late May, which then became late June and then late July. Still there was no reform plan. It wasn't until September 22 that the president made his major health care address to the nation. Within days, just as the president was beginning his all-out campaign to promote reform, he once again was distracted—this time by overseas crises and the battle to pass the North American Free Trade Agreement (NAFTA). All but one health care event scheduled for October was canceled. Actual legislation was not sent to Congress until November 20, the last day of the congressional session. Not until his January 1994 State of the Union address did the president return to health care. It was "a long hiatus," said White House Deputy Chief of Staff Harold Ickes.[10]

These fits and starts crippled his public relations plan. First, they enabled the health care industry to define the terms of debate. "While the White House fiddled, the Clinton health care opposition decided to burn up the news wires," a group of media observers commented.[11] By not having an actual plan to sell, the White House was unable to respond effectively to opposition attacks. And by failing to saturate the public with his core message, the President allowed reform opponents to do so. Among those filling the void was HIAA with its "Harry and Louise" ads. "They were terrific ads," said Deputy Chief of Staff Ickes. "People were confused and scared and we did nothing to counter that for a very long time."[12]

The delays caused other problems. Each day the White House dallied was another opportunity for frustrated task force members to leak an item to the press. Because of the substantive news vacuum, the leaks—whether accurate or not—assumed a disproportionate importance in the media. Moreover, without an actual proposal in hand, the media fell back on reporting the politics rather than the substance of health care reform, which diminished the president's ultimate message. Timing problems also hurt the organizing efforts of the Democratic National Committee and other reform proponents, who tried hard to build a coalition and an outreach campaign but never gained the momentum needed to counter the opponents.

For almost any public relations campaign, failure to manage the timing means failure to manage the message, the tactics, and the outreach to the media. Once President Clinton made the 100-day promise, he set in motion a timing problem from which his grand proposal never recovered.

## An Undisciplined Message

A fundamental principle of any public relations campaign is to keep the core messages clear, simple, consistent, and easy to understand. Message discipline is essential for public relations success. The White House did not practice it well with health care reform.

On the surface, the president's communications team performed textbook message development. They conducted polls and focus groups, they found "real people" who could poignantly illustrate the shortcomings of the current system, and they identified the visceral themes that drove the health care debate.

But unfortunately for the White House, they did not always communicate what they seemed to know. One week the motivation behind reform was the "price gouging, cost shifting and unconscionable profiteering" of the insurance and pharmaceutical industries, to quote Hillary Rodham Clinton.[13] Another week it was about the right of all Americans to health care. Yet another week it was about the security of having health care coverage if you were sick or lost a job. At other times it was about cost control. The messages spoke in dizzying ways to different audiences and sensibilities—to resentment, compassion, fear, and self-interest—without any unifying theme. This lack of message discipline gave reform opponents the opening they needed to cast doubt on key components of the Clinton plan. Would it eliminate the choice of doctors? Would it lower the quality of care? Would government meddle in the doctor-patient relationship? Is it going to hurt those of us who already have coverage? The Clinton team had persuasive answers for all of these questions but never presented them forcefully and coherently. By the time reform was declared dead, according to Haynes Johnson and David Broder, "the public came to see the Clinton reform as threatening the security of the middle class, not benefiting it."[14]

The administration also did itself no favor by presenting such a complex and weighty proposal. Although a plan to overhaul such a huge sector of the economy must by necessity be extensive, many observers wondered why the dotting of *i*'s and the crossing of *t*'s wasn't left to Congress. What the White House presented was a 1,342-page plan filled with bureaucratic acronyms, boards, and alliances. "We created a target the size of Philadelphia," White House aide Bob Boorstin told Johnson and Broder.[15] It enabled reform opponents to portray the plan as a complex, government-dominated, even authoritarian scheme that shifted power to bureaucrats in Washington. It became a plan about government, not "people like us." Senator Dole effectively exploited this theme in his televised response to the president's 1994 State of the Union message when he showed a flowchart depicting the many agencies and bureaus included in the plan. Filled with intersecting lines and acronyms such as NGFSFHP, NQMP, NHB, RHA, and CHA, the chart, according to the *New York Times,* "resembled a street map of Istanbul" and drove home the opposition message that the Clinton plan was big government run amok.[16]

The White House violated the cardinal public relations rule of keeping messages simple and digestible. Johnson and Broder write, "The absence of a few simple, structural principles, readily grasped by the public, was a crippling defect—and one that could have been anticipated." [17]

## The Pitfall of Secrecy

When it comes to government, wrote Supreme Court Justice Louis Brandeis, "sunlight is the best disinfectant." With the possible exception of national security, Americans have historically been distrustful of any government activity involving secrecy. People expect openness, full disclosure, and freedom of information. The news media, which depend on access to information, will rattle the chains of any government door that appears locked to the public. A government public relations campaign built on anything that smacks of secrecy is bound to face trouble. Secrecy—not the policy under consideration—will become the issue.

The Clinton administration committed a major strategic error when it steadfastly refused to discuss the work of the task force or to disclose the names of its participants. It is not clear why White House decision-makers chose this course. If they feared the public would misunderstand the reform process, they only had to look at the way Congress drew up legislation daily in full public view. If they feared leaks to the press or special interest meddling, that happened anyway. For reform opponents, it enabled them to say that the White House was trying to hide something from the public and was up to no good. "Opponents of Clinton-style reform used the secrecy issue to cast the first real doubts on the effort," the *Washington Post* wrote.[18] It also fueled what was already an adversarial relationship with the media, one that began early in Clinton's term when presidential aide George Stephanopoulos attempted to bar the press from White House corridors. Furthermore, secrecy would give the press little to write about besides the political battles of health care reform. And it would leave reporters beholden not to the administration but to their sources' interpretation of policy and events.

By blacking out rather than managing the news of the task force, the White House ironically participated in undermining public confidence in its effort. Disclosure to the public and press is a basic public relations principle, particularly for public officials. Refusal to disclose is often more damaging than whatever the press would report in the process.

## Choosing the Right Spokesperson

According to conventional wisdom, the president's health care reform initiative failed largely because of First Lady Hillary Rodham Clinton's leadership problems. The litany against her is that she was too arrogant, too confrontational, too inflexible, and too distracted by the Whitewater controversy to navigate reform through the rough political waters. But from a public relations perspective, the finger of blame is misdirected. The First Lady was not the problem. The president's decision to choose her was.

Initially, Hillary Rodham Clinton was a very popular choice to head the president's health care initiative. Throughout 1993, public opinion polls indicated that a majority of Americans approved of her efforts. At the president's September 1993 address to Congress, she was greeted with a standing ovation from both Democrats and Republicans. Pundits and politicians praised her testimony before five congressional committees that fall. "By the end of her first day on the Hill, the elevation of Hillary to icon had occurred," write Johnson and Broder.[19] By December of that year, her polls spiked toward 70 percent approval. Only in hindsight does she appear unpopular.

What made her a poor choice as reform leader is that she fit none of the public relations criteria for choosing a spokesperson. To be an effective spokesperson for a major national communications effort, one needs to be credible on the issue, above the partisan fray, beyond the potential for controversy, and dedicated to the cause without having anything personally to gain from it. In this case, with an issue that generated considerable emotion and reached deep into the lives of every American, the spokesperson needed to be someone who evoked trust, not politics. The First Lady's early popularity appears to have blinded the administration to her potential as a lightning rod on the issue. And she was a lightning rod the president could not relieve of her duties. By surrounding herself with C. Everett Koop and T. Berry Brazelton at the president's September 1993 speech, she implicitly recognized the need to inspire confidence and trust. They—or others like them—would have been more appropriate spokespersons for reform.[20]

## Understanding the News Media

A final flaw in the Clinton health care campaign is one common to many public relations efforts: a failure to understand how the news media shape and frame the issues they cover. Conflict, controversy, drama, novelty, and fear—these are the news hooks that too often govern media coverage today. This is not to suggest that news outlets ignore or disregard explanatory reports on substantive issues. But these stories are simply overwhelmed by breathless reports on the politics of an issue—who's winning, who's losing, whose poll numbers are up, whose are down, who's making a charge, who's making a rebuttal.[21] It is, as authors Edwin Diamond and Robert A. Silverman put it, "the old media habit of choosing conflict over context."[22]

According to Diamond and Silverman, *USA Today* published 41 articles on health care reform in a two-month period in early 1994; one dealt with cost issues, another provided an explanatory guide to various reform plans, and 29 covered the "battles," the "challenges," the politics, and the horse race. In a similar sampling of 35 articles in *Time* and *Newsweek* during 1993, nearly a third were concerned with the president's approval ratings and whether health care reform would "make or break" his presidency.[23] A study of nearly two thousand print and broadcast stories conducted by the Times Mirror Center for the People & the Press, in conjunction with the Kaiser Family Foundation and the *Columbia Journalism Review,* found that the politics of reform was covered twice as often as the impact of reform on consumers.[24]

It may well be possible that even the best-run media campaign could not avoid some of this coverage.[25] But the critical White House mistakes described above certainly fueled and reinforced it. Not having a clear message, shutting the press out of the policy-making phase, delaying the plan's introduction, and politicizing reform through the First Lady's appointment all paved the way for news coverage that focused on politics and personalities, not impact and substance. Although the president did a good job initially in showing the nation why reform was needed—and the media covered this side of the issue well—he did not follow up with clear and understandable explanations of how his reform plan would affect people's lives and wallets. Had he provided the media with a straightforward sense of why his plan would make health care in America better and less costly, and had he recognized the frequent need to feed the press new and different versions of this message, he might have had more success in shaping media coverage and swaying public opinion to his side. Instead, it was reform opponents who drove the media debate. And journalists obliged by framing their coverage as just another intramural battle among the warring interests of Washington, D.C.

## Conclusion

In retrospect, President Clinton acknowledges that he made key strategic mistakes in trying to pass his health care reform plan. He admits to misunderstanding Congress, to setting a naive legislative timetable, to underestimating the potential reaction to his wife, and to failing to recognize the inherent problems of the task force secrecy policy.[26] But he continues to believe that a majority of Americans, "if they're engaged and they understand what the options are," will make the right decision for the country.[27] Assuming the president is correct and it is indeed still possible to build consensus for political change, then the challenge for public officials is how well they engage voters and help them understand their options. Although President Clinton did not bequeath future generations a reformed health care system, his failure has taught a valuable lesson in the strategies and tactics of political communications.

## NOTES

1.  For the best account of the rise and fall of Clinton's reform plan, see Haynes Johnson and David S. Broder, *The System: The American Way of Politics at the Breaking Point* (Boston: Little, Brown and Company, 1996). Dole's quote on "a good beginning" is from Edwin Chen and David Lauter, "Clinton Unveils Health Reform," *Los Angeles Times,* September 23, 1993; his support for universal coverage is cited in James Fallows, "A Triumph of Misinformation," *The Atlantic Monthly,* January 1995. On the willingness of hospitals, insurers, doctors, and drug companies to acknowledge the inevitability of reform, see, for example, Judi Hasson, "All Players Have Ideas to Overhaul Health Care," *USA Today,* January 27, 1993: "Once opposed to any change, most of these industries now realize the health-care system will be overhauled whether they like it or not. So most are weighing in with their own ideas on how to fix it."

2.  Daniel Franklin, "Tommy Boggs and the Death of Health Care Reform," *Washington Monthly,* April 1995.

3.  See Johnson and Broder, pp. 194–195 for the amount opponents spent. Information on the "Harry and Louise" ad campaign can be found in Johnson and Broder, pp. 205–206 and in Dana Priest and Michael Weisskopf, "Health Care Reform: The Collapse of a Quest," *Washington Post,* October 11, 1994.

4.  Johnson and Broder, p. 53.

5.  Congress's failure to pass health care reform is best chronicled in Johnson and Broder. The book details the influence of various special interests, describes both the House Republican opposition strategy and the fragmentation of Democrats, and shows the rocky relationship between the president and Congress.

6.  Judi Hasson, "All Players Have Ideas to Overhaul Health Care," *USA Today,* January 27, 1993.

7.  Senator Thomas A. Daschle, D-S.D., was quoted in William Schneider, "No Score So Far in Health Care Game," *The National Journal,* February 12, 1994.

8.  ABC News Special, "President Clinton's Town Meeting," September 23, 1993.

9. Susan B. Garland, "Health Reform Hits the Campaign Trail," *Business Week,* August 30, 1993.

10. Ickes quoted in Edwin Diamond, Stephen Katz, and Cara Matthews, "Conflict v. Context in Covering Clinton's Health Care Proposal," *The National Journal,* November 19, 1994, p. 2738.

11. Diamond, Katz, and Matthews, p. 2738.

12. Dana Priest, "Flawed Sales Pitch Blamed for Health Reform Setbacks," *Washington Post,* March 30, 1994.

13. The First Lady was quoted in "Hillary Clinton Hits Hard in Health-Care Preview," *Minneapolis Star Tribune,* May 27, 1993.

14. Johnson and Broder, pp. 153–154.

15. Johnson and Broder, p. 229.

16. Michael Wines and Robert Pear, "President Finds He Has Gained Even if He Lost on Health Care," *New York Times,* July 30, 1996.

17. Johnson and Broder, p. 175.

18. Dana Priest and Michael Weisskopf, "Health Care Reform: The Collapse of a Quest," *Washington Post,* October 11, 1994.

19. Johnson and Broder, p. 185.

20. Sarah Brady of Handgun Control, Inc. is an example of a good choice of spokespersons. The wife of former White House Press Secretary Jim Brady, who was shot during the attempted assassination of President Reagan, she evokes trust and transcends partisanship on a divisive issue. On the other hand, Ross Perot was a poor spokesperson for opponents of the North American Free Trade Agreement (NAFTA). Not only was he controversial, but he also became too closely identified with the issue. His poor performance in a nationally televised debate with Vice President Al Gore was a fatal blow to treaty opponents.

21. An excellent analysis of how the news media look at news can be found in Kathleen Hall Jamieson and Karlyn Kohrs Campbell, *The Interplay of Influence,* 4th ed. (Belmont, CA: Wadsworth, 1997). See especially Chapter 2.

22. Edwin Diamond and Robert A. Silverman, *White House to Your House: Media and Politics in Virtual America* (Cambridge, MA: MIT Press, 1995), p. 67.

23. Edwin Diamond and Robert A. Silverman, p. 66.

24. The study is cited in Johnson and Broder, pp. 230–231.

25. Early in the debate, reform proponent Robert J. Blendon of the Harvard School of Public Health worried that the very nature of press coverage would undermine reform. "Given this media focus, the public's real questions with regard to a health care bill are left unanswered," he wrote. "Beware the Health Care Special Interests," *Boston Globe,* May 16, 1993.

26. President Clinton acknowledged his errors in interviews with Johnson and Broder for their book. See also Abigail Trafford, "Mistakes Sank Health Reform, Clinton Admits," *Washington Post,* April 21, 1996.

27. Johnson and Broder, p. 640.

*To enhance its credit card business and worldwide name recognition, MasterCard International became a sponsor of the 1994 World Cup Soccer Championship, a month-long tournament held in nine U.S. cities. MasterCard generated early interest in the games in 1993 by creating an "Ambassadors of Soccer" program, a series of World Cup Business Seminars to educate merchants in the nine tournament cities, and a major U.S. and European media relations program before and during the tournament. Exhibits 3-2a and 3-2b are news releases about the "Ambassadors of Soccer" program. Exhibit 3-2c is a news release announcing MasterCard's honoring of tournament players and contributions to charities, and Exhibit 3-2d is the MasterCard World Cup logo.*

**CASE 3-2**

## MasterCard's Sponsorship of World Cup USA '94

MasterCard International, Inc. with Alan Taylor Communications, Inc., New York, NY

### Background

The World Cup Soccer Championship is the largest sporting event in the world, taking place once every four years. In 1994, the World Cup was played on U.S. soil for the first time in history. For 30 days, the eyes of the world focused on the sport of soccer in nine U.S. cities as 24 countries competed in 52 matches to be the best soccer team in the world. An estimated 1.5 million soccer fans from around the world traveled to the United States contributing an estimated $4 billion in revenue. The month-long period of the tournament represented the culmination of a four-year sponsorship program for MasterCard International.

Courtesy MasterCard International, Inc.

## Research

MasterCard research, conducted by London-based Sponsorship Research International, showed that MasterCard's major competitor was ahead in several industry categories, including credit card volume and gross dollar volume, in addition to overall brand awareness worldwide. The research, which was used by the Harvard Business School in its preparation of a case study on MasterCard's sponsorship of World Cup USA '94, also showed that the World Cup was one of only two sporting events that were truly global. Based on this research, MasterCard decided to sponsor World Cup USA '94, viewing it as the basis for a totally integrated, worldwide marketing program designed to build brand awareness, stimulate card usage and provide business-building opportunities for its member banks.

Using this research, Alan Taylor Communications was challenged to develop a multitiered, multifaceted public relations program to be implemented primarily in the United States and secondarily, abroad. The programs were created to maximize media exposure for MasterCard's World Cup sponsorship and sponsorship support programs leading up to and through the World Cup tournament.

## Planning

### Objectives

MasterCard and Alan Taylor Communications established the following public relations objectives:

1. Develop a stand-alone public relations program to obtain maximum media exposure *throughout the United States* for MasterCard's World Cup sponsorship for *one full year prior* to the tournament that creates a natural tie-in to soccer interest in the U.S. and also appeals to a broad-based audience.

2. Leverage MasterCard's World Cup sponsorship:

    - as a business-building opportunity for MasterCard *member financial institutions.*

    - as a business-building opportunity for *merchants nationwide* with value-added card usage programs for cardholders.

3. Develop a multitiered public relations program that directly ties in with the 52 World Cup matches to ensure *worldwide* media coverage for MasterCard's sponsorship *during the one-month tournament.*

### Target Audiences

- Sports/soccer reporters—print and electronic media worldwide.
- Business/marketing reporters (major daily newspapers in the nine World Cup host cities).

- Banking trade media • Marketing / Advertising trade media • Major national / international consumer/business publications.
- Members—MasterCard is an association of 22,000 financial institutions worldwide.
- Merchants—MasterCard is accepted at more than 12 million merchant locations worldwide and 3 million in the U.S.
- Potential and existing cardholders—The MasterCard current cardholder base is 117 million in the U.S.

## Creative Strategy

1. Since most of the U.S. media had a lukewarm response towards soccer, one of our challenges was to create a program that would arouse the media's interest *one year prior to the World Cup*. Our plan was to involve sportswriters themselves as active participants in our program. We would conduct a nationwide search for *foreign-born* Americans who have made significant contributions to the growth of soccer in the U.S. A total of 24 "ambassadors," representing each of the countries competing in World Cup USA '94, would be selected by a panel of soccer writers from each of the nine venue cities, along with MasterCard spokesman, soccer legend Pelé (Objective #1).

2. To leverage MasterCard's sponsorship for its member financial institutions, merchants, and cardholders, we created a program to educate and market the event through a variety of regional and national marketing activities that were supported via print and electronic media placements. Included were business seminars; special World Cup "MasterValues" for cardholders; mall promotions, medallions, and a merchant decal/point-of-sale program (Objective #2).

3. With 52 World Cup matches to be contested during a 30-day period, the sports section of media outlets worldwide would be saturated with daily match results and upcoming match previews. We met this challenge by creating a multitiered media program to generate MasterCard stories considered newsworthy enough to crack the national and international sports pages DURING the tournament. We structured an award program; an all-star team; we set up a tv studio to accommodate interviews with spokesmen Pelé and English soccer legend Bobby Charlton; and we distributed spokesmen by-lined columns to key media outlets worldwide (Objective #3).

The total budget for the aforementioned programs was $630,000 (fee + expenses).

## Execution

1. MasterCard's "Ambassadors of Soccer": The initial portion of the program focused on finding media outlets and organizations (soccer writers nationwide, ethnic publications, newsletters of soccer organizations, soccer leagues, civic groups, etc.) from which to solicit nominees.

   In April 1993, more than one year prior to the World Cup, a press event was held in New York with Pelé to announce the program. At the same time, a news release announcing the search was distributed to the aforementioned outlets with strong follow-up made through January 1994. Following the January 31 deadline for nominees, a panel of New York–based soccer writers reviewed more than *450* nominees and selected finalists representing each of the World Cup countries. Press releases were prepared for all 90 finalists and distributed to local and national media outlets.

   A national media panel comprised of soccer writers from each of the nine venue cities was then assembled and joined Pelé in selecting one "ambassador" for each country. Ballots, categorized by country and including a brief summary of each finalist's contributions to the growth of soccer in America, were provided to the panel.

   On June 9, 1994, one week prior to the kick-off of World Cup USA '94, a press conference was held in New York to announce the selection of MasterCard's "Ambassadors of Soccer." The agency arranged for all 24 "ambassadors" to be in attendance (Objective #1).

2. *Marketing programs to LEVERAGE MasterCard's World Cup sponsorship:* More than one year prior to the World Cup, Master-Card hosted World Cup Business Seminars in conjunction with area Convention and Visitors Bureaus in each of the nine venue cities to educate merchants on ways to optimize the economic impact of the World Cup. These seminars also provided a platform to secure support among retailers for several MasterCard World Cup programs, including World Cup MasterValues, a card usage program in which cardholders saved from 10–25% instantly at the point-of-sale at more than 100 national and local retailers in the nine cities; MasterCard at the Mall, a World Cup–themed event held at malls in each of the nine cities that generated card usage and provided local member banks with an opportunity to acquire new cardholders. Pelé and members of the U.S. National Soccer Team were utilized to help spur attendance. The World Cup Merchant Decal/Point-of-Sale Program targeted 200,000 storefronts in the nine cities with point-of-sale materials that reflected MasterCard's global World Cup artwork. A sweepstakes component was built in to reward merchants and their respective member banks for utilizing the

materials. The World Cup Medallion Program offered specially created World Cup medallions and other merchandise to cardholders: the offer was included as an insert in bank statements as a revenue generator for member banks.

Press materials detailing the aforementioned programs and specific MasterCard World Cup cardholder services were prepared and distributed at the business seminars and to business/marketing reporters nationwide. Media interviews were coordinated for key MasterCard executives to discuss the programs prior to and following all seminars and in the months leading up to the World Cup (Objective #2).

3. *Multitiered public relations program implemented DURING the 52-match tournament:* The MasterCard Award was presented to one player in each of 52 matches who performed the most outstanding moment of the match, as selected by a panel of accredited media covering each match. Immediately following each match, the Award winner's name was provided by the panel and a press release was prepared and distributed to all media on-site in the stadium press room. An agency staffer in New York then faxed the release to dailies in the top 20 U.S. markets and to media outlets in the player's home country.

The MasterCard All-Star Team, the first-ever All-Star Team at a World Cup tournament, was selected by members of the Technical Study Group (TSG) of FIFA, the world governing body of soccer. Following the quarterfinals, a meeting was coordinated with the TSG to determine the potential finalists for the All-Star Team and a press release was prepared and distributed to all accredited media attending the semifinal matches in New York and Los Angeles. Following the semifinal matches, the 11 members of the MasterCard All-Star Team were selected. On July 15, two days prior to the championship match (when the international media was concentrated in Los Angeles), a press conference was held at the Ritz-Carlton Hotel in Pasadena to announce the final All-Star Team. More than *400* accredited media were in attendance, including *26* international television crews, as Pelé and Charlton announced the 11 All-Star Team members. To further its international goodwill, MasterCard donated a total of $100,000 to international charities on behalf of Award winners and All-Star Team members.

Pelé/Charlton By-Lined Columns: An agreement was reached with *USA Today* for exclusive by-lined columns written by Pelé to appear regularly leading up to and DURING the tournament. Sports editors of key newspapers in Europe, South America, and Asia were also offered columns written by Pelé and Charlton. In exchange for the free material, their affiliation with MasterCard was published with each column.

Pelé/Charlton Broadcast Interviews: We set up a studio on-site in Dallas (where more than 100 worldwide tv stations were based during the World Cup) and arranged interviews with Pelé and Charlton, who were positioned in front of MasterCard World Cup signage (Objective #3).

## Evaluation

1. *"Ambassadors of Soccer": April 1993–June 1994:* Ongoing publicity was generated in three phases ONE YEAR PRIOR to the tournament:

   a. A total of *120* stories were placed nationwide promoting *the search,* including *USA Today, NY Times, NY Daily News,* and Associated Press.

   b. More than *110* placements totaling *45 million* impressions were secured on the announcement of the finalists.

   c. The press conference to announce the 24 "ambassadors" generated more than *70* stories and *15* television placements, including international feeds WTN and Reuters TV. In total, more than *300* placements were secured on the program totaling *121 million impressions* (Objective #1).

2. World Cup marketing programs LEVERAGING the sponsorship:

   • Business Seminars: A total of 8,000 merchants attended the nine seminars and received information on MasterCard's World Cup programs.

   • MasterValues: Secured more than 200 merchants to participate in the program with a distribution of 200 million coupons.

   • Mall Promotions: Conducted promotions in 28 malls in the nine cities, which generated more than $1 million in Master-Card spending. These were member bank acquisition activities at every mall event. More than 3,000 merchants in total displayed MasterCard World Cup POS materials. An average of 2,000 people attended the mall event finales with Pelé or U.S. Team appearances.

   • Merchant Decal/POS Program: More than 200,000 retailers secured through 40 member banks received program materials.

   • Medallions: More than 3,000 orders were received for merchandise *prior to the event,* generating $300,000 in revenue for member banks.

   In addition, from January through July 1994, more than *170 placements* on MasterCard's overall marketing support programs received a total of *146 million impressions* in publications such as *Business Week* (3x), *The Wall Street Journal* (3x), *USA Today* (5x), the Associated Press

(3x), *Newsweek, Financial Times, Fortune* and the *International Herald Tribune.* Placements were also secured in the *business sections* of the major daily newspapers in the nine venue cities. A total of *23 stories* appeared in *banking/marketing trades,* including *American Banker* (5x), *Crain's Business Marketing* (2x), *Ad Age* (3x), and *Brandweek.* In addition, more than *60 stories* were placed in *European publications* totaling *30 million* impressions (Objective #2).

3. *Multitiered public relations program implemented DURING the World Cup:* June–July 1994:

- MasterCard Award: A total of *135 stories* appeared in U.S. daily newspapers nationwide totaling *65 million impressions* with *85* stories received from European publications totaling *46 million impressions.*

- MasterCard All-Star Team: More than *90 print placements* were secured in the U.S. and Europe totaling *43 million impressions.* In addition, 14 international tv spots were confirmed with an overall audience of *39 million.*

- By-Lined Columns: Pelé columns appeared in publications in 13 countries totaling *164 million impressions.* Charlton columns appeared in 12 countries totaling *56 million impressions.*

- Broadcast Interviews: Pelé conducted a total 10 international interviews reaching an estimated audience of *32 million.* In addition, interviews were coordinated with ABC Network and ESPN, which ran during the semifinal games and the championship match, reaching an audience of *35 million.* Charlton conducted a total of 11 interviews reaching an estimated audience of *18 million* (Objective #3).

The aforementioned programs generated *1.1 billion* media impressions for MasterCard's sponsorship of World Cup USA.

**Release Date**

FOR IMMEDIATE RELEASE

Contact

Marianne Fulgenzi
MasterCard International
212-649-5443

Tony Signore/John Liporace
Alan Taylor Communications
212-714-1280

## MASTERCARD LAUNCHES SEARCH FOR
## "AMBASSADORS OF SOCCER"

-- National program to honor America's 'melting pot' contributors to the sport --

NEW YORK - - To honor the debut in the United States of the World Cup,
MasterCard International, an Official Sponsor and the Official Card of the 1994
World Cup, has announced a nationwide search for soccer fans who have brought
their love of and commitment to the world's most popular sport from their native
homelands to the United States.

In conjunction with its World Cup sponsorship, *"MasterCard's Ambassadors of Soccer"*
program will honor one person, native-born, from each of the 23 countries traveling
to the United States to compete in the 1994 World Cup.   In addition, one
"representative at-large" will be selected from among the countries that competed in
the World Cup qualifying matches but did not qualify.  Each "ambassador" will be
chosen for their contributions to the growth of soccer in America.

"Because America is defined as the melting pot country, and soccer is truly a sport
involving all nations, MasterCard's Ambassadors of Soccer program seems the

(more)

*Official Sponsor*
*WorldCup*USA94⁻

**News Release**

Exhibit 3-2a
(*continued*)

"Ambassadors of Soccer"
News Release   (Courtesy MasterCard International, Inc.)

MasterCard's Ambassadors of Soccer - Page 2

for the NAIA Senior Bowl.  In 1965, he organized the first YMCA Youth Soccer League in Springfield, Illinois and also was responsible for the opening of Soccer World, an indoor soccer facility.

- a German immigrant, now living in the U.S. for 20 years, who organized the first Amateur Youth Soccer Organization (AYSO) chapter in his community and has received the AYSO National Green Thumb title for success in developing new AYSO regions around the country.

- a 91 year-old Dutch immigrant who came to the U.S. 45 years ago and organized the soccer team for his local university.  In 1972, when school budget cuts eliminated the full-time soccer coach, he volunteered for the job, spending five hours each day working with the team following a nine-hour work day at his full-time job.  Since 1977, he has voluntarily assisted every head soccer coach of the university.

Each of the 24 "Ambassadors of Soccer" will be chosen for their contributions to the growth of soccer in America.

Soccer legend Pelé, whose years playing with the New York Cosmos sparked the phenomenal growth of youth soccer in the United States, will serve on the judging panel for the program.  He is currently MasterCard's official World Cup spokesperson.

MasterCard will donate $1,000 to the charity of each ambassador's choice.  In addition, those selected will serve as honorary captains for their home country's World Cup team and attend a team practice session.  They also will receive tickets to their native country's opening-round World Cup match.

(more)

Nominees to *"MasterCard's Ambassadors of Soccer"* program must meet the following criteria. They must:

- be a full-time legal resident of the United States for at least ten years;

- have fostered the growth of soccer at either the local grass-roots level, or statewide, regionally or nationally in the U.S.;

- have been an administrator, teacher, coach, fund-raiser or promoter of soccer.

All entrants are required to submit a letter (or have one sent on their behalf) explaining their contributions to soccer and why they deserve to be honored, addressed to:

"MasterCard's Ambassadors of Soccer"
c/o Alan Taylor Communications
505 Eighth Avenue
New York, NY  10018
*For further information, call: (212) 714-1280*

All nominations must include the nominee's name, address, telephone number and country of origin, and indicate the number of years residing in the United States. Each letter will be reviewed and finalists will be selected per country.

All nominations must be submitted by January 31, 1994.

# # # #

**Release Date**

**Contact**

Marianne Fulgenzi
MasterCard International
212-649-5443

Tony Signore / Stephanie Wood
Alan Taylor Communications
212-714-1280

### FINALISTS SELECTED IN NATIONWIDE SEARCH
### FOR MASTERCARD'S "AMBASSADORS OF SOCCER"

**New York, March 22 —** More than 90 finalists from across the United States have been selected in a nationwide search for foreign-born Americans who have made significant contributions to the growth of soccer in the United States. The finalists were chosen by a panel of New York-based soccer writers from among the more than 350 nominations received representing 52 countries in "MasterCard's Ambassadors of Soccer" program. MasterCard is an Official Sponsor and the Official Card of World Cup USA 1994.

The program will honor one person representing each of the 23 countries traveling to the U.S. to compete in World Cup USA '94. In addition, one representative-at-large will be selected from among the countries that competed in World Cup qualifying matches but did not make the final World Cup field of twenty-four.

In phase one of the selection process, a soccer media panel chose finalists from each of the 23 countries and the representative-at-large category. The finalists were selected based on their contributions to the growth of soccer at either the local, regional or national level. During the second phase of the program which will take place in May, soccer legend and MasterCard's official World Cup spokesman Pelé, along with a panel of soccer journalists representing each of the nine World Cup host cities will select the final 24 ambassadors.

In June 1994, the 24 Ambassadors of Soccer will be announced at a press conference in New York, where they will be honored for their achievements by MasterCard and Pelé, whose years playing with the New York Cosmos sparked the phenomenal growth of soccer in the United States.

MasterCard will donate $1,000 to the charity of each ambassador's choice, and provide two tickets to one of their native country's World Cup matches.

# # #

*Official Sponsor*
*WorldCup*USA94™

**Release Date**

**Contact**

Marianne Fulgenzi
MasterCard International
212-649-5443

Tony Signore
Alan Taylor Communications
212-714-1280

### MASTERCARD INTERNATIONAL TO HONOR PLAYERS
### AND ASSIST WORLDWIDE CHARITIES DURING WORLD CUP USA 1994

**- - $100,000 to be Donated Through MasterCard Award
and first-ever All-Star Team at World Cup - -**

New York, June 9, 1994 - - MasterCard, an Official Sponsor and Official Card of World Cup USA 1994, will honor players for outstanding performances during the 1994 World Cup tournament, while continuing its commitment to assisting charities worldwide. Overall charitable donations totalling **$100,000** will be made through the MasterCard Award and MasterCard All-Star Team, the first-ever FIFA-selected all-star team at a World Cup tournament.

The **MasterCard Award,** which was established during the 1990 World Cup in Italy and implemented at various international soccer tournaments over the past four years, will be presented to one player in each of the 52 World Cup matches who contributes the most outstanding or memorable play of the match. A select panel of accredited World Cup journalists will determine each award-winning player. In addition, MasterCard will make a donation to the charity of each winner's choice in his name.

MasterCard will donate $5,000 to the award-winner's charity of choice for the championship match. A donation of $2,500 will be made for each of the two semi-final matches. Winners from each of the 49 other games will have $1,000 donated to their charity of choice.

The **MasterCard All-Star Team,** the first-ever all-star team at a World Cup tournament, will honor **11** players  - - one per position - - based on their performances **during** World Cup USA 1994. A panel comprised of members from the **FIFA Technical Study Group** (TSG) will select the MasterCard All-Star Team, which will be announced by MasterCard and the FIFA TSG at a press conference in Pasadena on July 15.

(more)

**Official Sponsor**
**WorldCup**USA94™

*Printed on Recycled Paper*

**News Release**

Exhibit 3-2c
(*continued*)

MasterCard Honors Players
News Release   (Courtesy MasterCard International, Inc.)

**Page two - MasterCard Award / MasterCard All-Star Team**

A donation of $3,000 will be made by MasterCard in the name of each All-Star Team member to his charity of choice. In addition, MasterCard will donate $8,000 on behalf of the All-Star Team to UNICEF / Children's Defense Fund, a program to immunize children in underprivileged countries around the world. UNICEF is the official charity of FIFA.

A variety of international charities have been the recipients of past MasterCard Award and All-Star Team donations. Mexico Hilfe, a village for orphans in Mexico, was the recipient named by German National Team Award winners during Italia '90. Dutch Award winners requested donations be sent to "Action for Hunger in Africa." Swedish players who were MasterCard Award winners during Euro '92 named "Catastrophe Aid for War Victims in Croatia and Bosnia" as their recipient charity.

"The MasterCard Awards in the past have brought merit to the game and its players, by encouraging senior and youth players alike to think of others in their moment of triumph," said **Joseph S. Blatter, General Secretary of FIFA.** "FIFA is grateful to MasterCard for helping promote the positive image of our sport in this way."

"MasterCard, working closely with FIFA and journalists worldwide, is proud to continue its support of programs that have helped benefit a variety of international worthy causes, while furthering our long-standing relationship with world championship soccer," said Alex McKeveny, MasterCard Vice President/Global Promotions.

MasterCard International Incorporated , headquartered in New York City, is a global payments franchise comprised of nearly 22,000 member financial institutions worldwide. Through its family of brands, MasterCard offers a full range of credit and debit products and services supported by a global transaction processing network. In 1993, 210.3 million MasterCard credit cards generated more than $320.6 billion in transaction volume at 12 million transaction locations worldwide.

# # #

Exhibit 3-2d

MasterCard World Cup Logo   (Courtesy MasterCard International, Inc.)

*In response to major midwestern flooding, the Monsanto Company partnered with the American Red Cross to provide almost $3 million in relief aid to farmers and towns in the stricken areas. Exhibit 3-3a is a news release announcing the company's contribution to the American Red Cross. Exhibit 3-3b is a letter to retailers encouraging their support for the program. Exhibit 3-3c is a photograph of Monsanto's contribution of a million-dollar check to the Red Cross.*

## CASE 3-3    Rural Flood Relief Fund

Monsanto Agricultural Group, St. Louis, MO, with Drake & Company, St. Louis, MO

### Background

In 1993, record floods devastated areas of nine Midwestern states. While this represented a relatively small percentage of Midwest farmers, thousands of farms and small towns were ravaged. Relief organizations, whose primary strengths were in urban areas, found their resources being depleted. As rivers neared record crests in July, Monsanto Company's Agricultural Group determined to provide $2 million in aid to its customers and their neighbors—i.e., farmers and rural communities.

### Planning

*Primary objectives:* (A) Donate funds to aid *rural areas* damaged by flooding—with half as a matching fund account. (B) Using communications, leverage the matching fund to attract further contributions.

*Second objective:* Demonstrate Monsanto's commitment to the agricultural and rural community.

*Key audiences* were identified: farmers, farm and commodity organizations, farm chemical dealers, agribusiness and other rural businesses, and the general public via the news media.

*Goals were:* 1. Achieve $2 million additional contributions. 2. Achieve broad recognition for Monsanto efforts.

Courtesy Monsanto Company

## Research

*Initial:* To ensure an appropriate use of funds, Monsanto directed an overnight telephone survey of 300 Midwest farmers and 200 rural (nonfarm) residents. Some 73 percent agreed that the American Red Cross was the best agency to employ the funds.

(Monsanto then worked with the American Red Cross to establish a unique fund, with total proceeds to go to small, *rural* chapters in the flood areas. Callers to a Red Cross 1-800 number could mention "Monsanto" or "Rural Flood Relief" to access the special fund and the matching dollars; a Red Cross P.O. Box also was established.)

*Mid-program:* To help guide use of funds, qualitative research was conducted with farm families. This uncovered a major communications need. The Red Cross and Monsanto contracted with Doane Agricultural Services to publish two special newsletters—"Road To Recovery"—to answer farmer questions about services.

*Follow-up:* In November, quantitative research was conducted among farmers to determine (a) recovery steps still needed, (b) assessment of relief efforts, (c) prevailing emotional conditions, (d) farmers' feelings about the future. Findings were presented in briefings to the American Farm Bureau, to U.S. congressional staffers, and to the Red Cross; they also were presented in a Washington press conference (see below).

## Execution

At a 7/18 news conference hosted by Monsanto and Congressman Dick Gephardt, a poster-size check for $1 million was presented to the Red Cross. The National Corn Growers and the American Soybean associations each immediately pledged $10,000 contributions. Television coverage on network affiliates led to inclusion of the event in ABC's "World News Tonight" and in CNN's "Moneyline." Monsanto employees were updated by e-mail and bulletin boards.

News releases resulted in heavy news coverage. Broadcast news was provided to the National Association of Farm Broadcasters, resulting in farm radio and television coverage.

Letters were sent from the Ag Group president to 8,800 ag chemical retailers across the U.S. enlisting their contributions *and* support; enclosed were a model customer letter for use with their own customers, display posters, and localized news release. Similar letters went to 60 primary suppliers, to major customers of the company's lawn and garden unit, as well as to competitors.

The American Red Cross issued a news release July 22 announcing the gift, with praise by Red Cross President Elizabeth Dole.

On a one-hour, 280-station telethon by the National Association of Broadcasters, Elizabeth Dole restated the Monsanto gift. More than

18,000 callers mentioned Monsanto, generating contributions of $1.2 million to Rural Flood Relief.

On August 1, Monsanto's vice chairman appeared on a telethon with Bob Hope to present a second $1 million check to the Red Cross. The presentation was featured in a *People* magazine photograph.

News coverage—and contributions—continued into October, with the ag press adding coverage and favorable editorials.

The November quantitative research findings were presented in briefings to the American Farm Bureau, to U.S. congressional staffers, and to the Red Cross. A Washington news conference announced the findings to the media, gaining coverage by the Associated Press, network radio, and the front page of *USA Today*.

## Evaluation

The goal of $2 million in additional contributions was exceeded by 50 percent, with almost $3 million raised.

News coverage ensured that residents of the rural Midwest were aware of the fund—and Monsanto's commitment. Editorials in agricultural publications cited and praised the effort.

Letters of support and congratulations from Monsanto employees, customers, farmers, and others provided convincing evidence that the company had done the right thing and was recognized for it.

# NEWS

# Monsanto

FOR RELEASE     IMMEDIATELY

Gerry Ingenthron (314) 694-3079
**The Agricultural Group**
*PUBLIC AFFAIRS DEPARTMENT*   Home 569-0359
Monsanto Company
800 N. Lindbergh Boulevard
St. Louis, Missouri 63167

MONSANTO SUPPORT TO FLOOD VICTIMS

ST. LOUIS, July 18 -- Monsanto Agricultural Group announced today that it will contribute up to $2 million to the American Red Cross to help support flood victims in rural areas of the Midwest.

Monsanto today contributed $1 million directly to the Red Cross and is setting aside another $1 million in an account that will be used to match individual or business contributions on a dollar for dollar basis, said Hendrik A. Verfaillie, President of Monsanto Agricultural Group.  Contributions will be directed to Red Cross chapters in rural flood-stricken areas.

"The flood devastation is incredible, and relief organizations are hard-pressed to meet the demands that have been placed on them," Verfaillie said.  "This contribution is intended to help the farmers and residents of rural communities who have been hard hit by the flood."

He said Monsanto is working with agribusiness across the Midwest to encourage those who were unaffected to contribute to flood relief for farmers and other rural residents.

-more-

A Unit of Monsanto Company

-2-

Contributions to this flood relief effort may be made
through Oct. 31, 1993.  A credit card contribution can be made by
calling the Red Cross at 1-800-842-2200 and designating "Monsanto
Matching Contribution."  Alternatively, a check can be sent to the
American Red Cross Rural Flood Relief, Monsanto Matching
Contributions, P.O. Box 66921, St. Louis, MO  63166-6692.  Checks
should be marked "Monsanto Matching Contribution" to be eligible for
matching funds.

"This gift will help meet emergency needs in the
agricultural areas so severely affected by the flooding," said Deborah
Patterson, Chapter Executive Officer of the St. Louis Bi-State Chapter
of the American Red Cross.

"Monsanto earlier was one of the first St. Louis
corporations to step forward with help.  This additional funding gives
an even greater sense of hope to the communities and the people who
have such desperate need as a result of the flooding."

In St. Louis, the Monsanto Fund -- the philanthropic arm of
Monsanto Company -- earlier contributed $100,000 to the St. Louis Bi-
State Chapter of the American Red Cross for its flood relief efforts.
The Monsanto Fund has announced that it will provide a special
additional match for contributions by Monsanto employees and retirees
to the Red Cross for disaster relief.

-o0o-

St. Louis
071893

Exhibit 3-3b    Letter to Retailers    (Courtesy Monsanto Company)

# Monsanto

**The Agricultural Group**
800 N. Lindbergh Boulevard
St. Louis, Missouri 63167
Phone: (314) 694-1000

July 19, 1993

Dear Monsanto Retailer,

We encourage your help in supporting disaster relief in the rural areas of the country that have been devastated by the flood of 1993. To facilitate this effort Monsanto, working with the American Red Cross, has established a special "Rural Flood Relief" fund.

Monsanto has committed up to $2 million to be sent to the American Red Cross Rural Flood Relief to be used by local American Red Cross chapters in the affected rural communities. We have already made a $1 million cash contribution and have committed another $1 million which will be used to match designated contributions from anyone else who wishes to participate. **All contributions payable to "American Red Cross Rural Flood Relief" are designated for the "Monsanto Matching Contributions" and will go to American Red Cross Chapters in rural communities.**

We hope you will help us by doing the following:

- Photocopy the enclosed letter and/or statement stuffer and send them to your grower customers.

- Display one of the enclosed posters in your business and place the other in a local coffee shop or other places where people gather.

- Ask your local paper or radio station to use the enclosed press release.

- We encourage you to make a matching contribution yourself and create a local press release with you presenting the check to the American Red Cross in a photograph for the local newspaper... please do it!

When one of us in the agricultural community is hurting, all of us feel the pain. Please do what you can to help our friends in need.

Sincerely

Hendrik A. Verfaillie
Corporate Vice President and
President of The Agricultural Group

d/enclosures

| Exhibit 3-3c | Photograph of Monsanto's Million-Dollar Contribution to the Red Cross |
| --- | --- |

Hendrik A. Verfaillie, right, president of Monsanto's Agricultural Group, presents a replica of a $1 million check to Deborah Patterson, executive officer of the St. Louis Bi-State Chapter of the American Red Cross, while Congressman Richard Gephardt (D-Mo.), left, looks on. Patterson accepted the $1 million on behalf of the Red Cross to be used for flood relief efforts in rural areas. In addition, Monsanto has set aside another $1 million to match contributions from others who want to support rural flood relief efforts.   (Courtesy Monsanto Company)

*The largest fiftieth anniversary reenactment of D-Day was not held on the actual landing site but in Virginia Beach, VA. Exhibit 3-4a is a news release announcing the event. Exhibits 3-4b and 3-4c announce the event's "Victory Dance" and parade. Exhibit 3-4d is a schedule, and Exhibit 3-4e is the "Back the Attack" poster used to promote the event.*

**CASE 3-4**

## The Commemoration of the Fiftieth Anniversary of D-Day

Department of Convention and Visitor Development, Virginia Beach, VA, with Brickell & Associates Public Relations, Virginia Beach, VA

### Program Objectives and Planning

In June 1994 Virginia Beach, VA, was the site for the largest reenactment of the 1944 Normandy landing. The event was scheduled for the "Omaha Beach" section of Fort Story, the training site for U.S. Army amphibious operations today and during World War II. The reenactment included 1,200 reenactors in authentic uniforms, vintage tanks, artillery, aircraft, and landing craft and was anticipated to draw 10,000 spectators. In addition to the reenactment, other weekend activities included a display of vintage military memorabilia, a parade with World War II equipment and units (and WW II star Van Johnson), an Operation Overlord Victory Dance, a '40s-era stage door canteen, and a wreath-laying ceremony to commemorate the war dead.

### Research

Based on several informal research programs, the Virginia Beach Department of Convention and Visitor Development (CVD) and its public relations firm, Brickell & Associates (B&A), made the decision to execute a major event to commemorate the Normandy invasion. Research revealed:

- The DOD-scheduled events worldwide showed that the reenactment recommended for the city of Virginia Beach had the potential to be the largest in the world.
- A large percentage of tourists to the resort area—as well as residents—are former members of the military.

Courtesy Virginia Beach Department of Convention and Visitor Development

- The first wave of battle at Normandy—with the most casualties—was led by the Army's Twenty-ninth Division, made up mostly of Virginians.
- The tourism infrastructure in Virginia Beach is very promilitary and receptive of the military.
- Virginia Beach is within a day's drive of most major population centers.
- Virginia Beach is still a major center of military operations today.

## Planning

### Goals and Objectives

- To create a meaningful and memorable event for the veterans of D-Day
- To create local, regional, national, and international publicity for the event and for Virginia Beach
- To increase the number of tourists to the resort city during the D-Day commemorative weekend

### Targets

- Local, regional, national, and international media
- Potential visitors to the city, focusing on World War II veterans and their families

In short, the objectives were to let the World War II veterans know that Virginia Beach recognized their sacrifice, to encourage the media to come to the city and report the reenactment as being broadcast from Virginia Beach, and to entice more visitors to the city.

### Strategy

The public relations strategy was very simple. Using news releases sent by phone, electronic distribution, and fax, and making follow-up phone calls, B&A was charged with informing as many local, national, and international media as possible. Once confirmed, B&A coordinated media interviews with World War II veterans and their families, active military, reenactors, volunteers, and city officials. The budget for public relations was nonexistent, because the time incurred was wrapped into the agency's retainer. The budget for materials did not exceed $10,000, because most everything was contributed.

## Execution and Cost Effectiveness

### Tactics

Before the event, standard publicity techniques were utilized to inform the media of this opportunity.

- A general news release was issued in March 1994 to 760 travel, military, and lifestyle writers.
- Follow-up news kits were sent out a week later.
- Follow-up phone calls to select media were made a week after the release of the news kit.
- A commemorative poster, "Back the Attack," was sent via Federal Express to targeted media, such as national radio talk show host G. Gordon Liddy.

The most immediate media response came from the first release, the list of authentic World War II equipment in the news kit, and the "Back the Attack" poster.

## Highlights and Possible Difficulties

D-Day was sponsored by a variety of participants: The War Memorial Museum of Virginia, the Kidney Foundation of Virginia, the U.S. Department of Defense, and the city of Virginia Beach. A committee of approximately 50, consisting of military representatives, World War II veterans, reenactors, city officials, volunteers, and B&A staff members met a year prior to June 4 for planning purposes. Because of the mechanics of the weekend, the actual role of overseeing D-Day eventually fell on the shoulders of the Virginia Beach Department of Convention & Visitor Development and Brickell & Associates Public Relations. In addition to coordinating the publicity—which the city was originally charged with—CVD and B&A were also involved with the following:

- Accommodating the World War II veterans. This encompassed everything from arranging for easy wheelchair access to the beach and comfortable seating at the reenactment to receiving a veteran's discount at the resort area hotels.
- Fielding and answering thousands of local and national calls.
- Acquiring funding for various supplies, including airplane fuel and bleachers.
- Acquiring off-duty police and medical attendants, coordinating traffic and provided buses.
- Housing the reenactors at a local military base.
- Reassuring environmentalists that everything was environmentally safe, tackling such issues as guaranteeing that explosives charged in the water would not disturb the sea turtles' breeding grounds and that the large number of attendees—and the explosions—at Fort Story would not destroy the sand dunes on the beach.
- Making sure residents were informed and received detailed fliers about the noise levels, danger levels, beach access, and other pertinent issues.

- Staffing a complex, portable news center on the reenactment site.

- The most challenging opportunity, from a public relations stand-point, was handling 125 worldwide members of the media at the command center. Press passes were issued by mail to media who responded to the event, and special clearance was made for them. Because the beach at Fort Story was wired with more than two miles of explosives, there were limited locations for event coverage. At the command center, each member of the media was assigned a particular post and was required to remain at the post until the event was over. Organization at the media command center was crucial, and the CVD staff, the B&A staff, the military police, and the public affairs officers at Fort Story, Fort Eustis, and Camp Pendleton kept things under control.

## Evaluation

By successfully cooperating with diverse publics and through the utilization of established public relations techniques, the city of Virginia Beach Department of Convention and Visitor Development and Brickell & Associates Public Relations accomplished the planning, coordination, and implementation of a major media event. Approximately $900,000 in print and broadcast media coverage (advertising value) was acquired locally, regionally, nationally, and internationally. Virginia Beach was featured or mentioned in such publications as the *Washington Post, USA Today, Life* magazine, the *Richmond Times-Dispatch*, the *New York Daily News*, the *Philadelphia Inquirer*, the *Atlanta Journal, USA Today International*, the *Baltimore Sun*, the *Cleveland Plain Dealer*, the *Iowa Antique Trader*, the *Lexington Herald-Leader* and the *Shreveport Times*. The event was covered by such broadcast media as NBC and ABC National News, National Public Radio, CBN, WJLA (DC), and French, German, Japanese, and Russian television. Typically, the total number of inquiries received by the city through its public relations and advertising efforts is about 300,000 annually. During the three-month media relations program for D-Day, inquiries through the city's 1-800 number increased about 3 percent. Approximately 15,000 people attended the event, which was limited by the space available at Fort Story.

## Research

Research for Virginia Beach's commemoration of the fiftieth anniversary of D-Day took several forms.

### *Historical*

The National Guard's Twenty-ninth Infantry Division continued to operate in the area. This Virginia army group was the first to hit the beach at Omaha in Normandy on D-Day and also suffered the most casualties. Many who survived the attack still lived in the area or within easy driving distance.

Reenactors were to use only period costumes and equipment. A display of memorabilia and equipment would attract substantial interest. Care would be taken to ensure authenticity.

Also a dance would be held featuring a period band, with those attending asked to wear period dress.

### Logistical

Many veterans' groups regularly booked into Virginia Beach for reunions. The tourism culture of the city was already dedicated to assisting the special needs of the veteran. In 1994, 73 military reunions attracted more than 11,000 veterans to the city. In 1993, only 48 veteran groups visited.

The military population, including retirees and private citizens working within the military, constitutes the largest segment of Virginia Beach, which is the largest city in the state. This very promilitary attitude indicated that a large-scale event would be successful.

Discussions with war reenactors showed that a full-scale mock invasion had not been planned. Military authorities, veteran groups, and reenactors were looking for a site, which Virginia Beach was happy to offer. The objective was to have the largest reenactment of the D-Day invasion in the world. Normandy, France, had a larger celebration, but no reenactment.

### Operational

Fort Story had limited space to accommodate spectators. It was determined that veterans of D-Day would have priority seating in viewing areas.

Media attention would be international. Special accommodations to handle it would need to be made for satellite feeds, translation services, and other requirements for more than 100 media who were estimated to attend.

## Planning

Planning for the D-Day commemoration in Virginia Beach took months of organization, involving dozens of different public and private groups working together. At one point, a veteran serving on the committee jokingly noted that the planning for the actual D-Day invasion 50 years earlier might not have been more strategic or complex.

More than 1,200 reenactors came from several different groups, most of whom had never participated with each other before. For most, this would be the largest event of its type in their lives. It involved every type of reenactor from Navy SEALs to Air Corps pilots to Army infantry.

Safety was a primary consideration. The pyrotechnic expert had wired more than 50 events, but the D-Day event was five times larger than any other in his career. Thousands of tons of ordnance were detonated.

Veterans of D-Day and WW II were to be given VIP treatment at all times. These heroes were to be offered special seating and ADA assistance to and from the beach, and media attention was to be focused on them at every opportunity. The event was in every way to be a salute to these brave men and women and their fallen colleagues.

More than 125 media from around the world were credentialed. Plans included creating and providing a media center for editing and filing stories via computer and satellite.

Informing citizens in Virginia Beach was important. Traffic, parking, and beach access restrictions on a busy summer weekend in the beach resort needed to be communicated in advance. Special attention was given to advance notice associated with the sound coming from the thousands of explosions in the reenactment.

Environmental concerns were anticipated. No explosions would be allowed that would harm sea turtles, other animals, or protective sand dunes or that would contribute to water pollution in the Atlantic Ocean or the Chesapeake Bay. Environmental groups were consulted in the planning process.

City leaders and hoteliers produced very special rate packages for veterans, many of whom were on fixed incomes.

Comprehensive information was provided to the city's tourism information center and public affairs department and to the Fort Story public affairs department. Inquiries in the thousands were anticipated.

Tourists who happened to be visiting Virginia Beach this weekend needed to understand that a real war had not broken out when the mock invasion began. Fighter planes, invasion ships, and explosions were all designed to look authentic. Extreme care was taken to keep anyone from misunderstanding the event.

## Execution

In advance of the D-Day event in Virginia Beach, Brickell & Associates Public Relations mounted a massive publicity campaign to reach local, regional, national, and international media.

The first phase of publicity was to generate awareness of the event so veterans could plan to attend. The second phase was for coverage of the event on reenactment day.

Media credentials were issued in advance. Media were divided into three groups, each of which would have a distinct vantage point from which to cover the reenactment. B&A staff were assigned to each group.

One group watched from the beach, directly in front of the mock invasion, but on a sand dune behind the veterans' VIP seating. This group had the best perspective of the defending German army's position. They also had access to interviews with and camera shots of veterans throughout the exercise.

A second group was positioned on a LARC (a land-and-water military vehicle that holds up to 60 people) on the beach just beyond the boundaries of the reenactment. This group had a long shot up the beach to capture the reenactment, which gave them a perspective on both the invading Allied troops and the defending German army.

The third group was positioned in a LARC in the water, just beyond the landing Allied forces. They had a perspective on the aerial attack and the Allied opposition as they reached Omaha Beach.

Military protocol was established throughout the event. Everything was explained in military terms, position assignments were given as orders, and all veterans were addressed as "Sir," regardless of rank.

A formal introduction and the playing of taps preceded the reenactment. These were performed by veterans who had served on D-Day.

Medical teams were on standby in the event that a veteran might need attention from heat or physical or mental exhaustion. These teams provided assistance for many.

VIP parking and seating for veterans was provided close to the event.

## Evaluation

The commemoration of the fiftieth anniversary of D-Day in Virginia Beach exceeded every expectation in the planning stages of the event.

Fort Story, limited by size, planned to keep attendance to 10,000. More than 15,000 were accommodated, however, owing to the large contingency of D-Day veterans and dependents who came to Virginia Beach for the celebration.

Weekend tourism normally declined the week after Memorial Day, but this time reservations were up dramatically throughout the resort. A large percentage of rooms was occupied by reunions of veteran groups.

Media from as far away as Japan, France, Russia, and Germany sent video teams for coverage of the event. More than 125 different media sources were given credentials, including ABC TV, NBC TV, CNN, National Public Radio, Associated Press, Virginia News Network, *Life* magazine, *USA Today,* the *Washington Post, New York Daily News,* the Philadelphia *Inquirer,* the *Atlanta Journal and Constitution,* the *Baltimore Sun,* and many others, including national publications dedicated to the military and veterans.

Satellite feeds were seen on dozens of local affiliate TV stations around the USA.

The advertising equivalency was $900,000 in publicity, on a production budget of $10,000, plus Brickell & Associates Public Relations' fees of less than $25,000.

The U.S. Department of Defense and Secretary of Defense William J. Perry awarded B&A a special certificate of appreciation "for outstanding support to the commemorations in honor of D-Day, the Allied Landings in Normandy, France, held at Fort Story, Virginia."

# Virginia Beach
# NEWS

April 18, 1994

FOR IMMEDIATE RELEASE

CONTACT: Deborah Barwick
(804) 466-0783
Sean Brickell, APR
(800) 333-6397

### VIRGINIA BEACH TAPPED AS SITE FOR D-DAY COMMEMORATION

VIRGINIA BEACH, Va. -- The resort city of Virginia Beach, Va., will host more than 10,000 veterans and participants in a 50th anniversary re-enactment of the D-Day Normandy invasion on Saturday, June 4, 1994. The event will be held on Omaha Beach at Ft. Story, Va., the U.S. Army's training site for amphibious operations during World War II and today.

The D-Day Normandy re-enactment is coordinated in conjunction with the 29th Division, Virginia, Army National Guard and the 29th Infantry Division Association to ensure maximum veteran participation. During World War II, the 29th Infantry Division was composed of citizen-soldiers from Maryland, Virginia, West Virginia and Washington, D.C., and was the first unit to land its troops on Normandy's Omaha Beach on June 6, 1944.

The commemorative ceremony begins at 1:30 p.m. Guest speakers include Sen. John Warner, R-Virginia, U.S. Senator; Dr. Brooks Kleber, retired deputy director, U.S. Army Center for Military History; and Dr. G. William Whitehurst, former U.S. Congressman and professor of history at Old Dominion University.

Immediately following the ceremony, the D-Day landing will begin at Omaha Beach with approximately 1,000 re-enactors storming

2

Department of
Convention and
Visitor Development

City of Virginia Beach
2101 Parks Avenue
Suite 500
Virginia Beach, VA 23451

Phone (804) 437-4700
FAX (804) 437-4747

the beach.   Of these re-enactors, 250 are actual National Guard soldiers of the current 29th Infantry Division (Light), headquartered at Fort Belvoir, Va.  Also featured will be current members of Seal Team 4, known as the Naval Combat Demolition Unit during World War II.  The scenario is authentic, and will include vintage tanks, artillery, aircraft and landing craft.  The re-enactment is expected to last from 2 to 3:30 p.m.

Following the re-enactment, a stage door canteen show featuring 1940's era entertainment will be held at Ft. Story.

The re-enactment is one of several activities planned to celebrate the 50th anniversary of D-Day.  To kick off the weekend, historic displays will be set up at nearby Camp Pendleton and Ft. Story, Friday, June 3 and Saturday, June 4.  Camp Pendleton is Virginia's state military reservation owned by the Virginia National Guard and Ft. Story is an official Department of Defense World War II commemorative community.  The displays will include current and vintage vehicles, weapons, and billets at the Camp Pendleton parade grounds.

An "Operation Overlord Victory Dance" is planned from 8 p.m. to 1 a.m. on Friday, June 3 at Oceana Naval Air Station.  The dance will be held in an aircraft hanger and will feature a Big Band concert by the Tommy Dorsey Orchestra conducted by Buddy Morrow.  The attire is black tie or period clothing.  The cost is

3

Exhibit 3-4a
(*continued*)

Reenactment News Release  (Courtesy Virginia Beach Department of
Convention and Visitor Development)

$75 per person and $65 for World War II veterans. For additional information contact Brac Gilbert at (804) 247-8523.

Saturday, June 4 will feature a parade on Atlantic Avenue and 16th Street with actor Van Johnson as Grand Marshall. The parade will showcase more than 100 units, including antique cars, bands and floats. Highlights include numerous World War II-era American vehicles, including a tank. World War II re-enactors will march in formation and pass out American flags along the parade route, and vintage aircraft and bombers will perform flyovers during the event.

A wreath laying ceremony is scheduled for 10 a.m. Sunday, June 5 at the Cape Henry Monument, Ft. Story, and will conclude the D-Day weekend.

The D-Day commemorative ceremony, re-enactment, stage show and wreath laying are free and open to the public. Due to a limited capacity of 10,000, those attending the D-Day ceremony and the re-enactment are advised to arrive early.

The D-Day Normandy Commemorative Celebration is co-sponsored by the War Memorial Museum of Virginia, Newport News, Va.; Ft. Story; Camp Pendleton State Military Reservation; the Virginia Army National Guard, and the City of Virginia Beach.

For additional information on the D-Day events or accommodations in Virginia Beach, call toll-free, 1-800-VA-BEACH (1-800-822-3224).

#    #    #

4

Exhibit 3-4b

"Victory Dance" News Release    (Courtesy Virginia Beach Department of
Convention and Visitor Development)

# Virginia Beach
# NEWS

April 18, 1994                          CONTACT:   Deborah Barwick
                                                   (804) 466-0783
FOR IMMEDIATE RELEASE                              Sean Brickell, APR
                                                   (800) 333-6397

**"OPERATION OVERLORD-VICTORY DANCE" PART OF D-DAY CELEBRATION**

VIRGINIA BEACH, Va. -- A black tie event, the "Operation
Overlord-Victory Dance" will be held from 8 p.m. to 1 a.m. on
Friday, June 3, 1994 at the Oceana Naval Air Station. The dance,
named after the World War II code name for D-Day, is part of the
D-Day Normandy Commemorative Celebration held June 3-5 in
Virginia Beach.

The dance will be patterned after a 1940's era social event
and will be held in a hanger at the air station. Patrons are
encouraged to wear either period costumes or black tie.
Highlights of the event include a big band concert by Buddy
Morrow and the Tommy Dorsey Orchestra, and a guest appearance by
actor Van Johnson, the Grand Marshall of the D-Day parade.

The cost for the dance is $75 per person and $65 for World
War II veterans. The event is open to the public.

For reservations or additional information about the dance,
contact Brac Gilbert at (804) 247-8523.

The D-Day Normandy Commemorative Celebration is co-sponsored
by the War Memorial Museum of Virginia, Newport News, Va.; Ft.
Story; Camp Pendleton State Military Reservation; Virginia
Beach; the Virginia Army National Guard, and the City of Virginia
Beach.                          5

Department of
Convention and
Visitor Development

City of Virginia Beach
2101 Parks Avenue
Suite 300
Virginia Beach, VA 23451

Phone (804) 437-4700
FAX (804) 437-4747

Exhibit 3-4b
(continued)

"Victory Dance" News Release (Courtesy Virginia Beach Department of Convention and Visitor Development)

For additional information on the D-Day events or accommodations in Virginia Beach, call toll-free, 1-800-VA-BEACH (1-800-822-3224). Virginia Beach, Va. is one of the East Coast's top resort destinations, offering more than 38 miles of ocean and bay beaches.

#    #    #

6

# Virginia Beach
# NEWS

April 18, 1994                          CONTACT:   Deborah Barwick
                                                   (804) 466-0783
FOR IMMEDIATE RELEASE                              Sean Brickell, APR
                                                   (800) 333-6307

### VAN JOHNSON, STAR OF WWII MOVIES,
### TO APPEAR AS D-DAY PARADE GRAND MARSHALL

VIRGINIA BEACH, Va. -- Van Johnson, who starred in such World War II era movies as "Battleground" and "30 Seconds Over Tokyo," will serve as Grand Marshall in a parade honoring the 50th anniversary of D-Day held June 3-5, 1994.

The 78-year-old actor will also participate in a black-tie "Operation Overlord-Victory Dance" at the Oceana Naval Air Station on Friday, June 3.

The parade, part of the D-Day Normandy Commemorative Celebration, begins at 9 a.m. on Saturday, June 4 at Atlantic Avenue and 16th Street in Virginia Beach. It will end at the Tidewater Veteran's Memorial across from the Virginia Beach Pavilion.

The parade will feature more than 100 units, including antique cars, bands, and floats. Highlights include numerous World War II-era American vehicles, including a tank. World War II re-enactors will march in formation and pass out American flags along the parade route, and vintage aircraft and bombers will perform flyovers during the event.

For additional information about the parade, contact Judy White at 587-0346.                    7

Department of
Convention and
Visitor Development

City of Virginia Beach
2101 Parks Avenue
Suite 500
Virginia Beach, VA 23451

Phone (804) 437-4700
FAX (804) 437-4747

Exhibit 3-4c
(*continued*)

Parade News Release   (Courtesy Virginia Beach Department of Convention and
Visitor Development)

The D-Day Normandy Commemorative Celebration is co-sponsored by the War Memorial Museum of Virginia, Newport News, Va.; Ft. Story; Camp Pendleton State Military Reservation; the Virginia Army National Guard; and the City of Virginia Beach.

For additional information on the D-Day events or accommodations in Virginia Beach, call toll-free, 1-800-VA-BEACH (1-800-822-3224). Virginia Beach, Va. is one of the East Coast's top resort destinations, offering more than 38 miles of ocean and bay beaches.

#     #     #

8

Virginia Beach

# NEWS

May 2, 1994                          CONTACT:   Deborah Barwick
                                                (804) 466-0783
FOR IMMEDIATE RELEASE                           Sean Brickell, APR
                                                (800) 333-6397

**D-DAY NORMANDY COMMEMORATIVE CELEBRATION WEEKEND**
**JUNE 3-5, 1994**
**UPDATED SCHEDULE OF EVENTS**
**PLEASE DISREGARD ANY PREVIOUS SCHEDULE OF EVENTS**

Friday, June 3, 1994

    9 a.m. - 5 p.m.      Historical Displays at Camp Pendleton
                         and Ft. Story

    8 p.m. - 1 a.m.      "Operation Overlord-Victory Dance" at
                         Oceana  Naval  Air  Station  (Aircraft
                         Hanger)

Saturday, June 4, 1994

    9 a.m.               Parade on Atlantic Avenue & 16th Street

    9 a.m. - 5 p.m.      Historical Displays at Camp Pendleton
                         and Ft. Story

    1:30 p.m.            Commemorative Ceremony - Ft. Story

    2 p.m. - 3:30 p.m.   Re-enactment

    4 p.m.               Stage Door Canteen Show

Sunday, June 5, 1994

    10 a.m.              Wreath Laying Ceremony

                          #    #    #

                            1

Department of
Convention and
Visitor Development

City of Virginia Beach
2101 Parks Avenue
Suite 500
Virginia Beach, VA 23451

Phone (804) 437-4700
FAX (804) 437-4747

Exhibit 3-4e "Back the Attack" Poster (Courtesy Virginia Beach Department of Convention and Visitor Development)

# Internal
# Communications

PUBLIC RELATIONS CONDUCTED INSIDE ORGANIZA-
tions falls into two general categories: employee relations and member relations. Employee relations includes all communications between the management
of an organization and its personnel. Member relations refers to communications inside a membership
organization between the officers and members.

# EMPLOYEE RELATIONS

Research, objectives, programming, and evaluation are useful problem-solving tools in employee relations.

# RESEARCH

Research for employee relations concentrates on client research, studying the reason for communication, and identifying the employee audiences to be targeted for communication.

## Client Research

Client research for employee relations focuses on *information* about the organization's personnel. What is the size and nature of the work force? What reputation does the organization have with its work force? How satisfied are the employees? What employee communications does the organization regularly use? Are any special forms of communication used? How effective are the organization's internal communications? Has the organization conducted special employee relations programs in the past? If so, what were the results of such programs? What are the organization's strengths, weaknesses, and opportunities regarding its work force? These questions might guide the initial research in preparation for an employee relations program.

## Opportunity or Problem Research

A second focal point for research is the *reason* for conducting an employee relations program. Is a new program really necessary? This question should be answered with care because it justifies the necessary expenditure for a program. Would the program be reactive—in response to a problem that has arisen in employee relations—or would it be proactive—taking advantage of an opportunity to improve existing employee relations?

A survey of employee attitudes may reveal a variety of issues, including: low levels of satisfaction and morale, dislike of the physical surroundings, and/or frustration with internal policies. The survey results may thus demonstrate a strong need for a reactive employee relations program.

## Audience Research

The final area of research involves precisely defining the *employee audiences* to be targeted for communication. These audiences can be identified using the following terms:

Management

Upper-level administrators

> Mid-level administrators
>
> Lower-level administrators
>
> Nonmanagement (staff)
>
> > Specialists
> >
> > Clerical personnel
> >
> > Secretarial personnel
> >
> > Uniformed personnel
> >
> > > Equipment operators
> > >
> > > Drivers
> > >
> > > Security personnel
> > >
> > > Other uniformed personnel
> >
> > Union representatives
> >
> > Other nonmanagement personnel

Effective research on employee relations is built on an understanding of the client's personnel, the opportunity or problem that serves as a reason for communication with the work force, and the specific identification of the employee audiences to be targeted for communication.

# OBJECTIVES

Objectives for employee relations include the two major categories of impact and output. Employee relations objectives may be specific and quantitative to facilitate accurate measurement. Optional percentages and time frames are included here in parentheses.

## Impact Objectives

Impact objectives for employee relations include informing employees or modifying their attitudes or behaviors. Some typical impact objectives are:

1. To increase employee knowledge of significant organizational policies, activities, and developments (by 60 percent during March and April)

2. To enhance favorable employee attitudes toward the organization (by 40 percent during the current fiscal year)

3. To accomplish (50 percent) greater employee adoption of behaviors desired by management (in a three-month period)

4. To make (60 percent of) the employee force organizational spokespersons in the community (during the next two years)

5. To receive (50 percent) more employee feedback from organizational communications (during the coming year)

Behavioral, informational, and attitudinal impact objectives may be used in any combination in a public relations plan. The chosen objectives should be carefully determined so they demonstrate the program's goals.

## Output Objectives

Output objectives in employee relations constitute the efforts made by the practitioner to accomplish such desired outcomes as employee recognition and regular employee communication. Some examples include:

1. To recognize employee accomplishments and contributions in (80 percent of) employee communications (during the current year)

2. To prepare and distribute employee communications on a weekly basis

3. To schedule interpersonal communication between management and a specific employee group each month (specify groups and months)

# PROGRAMMING

Programming for employee relations should include the careful planning of theme and messages, action or special event(s), uncontrolled and controlled media, and execution, using the principles of effective communication.

## Theme and Messages

The theme and messages for employee relations depend on the reason for conducting the campaign or program. Both of these elements should grow out of the opportunity or problem that accounts for the particular program. That is, themes and messages usually grow out of the problems faced by companies and the methods chosen to solve them. For example, a practitioner working for a company that is moving its facilities and offices to a new building could produce a brochure entitled "A Company on the Move."

## Action or Special Event(s)

Action and special events used in employee relations programs include:

1. Training seminars
2. Special programs on safety or new technology
3. An open house for employees and their families
4. Parties, receptions, and other social affairs
5. Other employee special events related to organizational developments

A bank, for example, could sponsor a surprise Dividend Day for participants in the employee stock program, and a company moving into a new facility could arrange an employee open house and party.

## Uncontrolled and Controlled Media

The use of uncontrolled media in employee relations is usually limited to sending news releases or announcements about employees' accomplishments to outside mass and specialized media as warranted. Actually, this is media relations, not employee relations, but it is often considered part of the employee relations program.

Controlled media, on the other hand, are used extensively in employee relations programs. The most frequently used controlled media are employee publications such as magazines, newspapers, and newsletters addressed to particular groups or levels of employees in larger organizations. These publications are often highly professional and creative, both in writing and design.

In addition to house publications, employee relations programs use a variety of other forms of controlled media, such as:

1. Bulletin boards
2. Displays and exhibits
3. Telephone hot lines or news lines
4. Inserts accompanying paychecks
5. Internal television
6. Films
7. Video cassettes
8. Meetings
9. Teleconferences
10. Audiovisual presentations
11. Booklets, pamphlets, brochures
12. Speakers bureaus (employees address community groups)

The use of media in employee relations differs from that in other forms of public relations because of the heavy emphasis on controlled media.

## Effective Communication

Principles of effective communication are virtually the same for employee relations as for most other forms of public relations, although two-way communication and audience participation should be stressed. Special events are an excellent way to employ these elements in employee relations.

# EVALUATION

Impact and output objectives in employee relations can be evaluated using the same tools of measurement as in other forms of public relations (see Chapter 2). In addition, a variety of research techniques have been developed to deal exclusively with internal organizational communication. These techniques include network analysis, which measures the effectiveness of internal communication channels using such methods as the ECCO (*episodic communication channels in organizations*) analysis. This method traces one message unit as it flows through an organization. A duty study involves employees recording their daily communication activities in a detailed diary. Observational studies use trained observers to record employees' communications during their work schedules, and cross-sectional interviews ask employees about their communication interactions.

The most extensive of these research activities designed to assess internal organizational communication is the communication audit developed by the International Communication Association (ICA). The ICA audit includes some of the network analysis techniques just mentioned and also queries employees about the nature of their communication experiences and their overall job satisfaction.

Follow-up surveys were used in most of the case studies in this chapter. These yield quantitative measures of the stated objectives. Objectives were also assessed through publicity placement and employee participation in the programs.

Again, remember that to be effective and useful to the organization, research—both initial and evaluative—should be conducted by trained, experienced professionals who work for reputable research firms.

# SUMMARY

The ROPE process provides a useful approach to the planning and execution of employee relations programs.

Research for employee relations concentrates on demographic data about the organization's work force, existing levels of employee satisfaction, the state of relations between management and employees, and the effectiveness of employee communication. The uniqueness of research in this form of PR is, of course, the focus on information gathering about the work force itself.

Both impact and output objectives are generally used in employee relations programs. Impact objectives include such desired outcomes as increasing employee knowledge of organizational matters and eliciting favorable employee attitudes and behaviors toward the organization. Output objectives are the efforts of practitioners to recognize employee contributions, distribute employee communications effectively, and otherwise enhance the impact objectives.

Programming for employee relations may include catchy themes; special events such as training seminars, special employee campaigns or programs, or social events for employees; and controlled media such as house publications, bulletin boards, displays, meetings, and a variety of electronic means of communication.

Evaluation of employee communication should refer back to each stated objective. Methods of assessment may include such specialized techniques as network analysis, duty studies, observational studies, or the ICA communication audit. Finally, follow-up surveys are a popular means of evaluating attitudinal and behavioral objectives.

Each element of the ROPE process should be tailored for the particular situation, as we will see in this chapter's cases.

# Employee
# Relations Cases

*Faced with an on-campus rape and murder, the University of West Florida (UWF) developed a low-key safety campaign around the concept of safety in numbers when using university facilities at night. Exhibit 4-1a is a "Dear Colleague" letter circulated among UWF faculty members. Exhibit 4-1b consists of "Teaching Tips" and a request for campaign suggestions. Exhibit 4-1c is a campaign poster. Exhibits 4-1d, 4-1e, and 4-1f are other print materials used in the program.*

**CASE 4-1**

### "Just 2 It!"

University of West Florida, Pensacola, FL

## The Challenge

In January 1993, the University of West Florida community suffered a wrenching tragedy. A student was raped and murdered on campus as she left night class. After immediately responding with improved lighting, security, and emergency systems, President Morris Marx and UWF's Safety Task Force called for increased safety awareness among campus community members. Communication Arts professors Martha Saunders (public relations) and Tom Groth (advertising) agreed to develop a comprehensive communication campaign to increase awareness and to encourage safe behavior on the UWF campus. The research-based campaign unfolded the following September.

## Research

Research methods included secondary research; media analysis; interviews with key informants among campus administrators and student leaders; student surveys; focus groups of student leaders, graduate students, and lower division students; and unobtrusive measures such as firsthand observation of student behavior. Our study revealed three important facts: (1) crime and fear of crime seriously threatens the quality of life on university campuses nationwide; (2) UWF students were complacent in their attitudes toward personal safety; and (3) some students perceived the administration to be uncaring and unresponsive to their safety needs. We concluded with the following problem statement:

> Overall increases in campus crime and attitudes of complacency and distrust at UWF combine to put our students and employees increasingly at risk for acts of violence.

## Planning

We chose as primary publics those most at risk—female students and employees using university facilities at night.

We set about developing our plan with two serious challenges: (1) finding a way to overcome complacency (our greatest enemy); and (2) finding a way to make students aware of *possible* dangers without making it appear that our campus operated in some kind of a war zone. We earnestly believed our student would still be alive had she not been alone in the parking lot that foggy night after class, so we chose as the centerpiece of our campaign the simple, time-honored wisdom most of us learned at our mother's knee—*there is safety in numbers*. Our behavioral goal was to have target audience members find partners when using university facilities at night. For them, the campaign needed to be positive, upbeat, and empowering. Our campaign theme, Just 2 It! provided a snappy slogan with an empowering message.

University populations virtually "turn over" every four years, so it was critical that we get the Just 2 It! concept normalized into the university's culture as soon as possible. For the 1993–1994 academic year we set four measurable objectives:

> Objective 1: To increase by 75 percent awareness of the Just 2 It! concept.
>
> Objective 2: To increase by 60 percent recall of the campaign theme.
>
> Objective 3: To increase by 55 percent comprehension of the Just 2 It! concept as meaning "safety in numbers."
>
> Objective 4: To increase by 50 percent audience members who find partners at night.

Additionally, we aimed to develop and maintain the continuity of message throughout all aspects of the campaign *and* to foster a caring relationship among the university community by communicating that we are all part of a quality, safety-oriented organization. The unspoken message: You're not alone at UWF.

Strategies centered around the communication patterns of our largely commuter campus and were designed to focus as much as possible on direct, personal impact. We set out to have the Just 2 It! message available wherever target audience members gathered. Creative tactics interrelated

1. UWF locations (classrooms, Commons, Rathskeller, computer center, dormitories, gym, swimming pool, nature trails, roads)
2. Time ("vulnerable times"; i.e., evenings, early mornings)
3. UWF events (presented as something positive to do in pairs instead of alone; e.g., studying, swimming, movies, exercise)
4. Action (messages featured dynamic duos; i.e., students, employees who "double up" because there is safety in numbers)
5. Headlines ("double-up" puns were designed to dramatize the 2-it message)

Visuals incorporated the Just 2 It! logo plus descriptor (safety in numbers) with art reflective of the lifestyle and tastes of the target public. We worked within an $18,000 budget.

## Execution

We used a roll-out method of introducing the campaign to avoid conjuring feelings of crisis. Every effort was made to deliver the Just 2 It! message personally whenever possible. The whole point was to get university members to "buy into" the concept and spread the word. Discussions with opinion leaders across the campus generated ideas for effectively spreading the word. Image Development Group, Inc., headed by a UWF graduate, offered pro bono and reduced rate production services. Hand-delivered professor packs for classroom use included teaching tips, brochures for class members, and a colleague-to-colleague letter from Saunders and Groth asking for participation in the campaign. Saunders met with the advisor and ad manager of the student newspaper and negotiated a greatly reduced rate for full-page campus ads. Volunteers set up table tents in the student center, the computer center, and the library. Students modeling for the ads earned mentions for their organizations and campaign t-shirts. Key individuals from every division pledged participation. Security people distributed information with parking permits; registration workers wore Just 2 It! t-shirts and distributed brochures; payroll clerks added the message to payroll vouchers; student activities coordinators made Just 2 It! announcements at the end of evening events and erected banners; bookstore personnel gave out Just 2 It! bookmarks with every purchase; physical plant workers framed and mounted posters near campus phones; the cafeteria commissioned Just 2 It! logos for beverage cups; and the Just 2 It! poster was featured on the back of the student handbook. Saunders gave presentations at freshmen orientation and met with department chairs, inviting their participation.

## Evaluation

By May 1994 it had become "cool" to "2-it!" The campaign received favorable media response, including featured articles in national publications, prompting numerous inquiries from universities around the country and abroad. A student survey revealed that we had exceeded our objectives, with 77 percent indicating awareness; 62 percent recalling the campaign theme; 99.9 percent understanding the meaning of the slogan; and 67 percent indicating that they now walk with a partner after dark. A phone survey of faculty and staff showed we had exceeded our objectives, with that group reporting 85 percent awareness, 70 percent recall, 99 percent comprehension, and 55 percent participation. We used this evaluation to revise our plan for the current academic year.

Communication Arts
Journalism
Public Relations
and Advertising
Radio, Television, Film
Communication
Studies
College of Arts
and Sciences


11000 University
Parkway
Pensacola, Florida
32514-5751

(904)474-2874

Dear Colleague:

Safety is everybody's business at UWF!  As classroom
instructors, we're in a unique position to encourage
our students to do the right thing when it comes to
personal safety.  Please join us in encouraging the
buddy system --especially in your night classes.

This packet includes brochures on UWF's "Just 2 It!"
campaign.  Give them to your night students so they'll
be reminded "it just takes two to stop a problem before
it starts."

In addition, we've enclosed some ideas for
incorporating the "Just 2 It" message into your class
activities.  The response card is for your ideas.  Your
thoughts are important.  Let us hear from you.

As always, thanks for your help.


The "Just 2 It!" Team
(Tom Groth, Professor)
(Martha Saunders, Asst. Professor)

*Tom & Martha*

The University of West Florida

An Equal Opportunity/Affirmative Action Institution

Exhibit 4-1b    "Teaching Tips"   (Courtesy University of West Florida)

# PLEASE!

Give us you ideas for including safety messages in your class activities! Just detach this comment sheet and send your suggestions to Martha Saunders or Tom Groth, Building 36.

PLEASE DETACH AND RETURN!

THE UNIVERSITY OF WEST FLORIDA

safety in numbers

THE UNIVERSITY OF WEST FLORIDA

safety in numbers

# TEACHING TIPS!

**1** Include a safety message in your syllabus.

**2** Discuss safety concerns during class orientation activities.

**3** Provide incentives for students to buddy up—2 points, 2 free assignments, or 2 days grace for an assignment—whatever suits you.

**4** Set the example. Just 2 it! yourself!

Exhibit 4-1c

Campaign Poster  (Courtesy University of West Florida)

Exhibit 4-1d    Program Materials   (Courtesy University of West Florida)

# 2night 2night

**EVERYNIGHT IS A 2NIGHT**. **UWF** REMINDS YOU TO JUST 2 IT!

THERE IS SAFETY IN NUMBERS. SO WHETHER IT BE AN EVENING

JOG, A TRIP TO THE RAT OR A STROLL FROM CLASS TO CAR,

DON'T GO IT ALONE - **DOUBLE UP**. IT JUST TAKES 2 TO STOP A

PROBLEM BEFORE IT STARTS.

safety in numbers

THE UNIVERSITY OF WEST FLORIDA

| Exhibit 4-1e | Program Materials   (Courtesy University of West Florida) |
|---|---|

| Exhibit 4-1f | Program Materials   (Courtesy University of West Florida) |
|---|---|

## *We Care About Your Safety at UWF*

**Please use the buddy system when walking to your car after work, especially now that it will be getting dark by 5:00 p.m. If you need an escort, call UWF SafeWalk at extension 2415.**

*Following a program of cost cutting, downsizing, and restructuring, the Eastman Kodak Company conducted a successful employee morale-building campaign. Exhibit 4-2a is a news release outlining the program. Exhibit 4-2b is an explanation of the program in the company newsletter,* Kodakery.

**CASE 4-2**

## Reshaping Benefits and the Corporate Culture

Eastman Kodak Company

*Instead of bettering morale, you make it worse! Keep cutting employees, benefits, etc. and you will have no company left to worry about.*
    —July 1994 employee response to monthly Kodak Opinion Trend Survey

### Background

For more than a century Kodak was viewed by its employees as the paternalistic "Great Yellow Father"—a caring company that provided generous wages and benefits, along with lifetime job security. But in recent years, Kodak, like many other companies, found itself facing stronger and more aggressive competitors and cost pressures that squeezed margins. Kodak's performance turned lackluster. In late 1993, the Kodak Board of Directors broke precedent and hired an outsider, George Fisher of Motorola, to restore company performance.

Fisher and his management team immediately undertook an aggressive program of cost cutting, downsizing, and restructuring to make Kodak financially healthy, performance driven, and marketplace competitive. Among the changes was the overhaul of three key benefits programs: the retirement plan, life insurance, and the much cherished Wage Dividend—a pioneering profit-sharing plan established by Kodak founder George Eastman. Independent assessments had shown that these programs were exceedingly rich when compared to similar plans at other blue-chip companies. A special management team, including representatives from Corporate Employee Communications, sought to reduce costs and to align the benefits better with business objectives.

## Research

As the management team developed its recommendation, a cross-functional communications team representing Corporate Employee Communications, Benefits, Organizational Development, Human Resources, and Manufacturing started on a parallel path to develop a communications strategy.

This team built on earlier best-practices research conducted through Jackson Jackson & Wagner as part of the restructuring of Kodak's communications organization. That firm provided additional recommendations regarding approaches for delivering difficult messages while trying to effect culture change. Towers Perrin, an international benefits consulting firm, also was engaged because of their extensive expertise in this area.

In addition, the team:

- Conducted telephone interviews with four Fortune 100 companies that had recently communicated major benefits changes.

- Conducted an extensive literature search, including a review of PRSA Information Center files and a Lexis/Nexis search, to gather background on benefits communications issues.

- Conducted a detailed demographic analysis of the employee population to better assess how the changes would affect the various populations within the company.

The confidential nature of the impending changes prohibited broad-scale employee focus groups, but the team engaged a small focus group to review communications approaches and key messages.

## Planning

### Objectives

(1) Get employees to understand the need to change key benefits and to believe the business case and competitive analysis that drove decisions. (2) Mitigate negative reactions by setting the context for the changes and conveying potential advantages. (3) Continue to build confidence in CEO Fisher and his leadership team.

### Strategies

(1) Position changes in the context of Kodak's newly emerging business and human resources strategies that focus on competitiveness. (2) Engage Kodak management as key communicators in face-to-face sessions with their employees, with corporate print and electronic media providing secondary support. (3) Develop evaluation mechanisms for assessment of the communications process and effectiveness of delivery. (4) Establish a process for continuing postannouncement communications,

including creation of individualized financial statements for all employees explaining the impact of the retirement changes.

### Key Audience

Primary—54,000 U.S. employees (34,000 in Rochester, NY, site of Kodak's headquarters and main manufacturing plant)—with special attention to early-career, mid-career, and retirement-eligible populations; secondary—Rochester community (because of financial impact of Wage Dividend change) and media.

### Budget

$100,000 for consultation fees and campaign materials.

## Execution

### Building Support

To build support for the communications strategy and a new face-to-face communications process, the communications team conducted briefing sessions with various management teams throughout the company during the months before the announcement. Feedback from the sessions helped refine the communications strategy. At the same time, print and video employee communications vehicles were used to improve employee understanding of key business issues underlying the impending changes.

### Rumor Control

Exaggerated rumors of drastic benefits cuts circulated throughout the summer, heightening employee anxiety and driving down morale. To help manage the rumor mill that was being fueled by speculative media reports, an "early alert" e-mail message was sent to all employees notifying them of the upcoming meetings.

### Resource Materials

The project team developed a management briefing notebook with overhead cells, talking points, and other resource materials that gave the managers a complete tool kit for conducting meetings with their employees. It included a videotaped message from CEO George Fisher explaining the business rationale for the changes and asking for employee support.

### Human Resources Staff Training

In an unprecedented training effort, nearly 250 human resources people from across the company were brought together in Rochester on a Friday, four days before the announcement, for an intensive eight-hour training session on the benefits changes and communications plans.

## Manager Training

The day before the announcement, more than 400 Rochester-based managers designated as key communicators gathered for a four-hour training session. It was telecast via the company's business television network to managers in 14 regional locations across the U.S.A. Two-way audio network permitted field questions.

## Announcement Day

Face-to-face meetings began at 6 A.M. on Tuesday, September 13, with manufacturing employees coming off the night shift and continued virtually around the clock in some locations for the next three days. A special issue of the company newspaper was issued the day of the announcement and the internal TV network as well as e-mail carried announcement news.

## Community/Media Relations

Key Rochester government and civic leaders were briefed the morning of the announcement. Company spokespeople refused specific comment to the media until the morning of announcement. A local paper quoted a Kodak spokesperson, "We want to have the opportunity to first share the details of the changes with employees face to face." A news release was issued after the employee meetings were well under way.

## Follow-up

In the weeks following the announcement, additional material was forwarded to all supervisors via e-mail to help them answer questions that flowed from the employee meetings. Both the company newspaper and the benefits newsletter provided additional information.

## Individualized Statements

Individualized financial statements were mailed in late November, explaining how the retirement changes affected each employee. This mailing, originally scheduled for March 1995, was moved up as a result of feedback from employee focus groups, which also suggested format changes.

## Evaluation

A five-phase evaluation effort was built into the communications plan: (1) evaluation of the manager/human resources training, (2) immediate anecdotal feedback following the announcement, (3) a "pulse survey" sent to 3,500 supervisors and managers nationwide within three days of the announcement, (4) a random survey of 2,000 employees nationwide in late November after they received their personal statements, and (5) a post-event, self-assessment by the communications team.

### Key Findings

- Within three days, some 46,000 employees nationwide (86 percent of the workforce) had attended a meeting with their manager.

- Four out of five employees said face to face was an effective way to communicate this message.

- 88 percent understood why the wage dividend was being tied to performance.

- 74 percent understood why the changes to retirement and life insurance were being made.

- 82 percent said the personal statement answered many/all of their retirement questions.

### Typical Survey Comments

- "I believe the reasoning behind the changes because I trust top management (Fisher)."

- "I think all information on significant change must be delivered in person as well as via other media."

- "Firsthand communication from supervision shows their commitment to the process."

As an outgrowth of this successful effort, Kodak has created for 1995 a quarterly face-to-face communications program to help managers convey company and unit performance information to their employees. In announcing the new program, George Fisher told employees, "It would be hard to build a performance-based culture without sharing performance expectations with everyone charged with delivering those results."

> *"I really understand what they're trying to do. I would rather do that and save our company and keep my job than to be out on the street."*
>
> —September 1994 Kodak television network interview with employee following benefits announcement

Exhibit 4-2a | Program News Release   (Copyright Eastman Kodak Company)

## KODAK MOVES TO LINK BENEFITS
## WITH COMPANY PERFORMANCE

ROCHESTER, N.Y., Sept. 13 -- Eastman Kodak Company today announced several new initiatives designed to better link employee benefits with the performance of the company.

"It is clear that for Kodak to succeed, we must fundamentally change the way we run the business," said George M.C. Fisher, Kodak Chairman, President, and CEO. "We must create a new Kodak that is world-class, performance-driven, and truly competitive when compared to other successful corporations."

For more than a year, Kodak has been studying how to better link employee benefits with company performance. As a result, a number of changes will be implemented. "The goal of these changes is to provide benefits programs that are competitive with the marketplace, fair to employees, and achieve some cost savings for the company," Fisher said. These initiatives will:

- Better link the company's annual wage dividend to financial performance.

- Change the company's retirement plan to encourage long-term employment.

- Increase company paid life insurance for employees.

- Amend life insurance benefits for future retirees.

- Modify health care benefits eligibility requirements for future retirees.

In a message to employees, Fisher explained that these changes are being implemented to help Kodak become a more performance-driven organization.

Eastman Kodak Company, 343 State Street, Rochester, New York 14650-0518

Kodak Moves to Link Benefits/page 2

"I recognize the pace of change at Kodak has been rapid over the last nine months," said Fisher. "But I truly believe that these changes are necessary to help create the new Kodak."

## Wage Dividend

In the future, the company's wage dividend, if declared, will be based on the company exceeding a specific return on net assets ( RONA ) target.

Under the new plan, there will be no minimum or maximum wage dividend payout. If the company is unable to meet specified RONA goals, there will be no wage dividend payout in the following year. At the same time, if company performance exceeds RONA thresholds, there will be no ceiling on the payout. If expectations for running the company are met, employees are likely to see a wage dividend payout over the next several years in the range of 3 to 10 percent of their participating earnings.

Currently, the wage dividend is based on a formula tied to the company's return on assets ( ROA ). The current formula also contains provisions for a minimum payout of 5% and a maximum payout of 15%.

The new wage dividend based on RONA targets will go into effect for any wage dividend declared for 1995 and paid in 1996. We expect a specific RONA target for 1995 will be set by the end of this year. At that time, employees will receive information enabling them to calculate what level of wage dividend would be achieved at various levels of RONA performance. Any wage dividend declared for 1994 and paid in 1995 will not be affected by the changes announced today.

## Kodak Retirement Income Plan Modifications

Effective January 1, 1996, Kodak will change its retirement plan to better support and encourage long-term employment, while generating financial savings for the company.

Under the new plan, the benefit formula is unchanged. What is changing is the point at which Kodak will subsidize early retirement and the level of that subsidy.

Under the current plan, employees are able to retire with unreduced benefits when age and service total 85 years.

Under the new plan, unreduced retirement benefits will be available to employees who are 60 years old with at least 30 years of service, or age 65 with any amount of service. Employees will be eligible for early retirement benefits at age 55 with at least 10 years of service.

Any pension earned after Dec. 31, 1995 will be available in the form of an annuity only. Pension earned before this date will continue to be available either as an annuity or as a lump sum.

The specific impact of these changes will vary from employee to employee depending on age and years of service. For example, as part of the new plan, an employee who is 40 years old with 15 years of service will need to work a few more years at Kodak -- under three years in most cases -- to reach the same levels achieved at full pension under the current plan.

No employee will have to leave the company to keep or hold onto a benefit. All employees, whether retirement eligible or not, will retain what pension they have earned. Therefore, any benefits earned through Dec. 31, 1995 will not be affected by the changes announced today. Because of this, for those closer to full pension who are older with greater years of service, even less additional service will be required to receive the same benefit. As a result, the majority of Kodak employees working today will still be able to retire prior to age 60 with a comparable pension if they so choose.

## Insurance Modifications

Kodak will increase the amount of company paid life insurance provided to current employees. Coverage will increase from one-half to one times an individual's annual rate of pay. Employees will be able to purchase additional insurance up to five times their annual rate of pay.

For employees who become eligible for retirement after Dec. 31, 1995, the company will reduce retiree life insurance benefits from two times to one times an individual's annual rate of pay. At age 70, company paid life insurance will be set at one-half an individual's annual rate of pay at the time of retirement, just as it is today.

Additionally, the post-retirement survivor income benefit will be eliminated for those who are not retirement eligible before January 1, 1996. The company will offer all employees the option to purchase Group Universal Life Insurance.

Kodak Moves to Link Benefits/page 4

Eligibility requirements for future retiree life insurance and health care benefits will also be amended.  For those employees who are not retirement eligible before January 1, 1996, these individuals must have a combined age and service totaling 75 years and must be at least 55 years old with at least 10 years of service in order to receive a company contribution to life insurance and health care benefits.

## External Comparison

With the changes announced today, Kodak moves closer to the average of its peer companies in terms of overall benefits offered.

In reviewing the company's recent benefit levels using an independent ranking survey, Kodak was found to offer benefits 13% above the average.  Others evaluated as part of the survey include companies like 3M, General Electric, and Motorola.

"We must realign compensation and benefits to make Kodak a more competitive, performance-driven organization," said Michael P. Morley, senior vice president and director, Human Resources.  "This is an essential step in enabling Kodak to grow and maintain leadership.  It will also help our company in our efforts to offer rewarding and long-term opportunities to employees, to enhance value for shareholders, and to meet our long-term commitment to retirees."

"These changes are well thought out and will go a long way to making us more competitive," added Fisher.  "But the biggest difference of all will come in our pulling together to build and sustain a Kodak which is performance-based and viable over the long-term for our customers and employees."

#

**Media Contact:**

David P. Beigie
Eastman Kodak Company
Corporate Media Relations
Phone: (716) 724-4244
Fax: (716) 724-0964

1994

Exhibit 4-2b

Excerpt from *Kodakery*   (Copyright Eastman Kodak Company)

*SEPTEMBER 13, 1994*

# KODAKERY

F O R   K O D A K   E M P L O Y E E S   A N D   R E T I R E E S

### BENEFITS ARE PART OF STRATEGY
## MAKING KODAK COMPETITIVE REQUIRES CHANGE

**To Kodak Employees:**

Since coming to Kodak, my first priority has been to put in place the process to improve Kodak's financial performance and make this company more competitive on a global basis.

Kodak is a tremendously powerful name that is respected throughout the world. But we cannot survive based on our reputation alone.

As an imaging company, we face intense new competitive challenges in the world market.

In the silver halide business, for example, pressure from competitors is becoming more intense. This pressure is holding down prices and reducing Kodak's profit margins.

As Kodak ventures deeper into the digital world, other marketplace challenges emerge including faster cycle time, shorter product life and slimmer profit margins.

It is clear that for Kodak to succeed as an imaging company, we must fundamentally change the way we run the business—we must create a "new Kodak." Our goal is to create a world-class, performance-driven company that is truly competitive when compared to other successful corporations.

While we have come a long way in a short time, there is more to do. We must continue to look at every opportunity to align all of our activities with our business goals.

For more than a year, a management steering committee examined our benefits programs with an eye toward recommending changes that would make Kodak benefits competitive with those of other top-tier companies while still generating cost savings for Kodak. And throughout this process, the overriding concern was to make sure that any changes were fair to Kodak employees.

As a result of this team's work and review by the Policy Committee, a number of changes will be made to better link compensation and benefits plans—from both a philosophy and cost standpoint—to the company's business and human resources strategies.

I recognize that the pace of change at Kodak has been rapid over the last nine months. But I truly believe that this change is necessary to create the "new Kodak."

I ask for your help and involvement in this process of change so that together we can build a company that will thrive and prosper into the 21st century and beyond.

*George Fisher*

George Fisher
Chairman, President and CEO

## MORE MANAGEMENT PAY TO BE TIED TO PERFORMANCE

Compensation plans for the company's middle and upper managers will be modified to better reflect Kodak's performance-driven focus and will be more closely aligned with business strategies.

While there will be no sweeping changes, the new plans strengthen the relationship between performance and pay. CEO George Fisher said results are the measure of reward for all Kodak people.

"Compensation is linked to how the company performs," he said, "and we are holding managers accountable for their commitments. That will be reflected in their compensation."

The Management Annual Performance Plan (MAPP), which has been in effect since 1987, will continue to place a certain percentage of management pay at risk—with incentive awards for performance that meets or exceeds specific goals.

Like the new Wage Dividend, one key measure of MAPP awards will involve the company's return on net assets (RONA) performance and reaching annual targets. If RONA is below acceptable levels, no payout will be made for that measure.

Another existing compensation-related program is the Management Performance Commitment Process (MPCP). In use for Imaging management

*continued on page 8*

## WHAT'S CHANGING

Following is a summary of the changes that are being announced to the Wage Dividend and benefits.

**Wage Dividend**—Any Wage Dividend approved by the Board for payment in 1996 will be based on return on net assets (RONA), with no minimum or maximum. Any Wage Dividend approved by the Board and paid in 1995 will not be affected by the changes. See page 4 for details.

**Kodak Retirement Income Plan**—KRIP will change effective January 1, 1996, to better support and encourage long-service. Benefits earned to that date will be protected and no one must leave before that date in order to keep a benefit. The new plan will allow employees to achieve the same benefit level as the current plan, but it will take longer. See page 6 for details.

**Life Insurance**—Life insurance will be adjusted to more appropriately balance pre- and post-employment coverages. Company paid life insurance for employees will increase from one-half to one times an individual's annual salary. Coverage for future retirees will be reduced. See page 5 for details.

Exhibit 4-2b
(*continued*)

Excerpt from *Kodakery*   (Copyright Eastman Kodak Company)

*SEPTEMBER 13, 1994*

## TRAINING INVESTMENT TO GROW

Kodak's investment in its employees will increase markedly beginning in 1995 as part of a new training initiative.

By the end of 1995, Kodak will be prepared to invest a minimum of 40 hours in the development of each employee every year. The company expects to achieve, at minimum, 50 percent of that goal during 1995.

"For Kodak to meet its business objectives, we must invest wisely—where the potential return is the greatest," said Mike Morley, senior vice president and director of Human Resources. "Highly skilled, knowledgeable employees are a competitive advantage."

Business needs and the requirements of current and future jobs will help determine the types of development activities that are pursued. Employees will be responsible for creating documented development plans that are aligned with and support the business needs of the organization. Supervisors will be responsible to work with employees to develop plans and ensure the necessary alignment, and will be accountable for providing the appropriate resources to implement the plan.

Some specific education will be required beyond the 40-hour minimum including supervisory and management education, training that is legally required, and programs to help employees understand company values and direction.

An Education and Development Advisory Board, chaired by George Fisher, will be established to address policies, principles and corporate direction for employee education and development.

"A performance-driven company uses training like fuel—to empower its people to achieve continuous improvement," Morley said. "An investment in each person is an investment in Kodak's future."

## COMPANY MODIFIES LIFE INSURANCE PLAN

Kodak will increase the amount of company-paid life insurance provided to employees as part of a number of changes within the company's life insurance program.

These changes will help make the life insurance program more balanced when compared with other companies and more equitable for current employees and retirees. Following is a summary of the changes:

❑ Company-paid life insurance for employees will increase from one-half to one times an individual's annual salary rate. In other words, if you earn $30,000 a year, under the new plan the company will pay for $30,000 in life insurance for you. Under the current plan, if you earn $30,000 the company paid for $15,000 in life insurance for you. Employees will still be able to purchase additional insurance up to five times their annual salary rate.

❑ For future retirees—those who do not have 75 in age and years of service or are not 55 with 10 years of service before Jan. 1, 1996—the company will reduce company-paid life insurance in retirement. Company-paid coverage will change from two

times to one times an individual's annual income. At age 70, the company-paid life insurance will be reduced to one-half an individual's annual income, just as it is today. Retirees will still have the option of purchasing additional life insurance, subject to age limitations.

❑ The post-retirement survivor income benefit will be eliminated for those who are not retirement eligible (i.e. do not have 75 in age and years of service or are not 55 with 10 years) before Jan. 1, 1996.

❑ The company will offer employees the option to purchase Group Universal Life Insurance, which is permanent insurance offered at group rates.

## CHANGES COMING TO RETIREE HEALTH CARE

In addition to the changes announced today, health care plans for current retirees will change effective Jan. 1, 1995.

The changes are consistent with the company's ongoing efforts to better manage health care costs while still addressing retiree needs. The changes include:

■ moving toward managed care, such as HMOs, as the basis for company contributions to health care, and

■ setting a future cap on company contributions to health care for some retirees.

**To help respond to retiree questions, a dedicated phone number and staff will be available beginning Oct. 3. That number and details of the changes will be provided in a special section in the Oct. 3 issue of *Kodakery*. Retirees should not call Benefits Information regarding these changes since representatives will not be able to answer questions on this subject.**

# MEMBER RELATIONS

Membership organizations include trade associations, professional associations, labor unions, interest groups, social and religious organizations, and thousands of other groups, large and small, which dot the societal landscape. Each has a need for communication between its officers and members. This process is called *member relations*.

# RESEARCH

Research in member relations includes the client, the opportunity or problem, and the member audiences to be targeted for communication.

**Client Research.** As a prerequisite for the member relations program, the practitioner needs a thorough understanding of the membership organization conducting the program. The precise nature of the organization, its purpose, its headquarters organization and personnel, its financial status, its reputation with the general public and especially with its own members, its present and past public relations practices, and its public relations or image strengths and vulnerabilities will be part of the organizational profile the practitioner must construct.

**Opportunity or Problem Research.** As in all other forms of public relations, the second research objective of member relations is a determination of the reason for conducting the program. Will it be a long-range, proactive program, or will it address a particular problem? The expenditure necessary for the program should be thoroughly justified at this point.

**Audience Research.** Identification of audiences to be targeted for communication is the last of the three aspects of research in member relations. Member publics can be categorized into six groups:

Organization employees
> Headquarters management
> Headquarters nonmanagement (staff)
> Other headquarters personnel

Organization officers
> Elected officers
> Appointed officers
> Legislative groups
> Boards, committees

Organization members

> Regular members
>
> Members in special categories, such as sustaining, emeritus, students
>
> Honorary members or groups

Prospective organization members

State or local chapters

> Organization employees
>
> Organization officers
>
> Organization members
>
> Prospective organization members

Related or other allied organizations

Member relations research, then, consists of an examination of the client or organization conducting the program, the opportunity or problem that necessitates the program, and the member audiences targeted for communication.

# OBJECTIVES

Impact and output objectives are used in member relations and, as in other forms of public relations, objectives should be specific and quantitative as far as possible.

**Impact Objectives.** For member relations, impact objectives consist of the desired outcomes of informing or modifying the attitudes and behaviors of the members of an organization. Some examples are:

1. To increase members' knowledge of organizational developments, policies, or activities (by 50 percent during the current year)

2. To engender (30 percent) more favorable member attitudes toward the organization (during the months of October and November)

3. To stimulate desired behavior modification among the organization's membership (by 30 percent during the next six months)

Impact objectives, in member relations, as in all types of communication, should be developed carefully for they are the standard against which the success of a program will be evaluated.

**Output Objectives.** Output objectives in member relations refer to the distribution or execution of essentially controlled forms of communication. Some examples are:

1. To prepare and distribute membership communications on a regular basis

2. To prepare and execute membership conventions, seminars, and other meetings on a timely basis

# PROGRAMMING

Programming for member relations includes theme and messages, action or special event(s), controlled media, and the use of effective communication principles. These factors are the same for member relations as for employee relations except for the types of action or special event(s) and the types of communication used.

Actions or special events for member relations concentrate on conventions, seminars, conferences, and similar meetings. The headquarters management of an organization has an obligation to schedule and execute such gatherings for the membership.

Other actions on the part of the headquarters officials of an organization usually include the promotion of industry research, preparation of industry statistics and data, development of professional standards and ethical codes, development of in-service education and training for members, and promotion of standards of safety and efficiency among the members or in the industry.

Member communications are limited to controlled media. These usually consist of newsletters and other member publications, reports, industry brochures, pamphlets, and other printed materials, some of which can be distributed to the members' clients. For example, the American Dental Association publishes dental care brochures for patients, and the American Heart Association prints materials for individuals who want to lower their levels of cholesterol.

Uncontrolled media in the form of news releases about employees or members are often considered part of the internal communication program. Strictly speaking, however, such communication falls into the category of external media relations.

Principles of effective communication are the same in member relations programs as in other forms of public relations.

Thus, programming for member relations shares many similarities with that for employee relations.

# EVALUATION

Evaluation of member relations directs attention back to the objectives established for such programs.

Success for programs may be directly linked to the objectives—informational, behavioral, and/or attitudinal—stated at the outset of a program. Was there favorable reaction from the membership? Did the number of members increase or decrease? Have requests for membership information increased?

# SUMMARY

Member relations is communication between the officers (management) of a membership organization and its members.

Research in member relations focuses on the demographics, information levels, attitudes, and behaviors of the organization's membership. A complete member profile should be constructed through such research, with special attention to the typical member's attitudes and behaviors toward the organization itself.

Both impact and output objectives are used in member relations. Impact objectives include the desired programmatic outcomes of favorable member attitudes and behaviors toward the organization. Output objectives catalog desired PR practices, such as effective planning, preparation, and distribution of member communications.

Programming for member relations usually includes such events as conventions, conferences, seminars, and such actions as promotion of industry research, preparation of industry statistics and data, and general promotion and development of the industry or profession represented by the membership. Commonly used forms of communication are member publications, reports, printed materials, audiovisual materials, and meetings.

As in other forms of public relations, evaluation consists of measuring stated objectives through surveys, observation, or other appropriate means suggested by the objectives themselves.

# READINGS ON INTERNAL COMMUNICATIONS

## Employee Relations

Conrad, Charles. *Strategic Organizational Communication: Cultures, Situations, and Adaptation*. New York: Holt, Rinehart & Winston, 1985.

Cronin, Michael P. "The Eye-Opening Employee Benefits Annual Report." *Inc* 16 (April 1994): 81ff.

Denton, Keith D. "Open Communication." *Business Horizons* 36 (September/October 1993): 64ff.

*Employee Annual Report: Purpose, Format, Content*. Chicago: Ragan Communications, 1984.

Farinelli, Jean L. "Motivating Your Staff." *Public Relations Journal* 48 (March 1992): 18ff.

Gonring, Matthew. "Communication Makes Employee Involvement Work." *Public Relations Journal* 47 (November 1991): 40ff.

Harris, Thomas E. *Applied Organizational Communication: Perspectives, Principles and Pragmatics.* Hillsdale, NJ: Erlbaum, 1992.

*How to Prepare and Write Your Employee Handbook.* New York: AMACOM, 1984.

Klubnik, Joan P. *Rewarding and Recognizing Employees.* Burr Ridge, IL: Irwin Professional Publishing, 1994.

Larkin, TJ, and Sandar Larkin. *Communicating Change . . . Winning Employee Support for Business Goals.* New York: McGraw-Hill, 1994.

McCathrin, E. Zoe. "Beyond Employee Publications: Making the Personal Connection." *Public Relations Journal* 45 (July 1989): 14–20.

McPhee, Robert D., and Phillip K. Tompkins. *Organizational Communication: Traditional Themes and New Directions.* Beverly Hills, CA: Russell Sage Foundation, 1985.

Milite, George. "Getting Staffers to Read Company Manuals." *Supervisory Management* 39 (April 1994): 1ff.

O'Connor, James V. "Building Internal Communications." *Public Relations Journal* 46 (June 1990): 29–33.

"Restructuring: Good and Bad News for Employee Communications." *Public Relations Journal* 45 (April 1989): 6–10.

Reuss, Carol, and Donn Silvis, eds. *Inside Organizational Communication,* 2nd ed. New York: Longman, 1985.

## Member Relations

"Association Public Relations" (special issue). *Public Relations Quarterly* 37 (Spring 1992).

Brett-Elspas, Janis, ed. *The Source: Guide to Communication Jobs.* Santa Monica, CA: Rachel P.R. Services, 1994.

*Career Guide to Professional Associations: A Directory of Organizations by Occupational Fields,* 2nd ed. Cranston, RI: Carroll Press, 1980.

Cutlip, Scott M., Allen H. Center, and Glen M. Broom. "The Practice: Trade Associations, Professional Societies, and Labor Unions." In *Effective Public Relations,* 7th ed. Englewood Cliffs, NJ: Prentice-Hall, 1994.

*Encyclopedia of Associations.* Detroit: Gale Research, published annually.

Fraser, Edith A. "Association Public Relations: The State of the Art." *Public Relations Journal* 37 (October 1981): 18–21, 30.

*National Directory of Corporate Affairs.* Washington, DC: Columbia Books, 1994.

Pace, Patricia Ewing, and Jo Culbertson. *Successful Public Relations for the Professions.* Edwardsville, KA: Professional Publishing, 1982.

*Reed's Worldwide Directory of Public Relations Organizations.* Washington, DC: Pigafetta Press, 1994.

*Rolles Blue Book.* Bethesda, MD: Rolle Communications, published annually.

## The ICA Audit

Goldhaber, Gerald M., and Donald P. Rogers. *Auditing Organizational Communication Systems: The ICA Communication Audit.* Dubuque, IA: Kendall/Hunt, 1979.

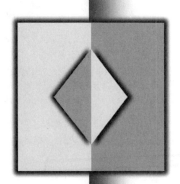

# Member Relations
# Cases

*The U.S. Chamber of Commerce represents a major segment of the U.S. business community and develops policy recommendations on domestic and international issues critical to U.S. business. The chamber's extensive program of communications includes print, broadcast, and interpersonal methods designed to inform both members and the population at large. Exhibit 4-3a is an excerpt from* Helping Your Business Thrive. *Exhibit 4-3b is from* GAIN—Grassroots Action Information Network. *Exhibit 4-3c is from the member publication* The Business Advocate, *and Exhibit 4-3d is a promotional piece for the TV show* "First Business."

**CASE 4-3** | The Member Relations Program of the U.S. Chamber of Commerce

Compiled by Adam Konowe, Associate Producer-Director, Broadcast Division, U.S. Chamber of Commerce

## Introduction

Recognizing the need for a central organization to define the business community's views to Congress, President William H. Taft took the first step toward forming the United States Chamber of Commerce at a meeting of more than 700 businesses, state and local chambers of commerce, and trade association representatives in Washington, DC, in April 1912. The initial membership comprised 82 businesses, trade associations, and state or local chambers of commerce. Headquarters for the chamber were built in 1922 across Lafayette Park from the White House, one of the most strategically valuable locations in the country, on a site where Daniel Webster once lived.

Today the U.S. Chamber maintains its eminent position as the world's largest business federation, with more than 215,000 business members, 3,000 state and local chambers, 1,200 trade and professional associations, and 75 American chambers overseas—all representing

Courtesy U.S. Chamber of Commerce

a broad spectrum of the business community. This diversity, as well as depth, is key to the continued success of the chamber. Whereas most of the nation's largest companies are active members, more than 96 percent of the members have fewer than 100 employees, and 85 percent have 25 employees or less. Chamber members come from each state and represent every major classification of American business—manufacturing, retailing, services, construction, wholesaling, and finance—with more than 10,000 members in each plan.

## Research

As a membership organization, the U.S. Chamber listens very closely to its membership. Through meetings, mailings, and surveys, members communicate their views. These exchanges provide information vital to volunteers and to the board of directors. The chamber looks to help define policy on domestic and international issues critical to American business. Once a policy is developed, the members, Congress, the White House, the regulatory agencies, the courts, and countries around the world are informed of the business community's recommendations on legislative issues and government policies.

A majority of these proposals originate in the U.S. Chamber's committees and councils. These specialized groups, comprised of member representatives from firms of every size, type, and geographic area, study the technical details of issues and judge their impact on business. A proposed policy statement is then submitted to the board of directors, the body that sets final policy positions. The board debates committee recommendations and adopts new policy positions by a majority of at least two-thirds. Interpretations of existing policy merely require a simple majority. A number of issues are submitted to the membership for guidance through polling both by mail and in conjunction with the chamber's publication, *Nation's Business* and *The Business Advocate.*

In addition to the standing policy committees, a special council representing small business interests exists to advise the board directly. The U.S. Chamber also has bilateral and multilateral councils working to improve the international climate for trade and investment abroad. And though any member may submit a proposed policy directly to the board, proposed policy must be "national in character, timely in importance, general in application, and of significance to business and industry." Thus, single industry or specific company issues are excluded.

## Objectives

As America's principal advocate for the business community, the U.S. Chamber is dedicated to championing the principles of private enterprise. Its mission is to "advance human progress through an economic, political, and social system based on individual freedom, incentive, initiative, opportunity, and responsibility." Thus, the chamber works on behalf of its members on a wide range of critical issues, including economic growth, the federal budget, health care, America's work force, technology and infrastructure, the removal of barriers to doing business, and the global marketplace. In the chamber's major areas of concern—domestic, economic, and international policy—more than 50 full-time experts in three policy units help advocate policies upon which this nation's enterprise system was built, consistent with the federation's mission.

Through a mail survey every two years, members help craft a National Business Agenda comprising those issues that matter most to business. The agenda, the ultimate statement of the federation's objectives, is then formally presented to government agencies, Congress, and the presidential administration by members at a function in Washington, DC.

## Programming

The U.S. Chamber has an extensive communications program. The entire range of print, broadcast, and interpersonal methods is utilized to bring timely and topical information to the members and to the population at large.

To further enhance chamber efforts before policy makers, four separately funded affiliate organizations have been founded. Because today's courts shape policies and interpret laws that affect business, the National Chamber Litigation Center (NCLC) gives business a voice in the judicial arena. The National Chamber Foundation (NCF) is a public policy research arm that anticipates trends and conducts studies on emerging issues. Established as the business representative in the National Endowment for Democracy, the Center for International Private Enterprise (CIPE) encourages the growth overseas of private enterprise organizations and principles. Finally, the Center for Workforce Preparation helps local and state chambers identify and implement strategies for communitywide education reform designed to develop the workplace for the year 2000 and beyond.

Chamber policy is implemented by nearly 70 staff specialists who are helped by thousands of members serving as activists in the chamber's Grassroots Action Information Network (GAIN). GAIN empowers the members through a comprehensive, state-of-the-art communications network. Regardless of size or industry, individual businesses and business groups can receive information on select issues, participate in instantaneous calls-to-action, and access Congress directly. But GAIN is only one of the many member services offered by the U.S. Chamber.

Through its publications, the chamber provides the inside track on the people and events that affect business decisions. *Nation's Business*, the chamber's monthly magazine, has a circulation of more than

860,000 and is read by more than 2.5 million people, a majority of whom are senior business executives. Also printed exclusively for members is *The Business Advocate,* published ten times annually, which relates chamber programs and positions on public policy issues. Distributed to over 700 newspapers, the "Voice of Business" columns written by the chamber president focus attention on breaking issues that affect economic growth and the business community.

The chamber's telecommunications facilities and division, known collectively as BizNet, have been acclaimed as the finest of its kind in the nation. Since 1979, the flagship television program "It's Your Business" has kept millions of American viewers informed about vital business and economic issues. The award-winning program is seen nationwide on more than 130 stations, which have a combined coverage of 65 percent of American households, representing 350,000 viewers per week.[1]

The chamber also produces the country's only news program focusing on small business owners and entrepreneurs. "First Business" airs every weekday morning on 75 stations, representing 50 percent coverage of American households nationwide, with 110,000 viewers per day.[2]

Special broadcasts are also produced for internal audiences. Live and taped programs addressing key policy issues are received by members around the world. The chamber's Quality Learning Services Division conducts special seminars in various elements of quality performance and leadership aimed at businesses with 50 or fewer employees. The sessions, featuring the most prominent experts on organizational change, are broadcast live by satellite, providing interaction by phone and fax with audiences throughout North America.

Enrollment in the Institutes for Organization Management represents a six-year commitment to strengthen leadership, management, interpersonal, and communication skills. The institute holds a variety of annual one-week courses individually designed for chamber or association executives. Over 2,200 executives a year attend these programs at sites around the country, receiving college and continuing education credit in addition to enhancing vital decision-making skills.

ConSern: Loans for Education enables members to offer employees and their families an attractive benefit free of administration or financial responsibility. The program provides long-term, competitive financing for the various costs of obtaining an education without any liability to the participating companies. So far, more than $500 million has been loaned to member employees and their families.

Members can receive research and development expertise through ChamberTech, which provides access to 100,000 federal lab employees

---

[1] Neilsen ratings, first quarter 1996.
[2] Ibid.

in 650 labs nationwide. The Federal Laboratory Consortium for Technology Transfer is also available to assist members in solving technical, manufacturing, design, research, and regulatory issues.

The U.S. Chamber's international programs respond to the critical need for global, economic, and business interdependence in U.S. enterprise. The federation shapes legislative and regulatory policies at home and abroad that lower barriers and open competition. A network of 11 bilateral councils around the world complement the chamber's efforts in the United States by producing agreements and shaping trade policies that improve business conditions in other countries. This network and 75 American Chambers of Commerce Abroad (AmChams) provide the chamber with the ability to communicate on key economic and commercial issues. Closer to home, the International Division Information Center provides one-on-one assistance with questions regarding trade policy and export promotion and services, as well as regional concerns and market opportunities. Hotlines and special publications provide up-to-date information on key actions affecting business, including export controls and bilateral and multilateral trade agreements. A new feature, IBEX, is a PC-based electronic network that allows users to find, qualify, and negotiate business transactions with partners domestically and internationally.

## Evaluation

The success of the chamber's programs, and of the federation itself, is contingent on the accurate measurement and implementation of member input. All of the programs listed above have opportunities for member feedback built into the process. For example, reader surveys are used in *Nation's Business* and *The Business Advocate;* telephone and on-line responses are solicited by all the broadcast operations; and GAIN uses a combination of all these methods and sends follow-up reports to members to explain the outcome of a program and the impact it has made.

The success of any federation rides on its ability to represent the opinions and interests of its members accurately over an extended period of time. In a sense, programming initiatives begin as well as end with evaluation of member opinion. It is this refined constant process of self-examination and improvement that has given the U.S. Chamber of Commerce a reputation for unyielding leadership for more than 80 years.

Exhibit 4-3a

Excerpt from *Helping Your Business Thrive*  (Courtesy U.S. Chamber of Commerce)

## THE UNITED STATES CHAMBER OF COMMERCE

## A WEALTH OF RESOURCES TO MEET YOUR NEEDS

# HELPING YOUR BUSINESS THRIVE

When you join the U.S. Chamber, you hire us to serve as your advocate in Washington — making your voice heard on the critical issues affecting the business community. But our efforts don't stop there. We function as your business adviser, providing needed information to give you every competitive advantage in the marketplace. Here's just a sampling of the valuable resources and benefits available to you as a member of the U.S. Chamber of Commerce.

Exhibit 4-3a
(continued)

Excerpt from *Helping Your Business Thrive*   (Courtesy U.S. Chamber of Commerce)

## RESOURCE GUIDES

To help you choose among the many benefits of your U.S. Chamber membership, a variety of resources guides are free to you as part of your membership investment. Among them are:

**A Guide to Membership Benefits**
An overview of the benefits and services available to you.

**A Guide to U.S. Chamber of Commerce Communication Tools**
A comprehensive listing of publications and services.

**U.S. Chamber Staff Specialists**
A list of issue specialists who can provide you with information, opinion and analysis on legislation, regulations and other programs.

**Workplace Training Resources**
A catalog of videotapes, audiotapes and books of quality training programs available in a self-study format.

**U.S. Chamber International Publications**
A sampling of materials to assist you in competing for trade and investment opportunities.

## PERIODICALS

As a member, you automatically receive two vital resources each month: **Nation's Business,** and **The Business Advocate.** These magazines are an invaluable source of information on federal legislation and regulations that affect you. In addition to forecasts on government action and economic trends, **Nation's Business** offers practical how-to information on running a business. **The Business Advocate** reports on the status of key business issues and contains a regular update on GAIN, the Chamber's Grassroots Action Information Network. Both magazines include regular surveys, used to direct U.S. Chamber policy decisions and to inform Congress of your views.

## PUBLICATIONS

Have you ever wondered where to turn when you're trying to decipher new laws? Or who can help when you're looking for ways to lower costs or expand your customer base? The U.S. Chamber offers specialized publications to give you detailed information and help clarify the issues. Here's just a sampling:

**What Business Must Know About The Americans With Disabilities Act: Compliance Guide**

**Concerns of Small Business**

**The Small Business Resource Guide**

**Risk Management: A Small Business Primer**

**Occupational Health and Safety in American Industry**

**100 Ways to Cut Legal Fees and Manage Your Lawyer**

**Analysis of Workers' Compensation Laws**

**Employment Law: A Checklist**

**Employee Benefits Survey Data**

**The National Business Agenda**

**The North American Free Trade Agreement: What it means for U.S. Business**

**A Strategy Handbook: Helping Small Businesses Through Chambers of Commerce**

**Guide to Municipal Solid Waste Management for Communities and Businesses**

**Managing Chemicals Safely**

**Making Your Family Business Outlast You**

# HOW-TO BROCHURES

The U.S. Chamber also offers easily understood "How-To" brochures as part of your membership investment. They contain tips on how to comply with new regulations and information about opportunities for your business. Here is a sampling of titles:

**How to Obtain Small Business Financing**

**How to Sell to the Federal Government**

**How to Manage Risk and Control Your Insurance Costs**

**How to Expand Your Market through Exporting**

**How to Obtain Good Legal Advice and Control Your Legal Costs**

**How to Comply with The Americans With Disabilities Act**

**How to Comply with the Civil Rights Act of 1991**

**How to Communicate with Your Congressional Representatives**

**How to Comply with OSHA**

**How to Locate Information for Your Family Business**

**How to Prevent Drug Abuse in the Workplace**

**How to Manage AIDS in the Workplace**

**How to Determine Independent Contractor Status**

**How to Succeed in Franchising**

**How to Test Your Benefit Plans for Discrimination**

# OTHER MEMBER BENEFITS

## GAIN
**Grassroots Action Information Network**

The U.S. Chamber created GAIN to keep you better informed and to help you have a real impact on legislation that affects your business. Our powerful grassroots network uses advanced technology to make it easier for you to communicate your views to members of Congress and the administration, as you attend to your day-to-day operations. The system is constantly expanding to meet our members' needs in many different ways, such as developing member to member networking opportunities.

## Membership Service Centers
**Helping You through the Federal Maze**

When you have a question about business, the U.S. Chamber's regional Membership Service Centers are a phone call away to provide the answers or locate the information you need. The Centers also can assist you with your communications to your members of Congress, saving you time and maximizing your impact on Capitol Hill.

## ConSern
**Loans for Education**

Employee benefits are important tools for hiring and retaining good employees, but they can be expensive. That's why the U.S. Chamber makes the ConSern loan program available to members, at very little cost. It's a valuable benefit you can offer your employees and their families. And, as an employer, you have no liability for the loans, and no administrative hassles.

## Quality Learning Services
**Training via Satellite**

The U.S. Chamber provides quality management training, educational and information services to help you run your business. Seminar series are available by satellite to U.S. Chamber members, either directly or through your local or state chamber, for a minimal fee. The sessions are also available on videocassettes.

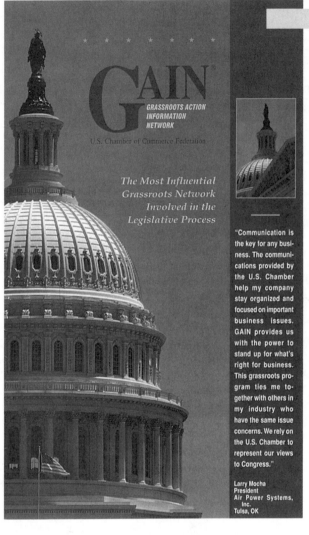

## Tailor GAIN

### *to Meet Your Needs*

★ ★ ★ ★ ★

**You Custom-Design GAIN to Work for You**

- *Choose* the issues that concern you.

- *Decide* how you want to receive legislative information — via fax or mail.

- *Spend* as much time and effort as necessary representing pro-business views to Congress.

- *Control* the amount and type of information that you want to receive.

- *Use* as much information as needed from the GAIN resources you receive to enhance your legislative programs and strategies — without attribution to the U.S. Chamber.

- *Obtain* direct access to U.S. Chamber issue specialists, who are available to you to discuss concerns you may have about your issues.

- *Help manage* your grassroots program through your participation in GAIN.

**Join Today!**

**For additional information, call the U.S. Chamber's Office of Membership Grassroots Management at (202) 463-5604**

*All Capitol shots by Dennis Swegart*

---

GAIN
GRASSROOTS ACTION
INFORMATION
NETWORK

U.S. Chamber of Commerce Federation

*The Most Influential Grassroots Network Involved in the Legislative Process*

"Communication is the key for any business. The communications provided by the U.S. Chamber help my company stay organized and focused on important business issues. GAIN provides us with the power to stand up for what's right for business. This grassroots program ties me together with others in my industry who have the same issue concerns. We rely on the U.S. Chamber to represent our views to Congress."

Larry Mocha
President
Air Power Systems, Inc.
Tulsa, OK

# GAIN

**GRASSROOTS ACTION INFORMATION NETWORK**

® U.S. Chamber of Commerce Federation

*Your Connection to Congress*

## Gain Power
### *through GAIN*

★ ★ ★

---

## GAIN: The Inside Advantage
### *on Capitol Hill*

★ ★ ★ ★ ★

As a member of the U.S. Chamber of Commerce, you have the opportunity to participate in one of the most powerful grassroots networks. GAIN — the U.S. Chamber's Grassroots Action Information Network — provides you with exclusive access to the latest developments on the legislative issues that concern you.

The business community has the force — at the grassroots level — to ensure that Congress works to protecting American free enterprise. GAIN works with you to help you do more than just comply with congressional mandates forced on business. As a GAIN participant, you will become involved in the legislative process and will help to enact laws that will have a positive impact on business.

Your members of Congress want and need to hear from you because it's their job to represent your concerns on Capitol Hill. And business leaders need strong representation from their lawmakers on important business issues that affect their community, industry, and the economy. GAIN participants have more clout with their members of Congress because they are recognized as interested and concerned constituents.

> "Pro-business lawmakers on both sides of the aisle know that the U.S. Chamber — with the breadth of its membership, the strength of its grassroots organization and the expertise and commitment of its staff — plays a critical role as an advocate for U.S. businesses and industry."
>
> **Rep. Charles Stenholm
> Texas**

---

## Stay Informed on the Latest Business Issue Developments

You select the issues on which you want to stay informed. U.S. Chamber issue specialists track your issues to provide you with the latest legislative developments. As your issues move through Congress, you will receive issue *Backgrounders, Updates, Action Calls,* and *Vote Watches.* This information will be timely, clear, and significant to your business or organization.

*Dennis Sweigert*

## Influence Members of Congress to Enact Pro-business Laws

Let your members of Congress know where you stand on issues that affect your business. GAIN makes it *easy* for you to take direct action on your issues. You will be notified — via fax or mail — as your issues move through Congress. We will let you know how best to communicate your message, who to contact in Congress, and how and when to contact your Senators or Representative. Your immediate action on GAIN issue information can result in legislative victories for business.

*Terry Ashe*

## Speak Out on Important Business Issues

GAIN gives you the facts on the issues, which makes it easy for you to speak out on specific concerns with confidence. You gain expert knowledge of all aspects of the issues that you select through the GAIN materials that you receive. Whether you plan to phone, write, or visit your members of Congress, GAIN prepares you to communicate effectively so that you can be heard on Capitol Hill. Use GAIN information to assist you with your legislative strategies and overall grassroots efforts.

## Monitor Congressional Voting

Hold your members of Congress accountable for their actions. GAIN encourages you to track your Senators' and Representative's voting records so that you know which members will best represent your views. As a GAIN participant, you will receive *How They Voted* and *Vote Watch,* both of which reveal how members of Congress voted on important business issues. Use these publications as your guides to monitor congressional voting.

> "The thousands of telephone calls and letters initiated by the Chamber's grassroots, as well as your [the U.S. Chamber's] television shows and magazine articles on the need for regulatory reform, were critical in garnering support for this much-needed legislation."
>
> **Rep. David McIntosh
> Indiana**

# The BusinessAdvocate

SUPPLEMENT TO Nation'sBusiness MARCH 1996

**Published By**
**U.S. Chamber of Commerce**

# Chamber Wins Legal Fight

The U.S. Chamber of Commerce has won another victory in its long-running court fight with President Clinton over striker replacements.

This latest win may prove to be the decisive round in the battle over the legality of an executive order issued by the president on March 8, 1995. Clinton's directive barred the awarding of most government contracts to businesses that have permanently replaced workers who were on strike for economic reasons, such as wages and employee benefits.

In response to an appeal filed by the Chamber, a three-judge panel of the U.S. Court of Appeals for the District of Columbia Circuit sided with the Chamber on Feb. 2 in ruling that the executive order could not be implemented because it was in violation of the National Labor Relations Act.

That 60-year-old statute, which governs U.S. labor-management relations, allows employers to replace workers who strike over economic conditions.

The appeals panel ruled that the Clinton executive order "is regulatory in nature and is preempted by the National Labor Relations Act, which guarantees the right to hire permanent replacements."

The ruling must withstand an expected administration appeal to the full appeals court or to the U.S. Supreme Court, but Chamber officials believe the decision is likely to stand.

"The appeals panel decision effectively ends the Clinton administration's blatant political attempt to circumvent Congress and nearly 60 years of labor law,"

> **"The new ruling on striker replacement provides business with a really big boost."**
> — Stephen A. Bokat

**Stephen A. Bokat, vice president and general counsel of the U.S. Chamber, sees this victory as the last nail in the coffin for the president's directive on the replacement of strikers.**

said Stephen A. Bokat, vice president and general counsel of the Chamber. "The new ruling on striker replacement provides business with a really big boost at a time when organized labor is becoming much more aggressive in organizing and making demands of employers," he added.

The executive order took effect immediately after the president signed it. It prohibited federal agencies from awarding federal contracts valued at more than $100,000 to companies that hire replacement workers for economic strikers.

The Chamber, backed by other business groups, quickly asked the U.S. District Court for the District of Columbia to bar federal contract officials from implementing the order. But in early May of last year, the District Court rejected the petition. The court reasoned that because no government contractor had yet been barred from receiving contracts, the order was not "ripe" for review.

The Chamber immediately appealed the decision to the Court of Appeals, which the following month ordered the District Court to review the case.

On July 31, the District Court blocked enforcement of the order, agreeing with the Chamber and other business plaintiffs that the order would unduly harm many firms contracting with the federal government. However, the District Court rejected arguments by the business groups that the order was unconstitutional and violated the labor-relations act.

The Chamber's appeal to the Court of Appeals on the constitutional issue resulted in the recent ruling in the business community's favor.

## 1995 HOW THEY VOTED
### Page 3A

Exhibit 4-3d

Promotion for the TV show *First Business*
(Courtesy U.S. Chamber of Commerce)

**First, Fast, & Factual!**

**Early & Effective.** First Business should be the beginning to your business day. A half-hour of fast-paced news from Washington, Wall Street and around the world. First Business is the wake up call for managers, business leaders and small business owners who want to keep their competitive edge.

**It's Fundamental to be First.** Because we are first, you don't have to settle for last night's news. Watch First Business for Capitol Hill agendas, investment do's and don'ts, even how to start a new business. Plus — business travel advisories, sports and weather and much more.

**The Fact Finder.** First Business is the small business owner's handbook to success. Find out what's working and what's not from others who make it their business to be first. Depend on First Business for the facts, and you'll get ahead every time.

**FIRST BUSINESS**

First Business is produced by BizNet, a service of the U.S. Chamber of Commerce, and is made possible by Connecticut Mutual.

*After a shaky start-up member relations program, the American Wood Preservers Institute (AWPI) refocused its communications efforts for a successful follow-up campaign. Exhibit 4-4a is an association fact sheet. Exhibit 4-4b is from the AWPI member newsletter. Exhibit 4-4c is a promotional piece for pressure-treated wood.*

**CASE 4-4**

## Credibility at Stake: Saving a Communications Program

W. Allan Wilbur, Director, Public Affairs, American Wood Preservers Institute

The American Wood Preservers Institute (AWPI), a small trade association representing 132 companies in the wood-treating industry and their chemical manufacturers, faced a challenge in 1994. AWPI, one of more than a dozen trade associations representing various sectors of the wood and timber industry, had developed a communications program to reach out to its members and the public. The idea of the program was to increase member support and public outreach through a proactive public relations and communications program that focused on positive information about the industry. The program, Campaign 2000, launched with much fanfare and promise in early 1994, had three goals: (1) to improve public awareness and the "image" of the AWPI and its members; (2) to respond to critics of the industry; and (3) to maintain industry markets against competitive building products (i.e., concrete, steel, and plastic).

Campaign 2000 sought to raise $1 million from members and non-members within the industry to finance the communications program. After public announcement of the program, the major effort focused on fund-raising within the industry. At the same time, public relations consultants, hired to develop communications strategies to achieve the announced goals, could not obtain a clear consensus from the association on what direction the communications program should take.

Campaign 2000 fell short of the stated goals during 1994. Months passed while staff and committee members debated what programs to pursue on behalf of Campaign 2000. By early 1995 the campaign

Courtesy American Wood Preservers Institute

lacked focus and was adrift. Growing dissatisfaction among member and nonmember contributors led to a change in direction. New executive leadership at AWPI and staff changes in the spring of that year led to efforts to refocus and make Campaign 2000 a successful communications program.

## The ROPE Model: Research

To address the challenge, AWPI staff analyzed extant research carried out by the association in preparation for Campaign 2000. In addition, AWPI interviewed key individuals in the wood and timber industry (1) to determine if Campaign 2000 had support and should continue and (2) to elicit opinions on how the campaign should proceed.

The responses indicated strong support for the idea and goals of the campaign. Respondents felt that too many promises had been made at the launch of the campaign and that few public relations results had been achieved between the announcement of the campaign and the end of 1994. They felt that there was little to show after a year's worth of financial contributions. The research pinpointed an undercurrent of discontent with the association because the campaign had not lived up to its early promise. Nearly 50 percent of all contributors to Campaign 2000 were not members of the association. The survey results suggested a "loss of faith" in the association among an important target group for membership.

## Objectives

The results led to six conclusions that influenced program planning and established the objectives for the campaign. First, the target audience for Campaign 2000 was no longer the public; that is, potential retail consumers of pressure-treated wood products. The focus shifted to members and nonmember supporters of Campaign 2000 and the industry at large who expected AWPI to deliver positive results. Second, the program had to produce high-visibility results in a hurry to regain member confidence in AWPI. Third, the campaign would continue in 1995 and 1996 as long as it produced results for the industry and the industry funded it. Fourth, the program components of the campaign had to be measured. Fifth, the program would focus initially on the trade press to address the concerns of contributors. Sixth, the budget for the remainder of 1995 was set at $100,000. The budget for 1996 was set at $160,000.

The revised objectives were (1) to increase industry, member, and nonmember awareness of Campaign 2000 through high-visibility programs and communications within the industry; (2) to improve public awareness and the image of AWPI and its members; (3) to address public concerns about pressure-treated wood proactively, and (4) to support members and potential members with a campaign message that promoted pressure-treated wood as an environmentally sound building material.

## Programming

The association planned and implemented several programs to address the objectives of Campaign 2000. Beginning in October 1995, AWPI began an advertising campaign in key trade publications that reached the treated wood industry. The target audiences selected were retailers, distributors, and those in the transportation and utility industries who used treated wood products (outdoor decks, marinas, docks, pilings, railroad ties, and utility poles). The publications also reached treated wood producers and suppliers who routinely read the trade literature their customers read.

A second component of the program was a direct-mail campaign to more than 40,000 individuals in several industries: contractors, construction material specifiers, engineers, landscape architects, and others who make decisions about what building materials to use. The purpose of direct mail was to promote the use of pressure-treated wood by providing accurate and positive information about the product. The direct-mail package included a pitch letter and a free copy of the basic information brochure about pressure-treated wood. The letter also made a free offer to provide two other information resource booklets on specific applications of pressure-treated wood. Ten percent of all direct-mail pieces included a business reply card that invited respondents to request information about specific applications of pressure-treated wood. The offer included a directory of available sources about treated wood and a printed summary of recent scientific research studies on treated wood in the aquatic environment. The goal was to achieve a 3 to 5 percent response rate. This program certified to both member and nonmember Campaign 2000 subscribers that AWPI was active in promoting treated wood products in a professional and consistent manner.

A third component of the program focused on AWPI publications. A revised monthly newsletter provided updates on Campaign 2000 activities. The association developed a new uniform graphic image and produced several new publications that provided new statistical and consumer information about the industry: a basic information brochure and an 80-page book that provided detailed information about treated wood. The book included a 20-page summary of the latest scientific research data attesting to the safety of pressure-treated wood. AWPI distributed both publications to members, nonmembers, and all Campaign 2000 subscribers.

A fourth element of the program was the development of a professional exhibit booth by AWPI to attend trade shows where potential markets for treated wood existed. The plan demonstrated to members that AWPI addressed industry concerns about losing potential markets to other building material producers. Trade shows provided opportunities to educate building material specifiers, engineers, and architects about pressure-treated wood.

A fifth element was the media outreach plan. A series of syndicated, three-minute radio programs distributed to several hundred stations focused on educating the public about pressure-treated wood and its safe and proper use. This radio programming was supported by a series of editorial pieces distributed by North American Precis Syndicate that provided credible and useful information about the environmentally sound uses for treated wood products. These programs targeted the general public, whereas the other programs focused on target groups within the industry.

The sixth element was the publication of a year-end progress report on Campaign 2000. The report included a three-page summary of all actions taken in support of the program and the results achieved by mid-December 1995. It also set out the objectives for the campaign during the upcoming year (1996). The report included color copies of the full-page ads that ran in seven different trade magazines between October and December 1995. The report included pictures of the covers of each trade publication that ran AWPI ads and graphic reports on other Campaign 2000 activities. AWPI distributed the report to members, potential members, and all Campaign 2000 contributors. The cover letter from the AWPI president included an appeal for continued financial support of the program.

## Evaluation

The feedback systems built into the programs provided quantitative results. To determine if the program had succeeded in changing opinions about AWPI and the success of Campaign 2000, AWPI surveyed the entire membership at the end of 1995. The survey asked members to grade the performance of AWPI on a scale of 1 to 5 (with 1 the highest score) on fulfilling the mission of the association. The survey contained 40 questions that asked members about AWPI's performance in legislative affairs, the success of several association meetings, the new Campaign 2000, and other association programs.

The survey results gave AWPI an overall rating of excellent (a 2 on the 1–5 scale). The Campaign 2000 program scored 2.5, halfway between satisfactory and excellent. It was clear from the survey that the campaign had an immediate and positive effect on both members and nonmembers. The campaign in three months time had scored other successes as well. Direct-mail response averaged more than 3 percent throughout the remainder of 1995. Phone calls seeking information about treated wood and its applications increased by 100 percent. To measure the increased level of response to the campaign, AWPI developed a "Treated Wood Hotline" (1-800-356-AWPI). Moreover, favorable media contacts and placements increased by a factor of 7 to 1. In four months, the association distributed 40,000 brochures and 7,500 copies of the 80-page book.

Members perceived a change in the vitality and the direction of the association and supported that change with membership dollars and with contributions to Campaign 2000. Membership, flat in 1994, showed signs of renewed strength as 1995 closed.

## Conclusions

Although it is perhaps too easy to overestimate the effect of one program or one activity, it was clear that the change of leadership, combined with the addition of new public relations staff, brought vigor and a professional approach to the challenge. Campaign 2000 succeeded in shifting member and nonmember perceptions about the association. The programs produced quantifiable measures of improvement and change. Results demonstrated the success of the program to the members. The year-end member survey verified that members viewed AWPI as an association back on track, representing their interests and fulfilling the mission of the trade association in an effective manner.

The public relations strategies utilized a basic public relations model to turn around a moribund communications program and to reestablish the credibility of the association in the eyes of members and the industry. Not bad for seven months work!

# American Wood Preservers Institute

**Tyson's International Building**
**1945 Old Gallows Road, Suite 150**
**Vienna, Virginia 22182-3931**
**Tel: (703) 893-4005  Fax: (703) 893-8492**
**Internet: 76202.2472@compuserve.com**

## Fact Sheet

**AWPI Objectives**  The American Wood Preservers Institute is a trade association representing 130 companies in the wood preserving industry. Member companies are wood treaters, chemical manufacturers and supporting companies working to conserve forest resources, preserve the environment and extend the life of wood products through the manufacture of pressure treated wood.

The objectives of the association are to improve public acceptance of preserved wood products, represent the industry on regulatory and legislative matters and address all questions about the manufacture, use, disposal and integrity of treated wood products.

**The Industry**  The pressure-treatment of wood is a process that forces preservatives into the wood cells under pressure in a tightly sealed cylinder. The result is a longer-lasting, more durable wood product protected against rot, fungal decay and termites.

Extending the service life of wood through preservation conserves an estimated 6.5 billion board feet of wood, the equivalent of building 425,000 new wood homes, or an estimated 26,000,000 trees annually.

**Economic Impact**  Preserved wood is a $2.5 billion dollar industry in the United States, with $50.5 million in annual exports. The total impact of the industry on the U.S. economy is an estimated $9 billion.

The nation's 550 wood treating plants employ more than 10,000 people.

More than 550 million cubic feet of lumber and industrial wood products are treated each year; that is 22 percent of the forest product industry's total value of annual shipments.

**The Preservatives**  There are three types of commonly-used wood preservatives in the United States: creosote, pentachlorophenol, and the inorganic arsenicals. Treated wood is not a pesticide. The preservatives are registered with the EPA. Pressure treatment increases the durability of the wood and does not alter the wood's characteristics. The selection of preservative depends on the end-use of the product. Wood preservatives have been used safely and effectively for nearly 100 years.

## Association Officers

**Chairman of the Board**
David T. Bryce
Atlantic Wood Industries
Savannah, Ga.

**Vice Chairman**
Paul A. Goydan
Osmose Wood Preserving, Inc.
Griffin, Ga.

**Immediate Past Chairman**
David L. Hatcher
KMG-Bernuth, Inc.
Houston, Tex.

**Treasurer**
Arthur Martin
Kerr-McGee Chemical Corp.
Oklahoma City, Okla.

**President**
Gene S. Bartlow
AWPI
Vienna, Va.

— over —

Exhibit 4-4a
(*continued*)

Association Fact Sheet   (Courtesy American Wood Preservers Institute)

**Government Affairs** AWPI monitors federal and state legislative and regulatory issues that affect members of the association. The range of issues includes environmental regulations, OSHA workplace rules, and other measures that impact chemical manufacturers, wood treaters, and the forest and lumber industry.

**Public Affairs** The association's public relations program provides accurate and timely information about the treated wood industry to the media, trade press, members, and consumers. The association publishes an all-member newsletter. Campaign 2000 is AWPI's strategic communications initiative to inform and educate consumers, specifiers, and retailers about the safety and benefits of pressure-treated wood.

**Answers to Often-asked Questions about Treated Wood** AWPI publishes a 71-page booklet that contains answers to consumer questions about treated wood. The booklet provides information on the wood preserving process and consumer information about the proper handling and uses of treated wood. It contains consumer tips on the characteristics of the wood and a discussion of environmental and safety information. The volume has a brief summary of scientific research data. For information on how to obtain a copy, call or write AWPI (list price $19.95, member price $9.95).

**Other Publications:**
*Management of Used Treated Wood Product.* This 14 -page booklet provides basic information needed for making cost-effective and environmentally-sound management decisions regarding the re-use or disposal of treated wood products. (free)

*Answers to Often-asked Questions about Treated Wood Products.* (Brochure) This 16-page pamphlet addresses the most frequently asked questions about treated wood. (free)

To order any of the titles listed above, contact AWPI at (800) 356-AWPI.

**Annual Meeting** The 1996 annual meeting is scheduled to be held in Amelia Island, Fla., September 30 through October 1. The Annual Washington Congressional Conference is scheduled to be held on April 22 through April 24, 1996.

**Other Meetings:**
AWPI sponsors regional environmental forums on current developments and regulatory requirements. These meetings provide legislators and members of the wood preserving industry with an opportunity to meet and share information on current environmental management obligations, and reporting requirements.

---

## Treated-Wood Products

*Some of the uses of
treated wood include:*

### Home Beautification and Recreation
*Decking*
*Landscaping*
*Boardwalks*
*Playground Equipment*

### Construction
*Foundation Piling*
*Home Construction*
*Retaining Walls*
*Mine Timbers*

### Agricultural Applications
*Fence Posts*
*Water Troughs*
*Barns*

### Communication and Transportation
*Railway Ties*
*Utility Poles and Crossarms*
*Bridge Construction*
*Highway Noise Barriers*
*Highway Guard Rails*

### Marine Construction
*Docks*
*Piers*
*Bulkheads*
*Sea Walls*

---

*For more information contact, W. Allan Wilbur, Director, Public Affairs,
AWPI, 1945 Old Gallows Road, Suite 150, Vienna, Va. 22182-3931
Treated-wood Hotline:  (800) 356-AWPI
Office: (703) 893-4005  Fax: (703) 893-8492*

Forest Conservation through Wood Preservation

December 1995 • Volume 1, Issue 6

# AWPI *news*

1945 Old Gallows Road • Suite 150 • Vienna, Va. 22182-3931

# NJ Proposes Second Treated-wood Ban

Once again, AWPI is fighting an attempt by the state of New Jersey to ban the use of treated wood products without cause. The New Jersey Department of Environmental Protection (DEP) has initiated a one-year study to determine the effect of residential docks on shellfish habitats and water quality. In the interim, the DEP proposed a policy that allows some homeowners to build a dock if they meet certain conditions. One of the conditions prohibits the use of pressure-treated wood.

### Flaws in the NJ Proposal

AWPI has identified problems with the study and the proposed interim policy on three levels. First, the interim policy lacks scientific basis. DEP admits that there is little scientific data to support banning treated wood; however, instead of generating data and making policy based on the results, the DEP is prohibiting the use of treated-wood products while they conduct this study.

Second, the proposed study is not unbiased, and the DEP is ignoring countervailing science. Rather than soliciting proposals from the scientific community at large, the DEP-funded study was sole-sourced to Judith and Peddrick Weis. The Weises are adamant critics of the use of treated wood products in any marine environment. Also, the DEP relies inordinately on the data and conclusions of the Weises. Other reputable scientists have come to completely different conclusions regarding treated wood in aquatic environments, even when using the Weises' data.

Third, the department has refused to provide information on a publicly-funded study. AWPI's request to review the Weises' proposal was denied. (A subsequent Freedom of Information request was filed by AWPI.) To date, AWPI is unaware of anyone outside of the DEP who has seen any justification for the expenditure of $75,000 in public funds to these researchers for this sole-sourced study.

### AWPI's Issue Management Strategy

AWPI developed a three-part strategy to confront the issue of DEP's apparent bias against pressure-treated wood. In Phase One, AWPI:

• Researched the "players" and gathered relevant information.

• Coordinated industry representation at all three public meetings. AWPI submitted questions and testimony to the DEP.

• Prepared a comprehensive compendium of scientific research reports and materials that reflect the current status of science on the use of pressure-treated wood in marine environments.

• Submitted written comments, including the research compendium, to the DEP identifying the problems with the study and interim policy. AWPI requested that the study be awarded to different scientists and insisted that the interim policy not include a ban on treated wood.

• Requested a meeting with the Commissioner of the New Jersey DEP. AWPI emphasized the scientifically unsubstantiated position and its effect on the citizens of New Jersey.

Phases two and three may involve some of the following actions: hiring a local lobbyist to work on a legislative solution to the issue; mounting a multi-media public affairs campaign in the state; and possibly litigation.

167

Exhibit 4-4b
(continued)

Excerpt from *AWPI News*   (Courtesy American Wood Preservers Institute)

**3**

# Campaign 2000 ads target industry consumers

November saw the unfolding of AWPI's advertising campaign in seven publications that reach more than 420,000 individuals who are potential users, retailers, or specifiers of pressure-treated wood products.

Four different, full-page, four-color ads appeared in the following publications: *Building Products Digest, Merchant, Building Material Retailer, National Home Center News, Builder, Architectural Record*, and *Transmission and Distribution*.

The color ads (See photo) focus on the specific message that treated wood is a safe, economical, long-lasting, and environmentally sound product. Four new ads are under development for 1996. During December the ad mix will be reviewed and revised to focus on other specific market segments likely to use pressure-treated wood.

While ads may be the most visible elements in Campaign 2000, the direct mail program targeted at specifiers in several industries and

to decision makers in city, county and state environmental agencies may have as much impact.

In November, 13,000 direct mail pieces were sent to key individuals who decide what building products to use. An additional 7,000 individuals will receive the mailing in December. The direct mail piece includes a letter urging them to consider pressure-treated wood and a free copy of the brochure, "Answers to Often-asked Questions about Treated Wood."

The pitch letter also urges recipients to write or call the AWPI Hotline (1-800-356-AWPI) for additional copies of the brochure or for specific information about pressure-treated wood applications. In 2,000 of the 20,000 pieces mailed, a business reply card is included urging recipients to send for more information about published information resources available on pressure-treated wood.

## AWPI wins national publication award

The AWPI's 1994 *Wood Preserving Industry Production Statistical Yearbook* took first place in a nationwide annual publications contest sponsored by *Association Trends*, the national weekly newspaper for association executives and suppliers. Jill Cornish, President and Publisher of *Association Trends*, said there were more than 650 entries in 19 publication categories. With an average of 34 entries per category, AWPI's entry won in the Statistical Yearbook category, combining excellent graphics and a compelling presentation of information that's important to the association and the industry.

The 1995 Statistical Survey forms will be mailed to all wood treating plants in January 1996. Do your part to make an award-winning publication even better, and remember to mail in your survey forms.

# On the road with AWPI...

The new AWPI exhibit booth made its debut trade show appearance at the American Society of Landscape Architects show in Cleveland, Ohio, Oct. 7-9. The exhibit was run in cooperation with the Southern Forest Products Association. Over 3,000 participants attended the convention where AWPI distributed literature to 10 percent of the attendees during the three-day show.

The most striking element of the show was the presence of many exhibitors displaying plastic products. With the exception of a few hardwood specialty exhibitors, AWPI was the only representative of the treated wood industry. One exhibitor even sold treated bamboo! It is clear that treated wood products should be represented at shows like the ASLA. AWPI will exhibit at five shows in 1996.

AWPI also exhibited at the one-day "Wood Solutions Fair" in Boston, Mass. on Oct. 24 (See photo). Nine thousand specifiers, were invited to the show from the New England and Mid-Atlantic regions.

The eight-hour exhibit proved to be an excellent opportunity to talk with an

audience of treated wood customers. More than 130 individuals stopped at the AWPI booth for information on publications as well as treated-wood applications.

**AWPI staffers Albert Lukban (r.) and Allan Wilbur (c.) pass on the good word about pressure-treated wood to an architect at the "Wood Solutions Fair" in Boston, Mass.**

AWPI staff distributed more than 500 pieces of literature during the one-day show and responded to 40 requests for specific information after returning to the AWPI office.

The Public Affairs Committee is gathering information for AWPI's 1996 trade show exhibit list.

Forest Conservation through Wood Preservation

# PRESSURE-TREATED WOOD

## The modern answer to your landscaping and decking needs.

**Pressure-treated wood... It's a safe, durable, and an economical building material that comes from a renewable resource.**

**Pressure-treated wood is safe.**

**It's economical.**

**And it's good for the environment.**

To order the brochure "Answers to Often-asked Questions about Treated Wood," call (800) 356-AWPI

**American Wood Preservers Institute**

5

# Community Relations

ONE OF THE MOST IMPORTANT AUDIENCES AN ORGA-
nization has is its community, the home of its offices
and operations. Maintaining good relations with
the community usually entails management and employees becoming involved in and contributing to local organizations and activities. In addition, the organization may communicate with the community in
other ways, such as distributing house publications or
meeting with community leaders.

Solving community relations problems may follow the usual sequence of research, objectives, programming, and evaluation.

# RESEARCH

Research for community relations includes investigation to understand the client, the reason for the program, and the community audiences to be targeted for communication.

## Client Research

Client research for community relations concentrates on the organization's role and reputation in the community. What is its level of credibility? Have there been significant community complaints in the past? What are the organization's present and past community relations practices? What are its major strengths and weaknesses in the community? What opportunities exist to enhance community relations? These questions provide a helpful framework for a community relations program.

## Opportunity or Problem Research

Why have a community relations program in the first place? Considering the cost and benefits involved, this is a question worthy of detailed justification. The public relations practitioner should assess problems the organization may have had with community groups and make a searching analysis of community relations opportunities. Many organizations conduct ongoing proactive community relations as a form of insurance against any sudden problem requiring a reactive public relations solution.

## Audience Research

The final aspect of community relations research consists of carefully identifying audiences to be targeted for communication and learning as much about each audience as possible. Community publics can be subdivided into three major groups: community media, community leaders, and community organizations. These categories can then be further subdivided as shown in Exhibit 5-a.

---

Exhibit 5-a

Community Publics

Community media
Mass
Specialized
Community leaders
Public officials
Educators
Religious leaders

Exhibit 5-a
(continued)

Community Publics

> Professionals
>
> Executives
>
> Bankers
>
> Union leaders
>
> Ethnic leaders
>
> Neighborhood leaders
>
> Community organizations
>
> Civic
>
> Business
>
> Service
>
> Social
>
> Cultural
>
> Religious
>
> Youth
>
> Political
>
> Special interest groups
>
> Other

In conducting community relations programs, it is important for the practitioner to develop contact lists of journalists, community leaders, and organizations.

The media contacts list will be similar to those discussed in Chapter 3, on media relations. These lists should include the type and size of audience reached by each media outlet in the community, the type of material used by each outlet, the name and title of appropriate editors who handle organizational news, and deadlines.

The list of community and organization leaders should be equally thorough. It should include the name, title, affiliation, address, and telephone number of all important community leaders. These data should be categorized according to occupational fields, such as public officials, educators, media people, or religious leaders. In addition to a listing of leaders alone, there should be a list of organizations that includes frequently updated names of officers, their addresses, and telephone numbers.

Research for community relations, then, consists of investigation of the client, the reason for the program, and the target audiences in the community.

## OBJECTIVES

Impact and output objectives for community relations, like those for other forms of public relations, should be specific and quantitative.

## Impact Objectives

Impact objectives for community relations involve informing the community audiences or modifying their attitudes or behaviors. Some examples are:

1. To increase (by 30 percent this year) community knowledge of the operations of the organization, including its products, services, employees, and support of community projects

2. To promote (20 percent) more favorable community opinion toward the organization (during a specified time period)

3. To gain (15 percent) greater organizational support from community leaders (during a particular campaign)

4. To encourage (20 percent) more feedback from community leaders (during the current year)

## Output Objectives

Output objectives consist of the efforts made by the practitioner to enhance the organization's community relations. Some illustrations are:

1. To prepare and distribute (15 percent) more community publications (than last year)

2. To be (10 percent) more responsive to community needs (during this year)

3. To create (five) new community projects involving organizational personnel and resources (during this calendar year)

4. To schedule (five) meetings with community leaders (this year)

Thus, both impact and output objectives are helpful in preparing community relations programs. They serve as useful and necessary precursors to programming.

# PROGRAMMING

Programming for community relations includes planning the theme and messages, action or special event(s), uncontrolled and controlled media, and using effective communication principles.

## Theme and Messages

The theme and messages for community relations are situational and grow out of research findings related to the organization, the reason for conducting the program, and the existing and past relationships with the targeted community audiences.

## Action or Special Event(s)

Actions and special events most often associated with community relations are:

1. An organizational open house and tour of facilities

2. Sponsorship of special community events or projects

3. Participation of management and other personnel in volunteer community activities

4. Purchase of advertising in local media

5. Contribution of funds to community organizations or causes

6. Meetings with community leaders

7. Membership of management and personnel in a variety of community organizations—civic, professional, religious

8. Participation of management and workers in the political affairs of the community—service in political office and on councils and boards

Involvement of the organization, its management, and its other personnel in the affairs of the community is the most significant aspect of a community relations program. With this kind of link to the community, there should be relatively smooth community relations, with few or no surprises.

## Uncontrolled and Controlled Media

In the communications part of a community relations program, the practitioner should think first of servicing community media outlets with appropriate uncontrolled media, such as news releases, photographs or photo opportunities, and interviews of organizational officers with local reporters.

The use of controlled media, on the other hand, should include sending copies of house publications to a select list of community leaders. The practitioner should also help the organization develop a speakers bureau, and publicize the availability of organizational management and expert personnel to address meetings of local clubs and organizations. It is also appropriate to target community leaders on a timely basis for selected direct mailings, such as important announcements or notices of organizational involvement in community affairs.

Both uncontrolled and controlled media in the community relations program should be focused on the eight types of community involvement listed earlier. These are the heart of the program.

### Effective Communication

Three principles of effective communication deserve special attention in community relations programs.

First, the targeting of opinion leaders or community leaders for communication is crucial to the success of such a program. The leadership provides the structure and substance of the community itself.

Second, group influence plays a substantial role in effective community relations. Organizations exercise varying degrees of cohesiveness and member conformity. The community relations program must cultivate community groups, their leaders, and their memberships. The effective speakers bureau is a primary means for accomplishing this.

Finally, audience participation is highly significant. Targeted community media, leaders, and groups can be encouraged to participate in the client's organizational events. Most important, the client should reach out to the community by sponsoring attractive activities.

## EVALUATION

If the objectives of the community relations program have been phrased specifically and quantitatively, their evaluation should be relatively easy. The success of a program should be directly linked to its attainment of the objectives stated at the program's outset.

## SUMMARY

Research for community relations assesses the organization's reputation and its existing and potential problems with the community. Targeting audiences usually includes a detailed analysis of community media, leaders, and organizations.

Impact objectives for community relations are such desired outcomes as informing or influencing the attitudes and behaviors of the community. Output objectives consist of a listing of public relations efforts to enhance the organization's relations with the community.

Programming concentrates on organizational involvement with the community through sponsorship of events, employee participation in community activities, contributions to community causes, meetings, and the like. The uncontrolled media used in community relations are aimed at servicing local journalists with appropriate news releases, photographs, and interviews with organizational officers. Controlled media usually include house publications, speakers bureaus, and appropriate direct mailings to community leaders.

Evaluation of stated objectives uses methods appropriate to the type of objective. Impact objectives are usually measured by a survey or other appropriate quantitative methods, while output objectives may call for simple observation of whether the desired output was achieved.

# READINGS ON
# COMMUNITY RELATIONS

Arkus, Connie. "Enhancing Community Relations in a Health Reform Environment." *Trustees* 46 (July 1993): 14ff.

Baker, W. R. "Houston Takes the Bus." *Public Relations Journal* (December 1985): 33ff.

Benedict, Arthur C. "After a Crisis: Restoring Community Relations." *Communications World* 11 (September 1994): 20ff.

Bickerstaffe, George. "What Companies Are Doing to Make Themselves Good Neighbors." *International Management* (May 1981): 30ff.

Center, Allen H., and Patrick Jackson. Chapter 4: Community Relations. In *Public Relations Practice: Managerial Case Studies and Practice,* 5th ed. Englewood Cliffs, NJ: Prentice-Hall, 1995.

"Community Relations: A Necessary Ingredient in Cleanups." *Environmental Manager* 3 (April 1992): 3–7.

Dyer, Sam. "The Story of a Community Relations Fiasco." *Public Relations Quarterly* 38 (Summer 1993): 33–35.

Harper, W. A. "A Rationale for Effective Community Relations." *New Directions for Institutional Advancement* (March 1982): 3ff.

Hirschhorn, Joel S. "A Model for Improved Community Relations." *Journal for Environmental Regulation* (Summer 1993): 387ff.

Kelly, D. C. "Decentralized Community Relations." *Public Relations Journal* (February 1984): 23ff.

Kipps, H. C. *Community Resources Directory.* Detroit: Gale, 1984.

Kruckeberg, Dean, and Kenneth Stark. *Public Relations and the Community: A Reconstructed Theory.* New York: Praeger, 1988.

Lowengard, Mary. "Community Relations: New Approaches to Building Consensus." *Public Relations Journal* 45 (October 1989): 24–30.

McDermott, David. "The 10 Commandments of Community Relations." *World Wastes* 36 (September 1993): 48ff.

Reish, Marc S. "Chemical Industry Tries to Improve Its Community Relations." *Chemical and Engineering News* (February 1994): 8ff.

Williams, Joe, ed. *World-Class Community Relations,* Vol. II. Bartlesville, OK: Joe Williams Communications Books, 1988.

Yarrington, Roger. *Community Relations Handbook.* New York: Longman, 1983.

# Community
# Relations Cases

*This is the story of an epic struggle between a modern-day Goliath, the Walt Disney Company, and a victorious contemporary David, the Piedmont Environmental Council, a determined citizens group that waged a Third Battle of Manassas (also known as Bull Run) in the rolling hills of northern Virginia to keep out Disney's unwanted theme park. Exhibit 5-1a is a press release used in the campaign. Exhibit 5-1b is a campaign advertisement. Exhibit 5-1c is a membership mailing used during the campaign, and Exhibit 5-1d is a campaign poster.*

**CASE 5-1**

## Disney, Take a Second Look

Leonard Steinhorn, Assistant Professor, School of Communication, American University

### Background

Virginia's Piedmont country is a quiet, peaceful area just 35 miles west of Washington, DC. With rolling hills, horse farms, vineyards, and small rustic towns that border some of the nation's major Civil War battle sites, the Piedmont offers a tranquil contrast to the bustling capital nearby. But in November 1993 that peace and tranquility was shattered by a surprise announcement from the Walt Disney Company that it had acquired control of 3,000 Piedmont acres near the small town of Haymarket to build an American history theme park. The park, to be called Disney's America, would draw upwards of 30,000 visitors a day. Within days of the announcement, the Piedmont would become the scene of a ten-month heated battle over the proposed theme park.

Although many local businesses and politicians initially welcomed Disney, grassroots opposition to the theme park grew quickly. At community meetings and forums, local citizens expressed concern about the potential disruption to the Piedmont way of life, citing the prospect of traffic congestion, increased pollution, strip mall development, desecration of historic lands, and off-season unemployment of theme park employees. A coalition of environmentalists, historic preservationists, landowners, and Piedmont citizens quickly organized under the umbrella of the Piedmont Environmental Council (PEC), a local conservation group. The coalition called itself Disney, Take a Second Look and soon outlined a campaign plan that ultimately would result in Disney's September 1994 decision to abandon its Haymarket theme park.

## Research

PEC had no illusions about the difficulty of its task. Take a Second Look staff and volunteers knew that Disney had vast resources and could draw on a reservoir of good will from the public. The fanfare surrounding Disney's initial announcement showed that Disney was taking nothing for granted and would launch an aggressive public relations campaign to promote its project. It would be difficult, PEC realized, to do battle with a venerated company that brought so much joy to America's children. The Take a Second Look name implicitly acknowledged this fact by not taking on Disney directly and instead urged Disney merely to reconsider its choice of locations.

Wisely, PEC leaders did not assume that the initial grassroots outcry against the theme park represented widespread opposition to it. Within weeks of organizing, they retained the Widmeyer Group, a Washington, DC public affairs firm, to conduct a series of focus groups to test public opinion about the Disney plan. To gauge general sentiment throughout Virginia, one focus group was held in Richmond; the other three were held in Manassas, within miles of the proposed site.

The focus groups revealed that the Disney name and image evoked positive feelings even from people skeptical about the theme park. But they also showed that Disney was extremely vulnerable once people began to hear various arguments from the opposition. According to the focus group report, opposition concerns about traffic, quality of life, the cost of infrastructure improvements, and Disney's general business approach evoked "a palpable shift in attitudes" toward both the theme park and the Walt Disney Company itself. To PEC, the focus groups clearly showed the potential power and effectiveness of a campaign message built on neutralizing Disney's magic dust image and portraying Disney as just another big corporation trying to get its way at the expense of taxpayers and the local community.[1]

Focus group research was one of many research tools PEC used to build its case. PEC knew it would have to substantiate its concerns about traffic, the environment, and the economy. It also wanted to poke holes in Disney's claims that the theme park would be an economic boon to the state and region. Therefore, early in the campaign PEC commissioned a number of studies. An economic study prepared by outside consultants concluded that Disney had overstated the fiscal benefits and the number of new jobs its proposed theme park would bring. Because Disney's own economic impact statement had come under criticism from various independent sources,[2] PEC saw an opening for its own report. Another study commissioned by PEC identified

32 alternative sites throughout the region that would create fewer environmental and traffic problems. PEC also teamed up with other Disney opponents to assess how the additional traffic from the proposed theme park would impact the region's ability to meet federal clean air standards. For PEC, these were not merely research studies; PEC made sure that they all received widespread coverage in the news media.

PEC also wanted to learn as much as possible about Disney's experiences with other communities. Campaign staff members and consultants researched Disney's relationship with Orlando, Florida, home of Disney World, and Anaheim, California, home of Disneyland. They also examined Disney's troubles with its Euro Disney theme park near Paris. And they sent feelers out to environmentalists who in 1991 successfully blocked a proposed Disney sea theme park in Long Beach, California. PEC learned one key lesson from this research: Disney seemed very concerned about its public image and viewed its good will with the public as a form of capital investment.

## Objectives

PEC had one overriding objective: to persuade Disney not to build its proposed theme park in Haymarket. But underneath this objective lay a major strategic objective for the campaign: to put as many roadblocks as possible in Disney's way, and to do it with enough publicity to generate concerns about Disney's image and intentions.

PEC's immediate task was to oppose Disney's request for $158 million in state funding for infrastructure improvements and other costs. Take a Second Look strategists knew this was an uphill battle, particularly with recently elected Governor George Allen visibly supportive of the project. But they also saw it as an opportunity to damage Disney's case and to demonstrate their determination to fight an aggressive battle. So PEC took its cause to the state legislature in Richmond. The campaign dedicated staff and financial resources to lobby against Disney's request and generate public concern about the proposed theme park.

PEC pursued a number of other campaign objectives. One was to slow down local approval of Disney's zoning request. Another was to raise concerns about the theme park's impact on the local environment, particularly the region's ability to comply with federal clean air standards. PEC also sought to build, initiate, and support local and national coalitions opposed to the theme park—coalitions that would create public relations headaches for Disney. One coalition of historians, journalists, and historic preservationists—called Protect Historic America—is credited with raising serious and decisive public doubts about the credibility of an American history theme park and its placement in a part of the country that the coalition described as hallowed by conflict and blood.[3]

Ultimately, PEC heeded the findings of its research: Keep Disney on the defensive and use the media and other public relations vehicles to chip away at the company's image and good will with the public. Fulfilling this objective, PEC believed, might make the price of the theme park too high for a company very protective of its public image.

## Programming

Just days after Disney's announcement, PEC began implementing an aggressive campaign to sway public opinion to its side. Among its first initiatives was a public meeting in a nearby town that was covered extensively by the press. PEC used the meeting to rally supporters and to articulate the campaign's basic themes in opposing the park. Within days, PEC ran radio spots urging Disney to take a second look. Bumper stickers calling Interstate 66 "Disney's New Parking Lot" began to appear on cars.

Knowing that many initial skirmishes would be fought in the media, PEC retained a number of public relations and political consulting firms to assist with media relations and advertising. A strong presence in the media also would be critical in providing support for PEC's effort to block state funding for the project. Beginning in mid-December 1993, PEC generated a cascade of news stories designed to shape the public debate and to discredit Disney's promotion of the theme park.

Among PEC's community outreach and media initiatives were:

- Public rallies cosponsored with other local coalitions opposing the theme park.

- A news event at the National Press Club in Washington, DC, on the adverse economic impact of the Disney theme park.

- A news event near Piedmont outlining alternative sites that would be more favorable for building the theme park.

- Briefings for state legislators to disclose the economic, environmental, and transportation findings of PEC studies.

- Editorial board meetings with major newspapers in the region, including the *Washington Post, Washington Times, Richmond Times-Dispatch, Norfolk, Virginia-Pilot, Roanoke Times and World News, Fredericksburg Lance Star,* and the *Journal* newspapers in northern Virginia.

- Placement of op-ed articles in regional, local, and national papers. Authors of these pieces included prominent journalists and former public officials.

- Radio and newspaper advertisements in local and Virginia outlets. One newspaper ad, under the headline "Brother, Can You Spare $158 Million?," depicted a likeness of Mickey Mouse's arm with its hand facing upwards as if asking for a handout; the ad listed the state capital switchboard number and urged concerned citizens to call their state legislators as well as the PEC.

- News events cosponsored with national environmental groups on the potential consequences for compliance with federal clean air standards.
- Outreach to national media outlets with the goal of turning the controversy into a national news story.
- Local and national talk radio outreach.
- A news conference and other events organized with Protect Historic America, a coalition of historians, journalists, and historic preservationists.
- A protest rally at the June 1994 Washington, DC, premiere of Disney's film *The Lion King*. The rally, featuring PEC placards calling Disney chairman Michael Eisner "the Lyin' King," received as much media attention as the opening of the film.[4]

These and other media initiatives kept PEC's cause not only in the news but in control of the message communicated to the public through the media. Such an aggressive media campaign was necessary, given Disney's own considerable efforts to build support, which included phone banks, newsletters, public opinion polls, media outreach, a Welcome Disney Committee organized by the local chamber of commerce, booths at county fairs, exhibitions featuring Disney's commitment to "environmentality," and special events targeted to public officials. Not wanting Disney to gain any public relations advantage, PEC made every effort to respond immediately to Disney's attempts to influence public opinion. For example, when Disney released a public opinion poll in January 1994 showing support for the theme park, PEC fired back with a news release calling the survey "biased" and stating:

> Given that Disney has been entertaining Americans for most of this century, no one should be surprised by polls showing support for its proposed theme park. But Disney's popularity is not the issue. The issue is whether this theme park is in the best interest of Virginia, and whether Virginia's taxpayers should be subsidizing one of the wealthiest corporations in the world.[5]

PEC's media strategy was clear: Use every opportunity not only to answer Disney but to reiterate the key messages of the opposition campaign.

## Evaluation

On September 28, 1994—a little more than ten months after Disney's initial announcement—the Walt Disney Company withdrew its plans to build the Haymarket theme park. PEC needed no better evidence to evaluate its success. That the campaign objectives were accomplished so well could be seen in the lead paragraph of the *Washington Post* story the day after Disney's withdrawal: "The Walt Disney Co. killed its Prince William theme park last night, apparently after deciding that an unexpected national debate over the location and concept of the $650 million Disney's America was hurting the company's image."[6]

For its part, Disney seemed unprepared for the vigorous and media-savvy campaign against it. Despite its textbook implementation of various public relations activities—the exhibits, newsletters, events, and welcome committees—Disney failed to gauge the intensity of opposition the theme park would generate.[7] The company's public relations researchers should have raised a red flag at the earliest stages of the project by alerting Disney to a similar battle in the region only a few years earlier, when grassroots opposition stopped a developer from building a shopping mall next to the Manassas National Battlefield Park, a Civil War site. Forced on the defensive almost immediately by PEC, Disney was never able to offer a win-win rationale for building the theme park. From a public relations perspective, Disney's final move made the most sense: Declare it a loss, stanch the bleeding, and put an end to what had become the Magic Kingdom's publicity nightmare.

# NOTES

1. The Widmeyer Group, *Focus Groups on Disney's America Theme Park*. Focus groups were conducted January 13 and 15, 1994.

2. William A. Rodger, "Disney Inflates Park Impact, Say Economists," *Washington Business Journal*, December 17–23, 1993. The article quotes economist and George Washington University professor Stephen Fuller—a self-described supporter of the theme park—as saying that Disney's economic impact statement "greatly exaggerates" the benefits to the community.

3. For an excellent article on the entire campaign, and especially the role of historians in defeating the theme park, see Larry Van Dyne, "Hit the Road, Mick," *The Washingtonian*, January 1995, pp. 59–63, 114–127. The article describes how the historians' campaign generated more than 10,000 newspaper and magazine clips.

4. Van Dyne, p. 123. See also Roxanne Roberts, "Disney's Animal Magnetism," *Washington Post*, June 17, 1994, p. B1.

5. Quoted from a press release issued by PEC's Disney, Take a Second Look campaign, January 27, 1994.

6. Peter Baker and Spencer S. Hsu, "Disney Gives Up on Haymarket Theme Park, Vows to Seek Less Controversial Virginia Site." *Washington Post*, September 29, 1994, p. A1.

7. The best overview of how Disney failed to anticipate and outmaneuver the opposition is Michael Wiebner, "The Battle of Bull Run: How Insurgent Grassroots Lobbying Defeated Disney's Proposed Virginia Theme Park," *Campaigns & Elections*, December/January 1995, pp. 44–48.

**DISNEY**
**TAKE A SECOND**
**LO K**
A PROJECT OF THE PIEDMONT
ENVIRONMENTAL COUNCIL

# PRESS RELEASE

*Embargoed for Release*
**11:OO A.M., Wednesday, February 2, 1994**

Contact:    Hilary Gerhardt
703/347-2334
Matt Wagner
Heather Hopkins
202/667-0901

## HAYMARKET THE WRONG SITE FOR DISNEY, NEW INDEPENDENT STUDY DOCUMENTS

An independent report released today names 32 other sites in the Northern Virginia and Washington metropolitan Region that are more favorable for the building of Disney's America theme park than the proposed location in Haymarket, Va.

"The Disney Corporation's choice of the Route 15/Haymarket site demands far too much public subsidy. Disney's America would be better served at other locations in the Region. These sites already possess needed infrastructure or the infrastructure could be provided at far less cost," said EM Risse, Principal of SYNERGY/Planning, Inc., which prepared the study.

The 50-page study, "Finding the Optimum Site for Disney's America -- The Basis for a Rational Site Selection Process and a Preliminary Summary of Potential Sites", addresses why it is necessary to look for alternative sites, establishes alternative site selection criteria, and examines the anatomy of the transportation infrastructure from a subregional and regional perspective.

The study notes Disney's America is only 95 acres plus access and parking. The remainder of the 3,000-acre Route 15/Haymarket site and the surrounding 8,000 acres would be occupied by urban uses, including retail, office, and "market" housing uses. The Region already has an oversupply of buildings and land with existing infrastructure for such uses. Given this, the study concludes there are more appropriate subregional and/or regional locations on which to build Disney's America, given the services they demand and the customers they support.

"This study shows that the Haymarket site is the wrong site for a development of this magnitude. There are simply too many problems associated with building the park on this site," said Bob Dennis of the Take A Second Look Campaign. "It would be too costly for Virginia's taxpayers and businesses, too costly for the environment, and too costly for the commuter."

45 Horner Street ■ Box 460 ■ Warrenton, Virginia 22186
703/347-2334 ■ (Fax) 703/349-9003

The report addresses six critical points:

- There are at least 32 better potential sites for the proposed park in the Region.

- There are limited public funds to provide infrastructure and support, and there is a long list of existing priorities.

- There is limited subregional demand for the retail/office/"market" housing that will be induced to relocate to the Route 15/Haymarket location.

- The total eventual public and private costs -- economic, social and environmental -- of supporting this major activity generator on a remote site will be very high.

- The more remote the site of a major new activity generator, the greater the loss to all the municipalities and citizens in the Region.

- If the park is built at the Route 15/Haymarket site, the biggest losers would be the municipalities, businesses, service users, and owners of homes, buildings, and land that will lose the market and tax base from the relocated uses.

The study contains four major elements, including the rationale for an alternative site analysis; the primary characteristics of the proposed park that affect the search for an alternative site; the nature of the regional infrastructure system that will serve any site for a major activity generator such as the proposed park; and the potential alternate sites for the proposed park.

The study also examines a number of issues surrounding the Route 15/Haymarket site, including the effect the park would have on the Region's existing tourism trade, the new demands the park would place on the Region's transportation system, as well as the eventual environmental pressures and costs associated with Disney's America.

"Under the current financial arrangements, Disney may have a more favorable short-term cash flow from Disney's America on the Route 15/Haymarket site given substantial public subsidies as compared to other sites. However, Disney states that the project is not feasible without yet-to-be-determined millions of dollars for yet-to-be-determined public infrastructure, beneficial interest rates on infrastructure debt and other support," the report states. "It is clear that lower public investment would yield higher public and private benefit on alternative sites."

The study lists eight sites which are currently served by METRO and have six-lane expressways and/or existing VRE service; ten sites which are served by a planned extension of METRO service and by six-lane expressways and/or VRE service; six sites which are served by existing six-lane expressways and VRE service; and eight sites that require extension of six-lane expressways and existing VRE services.

Risse noted that these sites would be less costly and more convenient to the public, and said that Disney could benefit as well from choosing an alternate site. He said Disney would not necessarily face construction delays if it moved its park to an alternative site. In fact, Risse asserts Disney could meet the many federal requirements associated with building a major activity generator faster and more easily by choosing one of the alternate sites.

"In the past, many private-sector owners and users of land have assumed that their best strategy to maximize profits was to select a site and then sell the concept to those who must help pay for the infrastructure," the study said. "Recent experience, especially in light of the need for broad public participation in the transportation planning, funding and implementation process, suggests that this may no longer be the most effective private strategy."

"This study shows that there are better ways of choosing a site for Disney's America than buying up land under assumed identities, engaging in a secret decision-making process, and using a well-oiled publicity campaign to sell a site to those who must pay for it," Dennis said. "We need a true public/private partnership in the location, planning, implementation, and execution of major new developments such as Disney's America."

SYNERGY/Planning, Inc., carries out strategic and tactical planning for the development of major land parcels. In the Washington-Baltimore region, these projects provide homes for over 50,000 residents, buildings for over 20,000,000 square feet of employment and retail space, as well as services, amenities and infrastructure to support these uses.

# # #

# BROTHER, CAN YOU SPARE $158 MILLION?

$158 million is a lot of money. But that's what the Walt Disney Company has asked Virginia's taxpayers to pony up for its proposed theme park in Northern Virginia. And it could end up costing a lot more.

Actually, Disney isn't asking. Its chairman, Michael Eisner, has threatened not to build the theme park if the taxpayers don't come up with the money by March 12.

This from a company whose 1992 profits exceeded $800 million, and from a man who recently cashed in $202 million in stock options.

$158 million could build schools, parks, and roads for Virginia's future. Or it could help build a theme park for one of the wealthiest corporations in the world.

Don't give our tax dollars to Disney.

**Call your legislator's office at 804-786-6530 and say you don't want to give your hard-earned tax dollars to Disney.**

**Or call the Take A Second Look Campaign at 800-341-2334 for more information.**

*D*isney's America, and the development that will inevitably ripple from it, will destroy one of the most historic and beautiful landscapes in the country.

—Richard Moe, President
—Henry A. Jordan, M.D., Chairman
National Trust for Historic Preservation

The Walt Disney Corporation is planning to build an urban complex in historic rural Virginia. This "edge city" will consist of millions of square feet of commercial space, several thousand hotel rooms and vacation units, more than 2,300 houses and a theme park.

As at Anaheim and Orlando, Disney's project will inevitably spawn vast sprawl development for miles around. Much of the secondary development will destroy historic towns, villages and Civil War sites which residents and landowners have carefully tended for hundreds of years. Highways, motels, t-shirt shops, fast-food joints and strip malls will pave over and invade this rural area if Disney gets its way.

Within a few miles of the Disney site lie 13 historic towns, 12 Civil War battle sites and 17 historic districts.

Haymarket, where Disney wants to locate, is an historic town chartered in 1739 and is located 35 miles west of Washington, D.C. It is a rural community surrounded by farms and Civil War battlefields; the famous Manassas Battlefield Park, for instance, lies four miles east. (It was setting for two of the most significant battles in the Civil War.)

The hamlet of Thoroughfare borders the Disney property. Thoroughfare is one of the earliest African-American communities in the nation. Much of the land there today is still owned by the same families to whom it was originally deeded.

The National Trust has designated all of this region

> *The Disney project "threatens to destroy the very historical landscape that it purports to interpret."*
> — James McPherson
> Princeton University
> President, Protect Historic America

as one of the most endangered areas of the country. And that's not the end of it.

☛ Disney is seeking coast-to-coast corporate welfare. In addition to the $163 million in financing approved by the Commonwealth of Virginia for the proposed Disney project, this avaricious corporation is also seeking up to $1 billion in California from the city, state and federal governments to build Westcot Center in Anaheim.

Bear in mind that Disney is one of the world's wealthiest corporations, with an average net income of $824 million over the past three years. Disney's CEO, Michael Eisner, was the nation's highest paid executive in 1993, with compensation of $203 million.

☛ Disney's project in Haymarket is a national test of the Federal Clean Air Act (CAA) and the Intermodal Surface Transportation Efficiency Act (ISTEA). Contrary to policy set forth in these laws, Disney's highway expansion projects will encourage inefficient patterns and densities of land use, pollute our air and waste our scarce tax dollars and our natural resources.

The Washington metropolitan area is *already* in violation of the Clean Air Act. A recently released

*continued on reverse*

study states that air pollution during the summer in the Shenandoah National Park is at times worse than in Los Angeles *(source: study conducted by the University of California at Davis).*

☞ This is not just a regional issue—everyone is affected. Virginia's history is America's history—think of Thomas Jefferson's Monticello outside Charlottesville, or George Washington's Mt. Vernon outside Alexandria. There are not many places left where history is so real and tangible. If taxpayer dollars are involved, they should be used to maintain real historic sites, not to subsidize developments that threaten their very existence.

☞ You will pay for Disney, because U.S. taxpayer dollars will be necessary to alleviate Disney-generated congestion on federal highways leading to Haymarket.

Diverting jobs and tourism from the developed areas of the region—including Washington, D.C.—will accelerate decay and underuse of the public facilities already in place. Instead of renewing our nation's Capital, we will be subsidizing its decline.

**Disney, back off!**

## Can Disney be stopped?
Yes. It was stopped at Long Beach, California. Disney wanted to develop a marine theme park outside Long Beach, but the public hue and cry prompted Disney to abandon the site.

## What *you* can do to stop Disney

☞ Detach, sign, date and stamp the attached postcards to federal officials expressing your concerns and urging a comprehensive environmental impact statement. Better yet, send your own letters, and also:

☞ Write letters to your state congressmen and senators.

☞ Write letters to the Editor and op-ed pieces in both your local papers and the national press.

☞ Encourage your local civic organizations to take a stand on this issue. Let the Piedmont Environmental Council in Warrenton, Va., know so that new names can be added to the more than 65 organizations already committed to fighting Disney, including the Sierra Club Legal Defense Fund, the National Trust for Historic Preservation and the American Farmland Trust, whose members believe that rural Virginia is worth protecting *(Piedmont Environmental Council, P.O. Box 460, Warrenton, VA 22186).*

☞ Form a local Save Historic Piedmont Virginia group. A group in Boston calls itself *YO*—for *Yankee Opposition.*

☞ Send your financial contributions to the Piedmont Environmental Council.

For more information on how you can help, contact the Piedmont Environmental Council at 1-800-341-2334.

> ### Virginians "should be so lucky as to have Orlando in Virginia."
> **—Disney chairman Michael Eisner in a nationally televised interview as reported in the June 3, 1994 *Washington Post*.**

*Tired of its role as Colorado's "second city," Colorado Springs made a national publicity splash with the grand opening of its new airport. In contrast to the overbudget and trouble-plagued Denver International Airport, Colorado Springs successfully and cost-effectively positioned itself as a serious, alternative "Gateway to the Rockies." Exhibit 5-2a is a news release announcing the airport's opening. Exhibit 5-2b is an airport advertisement. Exhibit 5-2c is an artist's rendering of the airport.*

**CASE 5-2**     Colorado Springs Airport Opening

City of Colorado Springs Public Communications Department with Heisley/LeGrand Advertising, Inc., Colorado Springs, CO

### Research

The citizens of Colorado Springs supported the Airport Improvement Project three times at the polls—in 1987, 1989, and 1991. In 1991, citizens approved the issuance of up to $64 million in revenue bonds to fund the city's share of building a new terminal (the remaining funds came from airport revenues and the FAA). Using research gathered before, during, and after these bond issue campaigns, we designed our public relations efforts with two key goals in mind:

- To reinforce voters' decision to support the new terminal by keeping them informed of the city's responsible fiscal management of the project—it opened on time, under budget, and at no cost to the taxpayer.
- Through ongoing media relations efforts and a series of special events, to ensure Colorado Springs residents' continued interest in and support for the new airport terminal.

### Planning

*Objectives*

- Create a sense of community pride and ownership in Colorado Springs' new airport.

---

Courtesy City of Colorado Springs Public Communications Department

- Raise community awareness about the benefits of the airport (compared to the old airport and Denver International).
- Raise national awareness of Colorado Springs as a destination and as a gateway to the Rockies.

### Key Audiences

- Colorado Springs community
- Communities in region surrounding Colorado Springs (from Pueblo to Southern Denver)
- Colorado Springs frequent outbound travelers
- Inbound Colorado travelers (skiers, tourists, business people)
- Colorado ski resorts and tourist destinations
- Local, regional, and national travel agents
- Colorado Springs business executives
- Airlines

### Strategies

- Build broad public anticipation of the airport by creating a constant stream of new information to the media for several months prior to the opening.
- Give community businesses and organizations across the spectrum a chance to participate in the opening.
- Position Colorado Springs as an alternative "gateway to the Rockies" for skiers, business travelers, and tourists who typically fly through Denver.
- Develop a grand opening celebration to draw at least 20,000 people to visit the new airport.

### Budget

| | |
|---|---|
| Public relations/special events (includes hard materials) | $78,500 |
| Direct mail | $18,000 |
| Collateral (brochures, support materials) | $26,500 |
| Educational materials | $64,000 |
| Advertising | $58,000 |
| Contingency | $13,500 |
| Total | $258,500 |

## Execution

### Program Tactics

- Prepared comprehensive media kit for distribution to key local, regional, and national media.

- Sent biweekly "fast facts" newsletter and regular news releases to regional media.
- Arranged for the Colorado Springs newspaper to run a 20-page special section on the airport.
- Stretched a tight budget by obtaining the support and contributions of more than 25 local organizations.
- Developed marketing co-ops and pricing discounts with Breckenridge Ski Resort and Ski Lift, a charter service from Colorado Springs to Summit County.
- Created a series of special events leading up to the grand opening celebration including:
  - Black-tie gala to benefit local charities
  - Reception and tour for local travel agents
  - Luncheon and tour for the Colorado Springs Press Association
  - Volunteer landscaping project
  - Breakfast and tour for the Colorado Springs Executives Association
  - Airport employees barbecue and tour
  - Dedication luncheon hosted by Mayor Bob Isaac
- Developed a grand opening day celebration full of activities, including an aviation display on the tarmac; and various interactive exhibits, sporting exhibitions, and music and entertainment for all ages and tastes throughout the terminal.

## Evaluation

### Results

- Despite cold, rainy weather that hampered some of the scheduled outdoor activities, more than 50,000 people came to the airport grand opening (more than twice the number expected).
- Direct-mail campaign for charity gala received greater than 100 percent response; more than 1,700 guests attended.
- More than 300 travel agents attended industry reception.
- Eighty-eight media and public relations professionals attended tour for Colorado Springs Press Association.
- More than 500 volunteers helped plant trees and shrubs along the airport's entryway.
- One hundred fifty business leaders turned out for the Colorado Springs Executives Association breakfast and tour.
- More than 500 airport and city employees came to an employee barbecue and tour at the new terminal.

- The dedication luncheon was attended by 650 business and community leaders.

- The Colorado Springs *Gazette Telegraph* ran 57 stories about the opening between August 12, 1994, and October 23, 1994 (the official opening was October 22).

- Altogether there were more than 300 media stories about the airport opening.

- The opening was covered by all Colorado Springs and Pueblo media, all major Denver media, dailies, and weeklies all along the front range, and twice by CNN.

- Colorado Springs radio and television stations aired 66 stories about the opening of the new airport.

- National print coverage included Reuter's Wire Service, *USA Today,* and the *Washington Post.*

- Television coverage outside Colorado included 28 stories about the airport opening carried by television stations in New York, Los Angeles, Dallas, St. Louis, Baltimore, San Diego, and West Palm Beach.

- The *International Herald Tribune* ran a story about the opening on October 24.

- Trade coverage included *Aviation News and Space Technologies, Agent Canada, Architect and Engineer, TravelAge West, Travel Weekly, Ski Magazine, Frequent Flyer, Tour and Travel News, Business Travel News, Meeting News, Insurance Conference Planner,* and *Professional Engineer.*

- Since the opening, a new commercial airline, Western Pacific, has chosen Colorado Springs as its hub; Northwest Airlines has established nonstop service between Colorado Springs and Minneapolis for the first time; Delta Airlines has established nonstop service between Colorado Springs and Cincinnati for the first time; and Reno Air has established direct service between Colorado Springs and San Jose and Las Vegas.

- According to travel agents, travelers in communities between Denver and Colorado Springs have begun flying in and out of the Colorado Springs Airport with much greater frequency.

**Exhibit 5-2a**

**CITY OF COLORADO SPRINGS**
# NEWS RELEASE

**SUBJECT:**   New Colorado Springs Airport Opens On-Time and Under-Budget

**CONTACT:**   George Dushan                                    Oct. 22, 1994

**RELEASE AT WILL**

The new Colorado Springs Airport is officially open for business.

Eight days ago (Oct. 14), Colorado Springs Mayor Bob Isaac, U.S. Rep. Joel Hefley, FAA Northwest Mountain Region Administrator Fred Isaac and other dignitaries dedicated the new airport and terminal building.  The following day (Oct. 15), more than 50,000 people -- approximately one in every six people who live in Colorado Springs -- attended the grand-opening Community Celebration to mark the event.  Then, the $39.5 million 12-gate terminal opened for business a week later (Oct. 22).

When 53-square-mile Denver International Airport opens, the Colorado Springs Airport (7,135 acres; 11.15 square miles) will be the second-largest airport in Colorado, though it is still larger than New York's La Guardia Airport, Los Angeles International, National Airport in Washington, D.C. and San Diego's Lindbergh Airport combined.  In 1991, Colorado Springs opened the longest (13,500 ft.) runway in Colorado to air traffic, during an earlier phase of the airport-improvement project.

But, those aren't the only reasons the Colorado Springs community celebrated the opening at the 270,000-sq.ft. terminal.  It was because the new airport and terminal were completed under budget and on schedule, and because the $140-million improvements (new runway, taxiways, aircraft-parking apron and other associated airfield improvements, in addition to the terminal) required no local taxpayer subsidy. The community's portion of the improvements ($80.5 million) was financed entirely with airport equity, citizen-approved revenue bonds (a total of $62.9 million in three series and a $3 passenger-facility charge. (**Note**:  One series of the bonds, for $9 million, was retired on an "early call" in January 1995.)

-more-

Exhibit 5-2a
(*continued*)

Airport Opening News Release   (Courtesy City of Colorado Springs Public
Communications Department)

Page 2

Passengers arriving in Colorado Springs today are greeted with the soft-hued colors of Southwestern and Rocky-Mountain motifs.  The architectural design, by the Van Sant Group of Colorado
Springs, features numerous windows and skylights to showcase the "plains-meet-the-mountains" vistas of
the Pikes Peak Region, a key access point to Colorado's mountains and ski areas.  Trees native to
Colorado and other Rocky Mountain plant life, rocks and cascading water accent the interior.  In addition,
the terminal's "great hall" displays a dramatic mobile sculpture by Boston artist Michio Ihara.

The facility more than doubles Colorado Springs terminal capacity for passenger convenience,
providing expanded passenger-waiting areas, baggage-claim and security areas and airline ticket-counter
space.  The larger terminal allows the airport to accommodate 2.5 million enplaned passengers a year.

The new terminal is located midway between the airport's 11,021-ft. north-south runway and its
longer new north-south runway two-and-one-half miles to the east.  The site of the new terminal makes
on-ground operations more efficient and economical for the airlines that serve Colorado Springs.

When Colorado Springs' new runway opened in 1991, it increased allowable take-off weights for
commercial airplanes, thus improving aircraft range and airline profitability.  That was important, as
summertime temperatures decrease air density and used to cause airlines to limit passengers to reduce
aircraft weights.  The runway's length greatly reduces this "density-altitude" factor, and makes it possible
for airlines to fill more of their available seats.

"The longer runway makes non-stop flights possible to just about anywhere in the U.S.  The new
apron and taxiways provide increased aircraft service and the larger terminal eases peak-period
congestion," explained Aviation Director Gary Green.

Approximately 3,000 acres of the Colorado Springs Airport are in use, or are scheduled for
projects.  That leaves more than 4,100 acres available for development, including 600 acres with direct

-more-

Page 3

runway access.

The new airport, its available acreage and recent air-service improvements have all combined to position Colorado Springs quite solidly as the community prepares to face the economy of the 21st Century.

-30-

# We Run Our Airport
# Like You Run Your Business.

The Colorado Springs Airport.

To get things done on time and on budget aren't just goals to a business — they're mandates.

And, when we designed and built an airport to meet the needs of business, they became our mandates as well. Not only does the new Colorado Springs Airport feature 12 gates with 94 daily flights and the longest runway in the state, it was completed ahead of schedule and on budget.

Remarkable? Not really. Just well thought out, well designed, and well implemented.

FOR A FREE PLANE FACTS FLIGHT GUIDE, CALL 1 800 GO COSPG OR 719 596 0188

Exhibit 5-2c

Artist's Rendering of the Airport (Courtesy City of Colorado Springs Public Communications Department)

*To enhance its relations with its home community, Bristol-Myers Squibb Company created a new community outreach program centered around the 50th anniversary of its Syracuse facility. Exhibit 5-3a is the logo of the program. Exhibit 5-3b is an internal announcement of the program. Exhibit 5-3c is a news release about the science student summer program. Exhibits 5-3d, 5-3e, and 5-3f are media alerts and a news release about the program.*

**CASE 5-3**

## "Lifting the Veil"

Bristol-Myers Squibb Company, Syracuse Divisions, with Eric Mower and Associates Public Relations Services

### Situation

The decades-old chain link fences circling Bristol-Myers Squibb's 70-acre site in Syracuse, NY, said it all: Stay off the property and out of our business.

Despite being one of the community's largest employers and one of its last remaining major manufacturers, neighbors, community leaders, media, and elected officials were in the dark about Bristol's remarkable achievements. They knew little of the Syracuse operation's historic role in pioneering the world's first wonder drug—penicillin—at the peak of World War II. And few people were aware of the company's modern-day breakthroughs in biotechnology and anticancer research.

It was no surprise, then, that by the early 1990s, most of the media and community focus was on Bristol's environmental troubles. In particular, the community's daily newspaper committed most of their Bristol coverage to environmental bashing.

This negative focus caught the attention of corporate leadership in New York City to such a degree that it jeopardized future investment in Syracuse. The message was clear: Without significant improvements in community relations, the future of the site and its 1,000+ jobs was in serious question.

In late 1992, on the eve of Bristol-Myers Squibb's 50th anniversary in Syracuse, the chain link fences came down, signaling a new direction for the facility. It was time to tell the Bristol-Myers Squibb story to the Syracuse community . . . before time ran out.

---

Courtesy Bristol-Myers Squibb Company

## Research

The Bristol-Myers Squibb/Eric Mower and Associates team turned to community opinion research completed in late 1991. The statistics confirmed that the sustained attention to negative environmental news combined with the "no comment/no access" mentality had badly damaged perceptions of the company.

- More than half of the community residents (51 percent) responding to a telephone survey held a negative opinion of the site.
- Only 26 percent had a positive opinion.
- 91 percent of those reporting a negative opinion cited environmental concerns as their reason for the rating.
- Readers of the daily newspapers were twice as likely as nonreaders to give negative overall opinions of the company.

Among all the negative findings, the research found one strategic positive:

- *Neighbors and the community were overwhelmingly supportive of the site's scientific research effort.*

This finding became a critical guide in developing community relations tactics that would emphasize the site's scientific leadership.

It was agreed at the start of the program that a post–community opinion survey would be conducted in early 1994 to measure results of the community relations initiatives and lay the foundation for future strategies.

## Planning

With corporate leadership prepared to pull the plug on future investment in the Syracuse site, the goal was clear: Demonstrate measurable improvement in community relations to Bristol-Myers Squibb decision makers.

### Audiences and Objectives

- Improve *community perceptions* among neighbors, elected officials, and community leaders . . . *as measured by the 1994 community opinion research.*
- Introduce a "balance" to *media coverage* beyond environmental issues . . . *as measured by a content analysis of news clippings.*
- Stimulate *employee and retiree involvement* in outreach activities . . . *as measured by actual employee/retiree participation.*

### Strategies

- Translate support for scientific research into demonstrable community pride in the site.

- Establish "linkages" with community partners to gain third-party support for the site.
- Invert "no comment/no access" mentality into "open/accessible" mentality.

## Execution

The Bristol-Myers Squibb/Eric Mower and Associates team planned and executed a year-long community relations program to capitalize on the 50th anniversary.

### Theme and Logo

A theme and logo consistent with the scientific message were developed for use with all outreach activities. "Project 2043: Science at Work" projected a forward-thinking message about the site's important work in the next 50 years.

### Community Outreach

*Site Brochure*—More than 5,000 neighbors, employees and retirees, elected officials, media, and community leaders received a four-color, 16-page brochure presenting the rich history and promising scientific future of the Syracuse site.

*Science Horizons: The Summer Science Adventure*—In a linkage with Syracuse University and the State University of New York College of Environmental Science and Forestry, the company launched an innovative, week-long science camp for 50 seventh- and eighth-grade students from all public and private middle schools in the county. An entire day was devoted to a visit inside the Bristol site. Students, parents, and educators gave high marks to Science Horizons, and the program generated a steady flow of print and broadcast media coverage.

*Community Open House*—For the first time ever, the company broke down traditional barriers and opened the site to hundreds of neighbors, elected officials, media, and community leaders. Guided by employee volunteers, visitors went inside laboratories and manufacturing areas that were previously "off limits."

*Bristol Omnitheater*—Bristol provided the community with a long-lasting symbol of its scientific leadership: a $700,000 naming grant to the local Museum of Science and Technology to build a high-tech omni-theater. More than 400 community leaders attended the announcement ceremony at the future site of the giant dome-screened theater. The contribution drew live TV and front-page coverage, including a newspaper editorial that called the gift "corporate citizenry at its best."

## Media Relations

*Media Briefing/Editorial Board*—To lay a solid foundation for future media coverage, site management held a "no holds barred" luncheon briefing at the site and a private editorial board meeting with the two daily newspapers. Bristol's corporate vice president for policy and planning attended both sessions. More than 20 news directors, editors, and reporters participated in the meetings, representing every major news organization in the region.

Post Standard *Feature Series*—Syracuse's morning newspaper was granted unprecedented access to the site's world-class research and development laboratories. The paper ran a three-day, front-page series entitled "Bristol Lifts the Veil," detailing the site's global scientific leadership.

*Ongoing Media Outreach*—An intense print and broadcast publicity campaign capitalized on each outreach initiative and emphasized science-related messages.

## Employee Involvement

*Employee Kickoff*—Recognizing the importance of employee participation, employee meetings were held to introduce the year-long slate of activities. All employees received a commemorative coffee mug bearing the "Project 2043" theme and logo.

*Volunteer Committees*—All major events and programs were directed by committees made up of employee volunteers.

*Project 2043 Report*—Bristol's corporate management and all site employees received a monthly update on the community relations efforts.

*Anniversary Luncheon*—A thank you luncheon for 1,200 employees, retirees, elected officials, and community leaders captured the attention of the community—and the corporation. The event featured presentations by the site's senior corporate officer and by two legendary retirees who were instrumental to the clinical and business development of the company. Twelve corporate officers who flew to Syracuse for the event were greeted by political, community, and business leaders.

## Budget

A budget of nearly $390,000 was set for the community relations program. Costs included all communications materials, site brochure, Science Horizons, open house, anniversary luncheon, and announcement of Bristol Omnitheater. Total costs at the end of the year were approximately $350,000.

## Evaluation

In clear, quantifiable terms the 50th anniversary community relations program met and exceeded all objectives.

### Community Perceptions

A comprehensive community opinion survey was conducted in February 1994 using the same methodology as in 1991. Additionally, interviews were conducted with media, community leaders, and elected officials. According to the research:

- Negative perceptions of the company were nearly cut in half to 29 percent from 51 percent in 1991.

- Positive perceptions increased by 50 percent.

- Readers of the two daily newspapers were *less* likely to hold a negative opinion of the company than nonreaders—a direct turnaround from the 1991 study.

- 85 percent of media, political, and business leaders interviewed had a positive perception of the company.

    Other measurements of community success were:

- The Metropolitan Development Association, Syracuse's most influential business organization, presented the company with a "Community Appreciation Award" recognizing five decades of achievement.

- Science Horizons received an international "Creative and Innovative" Special Merit Award from the North American Association of Summer Sessions Administrators.

- In concert with corporate decision makers, the local site has committed to sponsor Science Horizons for a second year. The hands-on program is also being considered a prototype for all Bristol domestic operations.

### Media Coverage

Media coverage and relationships dramatically improved from 1991 to 1993.

- 60 percent of coverage received in 1993 was unrelated to environmental issues, and negative environmental coverage decreased by 65 percent.

- Coverage on Bristol's community relations activities increased by 88 percent.

- 100 percent of reporters surveyed gave unaided, accurate descriptions of the company's products and business.

- Contrary to previous environmental reporting, an agreement with the state's top environmental agency received accurate and fair coverage. A *Syracuse Herald Journal* editorial called the agreement "the kind of public/private cooperation that will help Central New York prosper into the next century."

## Employee Involvement

Hundreds of employees played an *active* role in the community relations program.

- 100 percent participated in at least one initiative.

- Over 700 employees participated in the kickoff meetings at the start of the program.

- Nearly 20 volunteer employee committees and subcommittees were formed.

- 840 employees and 230 retirees attended the anniversary luncheon.

## Corporate Commitment

Corporate investment in and commitment to the Syracuse site have been solidified.

- In 1994, work will be completed on $110 million in new site construction.

- Another $10 million worth of projects will begin in 1994.

## Summary

Taken together, these concrete measurements verify Bristol's dramatically strengthened position within the community and among its media and political leadership. Among employees, the most important testimony to the increased stability of the Syracuse site comes from Kenneth E. Weg, the Bristol-Myers Squibb corporate president who oversees the facility. In praising the Syracuse site's "diversity and vitality," Weg told employees:

> "Syracuse has grown into a critical link in the Bristol-Myers Squibb structure."

Exhibit 5-3a

Program Logo  (Courtesy Bristol-Myers Squibb Company)

Bristol-Myers Squibb Company     Syracuse

# OFFICIAL NOTICE

April 15, 1993

### 50th Anniversary Program "Kick-Off Coffee Break"

As announced earlier, plans are underway to commemorate the 50th anniversary of the Syracuse site. Throughout the course of the year we plan to celebrate this milestone through a program comprised of several events.

To officially launch the program, you are invited to attend a "Kick-Off Coffee Break" on **Tuesday, April 20 in the Cafeteria. The gathering will be held in two sessions that day -- the first at 8:30 a.m. (for employees with last names beginning with the letters A-L), and the second at 9:30 a.m. (last name M-Z).**

During the gatherings you will have the opportunity to both learn more about plans for the anniversary commemoration, as well as to offer your services for any of the special events that will require volunteer involvement. Refreshments will be served and everyone in attendance will also receive a special gift as a memento of our anniversary year.

Knowing that all interested site employees may not be able to attend one of the Kick-Off Coffee Breaks, the following arrangements have been made to encourage everyone's participation:

- Second and third shift workers will have mementos and information forwarded to their areas for distribution.

- An area or departmental representative can be designated to attend the meeting. They can bring back information and mementos to anyone in the particular group who was not able to attend.

- If you are unable to participate in our "Kick-off Coffee Break", you may pick up program information and mementos in Bldg. 22, Room 216 during regular business hours through April 27.

**We encourage all employees' participation in the program.**

HUMAN RESOURCES

By: Public Affairs

**SCIENCE HORIZONS**
THE BRISTOL-MYERS SQUIBB
SUMMER SCIENCE ADVENTURE

**FOR IMMEDIATE RELEASE:**
June 28, 1993

**FOR MORE INFORMATION:**
Charles A. Borgognoni
Bristol-Myers Squibb Company
315/432-2404
-or-
Greg Loh/Michael Maurer
Eric Mower and Associates
315/466-1000

<u>FACT SHEET</u>

**BRISTOL-MYERS SQUIBB'S SCIENCE HORIZONS**
**The Summer Science Adventure**

| | |
|---|---|
| **PROGRAM DESCRIPTION** | Science Horizons is a pilot summer science program for 50 seventh- and eighth-grade students in Onondaga County schools. Created in cooperation with Syracuse University, Science Horizons encourages student interest in science and technology through exposure at an early age to a variety of scientific disciplines.  The program is presented and fully funded by the Syracuse Divisions of Bristol-Myers Squibb Company. |
| **PROGRAM HOST** | Syracuse University and the State University of New York College of Environmental Science and Forestry (SUNY ESF). |
| **PROGRAM PARTICIPANTS** | Fifty 7th- and 8th-grade students from public and private middle schools throughout Onondaga County.  Students have been nominated to attend by their middle school; selection was based on a demonstrated interest in science, evidence of creativity, proven problem-solving ability, a high degree of self-motivation, and academic achievement. |
| **PROGRAM STAFF** | The program is directed by Gloria Mabie, a science resource teacher in the Fayetteville-Manlius School District.  Staff includes area master science teachers, Syracuse University students in science and peer mentors from area schools.  Faculty from Syracuse University and SUNY ESF also will serve as resource people. |
| **PROGRAM DATES** | June 28 - July 2, 1993 8:30 a.m. - 5:00 p.m. daily |

-more-

 Bristol-Myers Squibb Company

**PROGRAM**
**ACTIVITIES**

o Presentations and discussions on science and technology topics
o Hands-on activities using problem-solving techniques
o Field trips within the campuses and the community, including the
Bristol-Myers Squibb Syracuse Divisions facility

# ## #

209

Exhibit 5-3d    Media Alert    (Courtesy Bristol-Myers Squibb Company)

PROJECT
**2043**
SCIENCE AT WORK
50 YEARS FORWARD

FOR IMMEDIATE RELEASE
OCTOBER 8, 1993

FOR MORE INFORMATION CONTACT:
CHARLES BORGOGNONI
ASSOCIATE DIRECTOR -
PUBLIC AFFAIRS
315/432-2404

**MEDIA ALERT**

P.O. Box 4755          **Bristol-Myers Squibb Holds**
Syracuse, NY 13221-4755   **Tours for Invited Guests**

EVENT:          Bristol-Myers Squibb, as part of its 50th anniversary celebration in
                Syracuse, will host site tours of its 65 acre Thompson Road campus
                for invited guests.  Community leaders, elected officials and
                neighbors have been asked to attend.

DATE:           October 9, 1993

TIME:           9 a.m. to 10:00 a.m. for media availabilities

PLACE:          Bristol-Myers Squibb
                Use entrance on Burnet Avenue near Thompson Road.
                After parking, report to the registration tent.

PEOPLE:         Tibor Racz
                Vice President, North American Operations
                and Biotechnology Development

 Bristol-Myers Squibb Company

| Exhibit 5-3e | Media Alert (Courtesy Bristol-Myers Squibb Company) |

**PROJECT**

**2043**
SCIENCE AT WORK
50 YEARS FORWARD

**FOR IMMEDIATE RELEASE:**
November 3, 1993

**FOR MORE INFORMATION:**
Greg Loh/Michael Maurer
Eric Mower and Associates
Public Relations Services
315/466-1000

**MEDIA ALERT**

**Bristol-Myers Squibb Syracuse Divisions**
**Celebrate 50th Anniversary at OnCenter**

P.O. Box 4755
Syracuse, NY 13221-4755

WHAT:    Nearly 1,200 employees, retirees and friends of Bristol-Myers
Squibb will gather at the OnCenter to celebrate the 50th anniversary
of the company's Syracuse Divisions. The luncheon is the crescendo
of a year-long anniversary celebration to commemorate the
company's half century in Central New York — from the first
breakthroughs in the production of penicillin to today's world class
research into anti-cancer treatments.

The program will include historical reflections by two leaders in the
growth of the Syracuse Divisions and a special presentation from
the Metropolitan Development Association recognizing Bristol-
Myers Squibb and its employees.

WHEN:    Thursday, November 4, 1993
Noon

WHERE:   OnCenter, Exhibit Hall A

WHO:     Tibor Racz, Vice President
North American Operations & Biotechnology Development
Bio/Chem Division

Julius Pericola, Retired President
Bristol Laboratories

Dr. Amel Menotti, Retired Vice President of Scientific Affairs
Bristol Laboratories

H. Douglas Barclay, President
Metropolitan Development Association

 Bristol-Myers Squibb Company

211

Capital Fundraising Campaign

MAKE THE MOST
OF OUR DISCOVERY

HOLD FOR RELEASE:
December 2, 1993, 5:00 p.m.

FOR MORE INFORMATION:
Stephen Karon, Executive Director,
Museum of Science & Technology
315/425-9068
-or-
Charles A. Borgognoni
Associate Director, Public Affairs
Bristol-Myers Squibb Co.
315/432-2404

### BRISTOL-MYERS SQUIBB GRANTS $700,000 TO MOST FOR BRISTOL OMNITHEATER

**Metropolitan Development Foundation
Transfers Ownership of Jefferson Street
Armory to the MOST**

SYRACUSE, NY -- Bristol-Myers Squibb Company, Syracuse, today announced a $700,000
grant to the Milton J. Rubenstein Museum of Science & Technology (MOST). The
contribution will support the construction of the Bristol Omnitheater at the MOST. The
grant was announced following the transfer of ownership of the Jefferson Street Armory
from the Metropolitan Development Foundation (MDF) to the MOST.

The 225-seat Bristol Omnitheater is a state-of-the-art, giant dome screen theater that
wraps the audience in images and sounds of unsurpassed size and impact. The theater, to
be located in the former Armory's drill hall, will show educational and entertainment films.
The Bristol Omnitheater is the first of its kind in New York state and one of only 16
nationally, and is targeted to open in spring of 1995.

-more-

Campaign Office
Post Office Box 1055
Syracuse, New York 13201-1055
315/422-3461
FAX: 315/472-4486

Bristol-Myers Squibb's senior executive in Syracuse, Tibor A. Racz, vice president, North America Operations and Biotechnology Development, Bio/Chem Division, presented the grant to the MOST Foundation and Board of Directors at a ceremony held at the MOST.

"Bristol-Myers Squibb presents the Bristol Omnitheater in appreciation of the community's support the Company has received during the last 50 years," said Racz. "Today we look to the future, and celebrate a theater and a museum that we hope will encourage the pursuit of science and technology for generations to come."

The Metropolitan Development Foundation gained ownership of the Jefferson Street Armory after negotiation and planning with county, state and federal officials in order to transfer title to the MOST. "The MDF's vision and perseverance has provided the MOST with a facility that will house the Bristol Omnitheater and support the museum's growth," said Thomas I. Paganelli, chairman, MOST Foundation Board.

Presiding over the MDF transfer of the Armory to the MOST was Metropolitan Development Association President H. Douglas Barclay. "The support of former New York state Sen. Tarky J. Lombardi, Jr. and former Assemblyman Melvin N. Zimmer were key to today's event," said Barclay. They had introduced legislation that provided for the Armory's transfer of ownership from the New York State Division of Military and Naval Affairs to the MDF. Barclay added, "U.S. Sens. Daniel Patrick Moynihan (D-N.Y.) and Alfonse D'Amato (R-N.Y.), and U.S. Rep. Jim Walsh (R-N.Y.) also backed legislation that provided for a new National Guard facility on Molloy Road."

-more-

BRISTOL OMNITHEATER/page 3 of 3


The naming of the Bristol Omnitheater is the largest corporate contribution to the Central New York community since the Carrier Corporation named the Carrier Dome. "Bristol-Myers Squibb's gift brings the MOST closer to reaching its $8.1 million goal to fund the completion of the MOST," said Edward S. Green, general chairman, MOST Capital Campaign. "When complete, the MOST will be one of the Northeast's premier centers for science education, scientific research and applied technology."


# ## #

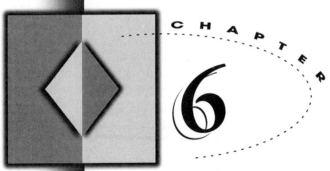

# 6

# Public Affairs and Government Relations

IN THE LAST 10 OR 15 YEARS MANY U.S. CORPORATIONS have subsumed what was formerly known as government relations within the broader enterprise now called public affairs. To add further semantic confusion, the U.S. government in the early 1980s decreed that the term *public affairs* would replace *public information* in all its departments and agencies.

Our principal concern here will be with how the enactment of legislation is influenced. This process includes the creation of political coalitions, direct and indirect lobbying, political action and political education activities, communication on political issues, and political support activities.

# RESEARCH

The research process of public affairs includes investigation of the practitioner's client or organization, the opportunity or problem that accounts for the need for communication—including the important area of issues management—and the audiences to be targeted for public affairs programs.

## Client Research

Client research for public affairs is similar to that for other forms of public relations. Background information about the client or organization should be obtained, including its personnel, financial status, and reputation, especially with government and community audiences. The practitioner should pay particular attention to past and present relations with the government and the community, along with any particular client strengths or weaknesses in these areas. Finally, the practitioner should catalog all opportunities for profitable communication with government or community audiences.

## Opportunity or Problem Research

In public affairs programs, the process of issues management can make assessment of the client's opportunity or problem much easier. *Issues management* consists of listing and giving priority to all issues of interest to the client and then determining options and strategies for dealing with them. This process includes assessing political risks and monitoring social and political developments of concern to the client at the local, state, national, and international levels. An examination of each of these areas on a priority basis is a useful means of targeting the client's public affairs program.

## Audience Research

The final aspect of research for public affairs consists of identifying target audiences, the necessary data regarding each one, and the methods of research necessary to obtain this information.

Public affairs programs target three audiences: community publics, government, and ancillary publics—this last group consisting of client allies, constituents of legislators, and media that reach both of them. Community publics were examined in the preceding chapter (see Exhibit 5-a). Government publics can be considered at the federal, state, county, or city level; they and the ancillary publics are listed in Exhibit 6-a.

Data necessary for understanding members of the legislative branches of government include officials' voting records on issues of concern to the client; their general attitudes or past and present reactions to the client; the size, location, and general demographics of their

| Exhibit 6-a | Government and Ancillary Publics |

## Government Publics

Federal
  Legislative branch
    Representatives, staff, committee personnel
    Senators, staff, committee personnel
  Executive branch
    President
    White House staff, advisers, committees
    Cabinet officers, departments, agencies, commissions
State
  Legislative branch
    Representatives, delegates, staff, committee personnel
    Senators, staff, committee personnel
  Executive branch
    Governor
    Governor's staff, advisers, committees
    Cabinet officers, departments, agencies, commissions
County
  County executive
  Other county officials, commissioners, departments
City
  Mayor or city manager
  City council
  Other city officials, commissions, departments

## Ancillary Publics

Allies
Constituents of legislators
Media
  Mass media
  Specialized media
    Trade
    Allied organizations' publications
  Constituent media

voting constituencies; their committee assignments; and their general interests and areas of expertise. Government officials in the executive branch may or may not hold elective office; this is their single most important characteristic. Beyond that, the nature and authority of the offices they hold, along with as much background about them as possible, should prove helpful. For officials in both legislative and executive positions, of course, the highest priority information about them is their degree of involvement with each issue or piece of legislation affecting the client, along with their stand and how they are expected to vote.

Methods of gathering information about government officials are usually nonquantitative. Voting records or accomplishments are public knowledge and easily accessible. Beyond that, conducting surveys among officials is usually not feasible. Thus, the practitioner must rely on other sources of information, such as conversations with staff people, the officials' past behavior, and their public statements regarding issues of concern to the client.

Research on the ancillary publics listed in Exhibit 6-a is also of considerable value. Allies of the client must be identified and cultivated with the goal of building a coalition. The home districts, communities, and constituents of legislators must also be identified and studied. Finally, mass and specialized media for reaching constituents and client allies should be identified, and media contacts lists should be prepared, as discussed in Chapter 3.

# OBJECTIVES

As in other forms of public relations, objectives for public affairs programs should be specific and quantitative.

## Impact Objectives

A sampling of impact objectives for public affairs includes such statements as:

1. To increase knowledge of the client's activities and field of operations among legislators (by 50 percent during the current year)
2. To create or enhance favorable attitudes toward the client among officials (by 30 percent before the February vote)
3. To influence a favorable vote on a bill (by 30 members of the House of Representatives during the current session)

## Output Objectives

Output objectives represent the effort of the practitioner without reference to potential audience impact. Such objectives might use such statements as:

1. To make oral presentations to 30 lawmakers
2. To distribute printed information to 45 lawmakers

# PROGRAMMING

Public affairs programming includes the same four planning and execution elements used in other forms of public relations: (1) theme and messages, (2) action or special event(s), (3) uncontrolled and controlled media, and (4) principles of effective communication.

## Theme and Messages

Always be aware that government audiences may be the most knowledgeable and sophisticated of all audiences for public relations communication. For this reason, the use of catchy themes or slogans may not be helpful; at times they can even be counterproductive. When addressing public affairs programming to ancillary audiences, however, more traditional use of themes or slogans may be appropriate. Messages, of course, should be carefully coordinated with the program objectives and actions or special events.

## Action or Special Event(s)

Public affairs programming, like other forms of public relations, is structured around actions and special events. The practitioner should review the types found in Exhibit 2-c.

The actions unique to public affairs programming are:

1. Fact finding
2. Coalition building
3. Direct lobbying
4. Grassroots activities (indirect lobbying)
5. Political action committees
6. Political education activities
7. Communications on political issues
8. Political support activities

**Fact Finding.**   Information gathering is an important aspect of public affairs. It includes attendance at openly conducted hearings, generally scheduled by both the legislative and executive branches of government when considering legislation or regulations. This monitoring function is indispensable for all public affairs programs.

In addition to monitoring hearings, fact finding often includes exchanging information with government officials, representatives of trade associations or interest groups, and other sources of reliable data. Fact finding may also include entertainment, since the relaxed atmosphere of most social gatherings can be conducive to exchanging information.

A final aspect of fact finding is the reporting of data and findings to the client, along with recommendations for appropriate responses.

**Coalition Building.** It is useful to organize groups or individuals with a common interest in the passage or defeat of legislation or regulations. Such coalitions can be much more effective in attaining goals than groups or individuals working alone. Coalitions can pool such resources as staff time, legal help, and printing and mailing costs. Working together, they can set priorities and devise operational strategies more effectively. In brief, the building of coalitions is one of the most important and effective tactics in public affairs.

**Direct Lobbying.** The two "core" activities of public affairs are direct and indirect lobbying. In direct lobbying, the practitioner contacts legislators or officials who can influence the passage or defeat of a bill or proposed regulation. It is an overt advocacy process, although it takes the sometimes subtle forms of information exchange and hospitality.

*Information exchange* includes providing the lawmaker or official with data about the client's field of interest and the effect the proposed legislation or regulation would have on this field. The practitioner, or lobbyist, usually makes an authoritative oral presentation, including the publicity potential for the legislator or official and the potential interest or impact of the proposals on constituents. These two aspects—*publicity value* and *constituent interest*—strike the most responsive chords in the ears of legislators or officials. They should always be central to a public affairs presentation. In addition to presentations, the practitioner usually offers the official a sample draft of the proposed legislation or regulation that incorporates the views of the client. Finally, information exchange may include providing authoritative testimony or offering witnesses for the hearings that are usually held in conjunction with proposed legislation or regulations. The practitioner often writes the testimony that is usually given by the client or the chief executive officer of the client's organization.

The second form of direct lobbying is still more subtle than information exchange. It involves offering *hospitality* to the legislator or agency official. The days of mink coats, yachting trips, weekends in hunting lodges, and the like have passed. Legislators and agency officials are now afraid of the ubiquitous investigative journalist, constantly in search of wrongdoing in high places. Nonetheless, hospitality still plays an important role in public affairs, or, more particularly, in lobbying. Lawmakers and agency officials often accept invitations to social functions sponsored by influential associations or corporations. These social gatherings provide a relaxed and conducive atmosphere for the subtle conduct of the business of public affairs.

A more recent and widespread variety of hospitality has turned the tables. Now, more often than not, the legislator provides the hospitality in the form of thousand-dollar-a-plate breakfasts, lunches, dinners, or other special events at which the corporation, association, or union representatives pay or make large contributions to attend, and thus gain access to the lawmaker.

Access is a major goal of all lobbying, and to an increasing degree, hospitality events—usually linked to fund-raising for the legislator—have become the most used avenue for reaching this goal.

**Grassroots Activities.** Indirect lobbying, or grassroots activities, is the second of the two core aspects of public affairs. This form of indirect lobbying involves mobilizing support for or opposition to proposed legislation or regulations at the state or local level, especially in the home districts of elected legislators. In the case of government departments or agencies, this grassroots level may be the location where a large agency is considering constructing or closing an installation that will profoundly affect the local economy.

Grassroots activities include working with national, state, or local mass media; the use of interpersonal communication; and the orchestration of campaigns to bring constituent pressure on legislators or officials.

The grassroots use of the mass media includes publicizing the client's position in national, state, or local media, demonstrating that this position will be beneficial to the media audience. This action is usually performed in cases where an elected official is in opposition to the client's position or is uncommitted. The practitioner, on behalf of the client, will use all feasible forms of media, including paid advertising, to generate news coverage about the situation. If the legislator has taken a stand contrary to that of the client's, the media messages will call attention to that, to voting records, and to the harm such a position will bring to the constituency. Care must be taken not to engage in overkill in this endeavor. In some cases, besieged legislators have also used the media, successfully portraying themselves as the victims of "fat-cat lobbyists."

A second effective type of grassroots activity is the use of various forms of interpersonal communication at the national, state, or local level. This includes targeting key groups of opinion leaders in the home districts of legislators and getting expert and highly credible representatives of the client's viewpoint invited to their meetings, conferences, or conventions as guest speakers.

In addition to addressing important grassroots audiences, the client can meet with key executives at breakfast, with editorial staffs of newspapers, or with small groups of community leaders. Dyadic interactions may include interviews and meetings with key public officials, executives, and/or union leaders.

Interpersonal communication, then, in the form of speeches, small group meetings, or dyadic interactions can be a highly useful form of grassroots activity.

Finally, grassroots activities culminate in the orchestration of campaigns at the national, state, or local level designed to bring pressure from constituents directly on legislators or officials. These campaigns can be orchestrated by small or large membership groups, associations, or other affected groups. They may take the traditional form of organized letter writing to a legislator from home district constituents; or they may use more contemporary forms, such as e-mail, faxing, or the formation of "telephone trees." The "telephone tree" consists of groups of constituents who each may call five to ten friends, who in turn each call five to ten more friends, and so on, all of whom then call or otherwise communicate with the office of the lawmaker with a common request or purpose.

The National Rifle Association is a membership group that uses all of these forms of constituent communication effectively to influence the course of national legislation. The NRA boasts the ability to mobilize its membership within 24 hours to flood Congress with enough constituent communication to shape the course of gun legislation.

Of the two public affairs core methods, grassroots activities usually prove more effective. These actions—working with mass media, interpersonal communication, and constituent communication campaigns—can provide legislators and other officials with unmistakable evidence regarding the will of the electorate.

**Political Action Committees.**  Political action committees (PACs) are an outgrowth of the reform in federal election campaign practices that followed the Watergate scandal. A PAC is a group established for the purpose of contributing an organization's money toward the election of political candidates. The Federal Election Commission permits PACs to contribute a maximum of $5,000 per candidate per election. Thus, PACs may contribute a total of $10,000 to a candidate who is in both a primary contest and the general election.

Since their inception in the mid-1970s, PACs have enjoyed phenomenal growth. Each year PACs provide funds to several thousand candidates for federal office. Such money may be solicited (but not coerced) from an organization's employees. Large groups, such as the banking and finance industry, labor unions, and the insurance industry, have the resources of hundreds of PACs at their disposal. Of course,

PAC money can be used collectively for candidates who support legislation favorable to an entire industry.

The use of such funds to support the campaigns of elected officials guarantees access to those officials. Thus, PACs have become a significant force in public affairs.

**Political Education Activities.**  During the past 20 years, corporations have increasingly attempted to politicize their employees. They issue newsletters on the major political issues confronting given industries along with the company's positions on these issues. Employees are instructed in the methods of grassroots lobbying: writing letters to legislators, taking action through membership groups, or visiting legislators in their home district offices. Moreover, some large organizations provide their employees with political education seminars. Elected officials and candidates are invited to corporate headquarters, where they make presentations and meet groups of employees. In return, the officials are often given honoraria, usually in accordance with legally allowable limitations. Political education activities, then, play an increasingly important role in the conduct of public affairs programs.

**Communications on Political Issues.**  Corporations communicate on political issues chiefly through advocacy advertising and targeted communications, such as direct mail to community leaders or special audiences.

Advocacy advertising has become increasingly popular since the early 1970s, when Herbert Schmertz, vice president for public affairs of Mobil, decided that major media outlets seemed interested only in condemning large oil companies for their alleged role in the creation of the gasoline shortages of the day. Schmertz abandoned the use of news releases and other uncontrolled media to give the oil companies' side of the controversy. Instead he began to buy advocacy advertising space in the nation's most prestigious newspapers and later bought time on cooperative broadcast networks. Schmertz's success in calling attention to his corporation's political views gave rise to a boom in the corporate use of advocacy advertising. Today it is impossible to read the editorial section of the Sunday edition of a major metropolitan newspaper without encountering myriad advocacy ads. Their proliferation has probably diminished their effectiveness, but they remain a major vehicle for corporate communication on political issues.

Political communications can also be aimed at community leaders or occupational groups. Professors of communication, for example, are frequently the recipients of slick reprints of speeches by the chief executive officers of television networks and other corporations. These reprints are only one of many forms of mailings to community leaders and members of various professions.

**Political Support Activities.** A final public affairs action is the support a corporation, association, or other organization offers an incumbent legislator or a candidate. Some organizations offer free media training, with expert consultants hired for the occasion. Guidance in effective public speaking, group communication management techniques, and other interpersonal communication skills are also offered. Some organizations provide volunteers to work on political campaigns. Additionally, political support can be offered in the form of expertise and other services needed for orchestrating election campaign events such as fund-raisers and testimonial dinners. Donations of facilities, recruiting celebrities to appear at the events, and any number of other services can be offered.

Like other forms of public affairs activities, political support can assure access to the officeholder at a later time.

Another form of political support called "soft money" has become the hottest—and most controversial—form of lobbying in the 1990s. Corporations and individuals are allowed to give unlimited amounts of money to national political parties for voter registration, television advertising, get-out-the-vote campaigns, and other party activities. This unlimited "soft money" can be contributed to support the party, but not specific candidates. Contributions to candidates for federal office are strictly limited by the Federal Election Committee. However, with increasingly close relationships between candidates, especially incumbents, and their political parties, the now commonplace multi-million-dollar contributions of "soft money" to political parties have become the most certain of all paths to officeholder access.

## Uncontrolled and Controlled Media

The practitioner's communication with public officials must largely be direct and interpersonal. The lobbyist or practitioner of public affairs uses uncontrolled media at the grassroots level. However, all forms of controlled media can be used both in direct contact with lawmakers and in grassroots communication with constituents. In general, then, the uniqueness of public affairs communication lies in the interaction that occurs directly with lawmakers and officials. To be effective, it should emphasize interpersonal, preferably one-on-one, communication.

## Effective Communications

The communication flow in public affairs is best described as triangular (see Exhibit 6-b). The flow is targeted ultimately at lawmakers, in the legislative branch, or at regulation-makers, in the executive branch. Thus, communication is generally initiated from the private sector and flows appropriately toward those two targets. In many cases, however, communication is initiated in the executive branch. Presidents,

| Exhibit 6-b | A Public Affairs Communication Model |
|---|---|

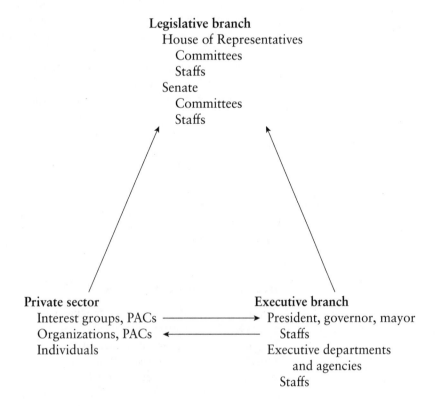

**Legislative branch**
House of Representatives
Committees
Staffs
Senate
Committees
Staffs

**Private sector**
Interest groups, PACs
Organizations, PACs
Individuals

**Executive branch**
President, governor, mayor
Staffs
Executive departments
and agencies
Staffs

governors, and mayors may lobby their respective legislative branches for the passage or defeat of a law. Sometimes officials in the executive branch lobby a particular audience in the private sector to bring pressure on the legislative branch. Legislators often refer to this as "going over their heads to the people." Some U.S. presidents have been particularly fond of this form of lobbying.

The nine principles of effective communication discussed in Chapter 2 all apply in public affairs. Of special concern, however, is *selective exposure*. Public affairs, more than other forms of public relations, deals with legislation and regulations that are controversial. Therefore, it is important that the practitioner categorize the targeted receivers based on their agreement or disagreement with the public affairs messages. As suggested in Chapter 2, the terms that coincide with the Likert scale can be useful in this process. Thus, targeted legislators or other officials should be rated as "positives," "somewhat positives," "undecideds," "somewhat negatives," or "negatives." The selective exposure principle is applicable in this situation. The practitioner should thus begin persuasive efforts with the positives. Next, to be targeted are the somewhat positives, then the undecideds, and last, if at all, the somewhat negatives. The pure negatives have hardened attitudes against the practitioner's cause and should not be targeted for communication. To communicate with those strongly opposed to the message is usually counterproductive; it simply makes them more determined and sometimes more active in their opposition.

Thus, the selective exposure principle of effective communication bears reiteration because of its special significance in public affairs. All other principles of effective communication should also be observed. Each one can contribute to the success of public affairs programs.

# EVALUATION

In public affairs, the measurement of impact and output objectives is somewhat different from the general methods of assessment presented in Chapter 2.

## Evaluating Impact Objectives

There are two differences in the measurement of impact objectives for public affairs. First, message exposure, message comprehension, and message retention are not measured in the same way. The primary target audiences for public affairs are legislators and officials. The media, however, are used essentially to reach the *constituents* of these public officials. And though the officials themselves are usually media sensitive, message exposure in public affairs usually refers to *constituent* exposure.

The second difference in the measurement of impact objectives is that surveys or other quantitative methods of research cannot be used with the primary target audiences because legislators and officials will not usually take the time to respond to such PR surveys. Thus, nonquantitative measurements of message exposure and message retention are used in assessing the results of informational objectives.

Message comprehension, of course, can be measured, as usual, by the application of readability formulas. This will give the practitioner an indication of the *potential* for comprehension, not actual audience comprehension, which can be measured using nonquantitative research methods.

These same generalizations are applicable to attitude and behavioral objectives. Surveys among the primary audience are generally impossible, so the practitioner must rely on the nonquantitative research methods discussed earlier in this chapter—voting records or accomplishments, conversations, use of the practitioner's materials, and public statements by the targeted legislators or officials. At the grassroots level, of course, surveys are useful and should be employed to evaluate the impact objectives.

### Evaluating Output Objectives

The practitioner needs to evaluate both forms of public affairs objectives. Output objectives can be measured through counting presentations and materials and through making qualitative value judgments. This is especially important in public affairs since surveys are impractical with the primary audiences. Evaluation of public affairs, then, ultimately focuses on observing the voting behavior or actions of legislators and other public officials. The practitioners in this chapter's cases accomplished all of their stated objectives remarkably well. In addition to informing their various targeted audiences, they also met their legislative or regulatory goals.

## SUMMARY

Research for public affairs concentrates on problem assessment through issues management and on identifying and understanding target audiences. Audiences are usually in the legislative or executive branch of government, at various levels. Information about these officials consists of voting records, accomplishments, and public stands on issues.

Impact and output objectives are both useful in public affairs. Impact objectives consist of providing the target audience with information or influencing its attitudes or behavior, in this case, voting behavior. Output objectives catalog the practitioner's communication efforts without reference to the desired impact.

The most essential activities in public affairs programming are fact finding, coalition building, direct lobbying, grassroots (indirect) lobbying, the use of political action committees, political education, communications on political issues, and political support activities. Of special significance in lobbying is the principle of selective exposure. Lawmakers to be lobbied should be categorized as "positives," "somewhat positives," "undecideds," "somewhat negatives," or "negatives." The positives through the undecideds should be targeted for lobbying; the somewhat negatives should be targeted with caution, and the negatives, not at all.

Evaluation is not the same for public affairs as for other forms of public relations. Media exposure or placement does not ensure contact with legislators, and legislators and officials are often unresponsive to PR surveys. Nonquantitative measurements of impact objectives are thus more useful. Output objectives, of course, are measured by the same means as usual—observation and quantification. The ultimate means of evaluation in public affairs, however, is the voting behavior of the target audience.

# READINGS ON PUBLIC AFFAIRS

Altschull, J. Herbert. *Agents of Power: The Role of the News Media in Public Affairs.* New York: Longman, 1984.

Bernays, E. L. "Operatives and Lobbyists vs. PR Professionals." *Public Relations Quarterly* (Summer 1985): 27ff.

Berry, J. M. *The Interest Group Society.* Boston: Little, Brown, 1985.

Chase, Howard. *Issues Management: Origins of the Future.* Stamford, CT: Issues Action Publications, 1984.

Clark, Joe. "Business-Government Relations: Opening the Systems." *Business Quarterly* (Summer 1985): 82ff.

Daly, James. "TRW Goes to Washington." *Forbes* (June 6, 1994): 127.

Dennis, Lloyd B. *Practical Public Affairs in an Era of Change.* Lanham, MD: University Press of America, 1995.

Gabriel, Edward M. "The Changing Face of Public Affairs in Washington." *Public Relations Quarterly* 37 (Winter 1992): 24ff.

Grefe, Edward A., and Martin Linsky. *The New Corporate Activism: Harnessing the Power of Grassroots Tactics for Your Organization.* Boston: Harvard Business School Press, 1994.

Gollner, Andrew. *Social Change and Corporate Strategy: The Expanding Role of Public Affairs.* Stamford, CT: Issues Action Publications, 1984.

Heath, Robert L., and Richard A. Nelson. *Issues Management—Corporate Policymaking in an Information Society.* Beverly Hills: Russell Sage Foundation, 1986.

"Issues Management in Public Relations" (special issue). *Public Relations Review* 16 (Spring 1990).

Koch, William J. "Public Affairs and Government: A New Generation Takes Charge." *Public Relations Journal* 49 (January 1993): 22.

Lammers, Nancy, ed. *The Washington Lobby.* Washington, DC: Congressional Quarterly (annual publication).

Mack, Charles S. *Lobbying and Government Relations.* Westport, CT: Quorum Books, 1990.

Masterson, John. "Looming Legislative Shake Up to Alter Public Affairs Practice." *Public Relations Journal* 48 (June 1992): 12ff.

Pedersen, Wes. *Winning at the Grassroots: How to Succeed in the Legislative Arena by Mobilizing Employees and Other Allies.* Washington, DC: Public Affairs Council, 1989.

Schafer, Peter. *Adding Value to the Public Affairs Function: Using Quality to Improve Performance.* Washington, DC: Public Affairs Council, 1994.

Shell, Adam, ed. "Winning in Washington Takes Luck as Well as Skill." *Public Relations Journal* 50 (February 1994): 6ff.

Tate, Sheila. "Prescriptions to Avoid Disaster in Washington." *Public Relations Quarterly* 37 (Spring 1992): 24ff.

Trento, Susan. *Power House: Robert Keith Gray and the Selling of Access and Influence in Washington.* New York: St. Martins Press, 1992.

Wise, Jim. "Tracking Legislation." *Public Relations Journal* 45 (September 1989): 43–44.

Wittenberg, Ernest, and Elizabeth Wittenberg. *How to Win in Washington: Very Practical Advice about Lobbying, the Grassroots and the Media.* Williston, VT: Blackwell, 1994.

# Public Affairs
Cases

*The Ohio Library Council prepared an effective lobbying campaign to prevent the state legislature from reducing taxpayer support of the state's public libraries. Exhibit 6-1a is a news release indicating the need to preserve existing levels of state funding for public libraries. Exhibit 6-1b is a fact sheet about public funding for libraries. Exhibit 6-1c is a graph representing increasing use of public libraries in Ohio. Exhibit 6-1d is a representation of the loss to libraries in the proposed state budget.*

**CASE 6-1**

## Never Take Your Eye Off the Goal: How Grassroots Activism Preserved the Funding of Ohio's 250 Public Library Systems

Ohio Library Council, Columbus, Ohio, with Edward Howard & Co., Columbus and Akron, Ohio

In 1991, business was brisk at Ohio's 250 public library systems. Thanks to a state funding formula that in 1986 substantially improved library service statewide, Ohio had the *highest per capita circulation of any state*. Materials, technology, and programs were in demand at record-breaking levels. But something threatened to turn back the clock. . . .

State officials, grappling with an unshakable recession and a budget shortfall of $500 million, were scouring the budget for spending cuts to plug the gaping deficit. The typical Ohio library is supported almost exclusively by state income tax revenue—6.3 percent of which is earmarked by law for libraries. Libraries learned that a proposal to reduce the funding formula to 5.7 percent was in the works. To prevent a major and possibly permanent diversion of funding, libraries—which previously had not participated actively in the governmental/political process—had to change their ways and become aggressive participants.

The Ohio Library Council (OLC) is a 4,800-member organization representing Ohio's libraries, library trustees, and Friends of the Library. As a matter of survival, securing adequate funding in the next budget cycle and preserving the 6.3 percent funding formula on behalf of its members became OLC's number one priority. Never before had this organization mobilized its membership to protect what they saw as their

Courtesy Ohio Library Council

lifeblood. Beginning with a program to school its members in basic legislative lobbying, then in tried and true public relations techniques, the membership of the OLC took its case to Ohio communities and to the statehouse, succeeding in preserving the funding formula and thus their superior service to all Ohioans.

## Research

To formulate the OLC's public relations program, two primary forms of research were involved: (1) commissioned research and (2) survey research. The results of both helped to shape the public relations strategy and the program ultimately developed.

An increasingly vocal core group of OLC membership felt the organization was too staff-driven and wanted there to be more avenues for member involvement—essentially, a grassroots approach to solving its problems. To address these concerns, the OLC in 1991 commissioned the American Society of Association Executives (ASAE) to conduct an evaluation of its operations and management, with an emphasis on communications and public affairs. One major conclusion stood out—libraries' stellar reputation and intrinsic credibility alone were not sufficient to protect their interests. Tapping member resources more extensively and helping libraries build relationships that would sustain them in both the short and the long term was vital to success.

A survey was conducted of all 250 library system directors to learn of ways in which the 6.3 percent funding formula—which replaced another funding source that favored urban over rural counties—improved their ability to deliver services valued in the community. Virtually all responded with stories that revealed in human terms how libraries were changing lives.

Two respected state tax policy consultants were commissioned to provide a detailed analysis of library funding in the 1980s and 1990s. OLC expected to use the results of this to communicate clearly to legislators and other state budget officials how libraries had fared financially under the old funding system and under different economic conditions with the current system, as well as describe the escalating negative impact on libraries' growth of the proposed reduction.

## Planning

To reach the objective of protecting their primary funding source, the OLC had to reach three key audiences: (1) its own membership—which needed to become articulate and steadfast in delivering the message; (2) library patrons—who stood to gain or lose the most in terms of service; and (3) the legislature and other state budget officials—who would ultimately decide the fate of the library budget.

Edward Howard & Co., working with the OLC's ad hoc Select Committee on Funding, developed a strategy based on grassroots activism. OLC agreed with ASAE's finding that libraries needed to tap their own constituencies—library patrons, Friends, trustees, and staff—in reaching out to the legislative audience. Yet the local library community was not by its nature equipped to rally support from people they didn't know; nothing in their training had prepared them to do so. In preparation for the battle they knew was coming, the OLC arranged special training in the political process for its members to help them participate meaningfully in what promised to be a grueling budgetary debate.

A simple theme unique to libraries—that they provide service to all—was created to focus the elements of the public relations plan. This core message, *"6.3 Percent Public Library Funding—Working for All Ohioans!"* was woven (along with a graphic logo) through all external communication, from testimony and speeches to media interviews and outreach to patrons. OLC then provided its members a "grassroots action kit" designed to help libraries communicate to their patrons, their local media, and their legislators how vital the funding source was to maintaining service levels. Two kinds of information supported the message: (1) the impact in human terms and (2) the financial realities of the anticipated revenue loss.

The human angle was emphasized in all public communication, referring to the concrete examples that had been provided during the earlier research. This enabled each library to customize its speeches or news releases with local anecdotal information. The financial angle was developed via the commissioned analysis and would be merchandised in face-to-face interaction with legislators as well as become one component of a proactive media relations campaign targeting local reporters and statehouse correspondents.

## Execution

The campaign was 18 months in duration (January 1992 to July 1993), beginning with a series of six regional workshops developed and presented to the library community by Edward Howard & Co. Legislators and statehouse reporters were incorporated into the day-long sessions to help demystify how business is conducted at the statehouse and underscore the message that being proactive is vital to becoming an effective lobbying force. More than 350 members attended—one of the largest turnouts for training ever organized by the association—setting the stage for the expanded public relations effort to come. More than 60 attendees were trustees or Friends, an unprecedented number of non-library personnel participants for an event of this type.

- The 6.3 Percent Grassroots Action Kits, showing how the message could be woven into speeches, news releases, and other suggested local activities, were distributed in all 250 public library systems.

- More than 150,000 signatures were collected in three weeks during a "Libraries Work for Us" petition drive statewide; these were presented during testimony before a key legislative subcommittee.

- The compelling conclusions of the independent tax analysis were announced in a press conference held in the capital. Representatives from more than half of all library systems flocked to Columbus to attend the conference, which was also well-attended by statehouse-based correspondents. Afterwards OLC members met individually with their own legislators to explain the findings face to face and to outline the local impact.

- The annual Ohio Libraries' Legislative Day held shortly before the budget bill went into conference committee had an unprecedented attendance of 570 librarians, trustees, Friends, and legislators. A "Technology Showcase" displayed some of the computer data bases the 6.3 percent funding formula made possible.

- A new monthly newsletter, *Access,* and a new legislative update, *Impact,* provided regular updates to the membership and streamlined communications within the OLC's Legislative Network.

The total program budget was under $75,000 for professional service fees and out-of-pocket expenses.

## Evaluation

The program succeeded on all fronts; the grassroots strategy proved to be solid. A balanced state budget was passed by the legislature on June 30, 1993, but not on the backs of Ohio's libraries. The dreaded deep cuts were averted; in fact, the legislature approved a final budget for libraries that was nearly *$11 million more* than originally proposed. Equally important, the 6.3 percent funding formula was preserved in permanent law.

Record grassroots participation of members was achieved in all aspects of the program. Media coverage of the libraries' message and activities was widespread and thorough, a first for library issues. Library patrons throughout the state demonstrated their personal support for library services.

Benefits to the internal audiences are perhaps most important of all. Members learned that personal participation and building relationships are vital to their cause, not just in the short term of a budget process but for the long-term well-being of libraries. The invigorated membership is transforming the association into one well-prepared to stake its claim aggressively during the next budget debate; already they have formed a special task force to build on the experience from the last round. They also learned the critical necessity of effective communications, even for an institution with an intrinsically high level of respect and credibility. As a result, the OLC is pursuing an ongoing effort to inform key decision-makers about the important role of the library and to persuade those same audiences to support the library actively in difficult times. Best of all, libraries were able to keep their promise of high levels of service for all Ohioans.

Public Library Funding

Working
For All
Ohioans!

FOR IMMEDIATE RELEASE
March 3, 1993

STUDY SHOWS LIBRARY SERVICES THREATENED
BY PROPOSED CUT IN LIBRARY FUNDING FORMULA

COLUMBUS -- At a time when demands for library services are at an all-time high, the state's financial funding formula has not kept the commitment which was made to libraries and their patrons when it became effective in 1986. Even more alarming, that funding formula would be cut by almost 10% if the proposed state budget is enacted, reducing library funding by approximately $62.7 million in the next biennium.

Those conclusions are contained in a special report commissioned by the Ohio Library Council (OLC), representing Ohio's 250 public libraries, and released today. The analysis was prepared by Levin & Driscoll, a state tax policy consulting firm in Columbus.

"These numbers, when combined with data confirming that libraries have stretched their resources to the limit to serve unprecedented patron demands, clearly show that Ohio's position as a leader in providing library services to all residents is threatened," said Steven Hawk, Librarian-Director of the Akron-Summit County Public Library and chair of the OLC's Select Committee on Funding. "On behalf of its patrons, Ohio's library community is asking state government not to cut the funding formula which allows us to serve all Ohioans effectively and efficiently."

The Library and Local Government Support Fund (the Library Fund) was created by the state legislature in 1985 to replace the locally-based intangible personal property tax, which was the primary source of library funding. In its extensive review of the state tax structure, a special legislative committee recommended that the method of financing Ohio's system of public libraries be changed, but added this specific statement:

> "It is the explicit intention of the committee that the funds currently available to the counties for library funding not be reduced as a result of this change."

The formula established by the Ohio General Assembly in 1985 dedicated 6.3% of the state's personal income tax collections for libraries, creating both a more stable base and one which would allow libraries greater growth potential while reflecting the state's overall economic conditions. However, the Levin & Driscoll report reveals that the commitment has not been kept.

-more-

67 Jefferson Avenue
Columbus, Ohio 43215
614/221-9057
FAX 614/221-6234

The report details that in 1990, the prediction for the intangible tax was $268.1 million. By contrast, the Library Fund in that year actually produced just $262.7 million, or $5.4 million less than the intangible tax forecast. In 1992, the fund received almost the identical amount that the intangible tax had been forecast to produce for 1990.

One of the key benefits of the Library Fund is the process known as equalization, whereby poorer libraries in the state receive a more equitable distribution of the fund, enabling them to bring needed services to their patrons. The report documents that, when sufficient funds were available to enable equalization to occur, that part of the formula worked very well, dramatically narrowing the gap between the richest and poorest libraries and thus providing better library services throughout the state. However, since 1990, the fund has not had enough revenue to trigger the equalization component.

Another significant drain on library funding was the freeze which was put in place during the last budget debate as the state struggled to balance its books in the recession. The Levin & Driscoll report shows that $31 million will have been lost to libraries during this freeze, which expires June 30, 1993.

The effect of the freeze on libraries would be compounded by the permanent reduction of the funding formula from 6.3% to 5.7% of personal income tax collections, as contained in the budget proposal. The Levin & Driscoll report estimates a $30.3 million loss in Fiscal Year 1994 and a $32.4 million loss in Fiscal Year 1995 if the formula is changed.

Hawk noted that total library circulation has increased more than 52% since 1986, going from 85.6 million items checked out in that year to more than 130.2 million in 1992. "This level of demand by the public was the highest in the nation, showing that Ohioans want and value the services and materials we provide," Hawk said. Total staffing (full time equivalency) increased just over 25% during those years, rising from 5,870 in 1986 to 7,853 in 1992. On a per employee basis, library staff were checking out 14,582 items per year; in 1992, that figure had increased 13% to 16,580 items per year. Book costs during the period increased approximately 21%.

"Ohio's libraries are asking only that state government lives up to the commitment it made in designing this formula. Now is not the time to decrease a system of financing which, when it is allowed to function properly, does what it is supposed to do. Keeping the 6.3% will allow us to continue to work for all Ohioans," Hawk said.

### 

For more information, please contact:

Lynda Murray  
Ohio Library Council    -or-  
(614)221-9057

Wayne Hill  
Edward Howard & Co.  
(614)224-4600

Exhibit 6-1b | Funding Fact Sheet   (Courtesy Ohio Library Council)

Public Library Funding

Working For All Ohioans!

**Facts and Figures About
the Library and Local Government Support Fund**

### What is LLGSF?

▶ Provides Ohioans in communities throughout the state with greater access to the resources of public libraries.

▶ Designed so that all libraries can offer a broad range of books, other materials and services, whether the libraries are in big cities or small towns.

▶ Derived from portion of state budget which is the equivalent of 6.3 percent of the current year's state personal income tax.

▶ Has expanded total library funding to $268.4 million (1991).

▶ Replaces the intangibles tax, which, in most areas, was inadequate for library funding and repealed in 1986.

### Why is this fund the best approach?

▶ Generates more financial resources for public libraries and ensures that those resources will be distributed more evenly in both urban and rural communities.

▶ Gives libraries the ability to plan responsibly for and implement new programs and purchase new materials, including new technology and equipment, to serve all Ohioans better.

▶ Provides a stable funding base and the potential for all library budgets to grow as economic conditions in the state permit.

### What kinds of improvements have been made under LLGSF?

▶ 13 million more books purchased statewide

▶ 19.2 million more items circulated from 1989 to 1991

▶ Technology acquired to improve cataloguing and information retrieval

▶ Increased hours of service, branch development

▶ Summer reading programs, evening story hours

▶ Investment in better trained staff to serve patrons

▶ Literacy services for adults

67 Jefferson Avenue
Columbus, Ohio 43215
614/221-9057
FAX 614/221-6234

- Expanded handicap accessibility

- Better periodical selections, computerized indexing

- Funds for bookmobiles, outreach to the homebound, senior citizens and correctional institutions

- Improved video and audio collections

- Photocopy and fax machines for public use

*How exactly does this work?*

- Fund is divided in two segments: the base share and the growth/equalization portion.

- Base share calculated by taking the amount distributed to a given county the previous year and adding an inflation factor to that.

- Growth/equalization portion exists when fund grows at a rate greater than inflation and is larger than the base share; this amount is distributed to counties according to a population-based equalization formula.

*How has the current economy affected the state budget?*

- For an 18-month period that ends June 30, 1993, libraries are operating under an LLGSF freeze imposed by the state legislature in response to the state's economic difficulties.

- Made libraries' long-range funding picture less clear.

- Uncertainty forces libraries to make cuts and defer action on plans to deliver better services to all Ohioans.

*How has the current freeze affected Ohio's libraries?*

Depending on the library system, these impacts have been reported:

- Budget cuts for books and other materials

- Delaying critical equipment purchases

- Reduction of service hours

- Deferring building expansion plans

- Deferring repairs to buildings

- Inability to fill vacancies or hire staff to meet expanding service needs

Exhibit 6-1c

Library Circulation Graph  (Courtesy Ohio Library Council)

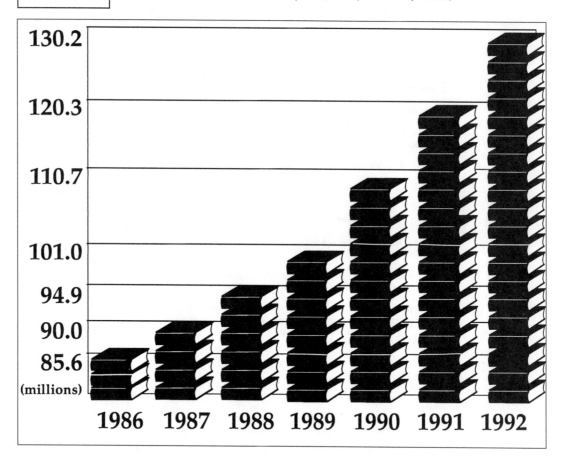

Exhibit 6-1d

Loss to Libraries in Proposed Budget  (Courtesy Ohio Library Council)

|          | 6.3%     | 5.7%     | Loss    |
|----------|----------|----------|---------|
| FY 1994  | $318.0   | $287.7   | $ 30.3  |
| FY 1995  | $340.6   | $308.2   | $ 32.4  |

*After a near loss of congressional funding, the Boeing Defense and Space Group waged a national awareness campaign to preserve its Space Station program. Exhibit 6-2a is an executive summary of arguments in support of NASA's International Space Station, along with other support materials used in the campaign.*

**CASE 6-2**

## Space Station: It's About Life on Earth, 1994 National Campaign

Boeing Defense & Space Group, Seattle, WA

### Summary

By the narrowest possible margin (216–215), the U.S. House of Representatives in the summer of 1993 barely averted a crippling blow aimed at one of the nation's most visible national treasures—the U.S. civil space program. By a single vote, an amendment that would have crippled space exploration by terminating funding for the International Space Station—centerpiece of NASA's near-term future in space—was defeated in a heart-stopping vote that flip-flopped until the last ballot was cast.

A year later, everything seemed to have changed. By overwhelming votes of 278–152 in the House and 64–36 in the Senate, continued funding for the Space Station was easily assured.

An aggressive national effort to forge public opinion and influence public policy toward the Space Station was a key factor in this dramatic turnaround. Newly appointed Space Station prime contractor Boeing Defense & Space Group had embarked on a national public relations campaign, focusing a well-developed arsenal of tools and tactics aimed at accomplishing three basic communication strategies:

1. *Bring the debate back to earth.* Deflect and avoid complex technical arguments, and make the Space Station an issue about life on earth.

2. Unify the vast—and formerly disparate—resources of the Space Station contractor community, and *begin speaking persuasively as a unified Space Station team.*

3. Tap into the vast wellspring of public support for the U.S. space program, and *mobilize public opinion to influence funding decisions.*

Courtesy Boeing Defense & Space Group

Only one measure of success would count: continued Space Station funding by the 1994 Congress. That success was achieved, and expectations delightfully exceeded, when commanding margins of approval were voted in both chambers.

## Research

The campaign plan was rooted in research on several important fronts. To validate the public relations team's assessment that techno-speak and multiple message confusion had polluted the communication environment, consultants Hill & Knowlton were retained to audit the 1993 message environment and make recommendations for 1994. To define the depth of public support for the program better and to understand which messages would best resonate with the public, the team turned to studies by Yankelovich & Partners and by the Bridgewater Group. Boeing lobbyists researched Space Station voting patterns in Congress, defining "swing districts" where grassroots efforts were most likely to bear fruit.

## Planning

Planning began in July 1993—before Boeing was even selected as the Space Station's new prime contractor. A mobilization plan detailing how Boeing would move quickly to take control of public relations for the industry team was reviewed with NASA and implemented immediately upon the August 1993 selection of Boeing to become the prime contractor. The public relations staff from major subcontractors McDonnell Douglas and Rockwell International were brought aboard the new Space Station PR team, joining with Boeing in planning and carrying out publicity, media relations, public appearances, advertising, and other tasks. For the first time, the communication efforts of the entire industry team were coordinated and centrally directed.

## Execution

The effort began with the establishment of a uniform set of Space Station messages, information tools, and communication tactics. While retaining clear control of the overall public relations effort, Boeing delegated the nationwide work load among the PR team members. Team leader Elliot Pulham (Boeing/Seattle) directed team activities and assumed responsibility for national news and media, policy, program issues, and outreach to the scientific community. Kari Thornton (Boeing/Houston) became responsible for program news and information, aerospace trade media, and outreach to congressional districts in the southwestern states. Jim Keller (Boeing/Huntsville) took on media responsibility related to Boeing manufacturing activities and outreach to congressional districts in the southeastern states. Anne Toulouse (McDonnell Douglas/Los Angeles) and Paul Sewell (Rockwell/Los Angeles) assumed media responsibility related to their manufacturing activities and outreach responsibility for congressional districts in California and key northeastern states. The effort was further broadened by providing public relations tool kits and training to dozens of smaller subcontractors distributed across the United States.

## Evaluation

The paramount measure of success was whether or not the 216–215 near-death vote of summer '93 was improved upon in the summer of '94. The astounding shift to a two-thirds majority of support in both houses of Congress assured continued funding and life for the Space Station program and proclaimed the Space Station 1994 national campaign a public relations success. Additionally, in-progress evaluation was provided by self-assessments during team meetings; management review periodically during the campaign; and peer review—the effort won numerous Public Relations Council of Alabama Medallion Awards and a Gold Award at the Worldfest/Charleston International Film Festival.

Exhibit 6-2a

# Executive Summary

## Science

▶ The purpose of the Space Station program is to establish an international orbiting laboratory for the advancement of a wide range of scientific and technical research.

▶ The benefits of Space Station research will improve the lives of a great portion of the world's population.

▶ The research to be performed on the Space Station cannot be accomplished on Earth.

▶ Hundreds of scientists throughout the world are waiting to use the unique capabilities for research offered by the Space Station.

## Life on Earth

▶ The secondary products or spinoffs that result from space projects have provided up to nine dollars to the U.S. economy for every dollar invested.

▶ Students from grade school to graduate school will be challenged by the frontiers the Space Station will open.

▶ The Space Station will have a stabilizing effect on aerospace jobs in a time when deep cuts are being made in defense and commercial sectors.

## Program Changes and Progress

▶ Changes have been made to the program which have resulted in considerable improvement in the management, engineering, and budgeting of the program.

▶ The International Space Station will have the capability to do more science, carry a larger crew, generate more electrical power for research, be maintained with less effort, and handle contingencies better than the previous design, and do it all for less cost-to-go.

## International Partnership

▶ International participation in the program builds bridges for peace and mutual prosperity.

▶ The addition of Russian technology to the Space Station increases scientific capability and flexibility while significantly reducing risk and cost.

## Affordability

▶ The Space Station has been reconfigured within Congressional budget limits designed to preserve other NASA priorities.

▶ The investment in space science through the Space Station is truly small when compared to the incalculable payoffs in health, ecology, technology, competitiveness, and world relations.

# I. International Space Station Science

## Humans and Space

▶ Space is an environment where humans learn to see their world and its mysteries in a completely new way.

▶ Scientific progress has been accelerated by 33 years of human space exploration.

▶ As important as our achievements in human space flight have been to date, we have barely dipped into what remains to be discovered.

▶ Currently, space scientists world-wide must compete and wait for the relatively few opportunities available to put their experiments on-orbit.

▶ Extended human space flight will allow scientists to conduct research more like they do on the ground. Modifying their experiments and taking advantage of unanticipated results, which have historically led to great scientific breakthroughs.

## U.S. Human Presence in Space

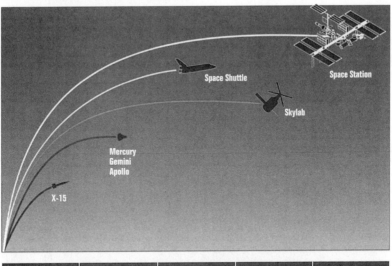

| Minutes | Days | Weeks | Months | Years |

Space Station will be the first permanent presence in space for the U.S.

4

# II. Life on Earth

## Products

▶ Beyond the immediate knowledge gained from space science, there has always been a synergistic effect with Earth technologies from which new and better products result.

▶ Even though Space Station science will be directed toward commercial applications, there will also be many spin-offs which will come about indirectly as a result of entrepreneurial efforts.

▶ Historically, the benefit of secondary applications of U.S. space technology has been to return up to nine dollars to the economy for every tax dollar spent.

## Education

▶ Hundreds of academic institutions throughout the U.S. have well-established ties with NASA which will allow them to participate in the Space Station program.

▶ Academic involvement will be encouraged through means such as the Graduate Student Researchers Program, as well as increasing the use of the Information Superhighway to share Space Station science results.

### "Why on Earth Do We Spend Tax Dollars on Space?"

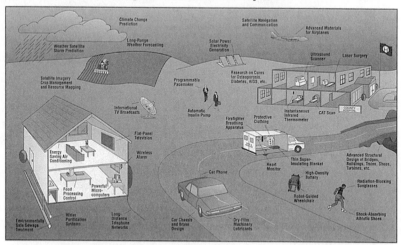

Each dollar invested in space programs yields up to nine dollars in new products, technologies, and processes on Earth.

18

- ▶ Space science is a catalyst for academic achievement as shown by the fact that enrollment trends of college students in advanced engineering and science programs track closely with the funding trends of the U.S. space program.

- ▶ Elementary and secondary school children are reached through programs like the Urban Community Enrichment Program and NASA Educational Workshops for Math, Science, and Technology Teachers.

- ▶ The excitement and wonder of the Space Station will encourage America's youth to be the next generation of technology leaders.

## Competitiveness

- ▶ Aerospace is the single strongest export sector in the U.S. economy.

- ▶ The U.S. is the current world leader in the design and manufacture of space hardware for research and commercial purposes, but several strong foreign interests are becoming very competitive.

- ▶ There is a strong correlation between the amount of non-defense research and development funding invested and the resulting trade balance of high-technology products.

**Positive Balance of Trade** U.S. Aerospace Sales

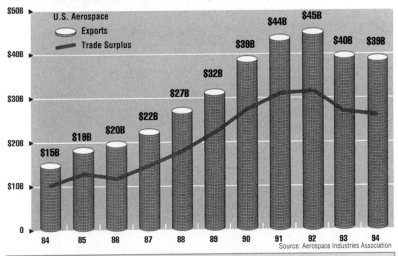

Source: Aerospace Industries Association

The large positive balance of trade provided by U.S. aerospace exports mitigates a $100 billion trade deficit for all manufactured goods.

19

Exhibit 6-2a
(*continued*)

## Arguments Supporting Space Station

(Courtesy Boeing Defense & Space Group)

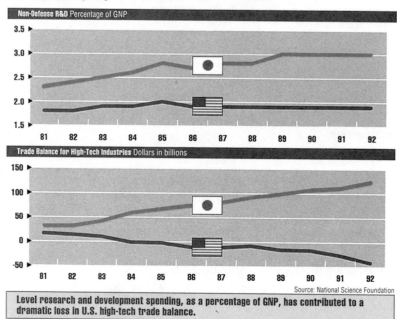

## R&D Spending Impact on International Trade

**Non-Defense R&D** Percentage of GNP

**Trade Balance for High-Tech Industries** Dollars in billions

Source: National Science Foundation

Level research and development spending, as a percentage of GNP, has contributed to a dramatic loss in U.S. high-tech trade balance.

## Employment

▶ The Space Station program has over 500 major suppliers in 39 states.

▶ There are 13,000 contractor and NASA employees working on the Space Station program and they in turn support about 32,000 secondary jobs nationwide.

▶ The total employment impact of the Space Station program includes contractor employees, NASA employees, and a share of Space Shuttle employees based on the number of assembly and utilization mission flights.

▶ Space Station employment helps maintain the important base of skilled and experienced aerospace designers, manufacturers, and administrators that is key to long-term U.S. competitiveness and vitality.

20

*When the U.S. Department of Agriculture (USDA) established new national guidelines for school meals, grains were initially omitted, despite grain foods having been an important and increased part of USDA's own pyramid of new dietary guidelines issued only three years earlier. With grain foods on the verge of being excluded from the school meal reform process, the Wheat Foods Council united the grain industry behind a public affairs program to turn the situation around. Exhibit 6-3a is a media alert on the revised school meal program. Exhibit 6-3b is a news release emphasizing the importance of grain foods in school lunches. Exhibit 6-3c is a news release explaining the success of the council's program, and Exhibit 6-3d is a fill-in-the-blank news release that can be used by school districts.*

**CASE 6-3**

## Balancing School Meals with Grains

Wheat Foods Council, Englewood, CO, with Fleishman-Hillard, Inc., Kansas City, MO

### Background

"We're deep-frying children's health," said then-USDA Secretary Mike Espy as he launched a food fight over the meals served to children at school. Armed with a new study revealing school lunches contained 38 percent fat—far higher than the 30 percent maximum recommended—the USDA set out to improve the 32 million meals dished up daily in 92,000 schools. Congress quickly followed suit, introducing legislation to police the USDA's meal-remodeling efforts. However, early scrutiny showed decision-makers were overlooking a crucial element in their recommendations. Along with nutrition advocacy groups, Congress and the USDA proposed boosting fruit and vegetable consumption as the *exclusive* means to balance meals. This shocked the nonprofit Wheat Foods Council. Just three years earlier, the USDA

Courtesy Wheat Foods Council

had issued new dietary guidelines suggesting that Americans base their lower-fat, high-carbohydrate diets on six to eleven daily servings of grain foods—up from four servings—while scrapping the "Four Food Groups" for a new Food Guide Pyramid. These scientifically based nutrition principles were left out of reform proposals for school lunches. In response, the Wheat Foods Council and Fleishman-Hillard began an opinion-leader educational program to move grain-based foods such as bread, cereal, and pasta to the center of the lunch tray.

## Research

The Wheat Foods Council set out to explore why rule-makers were overlooking grains.

### Issue Tracking

A media audit of school meal reform coverage found no mention of grains. Information checks with food and nutrition advocacy groups showed that grains simply were not addressed in early school meal reform recommendations. Measures by Congress to reform child nutrition programs made no reference to grains. USDA Assistant Secretary Ellen Haas's initial proposals contained no references to grains. Grains, it seemed, had become the forgotten food.

### Fact-finding Interviews

Interviews with key congressional committee staff, agency officials, and advocacy groups revealed that Washington leaders failed to recognize the role grains play in lowering fat intake; or how, by adding more grains to school meals, policy-makers could avoid the more draconian measures of attacking politically sensitive foods.

## Planning

With grain foods on the verge of being shut out of school meal reform, the Wheat Foods Council united its farmer leaders and grain industry officials behind a public affairs program to complement its larger nutrition education campaign.

### Goal

- To increase federal requirements for grain foods in school meal programs to help boost domestic demand for grain foods.

### Strategies

- Educate key decision-makers about the overlooked nutritional benefits of grains, positioning grain foods as the easy first step in balancing school meals because they are low-fat, nutritious, convenient, inexpensive, and popular.

- Advocate immediately updating school meal programs in accordance with the widely supported 1990 U.S. Dietary Guidelines and the 1992 Food Guide Pyramid, which position grains as the foundation for a healthy diet—a seemingly logical step ignored in initial government proposals.

- Build a broad base of health and nutrition opinion-leader support for the more-grain, less-fat connection to increase the chances that policy-makers would include more grains in school meals.

## Execution

The Wheat Foods Council launched an educational campaign that included:

- *Washington Briefings.* The Wheat Foods Council met with key officials involved in the school meal debate to walk through the rationale for a higher-grain, lower-fat diet. Briefings with more than 20 decision-makers opened the door for them to consider grains as a possible solution to cutting the fat in school meals.

- *VIP Roundtable on Grains.* To draw attention to the fact that Americans don't eat enough grain foods, the council invited respected officials from Congress, government agencies, academia, consumer media outlets, and trade associations to a day-long discussion of how to increase grain consumption. With the theme "From the Food Guide Pyramid to Reality: Grains and the Nutritional Needs of Americans in the 21st Century," the dialogue was summarized in a widely circulated report that helped the council garner a seat at the nutrition policy table.

- *White Paper Direct Mail.* To strengthen the case for increasing grains consumption, the Wheat Foods Council commissioned Tufts University's Dr. Jeanne Goldberg to draft a research summary entitled "Complex Carbohydrates, a Simple Way to Cut Fat." The white paper was mailed to 6,000 health and nutrition leaders, whose support could buttress positive changes in the school lunch and breakfast programs. It also was sent to health and nutrition editors with leading media.

- *Speaking Platforms.* The council provided keynote speakers at national conferences of both the American School Food Service Association, whose members must implement any changes made in the school meal program, and the Public Voice for Food and Health Policy, which led the charge for school meal reform. Remarks were publicized.

- *Legislative Input.* In addition to testifying at a USDA field hearing on school meal reform, the council issued written comments and rallied the grain foods industry to ensure that the grains message resonated during the comment period. The council also testified before the Senate Agriculture Committee on the importance of basing school meal requirements on USDA Dietary Guidelines and boosting grain consumption accordingly, with remarks carried on C-Span.

- *Media Relations.* To heighten awareness of the place of grains in a healthy diet, and specifically school meal reform, the council issued ten news releases and feature stories and made numerous individual calls alerting key trade and national consumer media to recent reform developments.

- *Gallup Survey.* To keep grains top-of-mind among nutrition policy-makers, the council released results of a 1995 Gallup survey on consumers' nutritional knowledge at a Washington luncheon involving 70 dignitaries, with guest remarks from Representative Pat Roberts of Kansas, whose Agriculture Committee oversees school meal programs. Dr. Marjorie Hogan, a spokesperson for the American Academy of Pediatrics, provided expert interpretation of the survey, which coincided with the release of the USDA's proposed school meal reform final rule.

## Evaluation

The council gained support from advocacy groups, trade associations, government agencies, and lawmakers, successfully increasing federal requirements for grain foods in school meal programs.

- The "Better Nutrition and Health for Children Act," signed into law by President Clinton November 2, 1994, requires the country's 92,000 school meal programs to meet federal nutrition guidelines reflected in the Food Guide Pyramid by the 1996–1997 school year. In addition to securing increased grain food requirements based on USDA Dietary Guidelines, the Wheat Foods Council was successful in incorporating specific language that references grains (where only fruits and vegetables were initially named) and that strongly endorses food pyramid–based nutrition education programs in schools.

- The USDA's proposed rule in the January 27, 1995, *Federal Register* calls for a significant increase in bread and grain foods requirements to reflect current dietary guidelines. The proposed rule increases the minimum recommended grains and breads servings in school meal patterns by 50 percent, from 8 to 12 servings for children in kindergarten through grade 6, and from 10 to 15 for children in grades 7 through 12, *and* positions grain foods as a low-fat source of calories to balance the loss of calories from fat.

- According to the USDA's Food and Nutrition Service's Regulatory Cost/Benefit Assessment model, the consumption of grain foods would increase nearly 80 percent as school officials achieve these nutrient goals without increasing budgets. For wheat growers, that means an increase of 15 million bushels of wheat, worth about $50 million annually. This reflects an approximately $350 million sales boost for grain food companies.

- Media coverage and reports by leading advocacy groups shifted to include "grains" as part of the solution to balancing school meals, helping the council teach all Americans about grains.

Exhibit 6-3a    Program Media Alert    (Courtesy Wheat Foods Council)

**WHEAT
FOODS COUNCIL**

Suite 111 • 5500 South Quebec
Englewood, CO 80111
Telephone: 303-694-5828 • FAX: 303-694-5807

## MEDIA ALERT

June 7, 1994

TO:      Carolyn O'Neill

FROM:    Nancy Karnopp
         Kami Jowers

SUBJECT:   **Revised School Meal Program Objectives**

USDA has been working to revise its School Meal Program nutrition objectives and may be
releasing them in the next few days. It's likely this announcement will cause some confusion,
especially because the objectives are expected to add a new approach to reducing fat intake
through "nutrient-based standards" rather than the traditional "meal pattern" approach. While
this concept may seem complicated, the simple secret to reducing the percentage of fat in
American diets remains the same -- eat more grains and other complex carbohydrate-rich foods.

As the foundation of the U.S. Food Guide Pyramid, low-fat grain foods provide children the
nutrients, energy and taste satisfaction needed for their active lifestyles. Therefore, it is
important that the nutrient-based standards guiding the School Meal Program reflect the
recommendations outlined in the Food Pyramid. Clinical research from the Cooper Institute in
Dallas supports the "more-grain/less-fat" solution as a successful and practical way to achieve the
recommended goal of 30 percent of calories from fat.

To explore this issue in greater detail, here are two individuals well versed on topics pertaining to
grains, fat reduction and weight control:

   **Judi Adams**, M.S., R.D., Executive Director, Wheat Foods Council (303/694-5828). Adams
   spearheads a national nutrition initiative encouraging Americans to include more      grains
   to achieve dietary balance.

   Jeanne Goldberg, Ph.D., Associate Professor of Nutrition, Tufts University (617/627-3223
   x2291). Goldberg is a widely respected nutrition columnist and professor who recently
   completed a paper on including more grains as a simple way to cut fat.

We can provide additional background or arrange interviews or meetings with these or other
related nutrition officials. Please call Nancy or Kami at 816/474-9407 for more information.

Exhibit 6-3b

Program News Release   (Courtesy Wheat Foods Council)

WHEAT
FOODS COUNCIL
Suite 111 • 5500 South Quebec
Englewood, CO 80111
Telephone: 303-694-5828 • FAX: 303-694-5807

FOR RELEASE JULY 27, 1994

**Cutting Fat in School Lunches Is Only Half The Story**

    **ST. LOUIS, Mo.** (July 27, 1994) -- Increasing the proportion of carbohydrates in the diet is a smart, simple solution to reducing percentage of fat in school lunches, according to Judi Adams, president of the Wheat Foods Council.  Speaking at the 48th Annual National Conference of the American School Food Service Association (ASFSA), Adams explained how schools can easily move closer to the USDA-recommended nutrient levels.

    "For 17 years, nutrition and health professionals have encouraged Americans to eat more grains as the first step to solving our fat consumption problem," stated Adams.  "Schools now have the opportunity to showcase what kids can eat *more of* for good health -- grains and produce -- but the best news is that kids already like these foods."

    Last month, the USDA issued School Meal Program nutrition objectives, replacing long-standing meal patterns with nutrient-based standards and limiting the amount of fat in school meals to 30 percent.  Adams said the nutritional "magic" in grain foods is that they are high in complex carbohydrates and low in fat -- just four calories per gram compared to fat's nine -- meaning people can eat more than twice the carbohydrates for the same calories as fat.

    American School Food Service Association is a nonprofit professional organization with 65,000 members who provide high-quality, low-cost meals to students across the country.

###

**WHEAT FOODS COUNCIL**

# NEWS RELEASE

Judi Adams, M.S., R.D.
Executive Director

Suite 111, 5500 South Quebec
Englewood, Colorado 80111

Phone: (303) 694-5828
FAX: (303) 694-5807

FOR IMMEDIATE RELEASE

Contact:  Barbara Witte-Scott
(303) 694-5828

### SCHOOL MEALS PYRAMID-BOUND BY 1996

**DENVER, CO.**  (November 8, 1994) — America's 50 million school children soon will be eating better as school food service directors comply with a new law that requires trimming excess fat from school meals while boosting consumption of high-carbohydrate foods.

The "Better Nutrition and Health for Children Act of 1994," which was signed into law by President Clinton last week, requires the country's 95,000 school meal programs to meet federal nutrition guidelines reflected in the Food Guide Pyramid by the 1996-97 school year.  That means children will be well on their way to getting a daily average of 5-9 servings of produce and 6-11 servings of grain foods.

"At school, our children will be eating a diet higher in complex carbohydrates and fiber, and lower in fat," said Judi Adams, president of the Wheat Foods Council.  "Now, if only children can teach the rest of us...."

Adams said school meal reform became a priority for the U.S. Department of Agriculture (USDA) and Congress after a 1993 government report indicated school meals contained about 38 percent fat — a level similar to most Americans' diets, but higher than the national goal of less than 30 percent fat.  At that time, school meal programs were based on outdated rules following the old "basic four food groups," which was discarded nationally in 1990 and replaced with the Food Guide Pyramid in 1992.

- more -

"We discovered that it requires a major effort to incorporate something as simple as the Food Guide Pyramid in the government's food and nutrition programs," said Adams.

To comply with the new requirements, school food service directors can use either the updated meal pattern plan or a computer nutrient analysis to assure children meet current nutrient goals by 1996. Both avenues require that school lunches and increasingly popular school breakfasts include:

✓ Less than 30 percent of calories from fat and 10 percent from saturated fat;

✓ Plenty of grain products, vegetables and fruits;

✓ At least one-third of the Recommended Dietary Allowances (RDA) for protein, calcium, iron, vitamin A and vitamin C; and

✓ An increase in the level of dietary fiber.

According to a USDA analysis, the consumption of grain foods and fruit would increase nearly 80 percent as school officials achieve these nutrient goals without increasing budgets. "Balance can be achieved," Adams explained, "by trimming fat calories and replacing them with carbohydrate-rich foods."

"Carbohydrates are the secret to satisfying, low-fat eating," said Adams. "Foods rich in complex carbohydrates are less likely to turn into body fat than foods with a high-fat content."

Adams said carbohydrates have just four calories per gram, while fat has nine calories per gram. "Bite for bite, one could eat more than twice the carbohydrates for the same calories as fat."

Because children already like carbohydrate-rich foods such as pasta, bread, cereal, crackers, tortillas, pretzels, dinner rolls and fruits and vegetables, Adams said she thinks school meal officials will find it easy to comply with the changes.

Approximately 25 million children eat lunch and 5 million children eat breakfast at school each day.

###

Exhibit 6-3d          Localized News Release   (Courtesy Wheat Foods Council)

FOR IMMEDIATE RELEASE

**WHEAT FOODS COUNCIL**

Suite 111 • 5500 South Quebec
Englewood, CO 80111
Telephone: 303-694-5828 • FAX: 303-694-5807

## WHERE TO FIND THE BEST MEAL IN TOWN

ANYTOWN, U.S.A. (Date) -- Looking for an affordable, nutritious lunch that will keep your kids full of energy throughout the day?  Look no further than the school cafeteria.

(_____ ), foodservice director for (school district name) said the district plans its lunch menus around nutrient-based standards that limit fat and increase servings of grains, fruits and vegetables.  Meals limit fat to 30 percent and saturated fat to 10 percent.

"We're cutting fat to help balance our students' diets," (_____) said.  "Rich in carbohydrates, grain-based foods provide time-released energy that keeps students going all day. And they supply essential B vitamins, iron and fiber."

A nutrient-based evaluation helps menu planners focus on foods rich in carbohydrates *and* protein, which reduce a meal's percentage of fat.  Complex carbohydrates, which contain less than half the calories of fat, are an integral menu component.  That means students can actually eat *more* of the foods they enjoy.

"Adults and children alike do not eat enough grain-based foods," (_____) said. "On average, we eat just 3 to 5 servings a day, although the U.S. dietary guidelines call for 6 to 11."

(_____ ) school district helps children reach 6 to 11 servings by filling its menus with such healthful selections as pasta with vegetables, club sandwiches, tortillas and low-fat crackers and toast.

###

# Investor and Financial Relations

Corporations that sell shares to the public must conduct a specialized form of public relations with the investment, or financial, community. Investor and other financial relations cannot be managed in the same aggressive manner that characterizes other forms of public relations. The U.S. Securities and Exchange Commission (SEC) prohibits the promotion of corporate stock under certain circumstances, and it has detailed regulations regarding the issuance of annual and quarterly reports and the timely disclosure of all information that will affect the value of publicly traded corporate shares.

How, then, does our four-stage process apply to this highly specialized form of public relations?

# RESEARCH

Investor relations research includes investigation of the client, the reason for the program, and the audiences to be targeted for communication.

## Client Research

The public relations practitioner needs to focus first on the company's past and present financial status, its past and present investor relations practices, and its strengths, weaknesses, and opportunities specifically related to the financial community.

## Opportunity or Problem Research

The second area of research involves assessing the need for a program of financial public relations. Most corporations engage in ongoing investor relations programs that may involve routine communication with the financial media, the annual report to shareowners, the annual meeting, as well as miscellaneous meetings with and tours for shareowners. When problems develop with particular publics, special programs may be devised reactively. Thus, the need for the program should be clearly justified and explained in this phase of research.

## Audience Research

Finally, research for investor relations involves identification of key audiences or groups that make up the financial community:

> Shareowners and potential shareowners
>
> Security analysts and investment counselors
>
> The financial press
>
>> Major wire services: Dow Jones, Reuters Economic Service, AP, UPI
>>
>> Major business magazines: *Business Week, Fortune*—mass circulation and specialized
>>
>> Major New York City newspapers: the *New York Times,* the *Wall Street Journal*
>>
>> Statistical services: Standard and Poor's, Moody's Investor Service
>>
>> Private wire services: PR News Wire, Business Wire
>
> Securities and Exchange Commission

# OBJECTIVES

Investor relations objectives, both impact and output, should be as specific and as quantifiable as possible.

## Impact Objectives

Impact objectives for investor relations include informing investor publics and affecting their attitudes and behaviors. Some examples are:

1. To increase the investor public's knowledge of significant corporate developments (by 40 percent during the current year)

2. To enhance favorable attitudes toward the corporation (by 30 percent this year)

3. To create (40 percent) more interest in the corporation among potential investors (during this year)

4. To raise (20 percent) more capital through the investor relations program (by our deadline of December 1)

5. To receive (45 percent) greater responses from shareowners and other targeted investor publics (during the next fiscal year)

## Output Objectives

In investor relations, output objectives constitute the distribution and execution of program materials and forms of communication. For example:

1. To distribute corporate news releases to 12 major outlets among the financial media

2. To make 18 presentations to security analysts during the months of March and April

Public relations directors often prefer to use output objectives exclusively. These clarify public relations actions and are much simpler to evaluate than impact objectives.

# PROGRAMMING

As in other forms of public relations, the element of programming for investor relations includes planning the theme and messages, the action or special event(s), the uncontrolled and controlled media, and the use of effective principles of communication in program execution.

## Theme and Messages

The theme and messages for an investor relations program will be entirely situational. Such programs usually provide assurances of credibility and attempt to enhance relations between the company and the financial community.

## Action(s) or Special Event(s)

Actions and special events unique to investor relations include:

1. An annual shareowners' meeting
2. An open house for shareowners or analysts
3. Meetings with members of the financial community
4. Special seminars or other group meetings with analysts
5. Special visits to corporate headquarters or plant tours for analysts and shareowners
6. Presentations at meetings or conventions of analysts, in and outside of New York City
7. Promotional events designed to enhance the company's image in the financial community

## Uncontrolled and Controlled Media

Uncontrolled media most frequently used in investor relations include:

1. News releases or feature stories targeted to the financial and mass media
2. CEO interviews with the financial and mass media
3. Media relations with key members of the financial press to stimulate positive news coverage of the company and its activities

Controlled media most often found in investor relations programs are:

1. Printed materials for shareowners, including the annual report, quarterly and other financial reports, newsletters, magazines, special letters, dividend stuffers, and announcements
2. Company promotional films or videos
3. CEO and other corporate officers' speeches to key audiences in the financial community
4. Company financial fact books, biographies and photographs of corporate officers, special fact sheets, and news releases

5. Shareowner opinion surveys

6. Financial advertising

Several examples of uncontrolled and controlled forms of communication are included with the cases in this chapter.

### Effective Communication

The most relevant communication principles for investor and financial relations are source credibility and audience participation.

Much of the effort of the investor relations program is directed toward enhancing the credibility of the corporation inside the financial community. The financial media, security analysts, shareowners, and potential shareowners must have a favorable image of the corporation. To accomplish this, organizations have changed their stock offerings from regional exchanges to the American or the New York Stock Exchange; have upgraded their printed materials, incorporating designs to convey a more "blue-chip" image; and have stepped up presentations to security analysts. Thus, corporate credibility must always be a paramount concern.

Audience participation is also a vital aspect of such programs. Prospective shareowners, financial media people, security analysts, and others targeted for communication are invited to as many corporate functions as possible. The ultimate form of "audience participation," of course, is the actual purchase of shares in the company.

## EVALUATION

Evaluation of investor relations programs should be goal oriented, with each objective reexamined and measured in turn. Although there is a great temptation to cite analyst reports about the company and the company's performance, especially its stock's price/earnings (P/E) ratio, these measures may not be related to investor relations programming, or there may be other intervening variables that overshadow the influence of such programming.

## SUMMARY

Research for investor relations aims at understanding the publicly owned company's status in the financial and investment community, the need for communicating with that community, and the makeup of that community as a target audience. The audience components are shareowners and potential shareowners, security analysts and investment counselors, the financial press, and the Securities and Exchange Commission.

Both impact and output objectives are used in investor relations. Impact objectives are oriented toward informing or influencing the attitudes and behaviors of the financial community, while output objectives cite distribution of materials and other forms of programming as desired outcomes.

Programming for investor relations usually consists of such actions and events as annual shareowners' meetings, an open house for shareowners, special meetings with analysts or other members of the financial community, and promotional events designed to enhance the company's image in the financial community. Uncontrolled and controlled media used in investor relations include news releases, interviews, printed literature, audiovisual materials, and/or speeches directed to targeted segments of the financial community.

Evaluation of investor relations should return to the program's specific, stated objectives and measure each one appropriately. Some practitioners attribute enhancement of the corporation's P/E ratio to the efforts of the investor relations program. However, the presence of intervening variables should always be suspected in such cases.

# READINGS ON INVESTOR AND FINANCIAL RELATIONS

Bernstein, Aaron. "Labor Flexes Its Muscles as Stockholder." *Business Week* (July 18, 1994): 79ff.

Braznell, William. "A Guide to Investor Relations for Emerging Companies." *Public Relations Journal* 50 (July 1994): 26ff.

"Corporate Public Relations" (special issue). *Public Relations Quarterly* 36 (Fall 1991).

Courter, Carol Lee. "When Annual Reports Get Hip." *Across the Board* (May 1994): 20ff.

Davids, Meryl. "How Now IR?" *Public Relations Journal* 45 (April 1989): 15–19.

Denmarsh, Robert I., and Francis R. Esteban. "How to Produce a Credible Annual Report." *Public Relations Journal* 44 (October 1988): 35–36.

Dunkel, Tom. "Keeping an Eye on Corporate America." *Working Woman* (April 1993): 56ff.

Elgin, Peggie R. "Announce Bad News Quickly to Keep Investor Confidence." *Corporate Cashflow* 14 (January 1993): 13ff.

Gringsby, Ed, and Ted Blood. "Shareholders as Ultimate Customers." *Financial Management* 22 (Spring 1993): 22ff.

Grunig, James E., ed. *Excellence in Public Relations and Communication Management*. Hillsdale, IL: Erlbaum, 1992.

Hutchins, H. R. "Annual Reports (Who Reads Them?)" *Communication World* (October 1994): 18ff.

"In the Trenches: Making Investor Relations Pay." *Corporate Cashflow* (July 1993): 28ff.

Johnson, Johnnie, and Win Neilson. "Integrating IR and Other Public Relations." *Public Relations Journal* 46 (April 1990): 26–29.

Johnson, Laura. "How to Succeed in a Close Proxy Vote." *Public Relations Quarterly* 39 (Spring 1994): 35ff.

Leeds, Mark B. "Why Wall Street Matters." *Management Review* (September 1993): 23ff.

Linden, Wechsler Dana, and Nancy Rotenier. "Perform or Else." *Forbes* 153 (January 3, 1994): 100ff.

Lowengard, Mary. "Coups of the Year." *Institutional Investor* (August 1993): 93.

———. "Relationship Angst." *Institutional Investor* (August 1993): 229.

Mahoney, William F. *Investor Relations: The Professional's Guide to Financial Marketing and Communications*. New York: New York Institute of Finance, a division of Simon & Schuster, 1991.

McMullen, Melinda. "IR: Staying on Top in the '90s." *Public Relations Journal* 46 (April 1990): 30–31.

Nichols, Donald R. *The Handbook of Investor Relations*. Homewood, IL: Dow Jones-Irwin, 1989.

"Pitching the Firm." *Institutional Investor* (February 1993): 34.

Poe, Randall. "Can We Talk?" *Across the Board* (May 1994): 16ff.

*The SEC, the Securities Market and Your Financial Communications*. New York: Hill and Knowlton, 1985.

Seely, Michael W. "Hit the Financial Bull's Eye with Well-Aimed IR Programs." *Corporate Cashflow* (July 1993): 26ff.

Stewart, Thomas A. "The King is Dead." *Fortune* (January 11, 1993): 34ff.

Taggart, Philip W., and Roy Alexander with Robert M. Arnold. *Taking Your Company Public: Red Lights and Green Lights for a Go/No-Go Decision*. New York: AMACOM, 1991.

Telsner, Julie, and Lori Bongiorno. "Turn the Page If You Can." *Business Week* (April 25, 1994): 40ff.

Upbib, Bruce. "What Your Annual Report and *Cosmo* Should Have in Common." *Communication World* (September 1993): 16ff.

Walker, Kenneth. "GIC Association Providing Education and Research." *Pension World* (May 1993): 40.

Walton, Wesley, and Charles P. Brissman. *Corporate Communications Handbook: A Guide for Managing Unstructured Disclosure in Today's Corporate Environment.* New York: Clark Boardman, 1988.

Webster, Philip J. "Strategic Corporate Public Relations: What's the Bottom Line?" *Public Relations Journal* (February 1990): 18–21.

# Investor
# Relations Cases

*Eastman Kodak Company decided to focus on imaging and sell its nonimaging health businesses. The company used a three-stage program to accomplish its divestiture. Exhibits 7-1a and 7-1b are a news release and a backgrounder explaining Kodak's divestiture program.*

CASE 7-1

## Project WINGS—Imaging Back in Focus

Eastman Kodak Company

"Virtually everything we have heard has made us more negative on EK."

—Prudential Securities, April 1994, one month prior to Project WINGS

### Situation

As 1994 began, Kodak was a company in quicksand. An earlier diversification into health-related businesses had mired the company in over $7 billion in debt. Earnings were down from a decade earlier.

Since coming aboard as CEO a month earlier, George Fisher had spent "every waking moment" studying Kodak inside and out. His research ranged from detailed financial analyses to customer visits. Communications research reflecting analysts' opinions, talks with major investors, and employee surveys supported Fisher's growing conviction that Kodak could not lead in both imaging *and* health. Instead, the company would focus on imaging and sell its nonimaging health businesses: Sterling Winthrop, maker of Bayer aspirin and other products; L & F Products, maker of Lysol and other products; and the Clinical Diagnostics Division, maker of blood analyzers and other health-related products. Proceeds from the sale would be used to pay down debt and strengthen the company's financial position.

The announcement would be the biggest news from Kodak in a decade. For employees and customers of the businesses being sold, it would bring concern, even fear. Shareholders and the financial community would likely welcome the new strategy. But the perceived failure of previous Kodak restructurings meant that many would greet this latest effort with skepticism, potentially undermining its success.

Courtesy Eastman Kodak Company

Communication would be critical in making Kodak's strategic decision understandable to all its stakeholders. With the May 3 announcement only weeks away, our communications team had to hit a home run on one swing—with no warm-ups.

## Research

- Our communications organization conducted reviews of analysts' opinions, face-to-face meetings with large investors, and employee opinion surveys, providing George Fisher with evidence of widespread discontent about Kodak's lack of focus and lackluster financial performance.

- A portfolio analysis conducted by Goldman, Sachs & Co., Kodak's investment banker, concluded that "as imaging goes, so goes Kodak."

- Among the factors in Fisher's divestiture decision were several studies that demonstrated that Kodak's financial health had been deteriorating. Our communications plan used this same research in developing key messages for the financial community.

- Two recent initiatives positioned us to respond rapidly to one of the biggest communications challenges in Kodak's history. Best-practices research conducted with Jackson Jackson & Wagner was part of a major restructuring of Kodak's communications organization. We also benchmarked our team against the communications departments of other leading health care companies.

## Planning

### Objectives

(1) To gain understanding among all audiences that focusing on imaging is in the best long-term interests of Kodak, its shareholders, customers, and employees. (2) To sustain employee morale, retain customer loyalty, and avoid disruption in the performance of divisions being divested. We also needed to reassure our Health Sciences Division customers, who might fear that Kodak's exit from nonimaging health businesses would somehow threaten its commitment to the X ray imaging market.

### Strategy

A corporate umbrella plan grouped communications activities into three stages: (1) An announcement stage to unveil intent; (2) an interim stage to reassure investors, customers, and employees while buyers were found for the businesses being sold; and (3) a final stage in which a series of divestiture transactions were announced. Subsidiary plans reflected and reinforced the corporate umbrella strategy.

### Key Messages

(1) Focusing on imaging will reduce Kodak's debt and align all the company's resources on Kodak's greatest strength and potential. (2) The units being divested are excellent businesses. (3) Kodak will protect the interests of customers and employees of these businesses by selling the units to buyers with the resources to help them achieve their fullest potential.

### Target Audiences

The investment community and financial media were key audiences, as were employees, especially those affected by the sale. Other important audiences included health customers, potential buyers, and government and opinion leaders in affected localities.

### Budget

$500,000 for internal and external communications; no paid advertising.

## Execution

A small "in-house" team designed and executed the communications plan. PR agencies were retained to assist with planning and implementation. Total secrecy was maintained prior to the announcement. In fact, many analysts and press accounts made special note of the fact that the event was a remarkably leak-free operation.

### Stage 1

On May 3, we unveiled the strategy with an investor meeting and press conference accompanied by a simultaneous employee news cascade inside Kodak and each of the affected businesses. Management meetings were held to reach employees firsthand. Sales organizations were provided with materials to reassure key customers. Government officials, suppliers, trade associations, and other influencers were informed on day one.

### Stage 2

(1) On May 11, Kodak's annual meeting reinforced key messages to shareholders and the investment community. (2) Ongoing employee communications in the health units included employee hot-lines, town meetings, site focus groups, and special transition newsletters. To assure credibility, division management communicated directly with employee teams. (3) Sales and marketing managers in the health units launched an intensive customer communications program to "keep customers sold" during the transition to new ownership.

## Stage 3

(1) Communications surrounding the sale of each business were closely coordinated with the acquiring companies but followed the successful pattern established in the first two stages. (2) Each announcement—there were 5 in all—was used to reinforce the key corporate message. Kodak was focusing on imaging, its core strength, its heritage, and its future.

## Evaluation

### Objective

To gain understanding among key audiences—customers, employees, and shareholders—that focusing on imaging is in the best long-term interest of Kodak. Persuading the investment community and financial media was critical to that objective. Initial media coverage was positive and conveyed our key messages. Reaction within the financial community was approving. Successive divestiture announcements—each for higher than expected prices—built growing approval for the company's strategy. A subsequent series of major articles in the national press included stories in *Fortune* and *Business Week*. The latter noted approvingly that the "photography cash machine is now available to fund growth, not debt payments." Shareholders also had reason to cheer. By the time the last major sale was announced, Kodak stock had risen over 25 percent in less than five months. Debt had been slashed from $7.1 billion to just over $1 billion. Morgan Stanley analyst Brenda Landry wrote, "Kodak is cooking with gas."

### Objective

To minimize loss of employee morale or disruption of performance of the businesses being divested. A constant communications flow during the months while sales were being negotiated created understanding and minimized employee anxiety. An overwhelming majority of employees stayed with the units being sold. Sales remained strong, reflecting customer confidence. The media communicated our message that the units we were divesting were "good businesses," helping the company negotiate without complication with a wide array of bidders. Perhaps the best indicator of success was the high value—nearly $8 billion—buyers placed on these businesses, indicating strong confidence in their performance and prospects.

> "A security and public relations triumph."
> —Michael Ellmann, Wertheim Schroder analyst, as quoted in the Gannett Newspapers, May 3, 1994

Exhibit 7-1a    Program News Release   (Courtesy Eastman Kodak Company)

## KODAK'S CEO UNVEILS
## NEW CORPORATE STRATEGY

Rochester, N.Y., May 3—Eastman Kodak Company today revealed a new corporate strategy that will focus the company's resources and management attention exclusively on its imaging businesses.

"Imaging offers Kodak tremendous opportunities for long-term success and growth. It is the business Kodak knows best, built on over a century of brand strength, marketing know-how, and technological leadership," said George M. C. Fisher, Kodak's Chairman, President, and CEO. "To achieve maximum success, we have concluded that we must commit our entire resource base to imaging opportunities and divest non-core businesses."

To realize this strategy, Kodak intends to divest the pharmaceutical and consumer health products subsidiary, Sterling Winthrop Inc.; the personal care and household products business, L&F Products; and the Clinical Diagnostics Division. These businesses currently generate approximately $3.7 billion of the company's annual revenues.

"Our goal is to divest these businesses in an orderly and responsible manner that optimizes value for Kodak," Fisher said.

Kodak will retain its X-ray film- and electronics-based medical, cardiology, and dental diagnostic imaging business, the Health Sciences Division, because it plays a vital role in its imaging strategy.

Eastman Kodak Company, 343 State Street, Rochester, NY 14650-0518

### Kodak Mission

Fisher noted, "Our mission must be to build a *highly-profitable, results-oriented* company based on a sound value system that emphasizes *five key values*. These values are the operating principles we will use with our customers, employees, shareholders, suppliers, and the communities in which we live and work." The key values are:

- Respect for the individual;
- Uncompromising integrity in everything we do;
- Trust;
- Credibility;
- Continuous improvement.

"We will rebuild this corporation on a platform based on those five values," he added.

He stressed that the company will focus on profitable participation in the five links of the imaging chain: image capture, processing, storage, output, and delivery of images for people and machines anywhere in Kodak's worldwide market. Kodak will emphasize the sale of imaging consumables in support of its mission, and will broaden its pursuit to include those digital electronic imaging arenas in which Kodak can profitably compete.

Fisher said the company will ensure that:

- Kodak's customers—and the ultimate consumer—are satisfied; and hence, Kodak's worldwide market share increases;
- Kodak's employees are energized, fulfilled, and productive, and hence continue to show their loyalty, dedication, and winning spirit;
- Kodak achieves superior financial results which provide attractive returns for its shareholders, and hence rewards Kodak with long-term investment in its stock.

New Corporate Strategy—Page 3

Fisher explained that Kodak will accomplish its business mission by driving three imperatives: total customer satisfaction, total employee satisfaction, and return on net asset (RONA) improvement.

### RONA Improvement Program

Fisher announced he is leading a new effort, the "RONA Improvement Program." This consists of ten initiatives that will significantly improve both after-tax profits and asset utilization, and deliver top-line revenue growth. Each project will have a team champion, with Fisher directly responsible for two: Growth of Market and Cycle Time Improvement. The ten RONA Improvement Program initiatives are:

- Growth of Market
- Asset Management
- Span-of-Control
- Cost of Quality
- R&D Productivity

- Marketing Opportunities
- Portfolio Review
- Process Reengineering
- Cycle Time Improvement
- Policy Opportunities

Fisher further explained, "Pursuing growth for Kodak is *not* synonymous with throwing money at the great information 'super highway in the sky,' or at digital electronics for imaging as we might have in the past. Our growth strategies must apply equally to our traditional silver halide film business as well as to our digital imaging opportunities.

"Rather than simply take an ax to budgets and manpower, we are trying to change, in significant ways, how this company operates," Fisher explained.

### Divestment Plans

By divesting the non-imaging businesses, three purposes are served. First and foremost, Kodak can move quickly to achieve significant debt reduction and a stronger balance sheet. Second, Kodak can commit its management attention and resources to improving the current performance of its core imaging businesses. And third, the company will strategically attack a broader array of imaging opportunities around the world to build an exciting and financially sound Kodak of the future—a company which is highly profitable with modest growth—and more profitable when it achieves better sales growth.

Fisher noted that the divestment plan also will better position the non-imaging businesses to achieve their full potential as central elements in core strategies under new ownership. Kodak noted that Sterling Winthrop's alliance partner, Elf Sanofi, has the right of first refusal to purchase the pharmaceutical alliance portion of the business. Kodak has retained the investment banking firm, Goldman Sachs, to assist in this transaction.

"The businesses we intend to divest are sound—with excellent prospects. Their current performance compares quite favorably with peer health and household products companies," Fisher added. "Kodak is now focused on its core strength, which is both our heritage and our future."

Fisher emphasized, "It's not going to be business as usual. There is a new Kodak, and it is moving swiftly and aggressively to achieve profitable growth."

#

Media Contact:
Paul H. McAfee
Director, Corporate Media Relations
Eastman Kodak Company
Tel: 716-724-4513
Fax: 716-724-0964

Exhibit 7-1b        Program Backgrounder   (Courtesy Eastman Kodak Company)

May 3, 1994

**BUSINESS BACKGROUND**

**KODAK'S CFO OUTLINES**

**NEW CORPORATE FINANCIAL OBJECTIVES**

Harry L. Kavetas, Senior Vice President and Chief Financial Officer of Eastman Kodak Company, presented Kodak's new financial management plans in a meeting with institutional investors on May 3, 1994. The plans will improve Kodak access to capital markets, improve cost and expense management, and reengineer the financial planning and control system.

Kavetas, George M. C. Fisher, and other senior managers outlined a strategy that will focus the company's resources and management attention exclusively on its imaging business. Following Fisher's presentation, Kavetas gave details of the intended divestment of the non-imaging Health businesses and the new financial processes that underpin the company's strategy.

**Divestment Intentions**

At the start of the meeting, Kavetas described the implications of Kodak's intention to divest its non-imaging health businesses. Sales revenues of the businesses that Kodak intends to sell total roughly $3.7 billion. The businesses employ approximately 18,500 employees.

Sales for 1993 for Kodak's Health segment (which includes the Health Sciences Division that Kodak will retain) were about $5.2 billion, with earnings

Eastman Kodak Company, 343 State Street, Rochester, NY 14650-0518 from operations of $618 million before restructuring charges. The businesses Kodak is selling have approximately $7.3 billion in total assets.

Outlining his expectations for the intended divestment, Kavetas said, "We would not expect any dilutive effect on continuing earnings per share as a result of these transactions. This is because decreases in interest expense—that we will realize by applying the proceeds to debt reduction—should offset the loss of near-term profit contribution from the sold units."

He explained that Kodak plans to have financial ratios that would support an A1/P1 commercial paper rating and a solid single-A long-term credit rating within a year, assuming proceeds from the sale of the non-imaging health businesses are available within that timeframe. Kavetas said, "We expect debt paydown from sale proceeds and cash from operations to be adequate to give us the interest coverage and debt-to-capital ratios commensurate with such goals."

## The Finance Function

Discussing Kodak's future financial plans, Kavetas concentrated on:

- Improvement of Kodak's access to capital markets—including the impact the health business divestiture is likely to have on Kodak's financial model;
- Cost and expense management;
- Reengineering of the financial planning and control system.

Business Background—Page 3

### Capital Market Access

Kavetas discussed Kodak's focus on improved access to capital markets. He outlined several actions that were aimed at improving Kodak's debt ratings, debt-to-equity ratio, interest coverage, and total debt.  These include:

- Calling the $1.2 billion LYONS issuance, resulting in an 8% conversion to equity and 92% redemption;
- Stopping the sale of receivables and terminating the Master Lease program, which will reduce economic funding costs;
- Developing a rational decision matrix to map the orderly reduction of Kodak's remaining outstanding debt as cash becomes available for debt reduction.

"The important news is that upon the receipt of the proceeds from the sale of non-imaging health businesses, debt reduction will occur much more rapidly," Kavetas stressed.  "This will be driven by the rate at which we receive those proceeds."

### Cost and Expense Management

"This management team is every bit as committed to cost and expense management as we are to driving technology and growth,"   Kavetas told the investors.  "The imaging-based strategy will lead to some additional rationalization and realignment, particularly between the corporate organization and the business group/unit structure."

He outlined progress on sales, advertising, distribution, and administration (SADA) and R&D expenses, in-line with goals previously set by Kodak.  "Reducing SADA expenditures, in particular, will continue to be a high priority over the next several years," he said.  He also indicated that the employment reduction of 10,000 people, announced in 1993, is on plan. Through the First Quarter of 1994, Kodak has a cumulative reduction of over 6,000 people.

As another key cost-reduction initiative, Kodak has begun implementation of an occupancy cost reduction program for its real estate on a worldwide basis.

### Financial Planning and Control

"We're putting in place, as part of our reengineered financial planning control system, a dedicated budget department that will report directly to me," Kavetas said. "This department's responsibility will be to drive performance analysis, measurements, and the operating plan process."

He outlined two ways to think about the new budgeting system:

- As an improved process with a better technology foundation that yields fewer defects and better cycle time;
- As a statement of the redefinition of the role of corporate finance in the overall Kodak management system, as a change agent and a competitive advantage for the company.

#

Media Contact:
Paul H. McAfee
Director, Corporate Media Relations
Eastman Kodak Company
Tel: 716-724-4513
Fax: 716-724-0964

*Its 1992 investor relations program successfully positioned the nonbeer businesses of the Adolph Coors Company as ACX Technologies, a diversified technology company that quickly became one of the "hottest stocks on Wall Street." Exhibit 7-2a consists of excerpts from an ACX Technologies brochure.*

**CASE 7-2**

## ACX Technologies 1992 Investor Relations Program

ACX Technologies, Golden, CO

### Research

In May 1992, the board of directors of Adolph Coors Company agreed in principle to spin off the nonbeer business of Coors in order to allow better access to capital sources to finance growth, enhance managerial flexibility, and permit investors, lenders, and other constituencies to better evaluate the separate businesses. On December 27, 1992, the spin-off was finalized and the distribution to stockholders of shares in the new company was completed. Initially, the new company, ACX Technologies, Inc., was unknown and had no Wall Street following. The company, with the assistance of its investment banker, helped create interest in the company and its shares through an aggressive investor relations campaign. The company first examined 35 public companies within five industry peer group categories and compared these companies with ACX Technologies. As a result of this study, it was decided to emphasize the proprietary technology, which was involved in the manufacturing of many of the products produced by the company. With its unique aluminum mini-mill process, high-performance consumer packaging, and advanced technical ceramic products business segment, along with several research and development businesses, ACX Technologies believed it should be considered a Diversified Technology company. This peer group has the advantage of attaining the highest price/earnings multiple next to the aluminum companies.

Courtesy ACX Technologies

## Planning

The following goals were set for the company:

- Establish ACX Technology as a Diversified Technology company because of the unique technologies employed. This category had the greatest price/earnings multiple of the industries examined.

- Create a personality or identity so that ACX Technologies would not be perceived as still being in the shadow of Coors, its former parent.

- Identify the target audience in terms of sell-side analysts most likely to be interested in covering the company and institutions concerned with investing in the stock based on their investment parameters.

- Establish third-party credibility through media placements and independent research reports from brokerage firms.

- Have an orderly market in the stock once it began trading.

## Execution

Planning for the launch of the new company began in early October. Several investor relations communications vehicles, such as a fact sheet, a seven-minute corporate video, and a slide show were created. A logo was developed, along with news release stationery and various "give aways" such as coffee mugs, pens, memo paper, and luggage tags, all with the ACX logo on them. A press kit folder containing camera-ready logo sheets, bios on top management, along with the fact sheet and appropriate news releases was prepared for the media. ACX management received media training and participated in meetings with sell-side analysts and the media. Company management also met with analysts in New York City and in Chicago, including several prestigious analysts on the *Institutional Investor* All-American Research Team. The meetings included large brokerage houses with vast retail coverage, such as Donaldson, Lufkin & Jenrette, First Boston Corporation, Merrill Lynch & Co. Inc., Morgan Stanley Group, Inc., Paine Webber Inc., Prudential Financial, and Salomon Brothers Asset Management. More formal meetings were arranged in December in a half-dozen other cities around the country, as well as a New York City media tour.

## Evaluation

The spin-off launch of ACX Technologies has been viewed by many analysts and money managers as one of the most successful they had seen. Third-party credibility for ACX Technologies came quickly, with extensive local and national business media coverage, including the *Wall Street Journal* and *Business Week*. Sample headlines included: "Coors spin-off ACX starting off on fast track." Analysts' acceptance of ACX Technologies on the two-week financial tour was very positive, as shown by the December 29, 1992, "soft soundings" of those individuals. Also, five research reports were in the process of being prepared. They included reports by Bear, Stearns & Co. Inc., C. J. Lawrence, Inc., Dillon, Read & Co. Inc., Merrill Lynch & Co. and The Robinson-Humphrey Company, Inc. The target audience was identified as both sell-side and buy-side analysts. Meetings have taken place with these individuals, and they are now on the company's mailing list. ACX Technologies was successfully accepted as its own company, with its own personality and style based on media stories, preliminary research reports, and soft-soundings. As the *Rocky Mountain News* article of December 16, 1992 stated: "A new Fortune 500 company has been born in Colorado. Adolph Coors Co.'s spin-off of its ceramics, packaging, aluminum and technology businesses into ACX Technologies, Inc. is the talk of Denver equities circles." ACX Technologies was effectively positioned as a Diversified Technology company, based on media stories, preliminary research reports and soft soundings.

| STOCK PRICE HISTORY | |
|---|---|
| DATE | OPENING PRICE |
| December 10, 1992 | $10.75 |
| | CLOSING PRICE |
| December 10, 1992 | $15.50 |
| End of December 1992 | $21.75 |
| End of January 1993 | $27.25 |
| End of February 1993 | $28.50 |

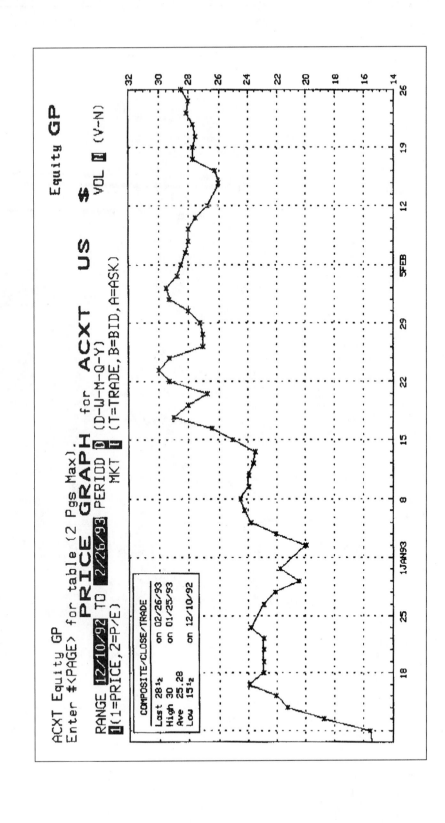

**Winter 1992**

## HIGHLIGHTS

★ HEADQUARTERS

■ GRAPHIC PACKAGING
CORPORATION

✳ GOLDEN ALUMINUM
COMPANY

● COORS CERAMICS
COMPANY

▽ DEVELOPMENTAL
COMPANIES

FOREIGN OPERATIONS (not shown):   Glenrothes, Scotland (Ceramic Manufacturing Plant)
Thun, Switzerland (Lauener Engineering)

*ACX Technologies is a new,*

*Fortune 500-sized Company, which applies*

*innovative technology in the manufacture*

*of superior industrial products.*

■ ACX Technologies manufactures value-added materials and products with unique or special properties for industrial markets worldwide. Its products include: high-impact, moisture-resistant packaging; advanced ceramics; and aluminum rigid container sheet.

■ ACX Technologies will be spun-off in late December 1992 as an independent, innovative technology company.

■ ACX Technologies utilizes environmentally sound, technically advanced manufacturing processes.

■ ACX Technologies is committed to focusing on earnings growth.

■ ACX Technologies manages a portfolio of seasoned core businesses that provide base earnings, as well as growth potential. The Company has a solid balance sheet and a high asset value.

| NASDAQ: ACXT | | Pro Forma 3rd Quarter 1992 | |
| --- | --- | --- | --- |
| Stock Distribution Date: | Dec. 27, 1992 | Total Assets: | $625,833,000 |
| Est. Shares Outstanding: | 12,537,000 | Current Ratio: | 1.6 |
| Est. Shareowners of Record: | 6,000 | 1991 | |
| Pro Forma 3rd Quarter 1992 | | Net Sales: | $543,503,000 |
| | | Operating Income: | $8,897,000 |
| Book Value Per Share: | $31.65 | Net Income: | $1,345,000 |

# TECHNOLOGIES

*EMPLOYS APPROXIMATELY 4,200 FULL-TIME EMPLOYEES, INCLUDING 3,000 IN MANUFACTURING AND 1,200 IN RESEARCH AND DEVELOPMENT, ENGINEERING, AND SALES AND ADMINISTRATION.*

## Graphic Packaging Corporation

H IGH-PERFORMANCE value-added folding carton and flexible packaging for major manufacturers of beverages, bar soaps, concentrated detergents, snack foods, photographic paper, pet food and other products. The folding carton market is a $5 billion industry. The flexible packaging market is a $13 billion industry. Both markets have grown at consistent, moderate rates, with higher growth expected in certain niches (e.g., bar soaps, concentrated detergents, microwave dinner entrees and snack foods such as soft cookies).

## Coors Ceramics Company

I N BUSINESS for more than 70 years, Coors Ceramics is the largest U.S. manufacturer of advanced technical ceramics, producing a wide range of product lines for thousands of structural and electronic applications. Industry data indicates substantial growth in the 1990s for the U.S. and world markets in the advanced technical ceramics industry.

## Golden Aluminum Company

F ORMED IN 1980, Golden Aluminum manufactures aluminum rigid container sheet (RCS) used by its customers to make can ends, lids, tabs and bodies for aluminum beverage and food use. The RCS market in North America has experienced moderate but consistent growth for the past several years with higher growth rates expected for international markets.

 **LOOKING TO THE FUTURE**

## R&D and Developmental Companies

G OLDEN TECHNOLOGIES is the company's R&D vehicle for the development of promising new technologies and is the parent company of the developmental companies. Golden Technologies intends to focus on commercializing promising technologies that have the potential for high profitability and significant growth.

Exhibit 7-2a
(*continued*)

Excerpts from ACX Technologies Brochure   (Courtesy ACX Technologies)

## TECHNOLOGY

USING COMPOSIPAC,™ a patented packaging technology developed internally, Graphic Packaging's folding cartons are manufactured with high-quality graphics and have enhanced moisture and air protection properties that preserve the integrity of the product inside. The use of a printed film allows recycled paperboard to be used while providing superior package graphics.

COORS CERAMICS continues to develop exciting new materials and new technologies, including automobile air-bag initiators, pressure sensors and fiber-optic connectors. The company has also developed zirconia and silicon carbide-based ceramic products and is developing other materials to complement its conventional alumina-based product lines.

GOLDEN ALUMINUM'S patented continuous-cast technology uses a higher proportion of recycled material and less energy than any other RCS process. In 1984, Golden Aluminum began manufacturing operations at its Ft. Lupton, Colorado, rolling mill. This facility proved, on a small scale, the commercial viability of its continuous block casting process to manufacture RCS end and tab stock using primarily used beverage can scrap.

GOLDEN TECHNOLOGIES uses a proprietary process to manufacture Bio-T™, a biodegradable solvent replacement for chlorinated hydrocarbons. Another new technology is the development of advanced electronic modules that are used in military and industrial applications.

## RECENT DEVELOPMENTS

RECENTLY COMPLETED and planned upgrades to printing, bag making and lamination equipment will enable Graphic Packaging to extend sales into personal care products and expand sales in existing flexible packaging markets, such as photographic and chemical packaging. A total quality management program is used to improve product quality and lower manufacturing costs.

THE COMPANY HAS COMPLETED a plant modernization program begun in 1988 that involved the construction of a number of new facilities and the modernization of several others. The company recently signed multi-year cooperative agreements that give Coors Ceramics exclusive rights to study and develop certain technology owned by the U.S. Department of Energy.

IN 1991, the company completed construction of its San Antonio rolling mill which is now in the start-up phase. This state-of-the-art mill is designed to manufacture RCS for food and beverage can bodies. The company has also entered into a joint venture with an Australian company to investigate the feasibility of constructing a 230 million pound annual capacity aluminum rolling mill in Australia.

GOLDEN TECHNOLOGIES has acquired the equipment and technology to research and develop low-cost, thin panel solar energy modules. The company is also involved in the co-development of a proprietary technology for the application of biodegradable polymers.

## CHALLENGES

AS THE COMPANY BEGINS to become a more significant player in the value-added packaging market, managing its growth and maintaining high-quality standards will be the major challenges. Competition is also a factor, with large suppliers dominating the folding carton segment and numerous suppliers in the flexible packaging segment.

THE COMPANY INTENDS TO BUILD ON its success in industrial markets by continued materials development and strategic international growth. International players and competition from manufacturers of lower cost alternative materials continue to challenge the ceramics industry.

THE SAN ANTONIO MILL is targeted to complete the qualification process, for certain customers, in early 1993. The worldwide aluminum RCS market is highly competitive and dominated by large multi-national integrated producers.

FINDING COMMERCIALLY VIABLE, untapped markets or utilizing new technologies is a high-risk, high-reward business. Some of these ventures will not succeed. Most will take years to develop.

## OPPORTUNITIES

GRAPHIC PACKAGING is targeting selected market segments which are expected to grow more rapidly than the overall industry. Individual products such as bags and pouches, and roll stock products such as labels, overwraps and lidding, used in medical, personal care, food, coffee and detergent products are Graphic Packaging's primary targets. Potential new product development efforts are expected in sift proof cartons, linerless cartons and liquid containment packages and environmentally friendly packaging innovations.

CERAMICS IS A MATERIAL OF THE FUTURE because of its inherent properties which include corrosion and wear resistance, hardness, non-conductivity and extreme temperature resistance. New applications and markets in the U.S. and abroad are being developed.

GOLDEN ALUMINUM'S FOCUS is to expand market share in North America and enter international markets where growth opportunities are greatest. When fully operational, the San Antonio plant will nearly triple the company's aluminum sheet capacity.

THESE DEVELOPMENTAL COMPANIES are working on several technologies that could become substantial future business opportunities.

## MANAGEMENT EXPERIENCE

DAVID H. HOFMANN, 54, has been president and chief executive officer of Graphic Packaging since October of 1989. He has more than 25 years of industry experience.

JIM WADE, 52, has been president and chief operating officer of Coors Ceramics since 1992 and 1991, respectively. He has more than 30 years of industry experience, having started his career with Coors Ceramics in 1959.

JOSEPH S. LAMB, 48, has been president and chief executive officer of Golden Aluminum since 1982. He has more than 25 years of industry and business experience.

DEAN A. RULIS, 45, president of Golden Technologies, has more than 25 years of engineering and business experience. He has held numerous positions in project management, facilities management and engineering.

Exhibit 7-2a
(*continued*)

Excerpts from ACX Technologies Brochure  (Courtesy ACX Technologies)

## SUMMARY FINANCIAL RESULTS

| (Dollars in Thousands) | 1991 | 1990 | 1989 |
|---|---|---|---|
| **Net Sales** | | | |
| Graphic Packaging Corporation | $188,141 | $155,809 | $136,848 |
| Coors Ceramics Company | 180,146 | 179,796 | 166,227 |
| Golden Aluminum Company | 95,996 | 113,445 | 94,173 |
| Developmental Companies | 76,956 | 69,866 | 69,570 |
| Corporate and R&D[1] | 2,264 | 2,313 | — |
| Total | $543,503 | $521,229 | $466,818 |
| **Operating Income (Loss)** | | | |
| Graphic Packaging Corporation | $17,185 | $ 9,804 | $ 772 |
| Coors Ceramics Company | 1,983 | 2,214 | 14,802 |
| Golden Aluminum Company | 6,346 | 16,322 | 9,110 |
| Developmental Companies | (4,805) | (3,394) | (7,897) |
| Corporate and R&D[1] | (11,812) | (8,998) | (1,906) |
| Total | $ 8,897 | $ 15,948 | $ 14,881 |
| **Assets** | | | |
| Graphic Packaging Corporation | $109,831 | $102,800 | $110,961 |
| Coors Ceramics Company | 167,330 | 147,915 | 151,175 |
| Golden Aluminum Company | 252,691 | 194,152 | 93,702 |
| Developmental Companies | 83,640 | 80,832 | 65,760 |
| Corporate and R&D[1] | 27,459 | 50,736 | 1,159 |
| Total | $640,951 | $576,435 | $422,757 |
| **Capital Expenditures** | | | |
| Graphic Packaging Corporation | $ 11,217 | $ 4,187 | $ 3,114 |
| Coors Ceramics Company | 26,668 | 14,356 | 32,960 |
| Golden Aluminum Company | 67,552 | 83,236 | 15,826 |
| Developmental Companies | 7,314 | 14,938 | 5,154 |
| Corporate and R&D[1] | 266 | 1,936 | — |
| Total | $113,017 | $118,653 | $ 57,054 |

Note (1): Corporate and Research and Development's (R&D) operating results include allocated corporate charges from the parent company and the historical results of certain efforts to develop and commercialize new technologies. Corporate and R&D assets include cash and cash equivalents and certain property, plant and equipment.

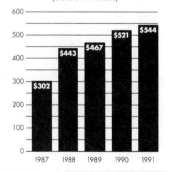

### Consolidated Net Sales
(Dollars in Millions)

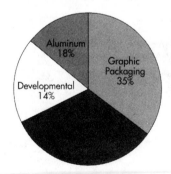

### 1991 Net Sales by Business

# 8

# Consumer
# Relations

A DEVELOPMENT ALMOST AS SIGNIFICANT TO BUSI-
ness as the Industrial Revolution has been the "Age
of the Consumer." This emphasis on consumerism
began with the establishment of the National Consumer's League in 1899. It received added impetus
with the establishment of the Consumers Union and
the publication of *Consumer Reports* in 1936. The
creation of government regulatory agencies such as
the Food and Drug Administration (FDA) and the
Federal Trade Commission (FTC) added to the movement's impact, and consumerism finally came of age
with the installation of a consumer affairs adviser in
the White House during the presidency of John F.
Kennedy.

Today, no corporation can ignore the need for a fully functioning program in consumer relations, or, as it is often known, consumer affairs. The ROPE process model is a useful means of preparing and executing a consumer relations program.

# RESEARCH

Research for consumer relations includes investigation of the client, the reason for the program, and the consumer audiences to be targeted for communication.

## Client Research

In the case of consumer relations, client research will be centered on the organization's reputation in its dealings with consumers. How credible is the organization with activist consumer groups? Has it been a frequent target of their attacks? What are its past and present consumer relations practices? Does it have a viable program in place? What are its major strengths and weaknesses in this area? What opportunities exist to enhance the organization's reputation and credibility in consumer affairs? The answers to these questions will provide a reasonably complete background for further development of a consumer relations program.

## Opportunity or Problem Research

Explanation and justification of the need for a consumer relations program is part of the research process. The need grows out of the client research phase in determining past and present dealings with consumers. If problems already exist, a reactive program will be necessary. If there are no problems with consumers at the moment, the practitioner should consider preparing a proactive program. The organization's "wellness" in its relations with consumers should be made a matter of priority concern to management.

## Audience Research

The final aspect of research consists of identifying and examining audiences to be targeted in a consumer relations program. These audiences usually include:

Company employees

Customers

Professionals

Middle class

Working class

Minorities

Other

Activist consumer groups

Consumer publications

Community media—mass and specialized

Community leaders and organizations

Information about the customer groups and activist consumer groups should be of particular interest. Their attitudes and behaviors toward the company and their media habits are especially important.

# Objectives

Consumer relations programs may use both impact and output objectives.

## Impact Objectives

Some likely examples of impact objectives are:

1. To increase consumers' knowledge about the company's products, services, and policies (by 30 percent during the current year)

2. To promote (30 percent) more favorable consumer opinion toward the company (before December 1)

3. To stimulate (15 percent) greater participation in the company's consumer relations programs (this year)

4. To encourage more positive feedback (20 percent) from consumer groups to the company's programs (in the coming year)

## Output Objectives

Output objectives for consumer relations involve the practitioner's measurable communication efforts with targeted audiences:

1. To distribute (10 percent) more consumer publications during the period June 1–August 31

2. To develop three employee consumer seminars for this fiscal year

3. To meet with five important consumer groups during the next six months

4. To prepare and distribute recipes for using the product to 12 major food editors in the state during the campaign

# PROGRAMMING

Programming for consumer relations includes planning the theme and messages, action or special event(s), uncontrolled and controlled media, and effective communication principles to execute the program.

## Theme and Messages

The theme and messages will grow out of the consumer relations situation and will reflect research findings and objectives for the program.

## Action(s) or Special Event(s)

Organizational actions and special events in a consumer relations program generally include:

1. Advising management and all employees about consumer issues
2. Developing an efficient consumer response system
3. Handling specific consumer complaints through a customer relations office
4. Creating a company ombudsman, whose role is the investigation and resolution of complaints
5. Maintaining liaison with external activist consumer groups
6. Monitoring federal and state regulatory agencies and consumer legislation that might affect the company
7. Developing emergency plans for a product recall
8. Establishing a consumer education program, including meetings, information racks with printed materials on product uses, training tapes on product uses, celebrity endorsements and tours, and paid advertising on consumer topics
9. Holding employee consumerism conferences, seminars, and/or field training

These actions and events form the basis of a thorough consumer relations program.

## Uncontrolled and Controlled Media

Community, and sometimes state or national, media should be targeted for appropriate news releases, photo opportunities or photographs, interviews, and other forms of uncontrolled materials reporting the company's actions or events in consumer affairs.

Controlled media for a consumer relations program usually include printed materials on the effective use of the company's products or on health, safety, or other consumer-oriented topics. In addition, specific printed materials are developed for meetings, conferences, and other special events. Audiovisual materials, such as training tapes and films, are often used as vehicles for consumer education. The cases included in this chapter illustrate a variety of forms of both uncontrolled and controlled media.

Finally, interpersonal communication should play a significant role in any consumer relations program. Ideally, the company can employ a consumer affairs spokesperson whose tasks may include conferring with consumer groups, addressing community organizations, or even representing the company in mass media appearances, including paid consumer advertising. Interpersonal communications should also be used generously in the company's consumer response system, its customer relations office, and other meetings and conferences in the consumer relations program.

## Effective Communication

The principles of special interest for effective communication in consumer relations are source credibility, two-way communication, and audience participation.

A major purpose of consumer relations programs is credibility enhancement. Consumers are increasingly quality-conscious in their purchases of goods and services. To cite one prominent example, U.S. automobile manufacturers have suffered a loss of public confidence and credibility in comparison with the high quality standards of their Japanese competitors. Because of this stiff overseas competition, the U.S. companies have been forced to improve their quality controls, their warranties, and their treatment of consumers in general. Once lost, corporate credibility is difficult to rebuild, but effective programs in consumer relations can be a decisive factor in that rebuilding process.

Two-way communication and audience participation go hand in hand in consumer relations. There can be no substitute for direct, interpersonal communication in some situations. The proper treatment of consumers demands that their grievances be heard and, in most cases, personally resolved. The most effective consumer education programs are those that go beyond mere distribution of literature on store information racks. The best programs involve the consumer personally in meetings, interviews, conferences, and/or other interpersonal presentations that allow audience feedback and participation.

# EVALUATION

There are no surprises and nothing out of the ordinary in the evaluation of consumer relations programs. The practitioner uses the previously discussed methods to evaluate the program's stated objectives.

# SUMMARY

Research for consumer relations concentrates on an organization's reputation with its consumers and on the reason for conducting a program of this kind. In some instances, the consumer publics are segmented, with different messages and media designed for communication with each group.

Consumer relations uses both impact and output objectives. Impact objectives propose outcomes that increase consumers' knowledge or influence their attitudes and behaviors. Output objectives propose outcomes in terms of measurable practitioner efforts without regard to impact.

Programming involves organizational actions such as advising management about consumer affairs, developing consumer-oriented programs, and/or holding meetings or conferences about consumerism. Communication for consumer relations includes uncontrolled, controlled, and interpersonal formats, although the use of controlled printed materials is often emphasized. But interpersonal communication is increasingly being used.

Evaluation, as in other forms of public relations, consists of discovering appropriate measurements for the program's stated objectives.

# READINGS ON CONSUMER RELATIONS

Austin, Nancy K. "Managing the Service Edge: How a Few Smart Companies Deliver What Customers Want." *Working Women* (July 1992): 26ff.

Baher, Connie. "Keeping Your Customers Satisfied." *Small Business Reports* (February 1992): 16ff.

Barrier, Michael. "Call It Supplier Satisfaction." *Nation's Business* (May 1994): 56ff.

————. "Innovations as a Way of Life." *Nation's Business* (July 1994): 18ff.

Bell, Chip R. *Customers as Partners: Building Relationships That Last.* San Francisco: Berrett-Koehler, 1994.

Cespedes, Frank V. "Once More: How Do You Improve Customer Service?" *Business Horizons* (April 1992): 58ff.

Farber, Barry J., and Joyce Wycoff. "Relationships: Six Steps to Success." *Sales and Marketing Management* (April 1992): 50ff.

Finkelman, Dan, et al. "Making Customer Satisfaction Efforts Pay Off." *Telephony* (March 30, 1992): 20ff.

Fornell, Claes. "A Method for Improving Customer Satisfaction and Measuring Its Impact on Profitability." *International Public Relations Review* 15 (1992): 6ff.

Haney, Camille, and Keith S. Collins. "Consumer Relations," in *Experts in Action: Inside Public Relations,* 2nd ed., edited by Bill Cantor. New York: Longman, 1989.

Julin, Jeffrey P. "Is PR a Risk to Effective Risk Communication?" *Communication World* (October 1993): 14ff.

Lesly, Philip. "Consumer Relations," in *Lesly's Handbook of Public Relations and Communications,* 4th ed., edited by Philip Lesly. New York: AMACOM, 1991.

Liebmann, Wendy. "The Changing Consumer." *Vital Speeches* (April 15, 1992): 409ff.

Maynard, Roberta. "What Do Customers Think of Your Firm?" *Nation's Business* (April 1993): 110ff.

Pare, Terrence P. "Finding Out What They Want." *Fortune* 128 (1993): 39ff.

Sellers, Patricia. "The Best Way to Reach Buyers." *Fortune* 128 (1993): 14ff.

Sjoberg, Goran. "Customer Satisfaction and Quality Control: What's in It for Public Relations Professionals?" *International Public Relations Review* 15 (1992): 5ff.

Skolnik, Rayna. "A Full Plate: Consumer Concerns Challenge Food and Beverage Practitioners." *Public Relations Journal* (October 1993): 24–27, 34–35.

Snider, James H. "Consumers in the Information Age." *Futurist* 27 (January–February 1993): 23ff.

"Targeting Black Consumers." *Public Relations Journal* 47 (February 1991): 20ff.

Thompson, Gary W. "Consumer PR Techniques in the High Tech Arena." *Public Relations Quarterly* 37 (Winter 1992): 21–22.

Trudel, Mary R. "Consumer Marketing Synergy: PR Comes of Age." *Public Relations Quarterly* 36 (Spring 1991): 26ff.

Walther, George R. *Upside-Down Marketing.* New York: McGraw-Hill, 1994.

Whitely, Richard. "How to Push Customers Away." *Sales and Marketing Management* (February 1994): 29ff.

Wylde, Margaret. "How to Read an Open Letter." *American Demographics* (September 1994): 48ff.

Zoda, Suzanne M. "Rebuilding Credibility with a Hostile Public." *Communication World* 10 (October 1993): 17ff.

# Consumer
# Relations Cases

*MasterCard International launched a consumer education campaign to increase public awareness of telemarketing fraud. Exhibit 8-1a is a campaign launch news release. Exhibit 8-1b is an advertisement stressing the campaign theme.*

**CASE 8-1**

## "Know the Difference. Hang Up on Fraud."

MasterCard International, Inc., Washington, DC, with Fleishman-Hillard, Inc., Washington, DC

### Background

Imagine you've just received a phone call announcing that you are the "lucky winner of the vacation of a lifetime." All you have to do to "reserve" your winnings is provide your credit card number to the caller. But the "exotic, dream vacation" never materializes. And when you get your credit card statement, hundreds of dollars of unauthorized charges have been made. Variations on this type of scam happen every day, costing American consumers up to $40 billion annually. Representing the interests of 5,000 member financial institutions, MasterCard's challenge was helping stop telemarketing fraud through a program that would help consumers identify fraudulent telephone solicitations.

### Research

Numerous sources pointed to the need for action. The National Consumers League research commissioned Louis Harris and Associates to conduct a study that ultimately concluded that more than 5 million Americans were victimized by telemarketing fraud in 1991 and 1992; less than one-third of those victimized reported the fraud to authorities, and one in six Americans found it difficult to resist a telephone solicitation. Congressional reports on telemarketing fraud went further. One finding suggested that for every case of fraud that is reported, an additional 10,000 cases go unreported. Another report highlighted the fact that Congress had been holding hearings and proposing legislation on the problem of fraudulent telemarketing since 1987, and yet no legislation had been enacted. Finally, the Justice Department concluded its 1993 report on telemarketing fraud, stating, "consumer awareness . . . and the consumer's ability to recognize these schemes, prior to being

Courtesy MasterCard International

victimized, are likely to be the most effective weapons in combatting telemarketing fraud."

## Planning

Based on the research, MasterCard decided to develop a campaign that would educate consumers, consumer groups, MasterCard member institutions, and the media about telemarketing fraud, while simultaneously moving policy-makers and law enforcement agencies to act on the problem. The campaign objectives were (1) to increase consumer awareness of telemarketing fraud and motivate consumers to act and (2) to encourage lawmakers to focus attention on this problem and pass legislation. The budget totaled approximately $375,000.

To meet these objectives, MasterCard created a three-pronged strategy:

- *Partner with a credible, national organization.* MasterCard selected as its partner a group established to fight telemarketing fraud nationwide—the National Fraud Information Center (NFIC), a subsidiary of the National Consumers League. With this partnership, MasterCard was able to take advantage of the NFIC's toll-free number, which served as a ready-made link to consumers. In addition, its computer data bank provided a mechanism to report consumer scams to law enforcement officials.

- *Leverage the campaign to gain credibility and lawmaker support.* Telemarketing fraud legislation pending in Congress provided opportunities to utilize the visibility and credibility of Washington policy-makers to promote the campaign and gain additional lawmaker support.

- *Promote a simple message through a high-profile personality.* Working with the NFIC, MasterCard developed a plan for a high-visibility PSA campaign that would grab the attention of consumers and receive free air time. Together, they chose actor Corbin Bernsen as the celebrity spokesperson because of his well-known role as an attorney on NBC's "L.A. Law." Mr. Bernsen's participation in TV and radio PSAs, a media tour, and the launch event gave the campaign outstanding media exposure for a relatively low cost.

## Execution

*Launch event:* Introduced the "Know the Difference. Hang Up on Fraud." campaign on May 12, 1994, at a Capitol Hill press conference. MasterCard and the NFIC were joined by Corbin Bernsen, Senator Richard Bryan (D-NV) and Congressman Al Swift (D-WA), who sponsored telemarketing fraud legislation, and other federal and state law enforcement officials. The launch event served as the public unveiling of the PSAs; it was attended by members of Congress and more than 100 representatives of consumer and law enforcement agencies, nonprofit consumer organizations, and financial institutions.

*Media:* Ensured the broadest possible exposure by booking Corbin Bernsen for interviews with local reporters around the country via satellite. Distributed mat articles, print PSAs, and press kits to hundreds of media outlets and reporters nationwide.

*Public service announcements:* Produced 10-, 20-, and 30-second TV and radio PSAs featuring Corbin Bernsen. The spots informed consumers to be cautious before purchasing goods or services over the telephone and to call the NFICs "800" number to obtain more information, screen dubious offers, or report a scam. Distributed the PSAs to 400 television and 620 radio stations nationwide.

*Consumer's guide:* Developed the consumer brochure "Schemes, Scams and Flim-Flams: A Consumer's Guide to Phone Fraud." Printed 400,000 copies and sent them to consumers who called either the NFIC or Master-Card's toll-free numbers.

*Posters:* Created eye-catching "Hang Up on Fraud" posters featuring the NFIC's toll-free number and information about telemarketing fraud. Distributed thousands to state consumer agencies, consumer groups, and MasterCard members.

*MasterCard members:* Expanded the boundaries of the program by providing more than 100,000 consumer guides to MasterCard member institutions to distribute to customers.

*State banking associations:* Motivated state banking associations to extend the campaign reach even further. State banking associations ran articles in newsletters to inform members about the campaign. The North Dakota Bankers Association, in partnership with the North Dakota Attorney General's office, used the campaign as a model for producing its own "Hang Up on Fraud" program.

## Evaluation

The program met the campaign objectives, and key audiences continue to embrace it enthusiastically.

*Increased consumer awareness of telemarketing fraud and motivated consumers to act*

- As a direct result of the campaign, calls to the NFIC have increased by 150 percent. In the seven months following the campaign's launch, more than 47,100 consumers had called the NFIC in response to the PSA.

- The NFIC has filed nearly 9,000 complaints and incident reports with federal law enforcement authorities on behalf of callers who responded to the PSA.

- More than 400 TV and radio stations in 47 states and the District of Columbia aired the PSAs, resulting in more than 540 million audience impressions.

- Major newspapers such as the *Washington Post* and *USA Today* reported the campaign's launch event, as did Cox newspapers and Gannett News Service.

- Corbin Bernsen's satellite media tour resulted in television coverage in more than 15 media markets.

- Requests from consumers and MasterCard members for the brochure have exceeded 450,000—a record for MasterCard consumer education campaigns.

- Due to the success of the initial campaign, MasterCard expanded its program to reach a Spanish-speaking audience. Calls to the NFIC hotline from Hispanic consumers increased from less than 3 per day to 30–40 per day and continue to increase weekly.

*Assisted policy-makers in focusing attention on telemarketing fraud and passing legislation*

- Senator Richard Bryan (D-NV) and Congressman Al Swift (D-WA) sent letters to all members of the U.S. Senate and House to inform them of the program and its usefulness to their constituents, as well as the need to enact legislation.

- The legislation passed and was signed into law by President Clinton on August 16, 1994.

- Congressman Jose Serrano (D-NY), Chairman of the Congressional Hispanic Caucus, wrote a congratulatory letter to MasterCard for producing the campaign in Spanish and "recognizing the special needs of ethnic minorities."

- An article in *American Banker* highlighted the campaign in reporting the passage of the Bryan/Swift telemarketing fraud bill.

The campaign is making a difference in people's lives. One example typifies its positive impact on consumers: A California woman was saved from being swindled out of $5,000 after a friend who saw the PSA told her to call the NFIC before sending any money; as a result, the con artist was arrested and she kept her money.

In the time it took you to read this summary, 15 more consumers called the NFIC, and MasterCard sent out another 200 brochures.

# Research

Research, both primary and secondary, demonstrated the magnitude of the telemarketing fraud problem.

## *Primary Research*

- The National Consumers League (NCL) in 1992 commissioned a survey conducted by Louis Harris and Associates, Inc., on consumers' experiences and knowledge of phone fraud. The Harris study found that 92 percent of consumers had received fraudulent or suspicious solicitations, 3 percent (5.5 million people) had purchased something that they now felt was misrepresented, and 17 percent of Americans find it difficult to resist a telephone solicitation. The survey also found that fewer than one-third of victimized consumers ever report the crime to the proper authorities.

- The Committee on Government Operations, U.S. House of Representatives, in its November 1991 report, *The Scourge of Telemarketing Fraud: What Can Be Done Against It?*, heard testimony from an expert who estimated that a scant one in 10,000 victims of telemarketing fraud ever reports the crime and that these scams cost Americans up to $40 billion per year.

- The Committee on Energy and Commerce issued its report in February 1993 to accompany the proposed legislation, H.R. 868. The report chronicled congressional attention to telemarketing fraud, the hearings held on the issue, and the reports issued. Although fraudulent telemarketing was well documented and a growing menace, Congress had failed to pass legislation aimed at combatting it.

- A 1993 Justice Department investigation, *Telemarketing Fraud*, further documented the problem and the tactics employed by the telemarketers. The report concluded, ". . . The first line of defense against telemarketing fraud is an educated American consumer."

## *Secondary Research*

Secondary research demonstrated the public's concern about crime and provided further indications that telemarketing fraud was indeed a real problem that needed to be addressed. Stories in prominent publications, such as the *New York Times, Time, New York Magazine,* the *Chicago Tribune,* and *USA Today,* highlighted the problem. Numerous other papers nationwide reported anecdotal stories about various scams.

## *Conclusion*

From this research, it was clear that a highly visible program that would cut through the clutter and educate consumers to identify fraudulent telephone solicitations was the best way to eliminate telemarketing fraud.

MasterCard International Incorporated
1401 Eye Street, N.W.
Suite 240
Washington, D.C. 20005
(202) 789-5960

**NATIONAL FRAUD**
INFORMATION CENTER

National Fraud Information Center
c/o National Consumers League
815  15th Street, N.W.
Washington, D.C. 20005
(202) 639-8140

<u>Embargoed until 10:30 am on May 12</u>

Charlotte Rush
MasterCard International
202/789-5960

Mike McGarry
Fleishman-Hillard
202/828-8836

or

Cleo Manuel
National Fraud Information Center
National Consumers League
202/639-8140

### *MasterCard, NFIC Launch Major Campaign to Stop Phone Fraud*
### *Advise Consumers to "Know the Difference.  Hang Up On Fraud."*

Washington, D.C., May 12, 1994 -- MasterCard International and the National Fraud Information

Center (NFIC), a project of the National Consumers League, today announced the launch of an

unprecedented national consumer education campaign designed to teach consumers how to spot,

stop and report telemarketing fraud.

The campaign -- largely a response to the public's mounting concerns about America's

skyrocketing fraud rate -- focuses on consumer empowerment.  The campaign tagline -- "Know the

difference.  Hang up on fraud." -- urges consumers to question callers' telemarketing pitches,

become fully informed about the company, product or service being marketed, resist pressure to

provide cash, checks or credit card numbers and report all suspicious calls to the proper authorities.

The problem of telemarketing fraud has grown to major proportions in recent years.  The NFIC

estimates its cost nationwide at $10 billion to $40 billion per year; precise figures are unavailable

since many victims never report or under-report their losses.

*- more -*

"Know the difference. Hang up on fraud."
**To Report Fraud, Call: 1-800-876-7060**

The demographics for the crime are similarly disturbing. While no American is immune to receiving fraudulent calls, scam artists <u>do</u> seem to prey heavily on the most vulnerable in our society -- the aged, the disabled, the poor and recent immigrants who have a poor command of the English language and American culture.

Despite the grim statistics, there is hope: Americans who feel powerless where crime is concerned <u>can</u> have an impact. Telemarketing fraud is an easily preventable crime, an area of criminal activity which we can all help to curtail.

The National Fraud Information Center's toll-free hotline advises potential fraud victims and processes hundreds of telemarketing fraud incident reports every day. Each report is filed electronically in the federal government's national fraud database and is instantly accessible by a variety of federal, state and local law enforcement agencies. Today, thanks to quick action on the part of victims and timely reporting of incidents, con artists are denied the sanctuary afforded by notification time lags.

"Being aware, informed and skeptical is the best way to detect and deflect fraud," said MasterCard U.S. Region President Peter Dimsey. "MasterCard's role in this campaign is rooted in our commitment to providing value to our cardholders, and we believe our alliance with the National Fraud Information Center will help consumers spot telemarketing fraud quickly and protect themselves from losses."

John Barker, Director of the National Fraud Information Center (NFIC), the campaign's co-sponsor, commented, "We applaud MasterCard for its leadership in this important national fraud prevention campaign.

"Alert consumers are our best weapon in reporting fraud and helping law enforcement to put crooks behind bars. We believe that taking this aggressive approach will help to make every American fully informed of the risks and consequences of phone fraud and of the preventive tactics they can take to stop scams," he added.

*- more -*

Telemarketing Fraud/3

Today's campaign kick-off on Capitol Hill featured several notable elements: the premiere screening of national public service announcements with "L.A. Law" star Corbin Bernsen (on hand to introduce the spots); distribution of the new and definitive booklet, "Schemes, Scams and Flim-Flams: A Consumer's Guide to Phone Fraud" and companion poster; and remarks by four of America's leading proponents of tough measures to crack down on fraudulent telemarketing operations -- Senator Richard Bryan (D-NV); Representative Al Swift (D-WA), Christian S. White, Acting Director of the Federal Trade Commission's Bureau of Consumer Protection and J. Joseph Curran, Jr., Attorney General, State of Maryland.

Senator Bryan (D-NV), who has led the fight in the Senate to combat telemarketing fraud commented, "This initiative on the part of MasterCard and NFIC is important to consumers, especially the elderly, who in some cases have been robbed of their life savings by telemarketing scam artists. This consumer education campaign in combination with my tough legislation will mean more consumers hanging up on telemarketing fraud."

"I applaud MasterCard International and the NFIC for their efforts to put an end to telephone scams," said Representative Swift (D-WA), sponsor of the Consumer Protection Telemarketing Act. "Too many consumers become victims of fraudulent telemarketers looking to make a fast and dishonest buck. We've all heard the pitches for free Caribbean holidays, contests and special promotions by phone. Remember -- if it sound too good to be true, it probably is."

FTC Consumer Protection Acting Director White also saluted the new campaign. "Telemarketing fraud is the consumer plague of the '90s. Credit cards are the lifeblood of fraudulent telemarketers. If consumers learn not to give their credit card numbers to telephone con artists, the flow of money to the crooks will shrink."

The FTC has brought more than 100 federal lawsuits against fraudulent telemarketing schemes, has put a stop to frauds estimated to have caused well over a quarter of a million dollars in injury and has returned more than $80 million dollars to consumers bilked by these scams.

*- more -*

"Telemarketing fraud is probably the fastest-growing illegal activity in this country. Attorneys General's offices around the country are being besieged by telephone calls from citizens who have been defrauded of hundreds, thousands, even tens of thousands of dollars," said Maryland Attorney General J. Joseph Curran, Jr. "An education campaign such as MasterCard's and NFIC's is a vital step in attacking this problem. The combination of education efforts and the passage of the Federal Telemarketing Fraud Act will ultimately lead to the elimination of this fraudulent virus."

The national radio and television PSAs -- :30, :20 and :10 television and :30 radio spots -- will air through the end of 1994. In each, spokesperson Bernsen advises consumers to ask questions, listen carefully, refuse to be pressured into sending cash, checks or providing their credit card numbers and report suspicious calls. All carry the campaign tagline and the NFIC hotline number for reporting fraud or requesting information.

To obtain copies of the new brochure, consumers should call **1-800-999-5136.**

MasterCard International Incorporated, a global payments franchise comprised of nearly 22,000 member financial institutions worldwide, is an advocate for the responsible use of credit and other payment options. In the United States, more than 5,000 financial institutions issue MasterCard credit and debit cards.

The National Fraud Information Center is sponsored by The National Consumers League, a private, non-profit organization. NFIC works to combat the growing menace of phone fraud. The Center provides information, referral services and assistance in filing complaints. It offers professionals involved in consumer fraud prevention and law enforcement access to advanced communications and data systems. The result has been improved regulation, prevention, apprehension and enforcement.

### #

# "Know the difference. Hang up on fraud."

*Dishonest telemarketers cheat American consumers out of billions of dollars a year.*

These swindlers often promise "guaranteed prizes" or the deal of a lifetime *if* you send cash, checks or provide your credit card numbers right away. *Don't do it!* Instead, ask lots of questions and report telemarketing fraud to the National Fraud Information Center:

## 1-800-876-7060.

Remember, the next time you get a phone call that sounds "too good to be true" — it probably is.

*For a **free** consumer guide on telemarketing fraud, call 1-800-999-5136.*

© 1994 MasterCard International Incorporated

**NATIONAL FRAUD** INFORMATION CENTER

MasterCard

*A message from the National Fraud Information Center, a project of the National Consumers League, and MasterCard International Incorporated.*

*Faced with declining egg consumption, the American Egg Board designed a program to educate consumers regarding new research indicating that, if they had normal cholesterol levels, they could safely eat eggs. Exhibit 8-2a is a news release announcing the new research, with the blessings of the American Heart Association. Exhibit 8-2b is a display of the campaign slogan and logo.*

**CASE 8-2**     "Eggs Are Back"

American Egg Board, Park Ridge, IL, with Aronow & Pollock Communications, Inc., New York, NY

### Summary

In 1994 strict food labeling restrictions were imposed by the Food and Drug Administration and adopted by the Federal Trade Commission. These restrictions essentially prohibited the American Egg Board (AEB) from capitalizing (through the medium of advertising) on encouraging results from emerging scientific research. This research had the potential to stem the tide of declining per capita egg consumption and to demonstrate that for people with normal cholesterol it's okay to eat one or two eggs per day.

Stymied by the advertising restrictions, the AEB turned to its public relations agency, Aronow & Pollock Communications, Inc., to design and implement a public relations campaign that would communicate this important scientific information to the American public both frequently and powerfully. A landmark article in the *New York Times* by Jane Brody and two separate segments on "Good Morning America" are just some of the highlights of this program. After reading the *New York Times* article, Arthur Schwartz of WOR radio in New York proclaimed over the airwaves, "Eggs are back, thank God!"

### Research

*Consumer Research*

Using the services of SMG North America, a San Francisco–based research firm (formerly Holen North America), one-on-one, in-person interviews were conducted to determine current attitudes about eggs and

Courtesy American Egg Board

related nutrition and health issues. Although most respondents believed that the cholesterol content of eggs is unhealthy, a large number of respondents also had powerful positive associations with eggs. Many respondents felt strong emotional ties to eggs and related eggs with families and nurturing atmospheres. The 1990s trend toward the family and traditional values such as "all things in moderation" seemed to provide an opportunity for eggs to reemerge as a vital symbol of family, integration, and harmony. Based on this research, it was determined that these trends could facilitate the efforts of the egg industry to educate the general public about the role of eggs in a healthy, balanced diet.

### Research by Health Professionals

Before embarking on an aggressive public relations campaign to promote the consumption of eggs every day, it was important to monitor the current thinking about eggs and cholesterol among opinion-leading health professionals. This was necessary in order to determine health messages that would be supported by this group and to avoid any negative backlash that could have the potential to thwart an aggressive consumer campaign.

Using the services of SMG North America, opinion-leading professionals were asked for their responses to 13 questions about eggs and a variety of health and nutrition issues. Respondents included such opinion leaders as the president of the American Dietetic Association; the chairman of the American Heart Association's Nutrition Committee; and the president of the American Medical Association.

Most of the respondents said that dietary cholesterol was not a problem for people with normal blood cholesterol. Many of the respondents also suggested that the egg industry had done an excellent job communicating that message to health professionals but should be more aggressive communicating it to consumers. With the directive to communicate more aggressively to consumers actually coming directly from the health professionals, Aronow & Pollock was ready to sweep the country with the message, "It's Okay to Eat Eggs!"

## Planning

### Target Audience

Women 25 and older who make food buying decisions for their families; general audience of men and women 18 and older.

### Program Objective

Create sweeping public attention for scientific research in order to combat limitations on egg consumption.

### Program Strategies

Research demonstrated that consumers had positive feelings and emotional ties to eggs but just needed permission to eat them. The research established that consumers consider authorities on dietary information to be doctors and other health professionals. A campaign was devised that would enable the American Egg Board to take its message to the public through both health authorities trusted by consumers and celebrity spokespeople who have the ability to secure appearances on major national television programming. Appearances on national television were important in order to sustain the same kind of audience reach created by television advertising. Working with these concepts, the following strategies were employed:

- Structure a campaign that is highly visible and powerfully and frequently reaches the target audiences
- Utilize individuals with celebrity status to deliver health messages supported by emerging research
- Support celebrity efforts with authoritative health professional spokespeople who deliver health messages supported by emerging research
- Develop and employ a variety of compelling news angles
- In addition to utilizing celebrities and health authorities, employ traditional public relations techniques to deliver campaign messages
- Tie in publicity campaign to ongoing public relations programs

### Budget

The budget for the campaign is $1.2 million. $650,000 is allocated for public relations fees and $550,000 for expenses.

## Execution

Recruit two celebrity spokespersons who have the potential to secure interviews on national television shows. In order to select appropriate celebrity spokespeople and to determine what health messages could be most credibly communicated by these spokespeople, research was conducted using the services of Copernicus, a Connecticut-based research firm. Other criteria for spokesperson selection included (1) an association with health and fitness; (2) high recognition among consumers and different segments of the target audiences; and (3) an ability to articulate health messages about eggs. Based on the research results, two spokespeople were selected: New York Jets quarterback Boomer Esiason and volleyball player/supermodel Gabrielle Reece.

Select leaders in the nutrition community and scientists involved with emerging scientific research on cholesterol and eggs to act as health professional spokespeople.

Conduct media training for celebrity athletes and health authority spokespeople.

Pitch a cadre of authoritative health spokespeople and a variety of compelling news angles supported by research to secure national media coverage.

Utilize a video news release to broaden the scope and increase the frequency of messages.

Utilize the existing American Egg Board scientific advisory panel and egg ambassadors (a group of registered dietitians from around the country) as medical and health professional advocates and support for media stories.

Develop a broad-reaching press kit to accompany campaign tactics, and blanket regional and local media, science writers, and physician broadcasters with information and news angles.

Make press kits available to the American Egg Board's state organizations to extend their reach further to local media areas.

Utilize ongoing public relations activities to augment the effectiveness of the consumer campaign.

## Evaluation

Create sweeping public attention for scientific research in order to combat limitations on egg consumption.

The public relations campaign has heightened awareness of new research that exonerates the egg to such a degree that even the American Heart Association (AHA) is rethinking its existing recommendations for egg consumption. The AHA has scheduled a meeting for the spring of 1995 to reevaluate dietary guidelines, including those regarding eggs and dietary cholesterol. In recognition of the conference's objectives, the AHA scientific conference, "Efficacy of Hypocholesterolemic Dietary Interventions," is sponsored by the American Egg Board.

A survey conducted by the Gallup Organization showed that 125 million Americans (or 65 percent of all Americans) have heard in the last six months that it's okay to eat eggs again.

Celebrity spokespeople Boomer Esiason and Gabrielle Reece have appeared on national television, reaching in aggregate more than 12 million viewers. Highlights of appearances include "Good Morning America" (ABC network) during the Friday before the Super Bowl; "Late Night with Conan O'Brien" (NBC network); "The Jon Stewart Show" (WOR syndicated); "Our Home" and "Live from Queens" (Lifetime); and the NBC Radio network.

Health professional spokespeople have generated media coverage reaching in aggregate more than 205 million Americans. As a result of Aronow & Pollock's efforts, a landmark article in the *New York Times* by health reporter Jane Brody delivered credibility and foundation to the public relations efforts. Aronow & Pollock used this article as a catalyst to facilitate the further communications of the egg health messages through other national media by health professional spokespeople. Other media coverage includes "CBS This Morning"; "Good Day New York"; "Consumer Reports"; "Popular Science"; "Weight Watchers" magazine; "Eating Well"; "Country Living"; "New York Daily News"; ABC Radio network news; WCBS radio, New York "Report on Medicine"; New York public radio (WNYC, New York); Bloomberg Information Radio, New York; and WOR Radio (Joan Hamburg and Arthur Schwartz). A segment on "Good Morning America" (ABC network)—this one featuring scientific spokesperson Wayne Callaway, M.D.—is scheduled for Tuesday, March 7. Upcoming print coverage includes *American Health* (June or July issue), the *Cleveland Plain Dealer* (March 12 or 19), the *Tampa Tribune* (March 9), and *Consumer Reports on Health*.

As a result of the campaign, the good news about eggs is sweeping into the mainstream as national television scriptwriters and show hosts are including eggs in their dialogue. During an episode of "The Simpsons," Homer Simpson told his friend, "While it has been established that eggs contain cholesterol, it has not yet been proven conclusively that they actually raise the level of serum cholesterol in the human bloodstream." Other outlets where eggs have been featured include "The Tonight Show with Jay Leno," "Wings," "First Loves" (FOX special), and "Friends."

The video news release that featured celebrity and scientific spokespeople aired during the week between Christmas and New Year's, reaching 2 million viewers on 41 stations in 33 television markets. Eight of the markets were top-20 ADI markets.

Exhibit 8-2a    Program News Release    (Courtesy American Egg Board)

FOR:        American Egg Board and Egg Nutrition Center
                  1819 H. St., N.W., Ste. 520
                  Washington, DC 20006

FROM:      Aronow & Pollock Communications
                  524 Broadway, Third Floor
                  New York, NY 10012
                  Contact: Harriet Shelare          212/941-1414
                          Maureen Ternus, M.S., R.D.    415/776-1610

**FOR IMMEDIATE RELEASE**

### STUDIES INDICATE AN EGG A DAY IS OKAY

**Healthy People with Normal Blood Cholesterol Levels Can Enjoy Eggs**

NEW YORK, NY -- Health authorities, including the American Heart Association (AHA), currently recommend limiting dietary cholesterol consumption. However, new research indicates that for healthy people with normal blood cholesterol levels, these guidelines may be too restrictive.

A study published in *Arteriosclerosis and Thrombosis*, a publication of the AHA, studied the effects of dietary cholesterol on blood cholesterol. Researchers at Columbia University monitored twenty healthy men who were fed four different diets for eight weeks. All the diets followed National Cholesterol Education Step I guidelines with 30 percent or less calories coming from fat. The *difference* between the diets is that they contained one, two, four or zero eggs per day.

The result of the study is that there was no significant difference in blood cholesterol levels when eating between zero, one and two eggs per day. It is possible therefore, for many healthy people with normal blood cholesterol levels to include one egg per day in a low fat diet, without significantly changing their cholesterol levels.

- more -

Investigator Henry N. Ginsberg, MD, points out that individual responses to dietary cholesterol in the study varied widely. In three cases, more eggs led to a *reduction* in total blood cholesterol. In others, there was no change and in some, blood cholesterol increased. "The variation is not surprising based on previous research. There is always a variation in response, most probably because of genetic variations between people," said Dr. Ginsberg. "It is very important for people to know what their blood cholesterol level is; they can then find out what happens if they alter their diets."

According to the study, increases in dietary cholesterol are also associated with modest, linear increases in LDL (low density lipoprotein, the major fraction of blood cholesterol) cholesterol, which are not of medical significance and are not likely to contribute to increased risk of atherosclerosis. The study showed that total blood cholesterol increased 1.47 mg/dl for every 100 mg of dietary cholesterol consumed per day, which is considered statistically and medically insignificant. Since an egg contains about 200 mg of cholesterol, consumption of one egg would raise serum cholesterol about 3 mg/dl, which is also statistically and medically insignificant.

Earlier studies have shown that responsiveness to dietary cholesterol is determined by the body's ability to compensate. According to Wanda Howell, Ph.D., R.D., of the University of Arizona, "Many people's bodies will cut back on the amount of cholesterol produced in the liver or increase cholesterol elimination when there is an increase in dietary cholesterol intake." According to Dr. Howell, as a result of this, most people can consume eggs without increasing their blood cholesterol levels.

- more -

Page 3

Nutrition experts stress that saturated fats have more of an impact on blood cholesterol levels than dietary cholesterol. A diet high in saturated fat may block the clearance of cholesterol from the bloodstream, promoting artery-clogging cholesterol deposition. While eggs contain 213 mg of dietary cholesterol, they are relatively low in saturated fat and total fat. It is possible to include one egg per day in a low fat diet. (see attached menus).

Previously, Dr. Ginsberg and co-workers studied a group of 48 healthy people and found that a reduction in dietary fat from 37 percent to 30 percent of calories did not lower blood LDL or total cholesterol levels unless the reduction of fat was achieved by decreasing saturated fats.

"Instead of concentrating on one particular food, such as the egg," said Dr. Howell, "we need to look at the diet as a whole." According to nutrition experts, following a low fat, high-fiber diet will help lower the risk of coronary heart disease. However, diet is not the most important risk factor. Smoking, a sedentary lifestyle and high blood pressure can all increase the risk for the nation's number one killer.

# # #

Exhibit 8-2b    Campaign Logo    (Courtesy American Egg Board)

*To help promote a more skin-conscious population, Vaseline Research developed a consumer-education program called Skin Awareness Month. Exhibit 8-3a is a news release announcing the program's mall tour. Exhibit 8-3b is the company's "skin tips" media release. Exhibit 8-3c is a drawing of the mall-tour exhibit.*

**CASE 8-3**

## Skin Awareness Month

Vaseline Research (Chesebrough-Pond's), New York, NY, with Cairns & Associates, Inc., New York, NY

### Situation Analysis

"As the U.S. population ages and becomes more concerned about the conditions of its skin, the hand and body lotion category accelerates its healthy growth."—*Mass Market Retailers,* September 20, 1993.

"We slather it on after showering or hand washing, expecting it to restore the skin we were born with. The top-selling mass market hand-body smoothers? Vaseline Intensive Care, Jergens, and Lubriderm." —*Health & Fitness News Service,* September 28, 1993.

Cairns & Associates (C&A) and client Vaseline Research designed a consumer-education campaign—Skin Awareness Month—to increase awareness of proper skin care and to elevate the consumer's perception of Vaseline—from trust and confidence to innovation and authoritativeness.

### Research

Among everyday hand and body lotion brands, three were securely established at the top of the list: Chesebrough-Pond's Vaseline Intensive Care, Andrew Jergens Co.'s Jergens, and Warner-Lambert Co.'s Lubriderm; therefore, it was imperative to develop and implement a program positioning Vaseline Research as an authoritative leader in the therapeutic skin-care category among females age 18–54.

• A survey commissioned by C&A (a representative sample of 270 women 18–54 years old) showed that 77 percent of total respondents claim that they check their skin irregularities 2.5 times per year. However, 63 percent have not visited a dermatologist in the past five years to check any skin irregularities. This illustrated a

Courtesy Chesebrough-Pond's, Inc.

lack of knowledge of the importance of routine skin exams for maintaining healthy skin.

- A 1993 National Benchmark study showed that shopping malls work as a marketing tool: Mall visits reach more than 100,000 consumers a mall on an average weekend. Visits typically last one to two hours and are the perfect vehicle for reaching consumers when they are open to new ideas.

- In a typical month, 170 million adults shop at shopping centers. Nearly two-thirds of shopping mall customers are female. The average household income of shopping mall customers nationally is $41,000.

- A Lexis review of business journals and newspapers confirm that consumers use 800 numbers to contact companies. Toll-free numbers are used by 71 percent of people to obtain product information, brochures, and other promotional literature, according to a Matrixx Marketing study.

## Planning

### Objectives

(1) Position Vaseline Research as a skin-care authority among a broad consumer audience; (2) generate high-profile, non-product-specific news for Vaseline Research; and (3) generate awareness/trial of new product introductions from Vaseline Research.

### Strategies

Develop a three-pronged program to convey a science-based authority image for Vaseline Research—vital to maintaining a strong presence in the competitive skin-care marketplace, including (1) an education program featuring the Skin Awareness Month Hotline (1-800-733-SKIN) and the Skin Wise Booklet; (2) 5-Market Mall Tour, and (3) a media relations program to reach consumers and the trade press.

### Audience

The audience includes women ages 18–54, consumer women's books, major market dailies, local broadcast, and trade publications.

### Budget

$175,000 program.

## Execution

### Educational Program

Work with media to increase awareness of proper skin care and to encourage consumers to see a dermatologist when necessary. To reach consumers with this message, a reader friendly brochure entitled "Skin

Wise" was developed and made available via a toll-free hotline (1-800-733-SKIN). Dermatologist referrals by area were also given when the number was called—to add credibility to the program.

### Five-Market Mall Tour

An interactive, state-of-the-art "skin science" booth was designed as the image-enhancing centerpiece for a five-market mall tour/local media tour. The aim of the mall tour was to reinforce Vaseline Research's positioning as the leading skin-care authority and to raise consumer awareness of Vaseline Research's ownership of Skin Awareness Month. Former beauty and health editor of *Glamour,* Chris Corcoran, delivered hard-hitting, consumer health messages during the mall tour and during local print and broadcast media interviews arranged in each city. Ms. Corcoran provided expert information, tips, and quotes for press materials and media interviews. In the first and last markets of the mall tour (Detroit and Boston), consumers had the opportunity to meet Judi Evans of "Another World" who shared her secrets for maintaining beautiful, healthy skin.

### Media Relations

To add credibility to the program, a well-respected New York dermatologist, Dr. Bruce Katz, and the core spokesperson, Chris Corcoran, were utilized in all aspects of the media campaign. Their tips, quotes, and expert input were incorporated into all press materials distributed to all media outlets.

Following are the media relations tactics executed on behalf of Skin Awareness Month:

- One-on-one presentations, with Dr. Katz, to key beauty and health magazine editors
- Individual pitches to major market dailies
- NAPS (mat) feature on healthy skin tips
- Video news release (produced and distributed to top 150 TV markets)
- Local print and broadcast media bookings to support five-market mall tour

## Evaluation

The public relations program has produced more than 97 million (97,905,538) print and broadcast impressions: television, 19,484,500; radio, 21,488,250; newspaper, 26,287,498; magazines, 30,125,450, and trade, 519,840.

This program produced measurable, traceable results: PR generated more than 30 percent of all calls to the Skin Awareness Month hotline (257,715 calls were received), which was a 580 percent increase in the number of calls received in 1993 when the public relations campaign included a simple newspaper effort; individual pitches to major market dailies; and a mat feature.

More than 60,000 calls were received as a direct result of the consumer magazine effort. This figure can be traced through the daily call counts. Furthermore, more than 219,000 Vaseline brand products were sampled at the local mall events.

Of the top ten cities/zip codes in volume of calls to the Skin Awareness Month Hotline, three were "mall tour" cities (Boston, Minneapolis, and Detroit) and five were in markets that received extensive regional publicity (Cleveland, Clifton, Brooklyn, Marietta, and Ann Arbor). Overall, 10 percent of all calls (25,421) were generated from mall tour regions.

By delivering authoritative messages stressing the importance of overall skin health via strategic tactical elements, Vaseline Research was able to position itself successfully as an authoritative leader in the therapeutic skin-care category.

| Exhibit 8-3a | Mall Tour News Release (Courtesy Chesebrough-Pond's, Inc.) |

# VASELINE RESEARCH

## "SKIN AWARENESS MONTH" TO SPONSOR

## A NATIONWIDE MALL TOUR

Interactive mall tour exhibit featuring skin care lectures and individual consultations, celebrity appearance, local print and radio advertisements, toll-free hotline, educational literature, free product samples and coupons.

New York, NY., January 31, 1994 - - Beginning February 25th through March 27th, **Vaseline® Research** will sponsor a five-city mall tour promoting March as "Skin Awareness Month". This month-long educational event is designed to increase awareness and encourage consumers to practice skin care techniques which will help detect as well as avoid potential skin problems.

The **Vaseline Research Skin Awareness Month Mall Tour Exhibit** will travel to malls in Detroit, Minneapolis, Denver, Houston, and Boston. The exhibit will remain in each city for three days, and will be open to the public during mall shopping hours, typically, 9:30 am to 9:30 pm.

At the exhibit, a skin care expert will utilize state-of-the art **Vaseline Research** technology to assess the condition of the consumers skin and offer daily maintenance advice. In the Detroit and Boston markets, consumers will also have an opportunity to meet soap star Judi Evans of "Another World", and discover her secrets for maintaining beautiful, healthy skin.

**Contact:** Cairns & Associates Inc. 641 Lexington Avenue New York, NY 10022 Tel. 212/421-9770

Additionally, consumers will receive the following when visiting the **Vaseline Research Skin Awareness Month Mall Tour Exhibit**: free samples and coupons towards the purchase of Vaseline® brand products; "Skin Wise," an educational brochure which details how to self-administer a skin check; an entry into a sweepstakes offering a chance to win a $250 mall gift certificate.

To support the **Vaseline Research Skin Awareness Month Mall Tour Exhibit**, local print and radio advertisements will promote the exhibit, as well as additional public relations support.

Below is the itinerary of the **Vaseline Research Skin Awareness Month Mall Tour Exhibit**:

| City | Date | Mall |
|------|------|------|
| Detroit | February 25-27 | Eastland Center Mall |
| Minneapolis | March 4-6 | Southdale Center Mall |
| Denver | March 11-16 | Southglenn Mall |
| Houston | March 18-20 | Sharpstown Mall |
| Boston | March 25-27 | Northshore Plaza |

During "Skin Awareness Month," consumers across the country can also receive the following by calling **1-800-733-SKIN***: The names of three recommended dermatologists in the area where they can go for a skin exam; "Skin Wise" brochure; $8 worth of coupons off the purchase of any of the Vaseline® brand products; free trial-size samples of new Dermasil™ Lotion and new Vaseline® Petroleum Jelly Cream; entry into the "Skin Awareness Month" Sweepstakes in which 200 consumers will win a free skin exam - up to a $150 visit fee.

The family of Vaseline® products consist of Vaseline® Intensive Care Lotion, Dermasil™, Vaseline® Petroleum Jelly, Vaseline® Petroleum Jelly Cream, Vaseline® Lip Therapy, Vaseline® Intensive Care Moisturizing Sunblock Lotion and Moisturizing Bath Products.

Chesebrough-Pond's USA is a manufacturer and marketer of personal products whose major brands include **Pond's, Rave, Aqua Net, Close-up, Mentadent, Brut, Fabergé, Power Stick, Q-Tips** and **Cutex.**

Headquartered in Greenwich, Connecticut, Chesebrough-Pond's USA is an operating unit of Unilever, one of the world's leading manufacturers of consumer branded products and packaging goods.

###

*The Skin Awareness Month toll-free number will be taking calls until April 15th.

**FOR FURTHER INFORMATION:**
Andrea Cantor/Karen Shnek
CAIRNS & ASSOCIATES
641 Lexington Avenue
New York, New York 10022          T013194
212/421-9770

Vaseline Research
MARCH
Skin Awareness Month

5 TIPS TO
MARCH YOUR SKIN
INTO SPRING!!!

1.      Protect your skin from the sun. Don't sunbathe or go out in the mid-day sun without using a sunscreen.  Don't forget to protect the lips too.

2.      Moisturize, Moisturize, Moisturize!  Use moisturizing lotions and creams liberally and frequently to help prevent moisture loss and make skin feel more comfortable.

3.      Be especially attentive to skin after swimming and sunbathing. Take a quick shower to remove chlorine or salt from the skin and moisturize from tip to toe to help counteract the drying effects of these activities.

4.      If you are in an air-conditioned environment constantly, avoid the drafts from air-conditioning outlets and make sure the humidity is regulated.

5.      Get an annual skin checkup from your dermatologist during Skin Awareness Month -- all of March.  Call the Vaseline Research Skin Awareness Month Hotline for the names of dermatologists in your area: 1-800-733-SKIN.

# # #

**Contact:** Cairns & Associates Inc.  641 Lexington Avenue  New York, NY  10022  Tel. 212/421-9770

| Exhibit 8-3c |

## The Vaseline® Research Skin Awareness Month Mall Tour Exhibit

Beginning February 25th and running through March 27th, Vaseline Research will sponsor a five-city mall tour promoting March as "Skin Awareness Month." This month-long educational event is designed to increase awareness and to encourage consumers to practice skin-care techniques that will help detect as well as avoid potential skin problems. At the exhibit (pictured), a skin-care expert will utilize state-of-the-art Vaseline Research technology to assess the condition of the consumer's skin and offer daily maintenance advice. The exhibit was created by Spaeth Design, the award-winning firm responsible for the famous Christmas windows at Saks Fifth Avenue and Lord & Taylor.
(Courtesy Chesebrough-Pond's, Inc.)

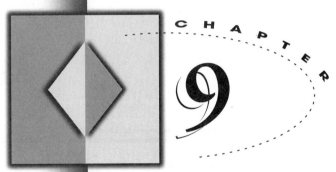

# International
# Public Relations

DURING THE PAST TWO DECADES, INTERNATIONAL public relations has become a major concern of practitioners. The two principal aspects of this field are counseling domestic clients in their programs to reach markets or audiences in other countries and counseling foreign clients, both corporate and governmental, in their efforts to communicate with American audiences.

International public relations problems should be approached using the ROPE process.

# RESEARCH

The research process for international public relations includes understanding the client, the opportunity or problem involved, and the audiences to be reached.

## Client Research

A thorough investigation of the client will begin with background information on their nationality or home country. The next need will be for knowledge of the client's reputation and status in the country of its target audiences, along with past and present public relations practices in that country. Finally, the client's public relations strengths and weaknesses in the host country should be assessed.

## Opportunity or Problem Research

In this phase of research, the practitioner should determine why and to what extent the client needs an international public relations program. The program may be either reactive, in response to a problem experienced in the host country, or it may be proactive in the interest of establishing a presence and creating good will in the host country.

## Audience Research

Whether domestic or foreign, the client—and more importantly, the practitioner representing the client—must understand various aspects of the target audience, including the language and its centrality to the culture of the host country, its cultural values, patterns of thought, customs, communication styles—both verbal and nonverbal, and the target audience's cultural norms. In addition, the public relations practitioner must become acquainted with the host country's various systems: legal, educational, political, and economic. Moreover, knowledge of the host country's social structure, heritage, and, particularly, its business practices will greatly benefit communicating with target audiences. Finally, audience information levels regarding the client and its products or services, audience attitudes and behaviors relevant to the client, and specific audience demographics and media use levels should be gathered as part of the research for an international public relations program.

As in audience research for community relations, international practitioners will need to investigate and understand the media, leaders, and major organizations of the host country. Collectively or singularly, they will often provide the key to success in communicating with a target international audience. Thus, audiences for international public relations will include those listed in Exhibit 9-a.

| Exhibit 9-a |
| --- |

International Publics

## Host Country Media

Mass

Specialized

## Host Country Leaders

Public officials

Educators

Social leaders

Cultural leaders

Religious leaders

Political leaders

Professionals

Executives

## Host Country Organizations

Business

Service

Social

Cultural

Religious

Political

Special interests

# OBJECTIVES

International public relations programs may employ both impact and output objectives. They should be both specific and quantitative.

## Impact Objectives

Impact objectives for international public relations involve informing target audiences or modifying their attitudes or behaviors. Some possible examples are:

1. To increase (by 20 percent) the international audience's knowledge of the client, its operations, products, or services (during a specific time period)

2. To enhance the client's image (by 15 percent during the current year) with the target international audience

3. To encourage (20 percent) more audience participation in the client's international events (during a particular program)

## Output Objectives

Output objectives for international public relations consist of the practitioner's measurable efforts on behalf of the client. They may include such operations as:

1. Preparing and distributing (20 percent) more international publications (than last season)

2. Creating (five) new international projects (during the current calendar year)

3. Scheduling (eight) meetings with international leaders (during a specified time period)

# PROGRAMMING

Programming for international public relations includes planning a theme and messages, actions or special events, uncontrolled and controlled media, and effective use of communication principles.

## Theme and Messages

The nature of the opportunity or problem and the research findings in the situation will govern the messages and theme, if any, to be communicated in the international public relations program.

## Action(s) or Special Event(s)

Client actions and special events for international programs often include:

1. Sponsorship of cultural exchange programs between the host and the client's countries

2. Establishment of institutes in the host country to teach the language and culture of the client's country

3. Meetings with leaders of the host country

4. Seminars or training programs held in schools, businesses, or institutions in the host country

5. Awards programs honoring leaders and other celebrities of the host country

6. Festivals in the host country celebrating the foods, dress, dance, art, or other aspects of the culture of the client's country. These may coincide with such holidays as creation of the client's country, its independence, victory in key battles or wars, birthdays of its founding fathers or heroes, and so on.

7. Participation of the client organization, its management, and its personnel in the special holidays and events of the host country.

A major key to successful international public relations is the client involvement and interaction that actions and special events in the host country can provide.

## Uncontrolled and Controlled Media

In international public relations, the practitioner should service the media of the host country with such appropriate uncontrolled media as news releases, interviews with officers of the client organization, and photo opportunities, all centered around the actions or special events comprising the program itself.

Controlled media may also use the client's actions and special events as a major focus, with related print materials mailed to a select list of leaders and a speakers bureau created to provide important organizations in the host country with oral presentations from officers of the client organization. Both uncontrolled and controlled media should be centered on the client's involvement with, participation in, and contributions to the interests of the host country.

## Effective Communication

The most important communication principles involved in the programming of international public relations are source credibility, nonverbal and verbal cues, two-way communication, the use of opinion leaders, group influence, and audience participation.

Nothing is of greater importance in international public relations than the perceived credibility of the client organization in the host country. Target audiences must believe that the practitioner's client has *their* best interests at heart and is not simply operating in the host country for purposes of exploitation of cheap labor, low production costs, lax environmental standards, and similar factors. In such situations, credibility enhancement requires tangible and visible contributions to the host country on the part of the client organization, its management, and its personnel. These organizational representatives simply *cannot* set themselves apart as an elitist enclave or separate community in the host country and expect to maintain their credibility. They must become active and constructive *participants* in the life and culture of the host country. This will be best reflected in constructive actions and special events as part of the organization's public relations programming.

Effective use of verbal and nonverbal cues in the programming will include an understanding not only of the official language of the host country but of that country's special applications or dialectical usage of the language. Although French is the official language of France, Canada's province of Quebec, and Haiti, its usage varies as widely among these countries as does Spanish usage from Madrid to Santo Domingo. The astute practitioner will understand such verbal nuances, as well as the many nonverbal cultural differences in the uses of time, spatial relationships, and visual and vocal cues. Failure to take these verbal and nonverbal distinctions into account can spell doom for international public relations programming.

Two-way, or interpersonal, communication is especially important in an international context. This presupposes the use of native speakers and writers in the public relations programming. The deadly public relations sin of overreliance on the mass media or other forms of one-way communication (mainly print) can take a serious toll on the effectiveness of international public relations efforts.

The inclusion of opinion leaders and groups is another indispensable element in international public relations programming. While important in most American contexts, attention to and communication with important leaders and groups can become magnified in the international context. This requires a thorough understanding of the complexities of the social and political context in the host country. It may require the employment of authoritative consultants in the host country. Though the cost of getting this right may be high, the cost of getting it wrong will, in the long term, be unbearable if not disastrous.

Finally, there can be no substitute in any public relations program for *audience participation*. If interactive programming is the norm for American public relations, it should be an absolute requisite of international public relations. This principle again underlines the significance of participative actions and special events as the core of effective programs.

Effective use of these communication principles cannot be overemphasized. They serve to heighten the practitioner's sensitivity to and awareness of the interactive and participative nature of public relations, especially in the international context.

# EVALUATION

The evaluation of an international public relations program should be driven by the monitoring and final assessment of its stated objectives. Both impact and output objectives can be evaluated using the same measurement tools as in other forms of public relations (see Chapter 2).

A significant difference may lie in the necessity to use research firms with credible reputations in the host country. It could be a serious mistake to bring in firms and employees from the client's country to conduct surveys, focus groups, and the like in the host country.

## SUMMARY

The ROPE process is a useful format for the conduct of international public relations. In all aspects of the process, unusual precautions must be taken to observe the social, political, and cultural norms of the host country of the program's target audience. Not only must successful practitioners understand effective public relations principles, they must also become working cultural anthropologists and sociologists versed in the host country's history and politics.

## READINGS IN INTERNATIONAL PUBLIC RELATIONS

Althen, Gary. *Learning Across Cultures,* 2nd ed. Tarmouth, ME: Intercultural Press, 1994.

Ambrecht, Wolfgang, and Ulf J. Zabel, eds. "Image as an International Public Relations Concept." *Journal of Public Relations Research 5* (2, 1993): 63–151.

Anderson, Stephen. "Successfully Working with International Journalists." *Communication World* 11 (September 1994): 30ff.

Arfield, George. "As the World Changes, So Must Communicators." *Communication World* (June–July 1993): 33–54.

Bates, Don. "Update on Japan: Tips on Dealing with the Press." *Public Relations Journal* 50 (October–November 1994): 14.

Black, Sam. "Chinese Update." *Public Relations Quarterly* (Fall 1992): 41–42.

Bovet, Susan Fry. "Public Relations in India Growing Exponentially." *Public Relations Journal* 50 (June–July 1994): 9ff.

———. "South Africa Open to Multinational Partnerships." *Public Relations Journal* 50 (August–September 1994): 26ff.

———. "Trends in the 'New' Europe: Four Practice Areas Will Dominate Business." *Public Relations Journal* (September 1993): 18–24.

Burk, John. "Training MNC Employees as Culturally Sensitive Boundary Spanners." *Public Relations Quarterly* 39 (Summer 1994): 40ff.

Chen, Ni. "Public Relations Education in the People's Republic of China." *Journalism Educator* 49 (Spring 1994): 14ff.

Chen, Ni, and Hugh M. Culbertson. "Two Contrasting Approaches of Government Public Relations in Mainland China." *Public Relations Quarterly* (Fall 1992): 36–41.

Crocket, Eddie. "A Single Europe: So Far and Yet So Near." *Communication World* (May–June 1990): 123–128.

Crowther, Connie. "Beyond the Borders." *Currents* (September 1994): 38ff.

Dempsey, Gerry. "Global Communication Comes into Its Own." *Communication World* (December 1992): 21–23.

de Souza, Cerena et al. "Navigating New Seas: Advice on Communicating Internationally." *Communication World* 11 (June–July 1994): 33.

Fawcett, Karen. "An Embassy Can Be a Communicator's Ally." *Communication World* (May 1993): 24–27.

———. "The (PR) Mouse That Roared in Six Languages." *Public Relations Journal* (December 1992): 13–16.

Fortner, Robert S. *International Communication: History, Conflict, and Control of the Global Metropolis.* Belmont, CA: Wadsworth, 1993.

Freivalds, John. "Creating a Verbal Identity." *Communication World* (December 1993): 32–33.

———. "Six Strategies for Doing Business in Former Soviet Republics." *Communication World* (July 1992): 20–24.

Fry, Susan L. "How to Succeed in the New Europe." *Public Relations Journal* (January 1991): 17–21.

Gargan, Edward A. "Chinese Propaganda Turns Black into White: Seeing Is Not Believing." *Far Eastern Economic Review* (July 13, 1989): 57–58.

Hagerty, Bob. "Trainers Help Expatriate Employees Build Bridges to Different Cultures." *Wall Street Journal* (June 14, 1993): B1, B3.

Howard, Carole M. "Perestroika from Pleasantville: Lessons Learned from Launching *Reader's Digest* in the Soviet Union and Hungary." *Vital Speeches* (April 15, 1992): 405–409.

Josephs, Ray. "Japan Booms with Public Relations Ventures." *Public Relations Journal* (December 1990): 18–20.

Josephs, Ray, and Juanita W. Josephs. "Public Relations in France." *Public Relations Journal* (July 1993): 20–26.

———. "Public Relations the U.K. Way." *Public Relations Journal* 50 (April 1994): 14ff.

Lublin, Joann S. "Companies Use Cross-Cultural Training to Help Their Employees Adjust Abroad." *Wall Street Journal* (August 4, 1992): B1, B6.

McCarthy, Michael J. "Pepsico Is Facing Mounting Lawsuits from Botched Promotion in Philippines." *Wall Street Journal* (July 28, 1993): B6.

McCoy, Charles. "Good Intentions: Chevron Tries to Show It Can Protect Jungle While Pumping Oil." *Wall Street Journal* (June 9, 1992): 1, 12A.

McLaughlin, James E. "Communicating to a Diverse Europe." *Business Horizons* 36 (January–February 1993): 54ff.

Moore, Tom. "A World of Differences Faces the International Communicator." *Communication World* 11 (October 1994): 7ff.

Morrow, David J. "Need Ink Abroad?" *International Business* (February 1992): 25–26.

Newsom, Doug, and Bob Carrell. "Professional Public Relations in India: Need Outstrips Supply." *Public Relations Review* 20 (Summer 1994): 183ff.

Nordstreng, Kaarle, ed. *Beyond National Sovereignty: International Communications in the 1990s.* Norwood, NJ: Ablex, 1993.

Pintak, Larry. "Counselors Eye Business in Asia." *Public Relations Journal* (July 1992): 8–9.

Reitman, Valerie. "Enticed by Visions of Enormous Numbers, More Western Marketers Move Into China." *Wall Street Journal* (July 12, 1993): B1, B12.

Sharlach, Jeffrey R. "A New Era in Latin America: Free Markets Force Changes in Five Key Nations." *Public Relations Journal* (September 1993): 26–28.

Sharpe, Melvin L., ed. "International Public Relations." *Public Relations Review* (Summer 1992): 103–221.

Shell, Adam. "American-Style Public Relations Greeted Warmly in Red Square." *Public Relations Journal* (November 1992): 6.

———. "Communications Revolution Reaches China." *Public Relations Journal* (July 1993): 4.

Vendrell, Ignasi B. "To Translate or Not to Translate." *Communication World* 11 (December 1994): 30ff.

"When It's Not the Media Doing the Sniping." *Inside PR* (December 1992): 43–44.

Wilcox, Dennis L., Philip H. Ault, and Warren K. Agee. "International Public Relations," in *Public Relations Strategies and Tactics*, 4th ed. New York: HarperCollins, 1995.

Wouters, Joyce. *International Public Relations.* New York: AMACOM, 1991.

# International
# Public Relations
# Cases

*Perceived by international investors as a small market remote from the heart of Europe and with an undeveloped infrastructure, Portugal waged a campaign to enhance its image and raise its profile in the U.S. business community. Exhibit 9-1a is a news release announcing a new Portuguese/American Advisory Board. Exhibits 9-1b and 9-1c are promotional materials used in the campaign.*

**CASE 9-1** Exploring Portugal: Opportunities for U.S. Business

Investimentos, Comercio e Turismo de Portugal (ICEP), New York, with Edelman Worldwide, Washington, DC

## Background

Portugal brings to mind images of picturesque fishing villages . . . sunshine and sandy beaches . . . and ancient seamanship that led to navigating the New World. Portugal has established an appealing image of the country as a *tourism* destination, but the Portuguese would like American business leaders *also* to think of technology parks and manufacturing plants. So ICEP called on Edelman/Washington at the end of 1994 to create and implement a multiyear program to encourage business investment in Portugal.

## Research

The Wirthlin Group conducted a series of interviews with business leaders (CEOs, senior management) to determine perceptions about Portugal. Generally, greater knowledge about a country results in greater investment interest. But in Portugal's case, the more that was known about the country, the less interest there was in investment! This meant Portugal suffered from an image problem among those who had enough information to form an opinion and a nonimage/noninterest among others. A double whammy. Overall, there was little awareness of positive attributes. Portugal was regarded as a small market, remotely located from the heart of Europe, with an undeveloped infrastructure. It was also a key finding that "personal contact" is the number one factor

Courtesy ICEP Portuguese Trade Commission

in foreign investment decisions, and the most trusted information is from perceived independent sources such as government and international organizations.

## Objectives and Audiences

Primary objectives of the multiyear international investment campaign were:

- To increase U.S. investment in Portugal
- To raise the profile of Portugal in the U.S. business community
- To engage decision-makers directly and to educate them about Portugal's key attributes
- To reduce negative views by communicating positive attributes and correcting misconceptions

The primary audience for the campaign was potential investors and decision-makers, including special sectors such as high technology, biotech/pharmaceuticals, and the film industry. Secondary audiences included decision-"influencers"—trade and vertical media reaching the target audience and independent information sources such as the U.S. Commerce Department.

## Planning

### Strategies

Strategies included initiating personal contact for ICEP with investors through one-on-one meetings with U.S. executives; targeting the most promising business sectors and vertical trade media; building on executive relationships via direct mail/newsletters, supporting media placements, and trade advertising; creating a credible advisory board; gaining inclusion in Commerce Department information sources; maximizing special events such as seminars, trade shows, hosted trips to Portugal, and visits by Portuguese officials to the U.S.; communicating success stories of American and foreign companies that have invested in Portugal; and utilizing favorable comparisons of Portugal and other countries.

### Campaign Creative

The creative approach sought to take established images of Portugal and then "surprise" the audience with the reality of Portugal's modern attributes and business advantages. Because the core message of the campaign was to persuade businesses to "locate in Portugal," the creative approach takes advantage of the connection between business location decisions and the country's heritage of navigation and exploration:

> For five centuries, Portugal's explorers discovered the world. Now the world is discovering Portugal's limitless business opportunities. . . .

The central creative strategy also sought to link the historical concept of "discovery" with the idea that there is a lot of information about modern Portugal for American business executives to "discover." A logo for the campaign was developed with the heading and themeline as follows:

Portugal Today: Discover the Difference. Explore the Advantage.

The modern-looking logotype was set over a background of an antique navigational map to enhance the concept. The lead brochure featured a square die-cut from the antique map appearing on the front of the brochure so that when opening it, the reader sees the modern "Portugal Today" logo in the middle of contemporary business images. The creative theme was carried out in all print materials, using the logo and the juxtaposition of old and new images. The "discover" and "explore" messages were carried out in all written materials.

### Key Messages

Specific campaign messages focused on Portugal's fast-growing economy; skyrocketing foreign investment; its stable, business-friendly political system; its skilled, low-cost labor force; its economic reform agenda; its incentives for U.S. business; and individual messages targeting vertical markets.

## Campaign Execution

Edelman developed a database of more than 7,000 potential business investors and began initiating meetings for ICEP with executives. Led by former Ambassador to Portugal Frank Carlucci, an advisory board was recruited to generate high-level referrals and business contacts. The board was launched in May 1995 at a press event where the Portuguese trade minister's upcoming visit to the U.S. was announced. Support materials included a lead brochure on investing in Portugal, a quarterly newsletter, press kits, a laptop computer presentation for ICEP one-on-one meetings, and translations in foreign languages. A trade advertising program included placement of one-page ads and business return cards (BRCs) featuring the discover/explore theme and placed in publications such as *Export Today, Trade and Culture, Site Selection, Area Development*, and *Institutional Investor.*

Initiatives targeting specific industries included materials created for each sector; a technology trade mission in which executives from tech companies, associations, and the Commerce Department were invited to tour Portugal; and a special visit to Portugal created for Motion Picture Association of America (MPAA) President Jack Valenti. Placement of stories about business investment in Portugal included publications from *Expansion Management* and *Business Facilities* to the *Journal of European Business* and *Newsweek.*

## Results

Following are highlights of the campaign's results to date:

- A total of 75 meetings have been arranged for ICEP with corporate decision-makers.

- Two of those resulted in deals currently under negotiation worth more than $100 million each.

- The one-on-ones have produced invaluable information on corporation incentives needed to make Portugal more competitive than other countries, which Portugal has in turn acted upon.

- The database of potential investors and influential people has been expanded from 7,000 to 10,000, with materials distributed to prospects on an ongoing basis.

- Advertising has resulted in 820 BRC responses for additional information.

- Media placements include more than 30 articles, primarily in niche and trade publications.

- Eight participants traveled to Portugal with the technology trade mission.

- Jack Valenti's visit resulted in additional counsel to Portugal on film industry incentives and information about Portugal distributed to the film industry via the MPAA.

- Primary contacts have resulted in a "multiplier effect," whereby word about the advantages of doing business in Portugal continues to grow and to generate more consideration and interest.

**ICEP**

*Investimentos, Comércio e Turismo de Portugal*

FOR IMMEDIATE RELEASE                              Contact:     Suzanne Pinto
                                                               (202) 326-1740

### PORTUGUESE/AMERICAN ADVISORY BOARD FORMED
### TO LAUNCH INVESTMENT INITIATIVE

WASHINGTON D.C. (MAY 1, 1995) - Former Ambassador to Portugal Frank Carlucci and former U.S. Congressman Tony Coelho will serve on the newly formed U.S. - Portugal Investment Advisory Board, Portugal's Minister of Trade and Tourism Faria de Oliveira announced today. Minister Faria de Oliveira and Ambassador Carlucci will co-chair the board, which will consist of 12 members – six from the United States and six from Portugal.

The advisory board is part of Portugal's new initiative and commitment to increasing U.S. - Portuguese trade and investment. The American members of the advisory board, high-profile business executives with operations in Portugal, will raise awareness of the opportunity Portugal presents to investors. As "honorary representatives of Portugal," board members will highlight the benefits of doing business with one of Europe's fastest growing economies over the past decade.

Minister Faria de Oliveira, who will be in Washington, New York and San Jose, CA to launch the initiative explained, "The purpose of the board is to reach out to American companies and invite them to come to Portugal to discover the difference and explore the advantage. Portugal's open-door policies to investors, competitive labor costs and $20 billion committed to infrastructure are just some of the advantages we offer that make Portugal an excellent business partner and the best investment opportunity in Europe."

As a full member of the European Union since 1986, Portugal has restructured its economy to open its domestic markets to increased external competition and direct foreign investment. The world's leading companies have taken advantage of Portugal's competitive edge over European countries.

Foreign direct investment increased 33-fold between 1986 and 1992, skyrocketing from approximately $164 million to $4.4 billion. The share of American investment increased 21 times between 1986 and 1991, and amounted to $116 million in 1993.

**ICEP Portuguese Trade Commission**
590 Fifth Avenue, 3rd Floor  NEW YORK, NY 10036-4702
Tel.: (212) 354-4610  Fax: (212) 575-4737  Telex: 640175 PGTO NY

Portugal

- Page 2 -

"American companies are still unaware of Portugal's economic success story. As a foreign investment target it offers a business-friendly environment, generous tax and financial incentives, great potential for growth, and access to the European Union's 360 million consumers," said Ambassador Carlucci. "Perhaps most important, the Portuguese people appreciate Americans and are eager to do business with us."

The Advisory Board will work closely with ICEP – the Portuguese Trade Commission, an agency of the Portuguese government, which promotes Portugal as a location for inward investment and tourism. Headquartered in Lisbon, with offices worldwide, ICEP can provide specific information on investment and will arrange meetings between potential investors and members of the Portuguese government. The other members of the advisory board will be announced in the coming months.

During his visit to Washington, the first part of a four city U.S. trade mission, the Minister will meet with Senate Majority Leader Bob Dole, Speaker of the House Newt Gingrich, Secretary of Commerce Ron Brown, and Jack Valenti, president of the Motion Picture Association to discuss foreign investment in Portugal. The Minister also will be meeting with American business leaders in New York, San Francisco and San Jose California.

###

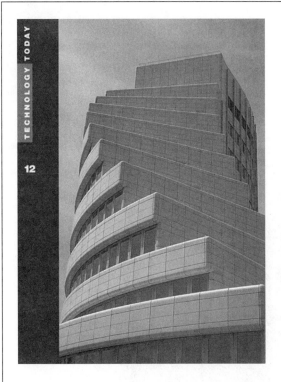

TECHNOLOGY TODAY

12

## THE TOTAL FOREIGN INVESTMENT PACKAGE

**Marconi Telecommunications Building**

Potential investors who talk to companies like Siemens, Texas Instruments, Samsung and Ford, will hear similar reasons why they chose Portugal. They also will hear similar success stories.

Texas Instruments chose Portugal because the investment incentives are competitive with other European countries. Because the company's high-value products required a highly skilled labor force that was both economical and efficient, Portugal was ideal. That choice has paid off. The Portugal facility is second only to the Japanese operation as the most productive TI semiconductor plant in the world, which includes production in Malaysia, Taiwan, Singapore and Mexico.

Ford Electronics chose Portugal because of the quality of the labor force, low union activity, and investment incentives in which the plant site was declared a "free trade zone." Non-EU-made components are shipped tariff-free directly to the Palmela plant, by passing customs at the point of entry. Conversely, products made from those components that are shipped back to non-EU markets remain tariff-free.

Siemens chose Portugal for a number of reasons — for a number of plants. Siemens currently has 13 separate facilities in Portugal. The quality of the labor force at the Corroios operation allowed the plant to open ahead of schedule and their "just in time" production schedule has increased their efficiency.

These companies are not alone in discovering the advantages of investing in Portugal. 3M, Abbott Laboratories, Allied-Signal, American Cyanamid, Data General Corp., Eastman Kodak, General Electric, General Motors, IBM, Unisys, and Xerox, to name just a few, have located operations or offices in Portugal. The combination of high-tech infrastructures, strong R&D facilities, unlimited market opportunities, competitive investment incentives, and efficient and cost-effective labor make Portugal the total package for foreign investors.

*Come discover the difference for yourself.*

PORTUGAL
TODAY

DISCOVER
the Difference

EXPLORE
the Advantage

*A premier manufacturer of surgical instruments, Baxter International, launched a campaign in Russia to overcome business obstacles and to educate Russian consumers. Exhibit 9-2a is a news release announcing the company's new plant in Russia. Exhibit 9-2b is a media advisory announcing Baxter International's participation in a Russian trade show. Exhibit 9-2c is a bilingual brochure about Baxter's program in Russia.*

**CASE 9-2**

## Coup or No Coup: Strategic PR Helps Baxter Overcome Obstacles to Establishing a Viable Business in Russia

Baxter International, Inc., Deerfield, IL, with Fleishman-Hillard, Inc., St. Louis, MO

### Background

Baxter is the world's leading manufacturer and marketer of health care products. International expansion is a key business strategy, as 40 percent of its revenues are projected to come from non-U.S. markets by the year 2000.

Russia represents an enormous, untapped marketing/sales opportunity: The population totals 150 million and the health care system is severely underdeveloped after decades of emphasis on military buildup. For example, only 30 percent of the demand for surgical instruments is being met; locally produced instruments often are of poor quality (scissors often fold over rather than cut) and last only a few months (compared to 3 to 5 years for Western-made ones). Baxter had been pursuing a Russian joint venture when the coup of August 1991 and subsequent collapse of the Communist Party killed the deal. Rather than give up, Baxter conducted market research and determined that a joint venture was still viable—*if* certain obstacles could be overcome. In November 1992, Baxter signed an agreement with a military-industrial concern to produce surgical instruments in a plant that once assembled guidance systems for the Soviet army. The plant renovation and the culmination of a strategic PR program led by Baxter, Fleishman-Hillard (F-H), and F-H's Moscow affiliate were scheduled for September 23, 1993—a date which proved fateful, as another attempted coup began two days earlier.

Meanwhile, in the U.S.A., Baxter needed to demonstrate to key con-

---

Courtesy Baxter International, Inc.

stituents—shareholders, analysts, customers, employees, and the media—that its dominance and future opportunities in the health care industry were as strong internationally as they were in the U.S.A. Baxter's entry into the Russian marketplace was a perfect way to strengthen the company's image as a truly global health care provider and competitor.

## Research

One-on-one, in-depth interviews with nearly 365 health care providers and 100 government officials (who control joint ventures) conducted by a Moscow consulting firm revealed that Baxter had virtually no image. Nearly all providers and bureaucrats who were interviewed had never heard of Baxter (however, many knew the names of its competitors), had no knowledge of its interest in partnering with a Russian firm, and were not aware of its products and services. The interviews also underscored the tremendous flux in the delivery of Russian health care—and specifically, in the acquisition of basic health care supplies. In addition, intelligence gleaned from F-H's Moscow affiliate revealed that Baxter would need to communicate credibly to audiences that were jaded by promises from foreign firms. In summary, the research revealed the following challenges:

- *Introducing an unknown U.S. company.* Baxter needed to gain credibility, generate goodwill, and build name recognition with customers and government officials. It wanted to be known as a premier health care company that was making a strategic, long-term investment of benefit to Baxter *and* to the Russian people and economy—*not* as one of the many foreign firms that make a "splash," turn a profit, and disappear. It also needed to avoid common pitfalls of doing business in Russia (for example, offending the Russians' national pride by appearing too patronizing or by presenting a business investment as a charitable gesture).

- *Overcoming the old guard/new guard clash.* Baxter needed to communicate credibly to government officials, other military-industrial concerns, and the public that a formerly top-secret military plant could be converted to a viable civilian enterprise and that such conversions were key to the country's future.

- *Identifying and communicating with customers.* Without Communism, the old customer—government—essentially no longer existed. In its place were diverse, far-flung customers who Baxter needed to reach.

- *Educating customers on Western-style sales concepts.* Baxter needed to educate customers about concepts that were virtually unheard of under Communism, such as value (Baxter instruments cost slightly more but are of higher quality and last longer) and product support (Baxter offers product warranties).

## Objectives/Target Audiences

- To build a positive image among Russian customers, government officials, and the general public
- To secure positive publicity in the U.S.A. to reinforce the company's presence and opportunities abroad to shareholders, analysts, plant communities, employees, customers, and U.S. media

## Planning

To lay the foundation for success in the Russian marketplace, the Baxter/F-H/F-H Moscow affiliate team believed that the company needed to make a cultural investment as well as a business investment. By embracing the Russian culture, the company could communicate credibly with its key Russian constituents and begin to overcome some of its business obstacles. A memorable, culturally appropriate and unique celebration to announce the company's entry into the Russian marketplace also would capture the interest of U.S. media, who continually report on the country's conversion to a free-market economy, including investments by U.S. businesses that aid this conversion. News reports in the major national media organizations would in turn influence and educate Baxter's other constituents about its global reach and opportunities.

## Execution

### National Symphony Orchestra Tour

When Baxter learned that the tour of Russia by the National Symphony Orchestra (NSO) was nearly canceled for lack of funding, it seized the opportunity to sponsor the NSO—and associate itself with its beloved, Russian-born music director, Mstislav Rostropovich, who was returning to his homeland to perform before retiring. The sponsorship became the program's centerpiece: It was leveraged to secure widespread publicity for Baxter (orchestra music has mass appeal in Russia); relationship-building events at each performance with constituents (the most influential constituents were invited with the hope that they could identify other constituents and spread "good news" about Baxter with credibility); and a long-term friendship with a national hero whose pet cause is health care and who could speak credibly on Baxter's behalf. The sponsorship also had a great deal of symbolic value: Just as the Rostropovich/NSO collaboration had led to a world-class orchestra, Baxter hoped its partnership with the Russian community would be equally successful.

### Plant Opening

The official plant opening was timed to the start of the concerts and included an "open door" tour for constituents and media (an anomaly in Communist Russia, where most plants were equipped with barbed wire fences and armed KGB guards) and a gala reception.

### TV Medical Documentary

To build its image further and to take advantage of Russians' love of education, Baxter arranged for Central Russian TV to broadcast (for no charge) a Baxter-underwritten, health care documentary, which included company "infomercials."

### Health Care Trade Show

To educate key constituents about its products and operations, Baxter merchandised its involvement in the Commonwealth of Independent States' largest health care trade show, and invited media, local officials, and customers to its booth for briefings.

### Media Relations

To communicate the company's entry into Russia and to reinforce its success internationally, an aggressive media relations program that included deskside briefings, plant tours, and proactive pitching was implemented in the U.S.A. and Russia.

## Evaluation

The NSO/Rostropovich sponsorship was an unparalleled vehicle for building a positive reputation and name recognition, generating goodwill, educating Russians about Baxter, and reinforcing the company's desire to embrace the Russian community. Russian media hailed the company for "saving" the tour and gave it extensive coverage. Central Russian TV brought an NSO concert in Red Square (and the Baxter name) to millions via a live broadcast. Every concert performance was sold out, and virtually all constituents Baxter invited to concert events attended (Boris Yeltsin viewed the Red Square concert from Baxter's VIP booth). Rostropovich attended every Baxter event and publicly applauded it, giving Baxter's efforts credibility and added recognition.

Baxter delivered key messages to constituents via a veritable flood of news coverage in Russia: In-depth, positive news reports were featured in major dailies, radio and TV stations, wire services, and consumer and trade magazines. (Several reporters printed Baxter's phone number so doctors could immediately order products.) The PR team also aggressively pitched domestic and Moscow-based American media, securing positive publicity in virtually all major U.S. media, including lengthy features in the *Washington Post* and *Chicago Tribune*.

The coup—which began two days before the festivities—ironically didn't affect Russian interest: 60 Russian reporters attended the plant opening and hundreds of health care providers visited Baxter's trade show booth—and many placed immediate orders. U.S. media based in Moscow were preoccupied, but by aggressively pitching a "business as usual" angle to domestic media and Moscow-based media, numerous positive placements appeared that reinforced key messages.

Exhibit 9-2a    Company News Release    (Courtesy Baxter International, Inc.)

## CORPORATE NEWS

Baxter International Inc.
One Baxter Parkway
Deerfield, Illinois 60015 U.S.A.

## *Baxter*

*For more information, contact:*
*For Baxter in Moscow (by 9/20), Shawn Ramsey, Palace*
*Hotel, 7095-956-3152*
*For Baxter in Moscow, Vladimir Ivanov or Galina*
*Tchernakova, 7095-119-6656*

### NEW BAXTER JOINT VENTURE PLANT WILL MANUFACTURE
### MUCH-NEEDED SURGICAL INSTRUMENTS IN RUSSIA

**MOSCOW,** September 1993 -- Baxter International and its joint venture partner in Russia, NIIAP, will open on Sept. 23 a manufacturing facility in Moscow to produce much-needed surgical instruments for hospitals and physicians throughout the country. The manufacturing operation is housed in a plant that formerly produced guidance systems for the Soviet military and space program.

The facility will manufacture hand-held surgical instruments such as vascular clamps, needle holders and surgical scissors. The plant will help meet the critical need for high-quality, affordable surgical instruments in Russia, where only one-third of the demand for such instruments currently can be met.

"For decades, Russia's focus on military build-up overshadowed other key industries, including health care," said Tony L. White, Baxter executive vice president, Global Businesses. "With the opening of this plant, Baxter will help meet the critical need for modern health-care products and materials, and at the same time, help the Russian economy."

The business venture, known as MosMed, is ruble-based and will rely on local equipment, supplies and labor -- initiatives designed to aid the Russian economy and ensure the long-term viability of the venture.

-more-

"Although high-quality surgical instruments are available from Western suppliers, Russian hospitals and doctors don't have the money to buy them -- even though they are desperately needed," White said. "Because our operations will have a Russian cost structure, we will be able to produce high-quality surgical instruments that are affordable."

The MosMed plant will eventually employ up to 100 Russians. In addition, Baxter has recruited and trained Russians for a Western-style sales and marketing team that will sell directly to health-care customers.

MosMed is 75 percent owned by Baxter and 25 percent owned by NIIAP (The Plant of the Research Institute for Automation and Instrumentation), a Russian manufacturing enterprise. Baxter contributed most of the manufacturing equipment, technology, and licensing and start-up costs -- an investment totalling about $10 million. Also, marketing, sales and distribution support will be provided by the newly established Baxter Russia and Baxter's V. Mueller Division, a leading global manufacturer and supplier of hand-held surgical instruments and endoscopy equipment.

NIIAP's contributions to the venture include land and approximately 30,000 square feet of space in its plant, which Baxter has renovated. NIIAP also contributed some manufacturing equipment, working capital (in rubles), and $1 million in hard currency for worker training.

The Russian Ministry of Health and the Department of General Machine Building assisted Baxter and NIIAP to establish MosMed.

White said that Baxter partnered with NIIAP because NIIAP workers are skilled in manufacturing precision, high-quality products -- characteristics critical in producing hand-held surgical instruments. More important, White said, NIIAP is an enthusiastic and progressive partner.

-more-

Exhibit 9-2a
(*continued*)

Company News Release  (Courtesy Baxter International, Inc.)

*Page 3*

"The plant management team at NIIAP recognized that its traditional 'customer' -- the state -- was refocusing its efforts away from defense build-up and toward other industries the country needs," White said. "Management knew change was necessary to ensure the future of the enterprise and the continued employment of its workers. Their attitude and dedication to this project have helped to make it a reality."

White said the plant opening represents a long-term investment in the Russian economy and people. "This may be just the beginning of our investment in the Russian health-care system," White said. "If we are successful in this venture, we may explore bringing other technologies -- including blood products, intravenous solutions and renal therapy -- to Russia."

Coinciding with the opening of the MosMed plant will be a Baxter-sponsored tour of Russia, Lithuania, Latvia and Estonia by the Kennedy Center's National Symphony Orchestra, led by internationally renowned Russian Music Director Mstislav Rostropovich. The tour is part of Rostropovich's farewell season with the NSO. A highlight of the two-week tour will be a free concert in Red Square at noon on Sunday, Sept. 26.

Also this week, Russian TV is airing a documentary series underwritten by Baxter that provides a historical perspective on the Nobel Prizes in physics, chemistry, physiology or medicine, literature and peace.

Baxter International Inc., through its subsidiaries, is the world's leading manufacturer and marketer of health-care products, systems and services. The company, based in Deerfield, Ill., offers products to health-care providers in 100 countries, and concentrates research and development programs in biotechnology, cardiovascular medicine, diagnostics, renal therapy and other medical fields. Baxter employs 61,300 people worldwide, and has 83 manufacturing plants, 148 distribution centers and 19 research facilities around the world.

###

# CORPORATE NEWS

Baxter International Inc.
One Baxter Parkway
Deerfield, Illinois 60015 U.S.A.

## Baxter

*For more information, contact:*
*For Baxter in Moscow, Vladimir Ivanov*
*or Galina Tchernakova, 7095-119-6656*
*For Baxter in Moscow (by 9/20), Shawn*
*Ramsey, Palace Hotel,*
*7095-956-3152*

### MEDIA ADVISORY

**WHEN:**    Friday, September 24
9:30 - 11 a.m.
(The show officially opens Thursday, September 23, and
runs through Thursday, September 30. The Baxter booth
will be open all three days and a media representative will
be available; however, Baxter senior managers will be
available only from 9:30-11 a.m. on Friday, September 24.)

**WHAT:**    Tour of Baxter exhibit at the Pharmaceutical, Medical
Equipment and Health-care Trade Show by Baxter's new
Russian sales and marketing team.

Briefings by Baxter senior executives on the company's
strategy and plans for selling its health-care products in
Russia.

**WHERE:**    Pavilion Forum/Krasnaya Presnya
Baxter Booth is in the U.S.A. Pavilion.

**DETAILS:**    Health-care providers from throughout Russia and the
ex-U.S.S.R. republics will attend this health-care trade show
to learn about new health-care techniques and products. It
is the largest show of its kind in Russia and is held once
every four years. There will be more than 600 medical
companies and organizations representing 34 countries,
including Russia.

Baxter's booth will include information and displays of the
health-care technologies and products it is now selling in
Russia. They range from blood and renal products;
cardiovascular diagnostic equipment; bed sheets, towels,
surgical gloves and other hospital supplies; and laboratory
testing equipment.

Baxter is currently manufacturing surgical instruments in
Russia and is exploring the possibility of manufacturing
some of its other product lines locally.

-more-

Page 2/Health-care Trade Show

Currently, Baxter's products are being sold by a
Western-style sales and marketing team -- a rarity in Russia.
Local physicians and professionals were recruited and
trained to sell directly to customers.

Baxter International Inc., through its subsidiaries, is the
leading manufacturer and marketer of health-care products,
systems and services worldwide.  The company, based
outside Chicago, Ill., offers 120,000 products to health-care
providers in 100 countries.  It concentrates research and
development programs in biotechnology, cardiovascular
medicine, diagnostics, renal therapy and other medical fields.

Baxter employs 61,300 people worldwide, and has
83 manufacturing plants, 148 distribution centers and
19 research facilities around the world.  It had 1992 sales of
$8.4 billion.

###

Exhibit 9-2c

Bilingual Brochure   (Courtesy Baxter International, Inc.)

## Attachment:  English-Russian Language Brochure

The primary purpose of the following "brochure" was to communicate Baxter's commitment to the Russian marketplace and unify the many elements of the communication program to launch its operations in the former Soviet Union.

The bilingual piece was included in mailings to invite constituents to concert performances and post-concert, relationship-building events, served as a handout at all concert events and at the plant opening, and became a marketing tool for the company's sales force after the opening festivities.

The collaboration of Russia's Mstislav Rostropovich and the United States' National Symphony Orchestra has led to one of the world's finest symphonic orchestras.

It is appropriate, then, that U.S.-based Baxter International sponsor the Kennedy Center's National Symphony Orchestra tour of Russia to commemorate its own collaboration with the people of this country. The company will open a facility in Moscow to manufacture much-needed surgical instruments for Russian hospitals and physicians.

The facility — called MosMed — represents a significant step toward meeting Russia's needs for high-quality, affordable health care. It will be operated in partnership with NIIAP (roughly translated, The Plant of the Research Institute for Automation and Instruments). Import-antly, the operation will be ruble-based, will use Russian raw materials and equipment, and employ Russian people — initiatives aimed at helping strengthen the nation's economy and making MosMed a viable venture over the long term.

The National Symphony Orchestra tour — which will coincide with the opening of the MosMed facility — is part of the farewell season of the orchestra's distinguished music director, Mstislav Rostropovich. Highlights of the concert series will include an historic public performance concert in Red Square, as well as performances in St. Petersburg, Vilnius, Riga and Tallinn.

The partnership of Maestro Rostropovich and the National Symphony Orchestra has resulted in a world-class orchestra. In this same spirit, it is our hope that Baxter's partnership with Russian business will help lead to the finest health care for its people.

Работая вместе, Мстислав Ростропович из России и Национальный симфонический оркестр из США создали один из лучших в мире музыкальных коллективов.

Именно поэтому американская фирма "Бакстер Интернэшнл" выступила спонсором гастролей по России Национального симфонического оркестра при Центре Кеннеди. Тем самым фирма намерена отметить начало своего сотрудничества с народом России, а именно-открытие в Москве завода по производству хирургических инструментов, столь необходимых для больниц и врачей всей страны.

Создание завода под названием "МосМед" является важным шагом к развитию качественной системы здравоохранения в России. Управление предприятием осуществляется с участием завода Научно-исследовательского института автоматизации и приборостроения (НИИАП). Важно отметить, что производство основано на рублевых расчетах; на заводе работают российские рабочие, а также используются российские сырье и оборудование. Цель такого подхода — содействовать укреплению национальной экономики и превратить МосМед в долговечное жизнеспособное предприятие.

Гастроли Национального симфонического оркестра, которые совпадают по времени с открытием завода МосМед, — это часть прощального сезона выдающегося дирижера Мстислава Ростроповича. В числе самых ярких выступлений будет и исторический концерт-представление для широкой публики на Красной площади, а также концерты в Санкт-Петербурге, Вильнюсе, Риге и Таллине.

Сотрудничество маэстро Ростроповича с Национальным симфоническим оркестром США привело к созданию музыкального коллектива мировой величины. Со своей стороны, мы надеемся на то, что участие "Бакстера" в российском бизнесе поможет России обеспечить ее граждан медицинской помощью высочайшего качества.

# 10

# Relations with Special Publics

SPECIAL PUBLICS ARE DEFINED AS THOSE UNIQUE OR distinctive groups with which an organization needs to communicate. These groups may be minority publics, such as African Americans, Hispanics, or Asian Americans. Practitioners should be aware of the extensive national, geographic, and ethnic subsets that exist within each of these broadly defined minority groups in the United States. For instance, practitioners might mistakenly lump all Hispanics together under the Mexican umbrella. For a Hispanic special event, they could employ a mariachi band and serve Mexican dishes. However, such treatment would easily offend Spaniards, Argentines, or Dominicans, all of whose home cultures differ sharply from one another and from that of Mexico, although all share Spanish as a common language. A similar mistake would be to treat Asian Americans as a singular group or, worse, to refer to them as Orientals. These Asian groups share neither common languages nor common cultural heritages. Many of them, in fact, have been enemies for centuries.

When dealing with a minority group with national origins outside the United States, practitioners would be well advised to consult in advance the embassy or consulate of that group's homeland and certainly the group's local leaders as well.

In addition to ethnic or national minority publics, practitioners may target for special communication such groups as women, students, educators, environmentalists, school-age children, the business community, municipal officials, or community physicians. The list of potential special publics can actually be extended to include all the segments of society.

The fastest growing and most significant of these special groups in the United States is the "senior citizen" segment of the population, a segment expected to double in size by the early twenty-first century. Age groupings such as 50–64 for the "active" seniors, 65–74 for the "less active," and 75-plus for the "elderly" are often used to describe subsegments of the senior citizen audience. These age groupings alone, though, are usually less useful in targeting senior audiences than are their organizational affiliations.

Organizations such as the American Association of Retired Persons (AARP), the National Council on the Aging (NCOA), the National Hispanic Council on Aging, the National Council of Senior Citizens, the National Senior Sports Association, and the Gray Panthers have chapter networks and affiliate organizations that can be used to reach their members. Thus, the key to reaching a senior audience lies in cosponsorship of an event or project with an organization such as the AARP or the NCOA.

As with other forms of public relations, the four-part ROPE process model is a helpful format for preparing and executing programs that target special publics.

# RESEARCH

Research for special programs includes investigation of the client, the reason for the program, and, most important, the distinctive audience to be targeted.

## Client Research

Client research for an organization's relations with a special public should focus on the client's role and reputation with the particular audience. How credible is the organization with this public? Have there been significant complaints against it from this public in the past? What are its past and present communication practices toward this audience? What are its major strengths and weaknesses relative to this public? What opportunities exist to enhance its relations with this public?

## Opportunity or Problem Research

Should a proactive public relations program be devised for this particular audience? Or has some problem arisen that must be addressed with a reactive program? Why should the organization communicate with this audience at all? Detailed answers to these questions will provide the necessary justification for the outlay of funds required for relations with a given special public.

## Audience Research

Obviously, the practitioner should learn as much as possible about a special public. One way to do this is to regard such publics as differentiated communities. In community relations, practitioners address community media, community leaders, and community organizations. These same audience subsets may also be applicable in defining a special public:

Media utilized by this public

Mass

Specialized

Leaders of this public

Public officials

Professional leaders

Ethnic leaders

Neighborhood leaders

Others

Organizations composing this public

Civic

Political

Service

Business

Cultural

Religious

Youth

Other

As in community relations, practitioners should develop special contact lists for the appropriate media and for the special public's leaders and organizations. These materials are indispensable in relations with a special public.

# OBJECTIVES

Programs that target special publics can use both impact and output objectives; and, as in all other types of public relations, the objectives should be specific and quantitative.

## Impact Objectives

Impact objectives represent the desired outcomes of informing or modifying the attitudes or behaviors of the special audience. Some examples include:

1. To increase the knowledge of the organization's minority-benefits program among members of this special public (by 50 percent before January 1)

2. To promote more favorable opinion (30 percent) toward the organization on the part of this special public (during the current year)

3. To stimulate greater participation (15 percent) in the organization's programs by this special public (during the summer months)

## Output Objectives

Output objectives comprise the specific efforts to enhance relations with special publics. For example:

1. To prepare and distribute materials to (30 percent) of the Hispanic community in Washington (during the coming year)

2. To schedule four meetings each year with leaders of the Chinese community in Houston

3. To develop five new projects for African American instructors' use in their classrooms (during the current school year)

# PROGRAMMING

Programming for relations with special publics includes planning the theme and messages, action or special event(s), uncontrolled and controlled media, and effective communication principles in the program's execution.

## Theme and Messages

Both the theme and messages should reflect the desired relationship between the organization and the targeted special public. They will also be an indicator of past and present relationships that exist between the organization and this public.

## Action(s) or Special Event(s)

Actions and special events should concentrate on the major interests of the targeted audience. The most successful actions and special events address the interests, needs, and problems of the particular target group. The special events in the cases in this chapter clearly meet this criterion.

## Uncontrolled and Controlled Media

As mentioned earlier, representatives of both the mass and specialized media aimed at the special audience are an important segment of the audience itself. Uncontrolled media in the form of news releases, photo opportunities or photographs, feature stories, and/or interviews should be prepared in the language of the designated media; they should be directed to media outlets known to be used by this special public.

Controlled media should be prepared with all the cultural, language, ethnic, age, or other demographic specifications of the target public in mind. As with other publics, there can be no substitute for personal interaction in the effective execution of programs.

## Effective Communication

Principles of effective communication are the same for special audiences as they are for most others. Extra care should be taken, however, in the matter of source credibility, which can be enhanced by the selection of a spokesperson from the same demographic group as the targeted audience.

In addition to source credibility, two-way communication and audience participation should also be given extra emphasis in relations with special publics.

Finally, the use of opinion leaders may be highly significant in relations with special publics, especially when the public is an organized ethnic or demographic group. In sum, all aspects of programming for relations with special publics are similar to those of community relations. The special public, in fact, can often be thought of as a community with its own media, leaders, and organizations.

# EVALUATION

The process of evaluating communications aimed at special audiences must take into account the program's objectives. Each one should be measured using previously discussed standards and methods.

Evaluation of special publics cases rely generally on the degree of participation by the target audiences and, in most instances, the amount of publicity generated by the program.

# SUMMARY

Research for programs that target special audiences focuses on the credibility of the client with a particular special public, along with the need or justification for the program. The audience itself can be analyzed using the same categories applicable to community relations—

media, leaders, and organizations. Special audiences can usually be treated as communities, or subcommunities, in their own right.

Objectives for relations with special publics may be impact or output in nature. Impact objectives express desired outcomes, such as augmenting the public's knowledge or influencing its attitudes or behaviors. Without reference to impact, output objectives consist of practitioner efforts to execute the program.

Programming for special publics often uses the significant events of the public's ethnic or cultural past. Along with this, of course, the programming must also address the problems or potential problems of the special group. Although standard controlled and uncontrolled media are used in this form of public relations, there can be no substitute for two-way communication with such audiences. More than others, they need to know that the organization cares enough about them to include a personal touch.

As with other forms of public relations, the special program's stated objectives must be evaluated appropriately. In general, the level of participation by the targeted group and the publicity generated by the program are used as benchmarks of success.

# READINGS ON
# SPECIAL PUBLICS

"A New Agenda." *Working Woman* (November 1992): 55ff.

Bouttilier, Robert. *Targeting Families: Marketing to and Through the New Family.* Ithaca, NY: American Marketing Tools, 1993.

Brimelow, Peter. "The Fracturing of America." *Forbes* (March 30, 1992): 74ff.

Crispell, Diane. "The Real Middle Americans." *American Demographics* 16 (October 1994): 28ff.

Deutschman, Alan. "The Upbeat Generation." *Fortune* (July 13, 1992): 42ff.

Dunn, William. "The Move Toward Ethnic Marketing." *Nation's Business* 80 (July 1992): 39ff.

———. *The Baby Bust: A Generation Comes of Age.* Ithaca, NY: American Marketing Tools, 1993.

Exter, Thomas G. "Middle-Aging Households." *American Demographics* 17 (July 1992): 63.

Frey, William H. "Boomer Magnets." *American Demographics* 17 (March 1992): 34ff.

Fry, Susan. "Reaching Hispanic Publics with Special Events." *Public Relations Journal* 47 (February 1991): 12ff.

Giles, Jeff. "Generation X." *Newsweek* (June 6, 1994): 62ff.

Holland, James R. "Reaching Older Audiences." *Public Relations Journal* 47 (May 1991): 14ff.

Korzenny, Felipe. *Mass Media Effects Across Cultures.* Newbury Park, CA: Sage, 1992.

Lazer, William. *Handbook of Demographics for Marketing and Advertising.* New York: Lexington Books, 1994.

Levine, Joshua. "Generation X." *Forbes* (July 18, 1994): 293ff.

———. "The Man in the Mirror." *Columbia Journalism Review* (March–April 1994): 27ff.

List, S. K. "The Right Place to Find Children." *American Demographics* 14 (February 1992): 44ff.

Longino, Charles E., Jr. "Myths of an Aging Population." *American Demographics* 16 (August 1994): 36ff.

"Mainstream Companies Address Hispanic Community's Needs." *Public Relations Journal* 47 (February 1991): 30.

Major, Michael J. "Dancing to a Different Drummer." *Public Relations Journal* 48 (November 1992): 20ff.

Mandel, Michael J., et al. "The Immigrants." *Business Week* (July 13, 1992): 114ff.

Morgan, Carol M., and Doran J. Levy. *Segmenting the Mature Market.* New York: Probus, 1994.

Oberdorf, Meyera. "The Changing Role of Women in the 21st Century." *Vital Speeches* (October 1, 1992): 751–754.

O'Hare, William P., and William H. Fry. "Booming, Suburban and Black." *American Demographics* 14 (September 1992): 30ff.

O'Neill, June. "The Changing Economic Status of Black Americans." *The American Enterprise* (September–October 1992): 70ff.

Palen, J. John. *The Suburbs.* New York: McGraw-Hill, 1994.

Pol, Louis G., et al. "The Eight Stages of Aging." *American Demographics* 14 (August 1992): 54ff.

Rabin, Steve. "How to Sell Across Cultures." *American Demographics* 16 (March 1994): 56ff.

Saindor, Gabrielle, et al. "The Other Americans." *American Demographics* 16 (June 1994): 36ff.

Schwartz, Felice N. "Women as a Business Imperative." *Harvard Business Review* 70 (March–April 1992): 105ff.

Tully, Shawn. "Teens: The Most Global Market of All." *Fortune* (May 16, 1994): 82ff.

Underhill, Paco. "Kids in Stores." *American Demographics* 16 (June 1994): 22ff.

Westerbeck, Tim. "Suppliers Zero in on a Growing Hispanic Market." *Public Relations Journal* 48 (July 1992): 7ff.

Wolfe, David B. "Targeting the Mature Mind." *American Demographics* 16 (March 1994): 32ff.

Zinn, Laura, et al. "Teen." *Business Week* (April 11, 1994): 76ff.

# Special Publics
# Cases

*Southwestern Bell Telephone Company (SWBT) targeted a special audience of lower-income "phoneless" Texans to provide needed discount telephone service. Exhibits 10-1a and 10-1b are news releases explaining the program in English and Spanish. Exhibit 10-1c is a 30-second radio public service announcement (PSA). Exhibits 10-1d and 10-1e are SWBT advertisements for the program. Exhibit 10-1f is a map showing phoneless households in Texas.*

**CASE 10-1**

## Throwing the "Phoneless" a Lifeline: Southwestern Bell Telephone Promotes Discount Phone Service

Southwestern Bell Telephone Company with Fleishman-Hillard, Inc., St. Louis, MO

### Summary

Southwestern Bell Telephone Company overcame fear, ignorance, illiteracy, and language barriers to provide a lifeline to indigent Texans. Texas leads the nation in the number of households without phone service, today's vital link to emergency and family services. By combining a federal program that provides free phone installation with its own monthly discount for households with incomes lower than the federal poverty level, Southwestern Bell helps many of Texas's half-million phoneless households to acquire a "lifeline." To increase awareness of this program, a monthlong public relations campaign was designed and executed, resulting in a fivefold increase in inquiries and a doubling of subscriptions.

### Research

The U.S. Census Bureau reports that more than 523,000 households—or 8.6 percent of all households in Texas—were without phones. Minority households were hit particularly hard, with 25 percent of Hispanic and 20 percent of African American households without phones. SWBT's own research showed that many in the target group

Courtesy Southwestern Bell Telephone Company

were distrustful of the government and major corporations. Many Hispanic households sheltered illegal immigrants. Proprietary demographic research into the values of the target group revealed that "family" and "family security" ranked extremely high. Literacy rates among potential subscribers were extremely low.

## Objective

To increase the rate of subscriptions to the Lifeline Discount phone service dramatically.

### Strategy

- Base the campaign on safety and security themes
- Weight the campaign to electronic media and direct forms of communication
- Create a system of icons that would communicate key messages visually
- Partner with credible and trusted third parties that held meaning to target groups
- Create a fully bilingual campaign (English/Spanish)
- Make it easy

### Execution

Fifteen markets in Texas were chosen for the October 1994 campaign: Dallas, Fort Worth, Houston, Corpus Christi, Victoria, Harlingen, McAllen, Laredo, El Paso, San Antonio, Lubbock, Abilene, Amarillo, Austin, and Odessa. Campaign elements included:

- *800 number:* The established 800 number was promoted in every communication, without exception. The 800 number became an easy point of entry for subscribers.

- *Logo and theme:* "Talking head" logos connected by a phone line became the central visual of the campaign. The talking heads communicated in icons (fire, police, and ambulance symbols). The campaign theme was "Lifeline Discount Phone Service. Now and Always."

- *Third-party endorsements:* The Lifeline team enlisted the endorsements of two groups that would become central to the campaign's theme of safety: the International Association of Fire Chiefs and the Texas Association of Chiefs of Police. The fire chiefs partnership was primary, and it provided grassroots outreach through thousands of firehouses in and near poor neighborhoods.

- *Public service announcements:* Spanish and English 30-second TV and radio PSAs were produced, using the talking heads, and were distributed to more than 350 TV and radio stations around Texas, accompanied by a letter from the International Association of Fire Chiefs to encourage their use. The dialogue emphasized the importance of the phone for safety purposes, the available discount, and the ease and convenience of obtaining the discount.

- *Celebrity involvement:* Singer Vikki Carr, entertainer Johnny Canales, and Texas Rangers catcher Ivan "Pudge" Rodriguez—celebrities with Texas connections who were familiar to the target audience—were recruited as celebrity spokespersons for Lifeline. Each appeared at kick-off media events, helped canvass nearby neighborhoods, and recorded localized, bilingual TV and radio PSAs about Lifeline. Canales promoted Lifeline on his television variety show, which has a large audience among Texas Hispanics, and during a concert in South Texas.

- *Educational campaign:* The Lifeline team developed an educational program in poster format for grades one through three. The program presented three lessons: telephone etiquette, using the telephone in emergencies, and telephone usage tips for children who are frequently home alone. Each kit included a camera-ready Lifeline information sheet for those teachers who desired to make reproductions for their classes. About 14,000 programs were distributed to Chapter One schools (so designated due to the poverty that surrounds them).

- *Retail partners:* Fiesta supermarkets and Popeye's fried chicken restaurants, along with local merchants in each market, supported the program. These partners provided space for Lifeline posters with tear-off fliers at their locations and, in the case of Fiesta, printed Lifeline information on 1 million shopping bags.

- *Volunteers:* Southwestern Bell volunteer organizations—Hacemos (Spanish for "the do-ers"), Network (African American group), and Pioneers (retirees)—supported the publicity campaign by canvassing neighborhoods and staffing booths at fairs and festivals in target markets.

- *Media events:* Media events kicked off the publicity campaign in each market. Generally they were held at fire stations or schools and featured fire and police chiefs and other local officials. In some markets, the celebrity endorsers participated in these events.

- *Radio promotions:* Radio was a prime channel for Lifeline messages. Leading Hispanic and African American radio stations were identified in each market, and near saturation-level promotions were conducted, including remote broadcasts from partners' retail sites.

- *Posters/fliers:* About 20,000 bilingual posters with tear-off pads, and more than 800,000 fliers, were distributed by volunteers, firefighters, and retail partners during the campaign.

## Results

- Daily calls to the Lifeline toll-free telephone line increased more than five times—up to 5,000 calls per day.

- The rate of subscription more than doubled as a result of the campaign, and subscription rates continue well above precampaign levels. More than 90,000 Texas households now are on "Lifeline."

Lifeline Discount Telephone Service
Lifeline – Servicio telefónico con descuento

## FOR IMMEDIATE RELEASE

Contact:  Thomas D. Pagano, 314/982-1702
Christopher R. Horner, 314/982-0597

**PROGRAM PARTNERS**

INTERNATIONAL ASSOCIATION
OF FIRE CHIEFS
*Chief T. L. Siegfried,*
*President*

THE TEXAS ASSOCIATION
OF CHIEFS OF POLICE
*Chief Richard Czech,*
*Midland, Texas*
*President*

SOUTHWESTERN BELL
TELEPHONE CO.
Hacemos
*Amanda Contreras,*
*President*
NETWORK
*Monica Conley,*
*President*

## SOUTHWESTERN BELL TELEPHONE'S 'LIFELINE' PROGRAM PROVIDES DISCOUNT SERVICE TO RESIDENTS IN NEED

**BROWNSVILLE**, Texas, October 5, 1994 --  While Texas leads the country in the number of households without telephones, the South Texas counties of Cameron and Hidalgo lead the nation with the highest percentage of households in metropolitan areas without phones, according to a study by the U.S. Census Bureau.

"Being 'phoneless' creates a very serious situation for these families," said Southwestern Bell Telephone Co. Service Representative Thelma Navarro. "If an accident occurs in their home, if they witness a crime, or a fire breaks out in their house, apartment or mobile home, there is no way to call the police, fire department or an ambulance. It's very risky.

"The state's phoneless also have a difficult time finding jobs because potential employers cannot call them for interviews," Navarro added. "Family communications are harder because, without a phone, they cannot call parents, children, brothers, sisters, or other loved ones."

According to the latest U.S. Census Bureau information, 523,034 Texas households -- or about 8.6 percent of all households in the state -- were without telephone service in 1990.  In South Texas, however, the problem was worse.

Cameron and Hidalgo counties had the highest phoneless rates in the nation, compared to other metro areas, according to the Census report.  The report shows that 17 percent of the households in Cameron County and 16.5 percent of the households in Hildago County -- nearly 30,000 households combined -- did not have telephones.

- more -

Ⓐ **Southwestern Bell** Telephone

Add One/Lifeline

"Southwestern Bell's Lifeline program was designed to help people obtain phone service
and change those statistics," Navarro said.  "By calling our toll-free number **(1-800-244-5993),**
people can learn about our Lifeline Discount Telephone Service to ensure that as many Texans as
possible -- especially those in the Rio Grande Valley area -- have phone service in their homes."

Persons with low incomes can receive a telephone service discount through the Lifeline
program, providing their income is at or below the federal poverty level.  Additionally, they must
be the head of the household and receive social service benefits such as food stamps, Aid to
Families with Dependent Children, Supplemental Security Income, Women, Infants and
Children, or other qualifying services.  Only one telephone line per household is permitted.

**The monthly phone rate with a Lifeline discount ranges from less than $2.50 for**
**basic, measured service to about $7.50 for unlimited, flat rate service.**

"Southwestern Bell's Lifeline program enables eligible Texans to receive a $7 discount
off their monthly telephone bill," Navarro said.  "With this discount, residents in the Rio Grande
Valley can definitely have immediate telephone access to emergency services, to family and
friends, and a better, safer lifestyle."

The effort to provide telephone service to as many South Texas residents as possible is
being strongly supported by the International Association of Fire Chiefs, local fire chiefs and
other authorities.

"Having a telephone in your home is vital," said Brownsville Fire Chief Ramiro Torres.
"It is a life-saving tool in the event of an emergency and a vital link to families, friends,
employment, and a better life."  Chief Torres urged all area residents without phones to call
Southwestern Bell's toll-free number to learn more about Lifeline and obtain telephone service.

# # #

Exhibit 10-1b "Lifeline" Program News Release in Spanish (Courtesy Southwestern Bell Telephone Company)

Lifeline Discount Telephone Service
Lifeline – Servicio telefónico con descuento

Genevieve Hilden, 214/953-0333

### EL PROGRAMA "LIFELINE" DE SOUTHWESTERN BELL OFRECE SERVICIO CON DESCUENTO A RESIDENTES CON BAJOS INGRESOS

**PROGRAM PARTNERS**

INTERNATIONAL ASSOCIATION OF FIRE CHIEFS
*Chief T. L. Siegfried, President*

THE TEXAS ASSOCIATION OF CHIEFS OF POLICE
*Chief Richard Czech, Midland, Texas President*

SOUTHWESTERN BELL TELEPHONE CO.
Hacemos
*Amanda Contreras, President*
NETWORK
*Monica Conley, President*

BROWNSVILLE, Texas, 5 de octubre de 1994 -- Mientras que Texas es el estado con el mayor numero de casas sin teléfonos, los condados en el sur de Tejas Cameron e Hidalgo tienen el porcentaje más alto del país de casas en zonas urbanas sin teléfono, según datos del censo.

"Estar sin teléfono es muy serio para estas familias," dijo Thelma Navarro representante de Southwestern Bell. "Si ocurre un accidente en su casa, ven un crimen, o tienen fuego, no pueden llamar a la policía, los bomberos o a una ambulancia. Es una situación peligrosa."

"Sin teléfono, es más difícil encontrar trabajo por que no se les puede llamar para entrevistas," añadió Navarro. "Las familias no se pueden comunicar porque no pueden llamar a los padres, los niños, hermanos o personas queridas."

Según datos del censo para 1994, hay 523,034 casas tejanas, o sea el 8.6 por ciento de todos los hogares en el estado, que no tenían servicio de teléfono en 1990. El problemas es más grave en el sur de Texas.

Los condados Cameron e Hidalgo tienen la tasa más alta de hogares sin servicio de teléfono, comparado con otras zonas metropolitanas, según datos del censo. El informe muestra que el 17 por ciento de hogares en Cameron y el 16.5 por ciento en Hidalgo, casi 30,000 hogares entre los dos condados, no tienen teléfono.

-sigue-

Ⓐ **Southwestern Bell** Telephone

371

Exhibit 10-1b
(*continued*)

"Lifeline" Program News Release in Spanish   (Courtesy Southwestern Bell Telephone Company)

Agregar uno
Lifeline

"El programa Lifeline de Southwestern Bell, fue creado para que los residentes puedan tener servicio de teléfono y cambiar estas estadísticas," dijo Navarro. "Llamando gratis al **1-800-244-5993**, se obtendrá información sobre el programa Lifeline de servicio telefónico con descuento. Es importante que los residentes, especialmente en el valle, tengan servicio de teléfono en su casa."

Las personas con bajos ingresos pueden recibir el descuento por medio de Lifeline, si sus ingresos están al nivel federal de pobreza o menos. Deben ser el encargado o la encargada de la familia y recibir estampillas de comida, Ayuda a familias con hijos dependientes, SSI, WIC u otro servicio similar. Solo se permite una línea telefónica por hogar.

**La tarifa mensual con Lifeline es menos de $2.50 para servicio básico y $7.50 para servicio con llamadas ilimitadas.**

"El programa Lifeline permite que los residentes elegibles reciban un descuento de $7 cada mes en su cuenta de teléfono," dijo Navarro. "Con este descuento, los residentes del valle pueden tener acceso a los servicios de emergencia, los familiares y amistades, y una vida más segura."

Este esfuerzo para ofrecer servicio de teléfono a todos los residentes cuenta con el apoyo de la Asociación internacional de bomberos, jefes de bomberos locales y otras autoridades.

"Tener servicio de teléfono en casa es vital," dijo Ramiro Torres, el jefe de bomberos de Brownsville. Puede salvar vidas en casos de emergencia y es esencial para comunicarse con el trabajo, la familia y las amistades." Torres recomendó que todos los residentes sin teléfono llamen al número 800 de Lifeline para recibir más información y obtener servicio de teléfono.

# # #

Exhibit 10-1c

Program PSA    (Courtesy Southwestern Bell Telephone Company)

Southwestern Bell Telephone Co.
Lineline Discount Telephone Service
Radio PSAs

*30 Seconds*:
A telephone at home can be a lifeline when emergencies happen, and a
comforting way to stay in touch with friends and family every day.  But the fact
is, more than a half million homes in Texas today don't have a telephone.

Lifeline Discount Telephone Service from Southwestern Bell Telephone offers
low-income residents a substantial discount on rates for basic monthly service.  If
you qualify, you can start getting phone service at a discount of up to $7 a month
*every* month.

To find out if you qualify for this new service, call toll free 1-800-244-5993.
Spanish-speaking operating are standing by to help you.

A public service message from this station and Southwestern Bell Telephone Co.

| Save up to $7 on basic phone service if you: | Ahorre hasta $7 en su cuenta mensual telefónica si Ud.: |
|---|---|
| Are head of household or spouse of head of household | Es cabeza de la casa o esposo o esposa de cabeza de la casa |
| Have income at or below federal poverty level | Sus ingresos no superan el nivel federal de pobreza |
| Receive benefits from one of the following programs: | Recibe beneficios de uno de los siguientes programas: |

- *Aid to Families with Dependent Children* / *Asistencia para familias con niños dependientes*
- *Food Stamps* / *Estampillas de comida*
- *Home Energy Assistance Program* / *Asistencia para energía en el hogar*
- *Medical Assistance Program* / *Asistencia programa médica*
- *Supplemental Security Income* / *Cheque suplemental*
- *Women, Infants and Children* / *WIC para la mujer*

| Have only one telephone line in the household | Solo una línea por hogar |
|---|---|

## 1-800-244-5993

Lifeline Discount Telephone Service
*Lifeline – Servicio telefónico con descuento*

Southwestern Bell
Telephone

Exhibit 10-1f

Phoneless Households (Courtesy Southwestern Bell Telephone Company)

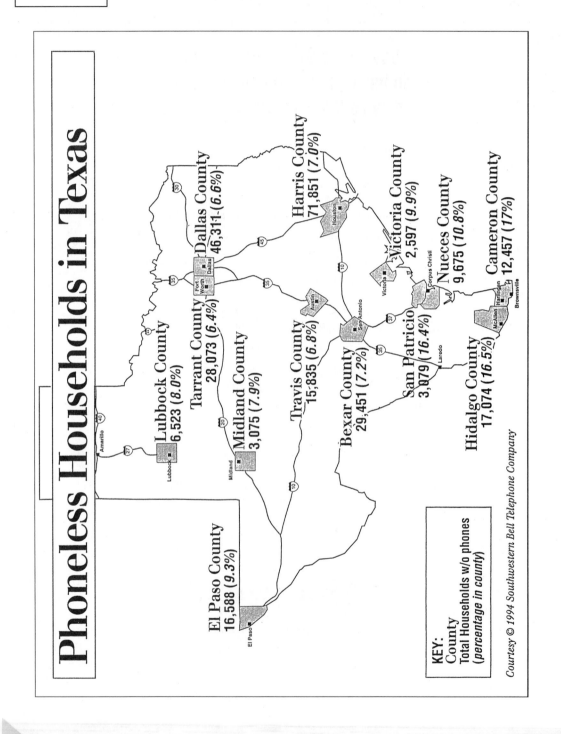

# Phoneless Households in Texas

**Lubbock County**
6,523 (*8.0%*)

**Tarrant County**
28,073 (*6.4%*)

**Dallas County**
46,311-(*6.6%*)

**Midland County**
3,075 (*7.9%*)

**Harris County**
71,851 (*7.0%*)

**Travis County**
15,835 (*6.8%*)

**Victoria County**
2,597 (*9.9%*)

**Nueces County**
9,675 (*10.8%*)

**Cameron County**
12,457 (*17%*)

**Bexar County**
29,451 (*7.2%*)

**San Patricio**
3,079 (*16.4%*)

**Hidalgo County**
17,074 (*16.5%*)

**El Paso County**
16,588 (*9.3%*)

KEY:
County
Total Households w/o phones
(*percentage in county*)

*Courtesy © 1994 Southwestern Bell Telephone Company*

*With child immunization rates below 50 percent in some parts of Atlanta, the Carter Center conducted a program to raise awareness about the importance of immunization and preventive health care for children. The program culminated in a successful "immunization week." Exhibit 10-2a is a media advisory about the campaign launch. Exhibit 10-2b is a program Q and A. Exhibits 10-2c and 10-2d are storyboards for 30-second television PSAs. Exhibits 10-2e and 10-2f are campaign posters.*

**CASE 10-2**

## Give Your Kids a Shot of Love

The Carter Center's Atlanta Project, Atlanta, GA, with CHD Public Relations, Atlanta, GA

### Background

Licensed dogs have a much better chance of receiving vaccinations than preschool children in the United States. Vaccinations are some of the most effective public health interventions available, and vaccination rates are a key indicator of the adequacy of child health services in a community. Ironically, the success of previous immunization programs in the United States has led to complacency.

Because all states require certain vaccinations for children to enter school, 95 percent or more of children over age 5 are fully immunized. But vaccination rates are much lower among preschool children. The CDC estimates that 40–60 percent of children under age 2—1.6 to 2.4 million infants and toddlers—are not fully immunized. African American and Hispanic children are less likely to be vaccinated at the appropriate age than Caucasian children, and vaccination levels among 2-year-olds in some inner city populations can be as low as 10 percent.

This alarming scenario profiles residents of The Atlanta Project (TAP), a program begun by former President Jimmy Carter to address many of the problems facing Atlanta's poorest communities. TAP was launched to empower citizens to deal with problems dividing families and urban neighborhoods—soaring drop-out rates, teenage pregnancy, unemployment, crime, drug abuse, inadequate health care, and home-

Courtesy The Carter Center

lessness, among others. Only 68 percent of Georgia's children were adequately immunized, with rates below 50 percent in many TAP neighborhoods. (TAP neighborhoods include approximately 200,000 adults and 50,000 children.)

TAP's Immunization/Children's Health Initiative aimed to impact low immunization rates and inadequate health care. The shots were to be a first step to get children into a computerized system, introduce them to a primary health care facility, and then follow up with other preventive measures.

## Research

Through research conducted with the Centers for Disease Control and Prevention, the Carter Center's Child Survival Task Force, Georgia State Health Department, and county health departments, CHD helped determine that lack of education, access, and cost were the major barriers to children receiving proper immunizations. CHD also considered the demographics and psychographics of TAP residents when planning media relations activities to ensure that the correct messages were communicated to applicable audiences.

In addition to immunizing preschoolers, studies revealed that TAP neighborhoods needed a system to provide for sustained immunization coverage. As of January 1993, no system existed for metro Atlanta counties to update and share health records. TAP and its initiative partners recognized early that a computerized tracking system linking the three counties, the community health centers, Grady Memorial Hospital, and other clinical sites in the TAP areas was a necessity.

With the problem clearly defined and obstacles identified, an independent research study was conducted to determine the most effective communication channels in sending messages throughout TAP communities. CHD also conducted a media audit of past publicity from other immunization campaigns across the country and spoke with representatives at Every Child By Two, a national immunization organization cofounded by Mrs. Rosalynn Carter and Mrs. Betty Bumpers, wife of Arkansas Senator Dale Bumpers. CHD applied its findings directly to the media relations plan.

## Planning

The initiative's Media/Public Relations Committee was formed three months before the launch and was charged with informing the public about the initiative and impressing upon TAP residents the importance of immunizations as the first step to fundamental health care for children. Research led the committee to place emphasis on broadcast coverage, urban radio sponsorship, and collaborative efforts with civic, county, and public organizations. The initiative would include the nation's first neighbor-to-neighbor community walk-through attempted in conjunction with an immunization program—volunteers were needed to visit every TAP household to identify children under 5 and help during immunization week. Finally, as an incentive to volunteers, children, and parents who took part in the initiative, a Kids' Celebration was planned. The celebration, hosted by Gladys Knight, with a special appearance by Michael Jackson, featured rap group TLC, Governor Zell Miller, Mayor Maynard Jackson, President and Mrs. Jimmy Carter, and local celebrities.

Primary initiative objectives included:

- Recruiting volunteers and informing TAP residents about the neighborhood walk-through.

- Raising awareness within the community about the importance of immunizations and preventive health care for children, as well as providing details about immunization week.

- Broaden the exposure of TAP and its cluster communities to the entire metro Atlanta area.

## Implementation

The communications team planned and implemented the program in phases:

### Initiative Launch/Start-Up

Tactics and tools:

- Conducted a major press conference staged at a TAP office/immunization site and featured TAP staff, cluster coordinators, President Carter, entertainer Michael Jackson, Atlanta Hawks basketball star Kevin Willis, and key local and state officials.

- Developed extensive media kit to explain all phases and distributed to a broad media list.

- Facilitated newspaper editorial board meetings to solicit positive opinion pieces.

- Conducted special briefing for public service directors from local radio and television stations to secure airtime for PSAs.

### Community Awareness and Volunteer Recruitment

Tactics and tools:

- Created a multifaceted, full-scale media campaign and materials around the theme "Give Your Kids a Shot of Love," featured on posters, billboards, educational materials, and PSAs.

- Created and produced two PSAs for all stages of the campaign. (All talent, creative, and production provided pro bono.)
- Designed and executed several ads and secured pro bono space in major newspapers and key minority publications.
- Developed and promoted a hot line to recruit volunteers.
- Scheduled multiple appearances for spokespeople on television and radio.
- Placed special inserts in telephone bills to promote campaign and recruit volunteers, and placed stories in public transportation news-letters for all bus and rail commuters.

### *Community Mobilization for Neighborhood Walk-Through*

Tactics and tools:

- Staged a news conference the morning of the walk-through at a TAP neighborhood site.
- Conducted a balloon lift-off at all sites to signal the start of a uni-fied effort across the city.
- Secured the involvement of top-rated local radio station as official sponsor of the walk-through to broadcast live throughout the day.
- Produced TAP t-shirts to identify volunteers traveling door-to-door in inner city neighborhoods.
- Wrote and produced educational materials.
- Formulated a comprehensive crisis communications plan to handle medical or security emergencies (the walk-through took place the morning that the Rodney King verdict was announced).

### *Immunization Week*

Tactics and tools:

- Organized postimmunization week roundtable with national media.
- Issued press releases announcing immunization activities and cre-ated posters, billboards, and educational materials.
- Promoted immunization sites by scheduling celebrities at various locations.
- Produced flyers for churches and other religious organizations.
- Developed banners and other signage for sites.
- Solicited promotional awards from local attractions as immuniza-tion incentives.
- Arranged for site listings in local media.
- Coordinated live and taped radio and television interviews through-out the week.

## Kids' Celebration

Tactics and tools:

- Identified a producer and coordinated with the support team to stage the event.

- Created the program, banners, and other promotional pieces for distribution at the event.

- Conducted a press conference on the day of the celebration, featuring President Carter, entertainers, and city officials.

- Coordinated local, national, and international press coverage.

- Facilitated video coverage of the event.

- Coordinated all celebrity and donor recognition programs and publicity.

The budget for the entire public relations campaign was $28,000, including time and out-of-pocket expenses. Because of the nonprofit nature of the client, CHD donated nearly $50,000 in professional fees.

## Results

The Immunization/Children's Health Initiative was an overwhelming success. The tangible results are easy to describe: Nearly 16,000 children were seen at area immunization sites; public health department and health professionals coordinated their efforts and were involved at all levels; some 12,000 volunteers turned out to serve others; and the comprehensive computer database to track children's immunizations is almost fully operational. The intangibles are harder to capture. The spirit of community that swelled around this effort was immense.

Hailed by the CDC and other national health experts as the most successful immunization program in the nation, in addition to the phenomenal turnout, more than 4,200 calls were placed to the immunization hot line.

Total media impressions for the two-month media relations effort amounted to 114,624,957 print and audiences of 55,504,490 in television and 22,163,400 in radio. Follow-up surveys cited the news media coverage and conversations with friends and neighbors as primary sources for learning about the immunization program.

The success of the TAP initiative impressed organizations around the nation, including Hillary Rodham Clinton's staff for health care reform. TAP advisers have been asked to testify before legislative committees about the details of the initiative. Materials and PSAs developed for the initiative have been supplied to the CDC and the Department of Health and Human Services for inclusion into a national immunization rollout.

Because of numerous inquiries from around the country, an 80-page report on the results of the initiative has been prepared for others to use as a model.

| Exhibit 10-2a | Program Media Advisory (Courtesy The Carter Center) |

NEWS F R O M THE CARTER CENTER

Contact:    Kathy Cosgrove        Gwen Davis
              CHD Public Relations    The Atlanta Project
              (404) 892-4505         (404) 881-3400

## MEDIA ADVISORY

### THE ATLANTA PROJECT LAUNCHES NEIGHBOR-TO-NEIGHBOR CAMPAIGN

**WHO:**    Former President and Mrs. Carter, sports figures, politicians, news media celebrities, Ronald McDonald and thousands of volunteers from The Atlanta Project (TAP) clusters and surrounding communities.

**WHAT:**    The most comprehensive immunization program ever attempted begins with a training session for volunteers in 25 different gathering sites in TAP. Following the training session, 2,500 balloons will be released to "kick-off" the day's activities. The balloons symbolically represent the many children and families the volunteers hope to visit during the day. Volunteers will attempt to visit the 203,000 homes within TAP to identify children under the age of six who are in need of immunizations.

**WHY:**    Immunization rates in TAP areas may be as low as 48 percent in Fulton County and 61 percent in DeKalb County for children under two years of age. Because all states require certain vaccinations as a condition of entry into school, 94 percent or more of children over age 5 are fully immunized. But vaccination rates are much lower among preschool children.

**WHERE:**    25 gathering sites within TAP (call (404)892-4505 for complete list of locations).

**WHEN:**    **Saturday, April 17, 9:00 a.m.** training session.
              10:00 a.m. multiple site balloon launch followed by door-to-door campaign.

**SPECIAL PHOTO OPPORTUNITY AT 8:15 A.M.:**
**Former President and Mrs. Carter will be joined by all celebrities at the Crim High School Theatre for a brief question and answer session for the news media. At 8:45 a.m. all will disperse to the different gathering sites. President Carter will remain in the Crim cluster for the training session and door-to-door campaign. Mrs. Carter will move to the Decatur cluster. Specific celebrity cluster assignments will be available at the photo op.**

Crim High School       Directions:   I-20 East to Maynard Terrace Exit. Turn left -- cross expressway.
256 Clifton Street, SE    From 75/85   Turn right on Memorial (at first light). Go one block. Turn right
Atlanta, GA 30317                on Clifton Street to enter parking lot. Crim High School is at
                                  corner of Clifton Street and Memorial.

Exhibit 10-2b    Program Q. and A.    (Courtesy The Carter Center)

NEWS F R O M THE CARTER CENTER

## The Atlanta Project's Immunization/
## Children's Health Initiative

**SEVEN KEY QUESTIONS**

**Q.**    Why has The Atlanta Project targeted Immunization and Children's Health for action?

**A.**    54,000 children under the age of five live within the boundaries of The Atlanta Project. Approximately one half are not adequately immunized against preventable childhood diseases. Adequate immunization and access to primary health care for all children are goals shared throughout the community. Additionally, immunization is cost effective. One dollar spent on immunization now saves ten dollars that would have to be spent later treating these preventable diseases.

**Q.**    Who is involved with this effort in addition to The Atlanta Project?

**A.**    There is a broad coalition that has been planning this effort since November, 1992. The coalition is called "The Immunization Resource Group." Representatives include: Scottish Rite Children's Medical Center's "Immunize Georgia's Little Guys", Rosalynn Carter's and Betty Bumpers' "Every Child By Two", the Centers for Disease Control and Prevention, the Task Force for Child Survival and Development, the State and County Health Departments, the Atlanta religious community, the area school districts, and others.

**Q.**    What immunizations will be provided during this campaign and what will they cost?

**A.**    The vaccines administered will begin/boost protection for the following diseases: Diphtheria, Tetanus, Pertussis, Polio, Measles, Mumps, Rubella, and H. influenzae type B. They will be given for free.

**Q.**    Will this initiative cost the taxpayers additional money?

**A.**    No. The entire program is being funded by either private donations or by contributions of services or material from businesses in the community.

Exhibit 10-2b
(*continued*)

Program Q. and A.    (Courtesy The Carter Center)

**Q.    What are the goals and the timetable of this initiative?**

A.    A complete list of the goals and a revised timetable are attached.  Basically, the goals are to mobilize the community through a "Neighbor-to-Neighbor" door-to-door campaign on Saturday and Sunday, April 17 and 18 and then to immunize as many children as possible during the week of April 24 - May 1.

**Q.    Is this campaign a one time effort?**

A.    No.  Both the community mobilization effort and immunization week are intended to serve as "kick-offs."  The immunization week, April 24 - May 1, is scheduled to coincide with the CDC's National Preschool Immunization Week.  The goal, however, is to assure that 90% of children under five living within the area of The Atlanta Project are adequately immunized by January 1, 1994.  Remember, this effort does not replace the service delivery system already in place.  Immunizations will be given by the county health departments and the community health centers.  Most important, we are all working to put a system in place that will track children from birth so that we can coordinate their immunization and help assure access to good primary health care.  That is what this effort is really about.  If we succeed, we will not need another "campaign" a year from now.

**Q.    What relationship does this effort have to the Clinton administration's immunization effort?**

A.    If the Clinton plan to increase funding for immunization is successful, resources will become available to help Atlanta and Georgia not only immunize those children who are currently not protected, but more importantly, will strengthen the infrastructure that is responsible to immunize our children.  We will not need "campaigns."

Our April initiative has generated some interest nationally and may serve as a model for other programs if we succeed.

Exhibit 10-2c    TV Spot Storyboard    (Courtesy The Carter Center)

C                          H                          D

"GRANDMOTHER" 30 SEC.

1.  GRANDMOTHER
    SEATED ON PORCH
    WITH TWO SMALL
    CHILDREN.  SHE
    SPEAKS TO CAMERA.

1.  SFX:  OUTDOOR
    SOUNDS PLUS CREAKING
    OF GLIDER GRANDMOTHER
    IS SEATED ON.

GRANDMOTHER:  You ready
for this weekend?  Well
something's happening ...
you're gonna have a visitor.
This Saturday or Sunday a
volunteer for The Atlanta
Project -- one of your
neighbors -- will be coming
to your door.  That neighbor
will tell you how to get
your kids immunized.
So you be sure to welcome the
volunteer -- and like they
say, Give your kids a shot
of love.  Immunize them.
Thank you.

2.  POSTER WITH
    THEME LINE

COLE HENDERSON DRAKE, INC   400 COLONY SQUARE   SUITE 500   1201 PEACHTREE STREET, N.E.   ATLANTA, GEORGIA 30361   (404) 892-4500   FAX: (404) 892-4522

Exhibit 10-2d    TV Spot Storyboard    (Courtesy The Carter Center)

C                                        H                                        D

"CHILDREN" 30 SEC.

1.    CHILDREN IN                         1.    SFX: TYPICAL CHATTER
      PRE-SCHOOL CENTER.                        & NOISES OF
      THEY'RE INVOLVED                          CHILDREN
      IN LEARNING & PLAY
      THRUOUT THE SPOT.

VOICE OVER:  You're looking

at a future secretary of

state... a surgeon...

prima ballerina...supreme

court justice... a chairwoman

of the board...

But first, you've got to

protect them -- against

childhood disease.

Give your kids a shot

of love.

2.    POSTER WITH                  Immunize them. It's

      THEME LINE                   free.  It's quick.  It's safe

and simple.  So immunize...

April 24 through May 1.


FREEZE FRAME.

GIVE YOUR KIDS
A SHOT OF LOVE.

Immunize them.    April 24-May 1.

COLE HENDERSON DRAKE, INC.  400 COLONY SQUARE  SUITE 500  1201 PEACHTREE STREET, N.E  ATLANTA, GEORGIA 30361  (404) 892-4500  FAX. (404) 892-4522

Exhibit 10-2e | Campaign Poster (Courtesy The Carter Center)

Exhibit 10-2f | Campaign Poster  (Courtesy The Carter Center)

**THE ATLANTA PROJECT**

# Kids' Celebration

**MISTRESS OF CEREMONIES**
**GLADYS KNIGHT**

**FEATURING**

BOOKER T. WASHINGTON HIGH SCHOOL BAND
ALLEN WARD, DIRECTOR

GOVERNOR ZELL MILLER

MAYOR MAYNARD JACKSON

THE HONORABLE JIMMY CARTER & ROSALYNN CARTER

KIDSGYM USA

SOWETO STREET BEAT DANCE COMPANY

TLC

KIDS' CELEBRATION SINGERS
ROBIN BROWN, MUSICAL DIRECTOR
FEATURING
DOUGLASS HIGH SCHOOL CHOIR
NANCY BISHOP, CHOIR DIRECTOR

JOHNTÁ AUSTIN
KAYCEE GROGAN
USHER RAYMOND
CHIMERE SCOTT

**AND A SPECIAL APPEARANCE BY**
# MICHAEL JACKSON

*Many senior citizens do not recognize stroke warning signs. The Upjohn Company developed a stroke medication that must be used within the first six hours following stroke onset. Upjohn teamed up with the National Stroke Association to educate consumers about stroke warning signs and the need for immediate treatment. Exhibit 10-3a is a news release announcing the consensus on stroke emergency treatment. Exhibit 10-3b is a flyer used in the campaign.*

**CASE 10-3**

## When Stroke Strikes: The First Six Hours

The Upjohn Company and the National Stroke Association with Ketchum Public Relations

### Situation

Imagine feeling numbness in your right arm and experiencing blurred vision. You don't know what's wrong, so you lie down and wait for the symptoms to pass. Later that day, you call your doctor, who sends you to the emergency department. Your doctor fears you are having a stroke. At the emergency department, your family is told that there is little that can be done. Everyone will have to "wait and see" the extent of the brain damage.

This scenario is far too common. A recent study shows that most Americans don't reach the emergency department until 24 hours after stroke onset. Ninety-seven percent don't recognize stroke warning signs. In addition, because most health care professionals believe that there is little that can be done to treat a stroke patient, treatments vary from hospital to hospital, and most adopt a "wait-and-see" approach. The Upjohn Company is developing a new medication called Freedox that will lessen the neurological damage caused by a stroke. However, in order for the drug to be used effectively, it must be administered within the first six hours following stroke onset. Upjohn teamed up with the National Stroke Association (NSA) to educate the public and health care professionals about the importance of responding to stroke as a medical emergency. The partnership's mission was to educate Americans to identify the signs and symptoms of stroke, encourage those who

Courtesy the Upjohn Company and the National Stroke Association think they are having a stroke to call 911 or their local emergency hotline, and establish a national consensus on the emergency evaluation and treatment of stroke.

## Research

In evaluating various secondary research sources, we learned that (1) Americans don't recognize stroke warning signs and are not prepared to handle stroke as a medical emergency and (2) most emergency departments don't treat stroke as a medical emergency.

- 1991 Gallup survey revealed that 97 percent of consumers age 50-plus don't recognize stroke warning signs.
- 1992 (December) Yankelovich survey showed that 46 percent of Americans can't identify 911 or don't know the difference between the 911 emergency hotline and 411 directory information. The survey was cosponsored by Upjohn and the American College of Emergency Physicians.
- 1992 news articles about stroke failed to position it as an emergency condition.
- Studies in the *Journal of the American Medical Association* highlight the need for faster stroke treatment.

## Planning

### Objectives

1. To initiate efforts to standardize the treatment of stroke in U.S. emergency departments
2. To educate consumers about stroke warning signs and the need for immediate treatment
3. To generate "stroke is an emergency condition" and "treat stroke within the first six hours" coverage in targeted national consumer and medical trade media

### Strategies

1. To establish a national hospital consensus on the emergency evaluation and treatment of stroke
2. To launch a program to educate consumers to identify stroke warning signs and call 911 at the first hint of stroke symptoms
3. To seek endorsements from third parties to establish credibility and to increase distribution/communication channels
4. To promote consensus and consumer education programs on stroke warning signs to media

## Budget

$85,000 ($65,000—fee, $20,000—OOP)

## Audiences

Potential stroke victims (strong focus on the 50-plus group), their family members; medical professionals (emergency health care professionals, neurologists); media that reach these audiences

# Execution

NSA's credibility and contacts and Upjohn's non-product-specific financial support were key to the success of "The First Six Hours" program. It consisted of three initiatives: (1) the creation of a consensus statement for hospital emergency departments, (2) the creation of a consumer education kit on stroke warning signs, and (3) a media event.

## Consensus

Through the NSA, leading independent stroke experts were recruited to join a consensus panel and draft "Stroke: The First Six Hours—Emergency Evaluation and Treatment." The panel chair/NSA president and Upjohn's medical science liaisons attended the consensus panel meetings and provided insight that helped focus the consensus on the emergency nature of stroke and the importance of the first six hours. As a testament to the need for the first consensus, it was completed in five months—eight months sooner than originally projected—and was endorsed by medical organizations including the National Institute of Neurological Disorders and Stroke, the American Academy of Neurology, the American Association of Neurological Surgeons, the American Society of Neuroimaging, the Congress of Neurological Surgeons, and the International Stroke Society.

## Education Kit

To educate consumers about stroke warning signs and the need to call 911, NSA and Upjohn created the "Preventing Stroke in Later Years" education kit. Each kit contained a "Brain at Risk" videotape and copies of the brochure "Preventing Stroke in Later Years" (which was given to seniors). After gaining endorsement by the American Association of Retired Persons (AARP), the National Association of Area Agencies on Aging (NAAAA), and the National Council on the Aging (NCOA), more than 10,000 stroke education kits were distributed through these organizations and other networks on aging.

## Media Event

To announce both the stroke consensus and the stroke warning signs education kit, a press conference was held at the annual meeting of the

American Academy of Neurology. Members of the consensus panel—leading experts on the evaluation and treatment of stroke—presented details of the consensus and consumer program. A particular coup was the appearance of Michael Walker, director, Division of Stroke and Trauma, the National Institute for Neurological Disorders and Stroke. The press conference was supported with a telephone press briefing and a radio news release. Media attendance was "standing room only," and included such notable reporters as Larry Altman of the *New York Times* and Malcolm Ritter of the Associated Press.

## Evaluation

### Objective #1

*Initiate efforts to standardize the treatment of stroke in U.S. emergency departments.* We coordinated and confirmed the "Stroke: The First Six Hours—Emergency Evaluation and Treatment" consensus with five of the top neurological associations. The content of the consensus effectively outlined for the first time how the medical community evaluate and treat patients with stroke. More than 95,500 consensus statements were initially distributed to the medical community, including neurologists, emergency physicians and nurses, and hospital trauma center administrators. Following this initial mailing, NSA received 10,000 additional requests from the medical community for copies of the consensus.

### Objective #2

*Educate consumers about stroke warning signs and the need for immediate treatment.* More than 10,000 "Preventing Stroke in Later Years" kits were distributed to NSA, AARP, NAAAA and NCOA senior groups and affiliated senior centers nationwide. Additionally, nearly 20,000 "Preventing Stroke in Later Years" brochure requests were fulfilled through publicity of NSA's 1-800-STROKES hotline number.

### Objective #3

*Generate "stroke is an emergency condition" and "treat stroke within the first six hours" coverage in national consumer and medical trade media.*

- 100 percent of placements communicated that stroke is an emergency condition and should be treated within the first six hours following symptom onset in order to improve outcome.

- A carefully planned media effort generated more than 18 million media impressions. Coverage included: "CBS This Morning" (3:10-minute segment), the *New York Times, USA Today,* the *Washington Post,* the *Los Angeles Times,* the *Record, Kansas City Star, Medical World News,* the *Lancet,* the ABC Radio Network (covering more than 760 stations nationwide), the CBS Spectrum Radio Network (covering approximately 150 stations nationwide), the UNISTAR Ultimate Radio Network (covering approximately 1,034 stations nationwide), MEDSTAR (network feed is distributed to 52 television stations nationwide), and WFTV-TV (Orlando, FL) (three-part series was a feature news story on three consecutive broadcasts).

The NSA and Upjohn pubic/private partnership proved so successful that an extension to this stroke program was launched in 1994.

Exhibit 10-3a

Program News Release   (Courtesy the Upjohn Company and the National Stroke Association)

# National Stroke Association

8480 East Orchard Road, Suite 1000 • Englewood, Colorado 80111-5015
(303) 771-1700 • FAX (303) 771-1886 • TDD: (303) 771-1887

FOR IMMEDIATE RELEASE

FOR INFORMATION:
Wendy Werblin, Ketchum PR
212-536-8762

Gary Houser, NSA
303-771-1700

### *New Hope for Stroke Victims*

NATIONAL STROKE ASSOCIATION ANNOUNCES
THE FIRST NATIONAL CONSENSUS ON THE EMERGENCY EVALUATION
AND TREATMENT OF STROKE

New York, NY, April 28 -- Stroke victims, who traditionally have received insufficient or inconsistent medical treatment, are being given new hope with the release of the first national consensus statement providing guidelines for the emergency evaluation and treatment of stroke.  Through a collaboration of seven leading medical organizations, including the National Institute of Neurological Disorders and Stroke, the consensus establishes a universal protocol defining how stroke victims must be treated within the first six hours following symptom onset in order to improve outcome.  Titled *"Stroke: The First Six Hours -- Emergency Evaluation and Treatment,"* the consensus was announced today by the National Stroke Association at a press conference during the annual meeting of the American Academy of Neurology.

Consumers and the medical community currently do not respond to stroke as a medical emergency.  According to a 1991 Gallup survey, 97 percent of consumers age 50-plus are unable to recognize stroke warning signs.  The result is that most stroke victims present in the emergency department 24 hours following symptom onset; far beyond the "golden six hours" specified in the consensus.  Until recently, hospitals felt that little could be done to treat stroke victims.  Many hospitals adopted the "wait and see" approach.  This thinking has resulted in treatment variations from hospital to hospital and lack of a universal treatment protocol.

-more-

BE STROKE SMART

According to Fletcher McDowell, M.D., president, National Stroke Association, and chairman of the consensus panel, "Research shows that if a stroke is treated aggressively within the first six hours following symptom onset, chances of recovery significantly improve. Stroke symptoms should be identified as a brain attack, much as chest pain signals heart attack. Both should receive emergency treatment. This is the message we are bringing to hospitals, physicians and the public."

The consensus calls for rapid transport of the stroke victim to the hospital, speedy diagnosis to determine the stroke's cause and immediate treatment. Early consultation with a neurologist and a CT (computed tomography) scan are recommended for stroke diagnosis. "The CT scan helps to determine whether a stroke is ischemic or hemorrhagic in 95 percent of patients, which is the basis for further treatment measures," said James Robertson, M.D., professor and chairman, Department of Neurosurgery, University of Tennessee; chairman-elect, AHA's National Stroke Council; and consensus panel member. Further neuroimaging tests, including MRI (magnetic resonance imaging), angiography or a cerebral angiogram can further isolate the source of bleeding or blockage in the brain.

Once the cause and location of a stroke is determined, emergency surgical and/or medical treatment can begin. "There is a belief that stroke treatment, particularly surgery, need not be undertaken in the first six hours except in critical cases," said Dr. Robertson. "However, research has shown that the earlier we stop the injury and restore blood flow to the brain, the greater the chances are for recovery."

The statement outlines several current and future treatment choices depending on the cause of the stroke, including surgery and treatment with blood thinners, antihypertensives and clot busters (thrombolytics). Experimental drugs which show promise for treating stroke, such as agents which protect brain tissue from secondary injury, are also discussed. These important new drugs will require usage within the six hour window to be effective and may mean the difference in recovery for many stroke victims.

The new consensus is being distributed by the National Stroke Association to nearly 100,000 physicians, nurses and hospital medical directors in an effort to educate hospital-based practitioners about the guidelines and encourage them to adopt the guidelines in their own hospitals.

-more-

Exhibit 10-3a
(*continued*)

Program News Release  (Courtesy the Upjohn Company and the National Stroke Association)

-3-

To address the educational needs of the public, the NSA is launching a nationwide stroke awareness and education program to teach older Americans -- the high risk group -- how to lower stroke risk, identify stroke warning signs and call 911 for help.  According to Jim Lannon, executive director of the NSA, "These symptoms include numbness or paralysis on one side of the body, sudden decreased or blurred vision, difficulty speaking or understanding speech and loss of balance or coordination.  Usually, several stroke symptoms are experienced at once."

An educational kit, *Preventing Stroke in Later Years,* is being distributed to 10,000 senior centers and AARP health promotion coordinators nationwide.  The kit contains a videotape, "The Brain at Risk -- Understanding and Preventing Stroke," which dramatically illustrates stroke warning signs and emphasizes the emergency nature of stroke; and "Preventing Stroke in Later Years" brochures, which highlight key stroke facts, prevention tips and warning signs, and which encourage older adults to call 911 for help if they experience stroke symptoms.  Consumers can also receive the free brochure by calling NSA at 1-800-STROKES.

*Preventing Stroke in Later Years* is also sponsored by the American Association of Retired Persons, National Association of Area Agencies on Aging and the National Council on the Aging.

The consensus was developed by the National Stroke Association, and is cosponsored by the National Institute of Neurological Disorders and Stroke; American Academy of Neurology; American Association of Neurological Surgeons; Congress of Neurological Surgeons; American Society of Neuroimaging; and the International Stroke Congress.  Both the consensus and the public education program were supported through an educational grant from The Upjohn Company.  The National Stroke Association is a national, nonprofit organization dedicated to reducing the incidence and impact of stroke.

# # #

# Know the Warning Signs of Stroke

Some strokes are preceded by warning signs called transient ischemic attacks (TIAs). TIAs cause a *temporary* interruption of blood flow within or leading to the brain (a stroke is a *permanent* cutoff of blood to a region of the brain). TIAs or stroke warning signs include:

- *Numbness, weakness, or paralysis of face, arm, or leg — especially on one side of the body*

- *Sudden blurred or decreased vision in one or both eyes*

- *Difficulty speaking or understanding simple statements*

- *Loss of balance or coordination when combined with another warning sign*

It's important to learn to recognize these serious warning signs. Although these symptoms eventually go away, they are clear warnings that a stroke may follow.

**For more information about stroke, please contact your local NSA chapter or National Stroke Association at 1-800-STROKES. Join NSA in the fight against stroke!**

## *Stroke is an emergency! If you experience any stroke warning signs,*

## *call 911 immediately.*

Supported through an educational grant from

**Upjohn**

*The crisis in the science literacy of American students provided the Dow Chemical Company an opportunity to respond to this problem with a touring MTV-style science education road show for high school students. Exhibit 10-4a is a localized news release announcing the program and its itinerary. Exhibit 10-4b is a photograph of the cast in performance. Exhibit 10-4c is an excerpt from the program's promotional material. Exhibit 10-4d is a synopsis of the show.*

**CASE 10-4** Chem TV! Dow's Answer for Sparking Student Interest in Science

The Dow Chemical Company, Midland, MI, with Ketchum Public Relations, Washington, DC

## Situation Analysis

Over the past two decades, the science literacy scores of America's students have plummeted in comparison to students from other countries. In the last *International Assessment of Education Progress,* U.S. students ranked 19th in a survey of 20 industrial nations. This ranking is particularly disturbing on the edge of a century where a mastery of science and technology may be the most important keys to our nation's economic competitiveness and prosperity. Educators and government officials are aware of the magnitude of this national crisis and have been searching for the formula to bring science education back on track.

The Dow Chemical Company also recognizes the importance of science literacy—to the nation's future and to Dow's future. But at Dow, it is more than an issue of being able to hire an educated work force, cultivate future patent winners, and assure increased market share. Dow believes that science literacy is crucial to understanding the world and how it works.

Dow is concerned that citizens with little or no understanding of science are reacting to or influencing policy decisions about complex issues that affect the chemical industry. Dow believes that improved scientific literacy will help citizens make educated decisions about issues related to the industry and its future.

Courtesy the Dow Chemical Company

The biggest challenge to improving scientific literacy in the future is getting students interested in the sciences *now.* Fortunately, educators, government officials, and business leaders believe they've found a way to turn around this perspective. They think the answer to our science education crisis lies in innovative science programs—programs that encourage hands-on exploration and show how sciences are tied to everyday life.

To implement new teaching standards and to bring innovative science programs into the classroom, teachers will need additional resources and materials. Increasingly, educators are looking to the private sector for those resources.

In response, Dow set out to create a program that sparked interest in sciences and a curiosity about how the world worked—to create a program that showed students that chemistry holds the power to understand and improve the world—to help create a scientifically literate generation that could make informed decisions about the future of the chemical industry.

## Research

### Media Analysis

Ketchum analyzed the 1993–1994 media coverage regarding science education to assess what measures were being implemented to improve it. *Findings:* Teaching science as it relates to everyday life is the key to keeping students interested in science and math; "learning by doing" is the new philosophy embraced by many schools; and in their 1994 draft of the national science education standards, the National Science Foundation, in conjunction with a myriad of national teaching organizations, put a new focus on interactive science programs that encourage hands-on experimentation.

### Secondary Research Analysis

Ketchum reviewed the results of various science education performance surveys, including the International Assessment of Education Progress, Science Report Card, and Science and Engineering Indicators. *Findings:* 48 percent of the high school students polled believed that science is not useful in everyday life—34 percent believed that this information would not be useful in the future; only 7 percent of high school seniors had sufficient skills to do well in college-level science courses; and, in science literacy, U.S. students ranked 19th out of 20 industrial nations.

### Influentials' Research

Ketchum interviewed science education leaders and chemistry teachers to determine how Dow could create a program to renew interest in science and support the new teaching philosophy. *Findings:* Tie the teaching messages to life; use interactive elements that involve the students;

entertain and engage while educating; provide follow-up materials to maintain the momentum after the performance.

### Four Focus Groups

Focus groups were conducted with more than 40 high school students in Charlotte and Seattle. *Findings:* Students thought that chemistry was a boring and difficult school subject; few students had any interest in the sciences, especially chemistry; few students had any knowledge of chemistry's role in everyday life; students want to hear from their peers; they don't want to be preached to; music, comedy, skits, and video were deemed effective methods for delivering educational messages.

## Planning

Based on the research results, Ketchum and Dow set out to create a program that wasn't the same old chemistry lecture—no adults in lab coats on stage lecturing about equations and formulas in this production. The program, called "ChemTV," would be an interactive, exciting "Broadway-style production" that brought chemistry to life through music, comedy, live actors, and a game show where contestants are pulled from the audience to participate. Students would learn from their peers through their own music, culture, and language.

Research, development, and planning activities began in September 1993. "ChemTV" debuted its three-year, national high school tour in May 1994.

### Objectives

- To fuel student interest in chemistry
- To create an awareness of the critical importance of chemicals to life
- To support national education efforts to teach through innovative, interactive programs

### Strategies

- Create a high-energy, motivational production to illustrate the importance of chemistry to everyday life
- Create an understanding that everything is chemical and the result of chemistry—our bodies, the earth, and every product around us
- Help educators maintain enthusiasm about the sciences throughout the school year

### Audiences

Primary audience: high school students and educators. Secondary audience: the general public through media coverage.

### Budget

$300,000 for the concept development, planning, research, script revisions, educator outreach, school bookings, materials development, and publicity—75 percent for staffing, including all activity from research and creation of the program to on-the-road publicity of it; 25 percent for expenses, including design, production, and printing of all program materials and student/teacher resources. Set design, equipment purchase, script development, and staging were handled by a third-party contractor that was hired by Dow.

## Execution

Ketchum and Dow developed the concept, determined the relevant chemistry teaching points, and outlined the elements of the program, including skits, songs, and the game show involving audience participants. Dow then hired a professional producer to script and stage the show. "ChemTV," a 45-minute live performance, involves a cast of five and a crew of five and uses music, humor, dance, and skits to deliver more than 75 separate chemistry teaching points.

To ensure the high educational value of the program, Ketchum solicited critiques of the teaching points and script from the American Chemical Society, the American Association for the Advancement of Science, and an independent panel of chemistry teachers. In May 1994, Ketchum booked "ChemTV" performances in four test markets to gauge student and teacher response and to refine the program content. Based on the comments received in these markets, two skits were dropped from the program and additional examples of chemistry's role in everyday life were added.

Once the program was finalized, Ketchum booked the 1994 fall tour of "ChemTV" in 18 midwestern and southern cities. Ketchum and Dow targeted large, urban high schools to reach the maximum number of students in areas that typically have the fewest resources for innovative programming and the lowest enrollment in science courses. A highlight of the fall tour was a three-day booking at the Indianapolis Children's Museum, where students from across the state were bused in to see the production. Ketchum also booked performances in 36 cities for the 1995 spring tour.

To maintain the enthusiasm and to drive home the point of the program, "ChemTV" audiences received cassette tapes with a sample of "ChemTV" tunes. Important messages about the relevance of chemistry to everyday life were included on the cassette jacket as well as Dow's 800 information number. Interested students and teachers could call Dow to request further information about chemistry and additional chemistry teaching materials.

To foster further chemistry exploration, Ketchem secured approval from the American Chemical Society's educational division for Dow to distribute free copies of excerpts from their acclaimed chemistry textbook, *ChemCom,* to teachers who wanted hands-on experiments and innovative curricula that tie chemistry to everyday life.

In addition, Ketchum extended the reach of the message that everything is chemical and the result of chemistry to the general public by pitching the local media in each market visited.

## Evaluation

"ChemTV" will be on the road for three years, but already, in its inaugural tour, "ChemTV" has moved minds.

### Student Response

Live performances of "ChemTV" will reach more than 87,000 students by June 1995. Student surveys, administered before and after "ChemTV" performances, show that the program is changing the way students think about science and the importance of chemistry to everyday life. *Before* "ChemTV": Chemistry is boring, dull, and hard; the periodic table is "a list of chemicals"; and chemicals are "dangerous and poisonous." *After* "ChemTV": Chemistry is "power" and "important to life"; the periodic table is "the table of life" and "the ingredients of the earth"; and chemicals are "what everything is made from." In addition, students are writing to Dow to thank the company, to request additional information, and to share the most important points they learned through the program.

### Teacher Response

Administrators and teachers also have sent letters praising Dow for creating a high-quality, credible, and entertaining educational production that brings chemistry to life and illustrates the importance of understanding chemistry. Several administrators are preparing for increased enrollment in the sciences in the next school year, based on the interest generated by "ChemTV."

### Maintaining the Momentum

Dow has received more than 500 calls on its 800 number since the tour began. Callers have requested additional information on chemistry, chemistry teaching materials, and live "ChemTV" performances. After hearing rave reviews about the production, the Society of Plastics Engineers booked spring performances at the Chicago Museum of Science and Industry. The American Association for the Advancement of Science (AAAS), in conjunction with Georgia Tech's Engineering Department, booked "ChemTV" at the AAAS annual meeting in Atlanta for February 1995.

## Extending the Reach

In addition, the local media have been carrying the messages that chemistry is important to everyday life and that everything is a chemical and a result of chemistry to a broader audience. "ChemTV" media coverage blanketed the local markets—television, radio, and print reporters turned out in every city. An additional 5.1 million Americans have heard "ChemTV's" messages.

To meet the growing demand for "ChemTV" performances—250 requests, to date—Dow has created a network-quality, 45-minute video of the program for schools that Dow cannot visit due to time and cost constraints. The video is available, free of charge, to any school requesting it.

Exhibit 10-4a    Localized News Release   (Courtesy the Dow Chemical Company)

# News Release

<br />

Dow Corporate Communications
Midland, MI 48674

FOR MORE INFORMATION CONTACT:
Doug Draper
The Dow Chemical Company
2030 Dow Center
Midland, MI 48674
517/636-2876

November 7, 1994

**CHEMTV BRINGS A NEW TWIST AND SHOUT TO SCIENCE EDUCATION**

An innovative science education program called ChemTV will have

Saginaw, Bay City and Midland students taking a fresh look at chemistry

when the live theatrical production visits local schools.  Designed to

capture the imagination of today's teens, ChemTV uses, music, comedy

and an interactive format to show the vital role chemistry plays in

everyday life.

ChemTV appears at Saginaw's Heritage High on Nov. 14, Bay City's

Central High on Nov. 16 and Midland's Central Intermediate on Nov. 18.

At Central Intermediate, shows provided for students during the day will

be supplemented with a 7:30 p.m. performance open to the public.

Admission is free.

"What does chemistry mean to me?" and "Why should I care about

science?" are common questions from high school students that

challenge educators across the country.  The Dow Chemical Company

created ChemTV to answer those questions and illustrate how intricately

chemistry is entwined with our lives -- from our environment, to our

bodies, to the products we use every day.

(more)

According to the National Science Foundation's 1993 Science and Engineering Indicators, the perception that science is not relevant to students' lives or future aspirations may account for their lack of interest in science courses. Forty-eight percent of the students polled by the foundation believed the information learned in science classes is not useful in their everyday lives, and 34 percent believed that the information will not be useful to them in the future.

ChemTV battles that perception by showing how science is used to improve the quality of life, and develop solutions to many of the health, environmental, economic and other social issues that concern teens most. ChemTV drives home the message that chemistry is the power to understand and improve our world.

"Whether or not students plan to pursue careers in chemistry, they need to be able to understand the world around them and that means understanding science and its applications," said Doug Draper, manager of external communications at Dow. "ChemTV brings that message to students in an unexpected and entertaining way."

When creating ChemTV, Dow worked with an independent panel of chemistry teachers and the education division of the American Chemical Society to develop the teaching points and ensure the high educational standard of the production. Their review of the program has been enthusiastic.

(more)

"ChemTV is a valuable program that shows how exciting and useful chemistry can be," said Sylvia Ware, education director for the American Chemical Society. "The same enthusiasm that students feel when they leave a performance of ChemTV can be created through the high school chemistry lab."

Saginaw, Bay City and Midland are some of the first cities to host ChemTV as it begins a two-year tour. The production will tour junior and senior high schools in the U.S. and Canada through the spring of 1996. Schools that can't be reached through the live performance have the option of viewing the ChemTV video, which may be ordered by calling Dow at 1-800-258-2436.

ChemTV is one component of Dow's ongoing commitment to improve and reform education and stimulate interest in the sciences.

# # #

Exhibit 10-4b

Photograph of Cast in Performance  (Courtesy the Dow Chemical Company)

Exhibit 10-4c

Program Promotional Material   (Courtesy the Dow Chemical Company)

Exhibit 10-4d    Chem TV Synopsis    (Courtesy the Dow Chemical Company)

# Act One

Pre-Show—Popular music videos play as the audience enters the auditorium. News footage showing researchers tackling science, health and environmental problems is scattered throughout the videos. An "infomercial" spoof—supermodel Fabulo's National Institute of Home Study Science — introduces the basics of chemistry.

Edge Of The Century—Live music and video illustrate the complexity of the issues the world faces and urge students to become part of the search for solutions.

Vicki Lake Show—A humorous cast of talk show guests (Rush Trimbaugh, Dr. Bluth, Dr. Tray) uncovers the "chemistry conspiracy!" Chemistry is used to create a multitude of products around us.

Lethal Water Warriors—Students learn how and why drinking water is disinfected through the hottest new home video game.

# Act Two

Method To The Madness —The rap song explains the importance of understanding and embracing a scientific method (forming hypotheses, challenging ideas, making observations and creating solutions).

Il Tablo Piriodico—An Italian operetta presents a fun, easy-to-understand explanation of the periodic table. The elements are shown as the building blocks of everything in our world.

Check It Out!—*ChemTV's* gameshow segment challenges the "chem quotient" of student participants. Students test their knowledge of chemistry and the exciting areas related to it.

Operator, Give Me Information—The technological revolution of the information superhighway is the focus of this soulful skit.

Change The World—The show closes with a call for students to take action and become a part of the solution. An understanding of the sciences and the impact they have on our lives is vitally important. To make a difference, students must explore, they must challenge, they must form educated opinions, and they must act.

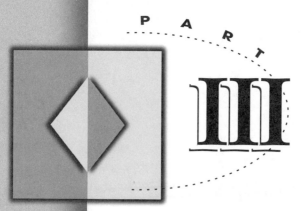

# III

# Emergency
Public Relations

**Chapter 11**
Emergency Public Relations

# 11

# Emergency
# Public Relations

IN PREPARATION FOR EMERGENCIES, THE PRACTI-
tioner should be generally aware of the four aspects
of the process model, although its use in this form of
public relations will be limited.

# RESEARCH

Some research will be helpful in reaching a state of readiness for an emergency. The three types of research used for other forms of public relations are appropriate.

## Client Research

Client research should focus on preparing as many "worst-case" scenarios as possible. What can go wrong? Is the organization's physical plant vulnerable to fire, explosion, or other crises? Is dangerous equipment located on the premises? All division heads in the organization should be asked by the director of public relations to prepare a list of potential trouble spots that could erupt in their respective areas. Whenever possible, corrective action should be taken to neutralize these problems before an emergency can occur. Research may also examine the client's handling of past crises.

## Opportunity or Problem Research

Emergency public relations is generically reactive in nature. Some practitioners argue that it is impossible to really get ready for a sweeping disaster. Emergency planning, however, must be proactive in order to be prepared for a proper reactive response to an emergency.

## Audience Research

The practitioner should make a list of internal and external publics to be immediately notified in case of an emergency. Internal publics would include the chief executive officer and other top organizational officials on a "need-to-know" basis at first. As the emergency progresses, the entire work force can be notified through existing internal channels of communication. External audiences in an emergency should include, in priority order, law enforcement officials; the next of kin of the injured or dead, notified before the public release of their names; the mass media; governmental agencies, if appropriate; and trade publications. These internal and external audiences are a suggested starting point. The practitioner needs to be much more specific in creating an emergency contacts list designed to notify all concerned parties in a timely fashion.

# OBJECTIVES

Because of the exceptional nature of emergencies, objectives for this form of public relations cannot be carefully planned. Nonetheless, some general guidelines are applicable:

1. To provide accurate, timely information to all targeted internal and external audiences

2. To demonstrate concern for the safety of lives

3. To safeguard organizational facilities and assets

4. To maintain a positive image of the organization as a good corporate or community citizen

These guidelines will serve the practitioner well in preparing for the two areas of responsibility involved in programming.

# PROGRAMMING

Programming for emergency public relations should focus on two major actions or areas of responsibility: establishing a public relations emergency headquarters and a media information center.

## The Public Relations Headquarters

The public relations emergency headquarters (PR HQ) will probably be the regular public relations office itself. If more space is needed, other offices may also be designated as part of the PR HQ. This office will be responsible for notification of all internal and external emergency audiences, for preparation of material for the media, and for the establishment of a public information center to answer inquiries and to control rumors. The director of public relations should remain in the PR HQ to supervise these three functions.

Notification, the first function of PR HQ, will be the top priority of this office as soon as a crisis occurs. The internal and external audiences were discussed above and will be reviewed in Exhibit 11-a, the "Emergency Public Relations Checklist."

Names of the injured or dead should be withheld from public release until the next of kin are notified or for 24 hours, whichever comes first.

The second function of the PR HQ will be preparation of materials for the media. A company or organizational backgrounder, fact sheet, biographies of major officers, and their captioned photographs should already be prepared and waiting in the files. Along with assembling these background materials, the public relations staff should immediately begin the task of preparing its first basic news release on the crisis. A good rule of thumb is that this should be ready for release *no more than one hour* after the occurrence of the emergency. The release should include all known facts, such as what happened, how, when, where, who, and how many were involved. The question of why may be omitted since the organization may run the risk of involving itself in litigation through an admission of fault. This matter should be handled by the legal department. The release should be cleared as quickly as possible with senior management, the legal department, and possibly the personnel department. Then the news release should be issued immediately to local and national mass media, specialized publications, employees, community leaders, and pertinent government agencies. In addition to the first basic release, PR HQ should issue frequent statements to the media in ongoing crises and should coordinate media interviews with the CEO as warranted.

Through all of these emergency public relations procedures, two principles are recommended: a *one-voice* principle and a *full-disclosure* principle. Above all other considerations, the organization should *speak with one voice*. All employees should be briefed to give information to the media or other concerned parties only from official organizational statements, issued by PR HQ. The full-disclosure principle refers to giving all known information, with the exception of why the emergency occurred if this might involve admission of fault.

The third function of the PR HQ is to establish a *public information center (PIC)*. The responsibilities of the PIC include responding to telephone inquiries with accurate information, providing information to groups to combat rumors, and holding meetings with groups as needed to clarify misinformation. The organization's switchboard should be briefed in advance to refer all calls in an emergency to the PIC, and the one-voice and full-disclosure principles should be observed at all times in its operation.

## The Media Information Center

If media people will be gathering at the site of an emergency or disaster, the director of public relations should set up a *media information center (MIC)* at some location near the crisis area but away from the PR HQ. Public relations staff members at the PR HQ must be allowed to perform their required tasks without the interruption of news people wanting information. The MIC should, if possible, designate some staff people to escort media representatives if there is a hazardous disaster area. Reporters should not be permitted to wander freely through a dangerous zone, although they usually want unrestricted access to everything. The MIC should be a suitable room, preferably an auditorium if available, where journalists can remain to receive news releases about the emergency. A high-credibility spokesperson and several alternates should be designated in advance and, once chosen, a single spokesperson should be on duty as long as necessary at the MIC to read news releases. Directors of public relations should never be designated MIC spokespersons. They should remain at the PR HQ to supervise all operations. The spokesperson, however, should be a high-ranking officer in the organization; otherwise, the organization's credibility could suffer. Needless to say, the one-voice and full-disclosure principles should be stringently applied in the operation of the MIC.

## Uncontrolled and Controlled Media

In an emergency situation, most of the communication will be uncontrolled in the form of news releases, interviews with organizational officials, and perhaps photographs, although the media representatives will usually take their own photos. Controlled media will be used sparingly, usually as prepared background material or as in-house bulletins posted for employees.

## Effective Communication

Two-way communication and audience participation may assume greater than usual importance in a crisis. The targeted audiences, especially the media, will want to be involved and interact with the spokesperson as much as possible. But in general, all the previously discussed principles of communication should be observed.

Programming for emergency public relations, then, concentrates on the two major responsibilities of creating a public relations emergency headquarters and a media information center (see Exhibit 11-a). Beyond that, customary use of uncontrolled and controlled media and principles of effective communication are appropriate.

---

| Exhibit 11-a | Emergency Public Relations Checklist |
| --- | --- |

I. Public relations emergency headquarters (PR HQ). The PR director stays in PR department or designated PR HQ and supervises:

   A. Notification and liaison

      1. Internal: Notify the CEO and other top officials on immediate "need-to-know" basis

      2. External: Notify the media; law enforcement officials; governmental agencies; next of kin of injured or dead, before public release of names (24-hour rule suggested)

   B. Preparation of materials for media

      1. Have company backgrounder, fact sheet, and bios of officers already prepared

      2. Prepare basic news release on crisis as soon as possible (one-hour rule suggested)

         a. Include all known facts—what happened, how, when, where, who, and how many involved—not why (fault)

         b. Be certain all information is accurate; never release unconfirmed information

         c. Withhold names of victims until next of kin are notified (or 24 hours, whichever comes first)

           d. Clear release with senior management, legal department, personnel department

           e. Issue release immediately to local and national mass media, specialized publications, employees by bulletin boards and phone, community leaders, insurance company, pertinent governmental agencies.

    3. Issue timely statements to media in ongoing crises

    4. Use *one-voice principle*—information only from official organizational statements

    5. Use *full-disclosure principle* (except admission of fault)

  C. Public information center (PIC)

    1. Establish and announce a public information center in PR HQ

    2. Respond to telephone inquiries with accurate information

    3. Provide accurate information to groups where rumors are circulating

    4. Hold meetings with groups as needed to clarify misinformation

    5. Have switchboard refer all pertinent calls to PIC

    6. Direct company employees to make no unauthorized statements to media people

    7. Use *one-voice principle*—information only from official organizational statements

    8. Use *full-disclosure principle* (except admission of fault)

II. Media information center (MIC)

  A. Designate a place for media people to gather, if necessary

  B. Locate MIC at site near crisis area, but away from PR HQ. (Media people admitted to disaster site must be *escorted* by PR personnel)

  C. Have sole spokesperson on duty day or night at MIC

    1. Use *one-voice principle*—information only from official organizational statements

    2. Use *full-disclosure principle* (except admission of fault)

## EVALUATION

The evaluation of emergency public relations will be less precise than for other forms of the discipline. Since emergencies are unplanned, the PR objectives must be, at best, general and nonquantitative guidelines. In a quiet period well after the organization's recovery from the emergency, it will be appropriate to review the general guidelines previously mentioned and informally assess the PR department's degree of success in meeting them. Such a review should also include analyzing media coverage; tracking complaints from consumers, community, employees, and other relevant publics; holding internal meetings on the crisis plan and its implementation, and assessing damage to the organization's image. Of course, a formal survey of all participants can also be taken. The results may be used for a variety of purposes, possibly including improvement of emergency public relations procedures.

## SUMMARY

Although the ROPE process has limited applicability in emergency public relations, it should not be forgotten or discarded.

Research is useful in preparing for emergencies. Worse-case scenarios should be prepared to determine what problems could possibly develop. Although emergency public relations is inherently reactive, planning for such crises should be proactive. Emergency contacts lists should be made, including all internal and external individuals, groups, and agencies that are to be notified in a crisis.

Objectives for emergency PR tend to be of an impact nature. They usually concentrate on providing information to important audiences as needed; safeguarding lives, facilities, and assets; and protecting the credibility of the organization.

Programming should include establishing a public relations emergency headquarters and, if necessary, a media information center. The functions of the emergency headquarters include notification and liaison and preparation of materials for the media. If reporters will be gathering at the site of a disaster or crisis, a media information center should be established near (but usually not on) the site, and an organizational spokesperson should be designated to be on duty to read statements to the journalists as long as the crisis lasts.

Evaluation for emergency PR is usually less formal than for other types. If objectives have been set before a crisis occurs, each should be appropriately evaluated. If not, the organization should, after the emergency, want to review its notification functions, its general accessibility and service to the media, and, of course, its media coverage during the event.

## READINGS ON EMERGENCY PUBLIC RELATIONS

Barton, Lawrence. *Crisis in Organizations: Managing and Communicating in the Heat of Chaos.* Cincinnati, OH: South-Western, 1993.

Bergman, Eric. "Crisis? What Crisis?" *Communication World* 11 (April 1994): 19ff.

Bernstein, Alan B. *The Emergency Public Relations Manual,* 3rd ed. Highland Park, NJ: PASE, 1990.

Berzok, Robert M. "Recipe for Effective Communication: Substitute Emotion for B.S." *Communication World* (October 1993): 22ff.

Birch, John. "New Factors in Crisis Planning and Response." *Public Relations Quarterly* 39 (Spring 1994): 31ff.

Carney, Ann. "Prepare for Business-Related Crises." *Public Relations Journal* 49 (August 1993): 34ff.

Carney, Bill. "Communicating Risk." *Communication World* (May 1993): 12ff.

Dilenschneider, Robert L. "You: Ready for Trouble." *Public Relations Quarterly* 38 (Spring 1993): 29ff.

Dougherty, Devon. *Crisis Communications: What Every Executive Needs to Know.* New York: Walker, 1992.

Fink, Stephen. *Crisis Management: Planning for the Inevitable.* New York: AMACOM, 1986.

Gottschalk, Jack A., ed. *Crisis Response: Inside Stories on Managing Image Under Siege.* Detroit, MI: Visible Ink Press, Gale Research, 1993.

Green, Peter Sheldon. *Reputation Is Everything.* Burr Ridge, IL: Irwin, 1994.

Guth, David W. "Crisis Plans in Short Supply." *Public Relations Journal* 49 (August 1993): 12.

Horne, G. N. "Mediating Conflict in a Crisis." *Public Relations Journal* 39 (January 1993): 22ff.

Jackson, Janice E., and William T. Schultz. "Crisis Management Lessons: When Pushed Shove Nike." *Business Horizons* 36 (January–February 1993): 27ff.

Katz, Anthony R. "Checklist: 10 Steps to Complete Crisis Planning." *Public Relations Journal* 43 (November 1987): 46–47.

Kaufman, Jeffrey B., et al. "The Myth of Full Disclosure: A Look at Organizational Communication During Crisis." *Business Horizons* 37 (July–August 1994): 29ff.

Lerbinger, Otto. *Managing Corporate Crises: Strategies for Executives.* Boston: Barrington, 1985.

Levy, Robert. "Crisis Public Communications." *Dun's Business Review* (August 1983): 50ff.

Lukaszewski, James E. "Checklist: Anatomy of a Crisis Response." *Public Relations Journal* 43 (November 1987): 45–46.

"Managing Environmental Information and Crises Is Called Environmental Challenge of the '90s." *Supervision* 54 (March 1993): 6ff.

Newton, C. *Coming to Grips with Crisis*. New York: AMACOM, 1981.

Patterson, Bill. "Crises Impact on Reputation Management." *Public Relations Journal* 49 (November 1993): 28.

Pines, W. L. "How to Handle PR Crises: Five Dos and Don'ts." *Public Relations Quarterly* (Summer 1985), 16ff.

Pinsdorf, Marion K. *Communicating When Your Company Is Under Siege: Surviving Public Crisis*. Lexington, MA: Lexington, 1987.

"Play It Straight with the Press." *The Magazine for Senior Financial Executives* 9 (March 1993): 28.

Reinhardt, Claudia. "How to Handle a Crisis." *Public Relations Journal* 43 (November 1987): 43–44.

Ressler, Judith A. "Crisis Communications." *Public Relations Quarterly* (Fall 1982): 8ff.

Shell, Adam. "In a Crisis, What You Say Isn't Always What the Public Hears." *Public Relations Journal* 49 (September 1993): 10ff.

Walters, Lynne Masel, and Lee Wilkens, eds. *Bad Tidings: Communications and Catastrophe*. New York: Erlbaum, 1988.

Werner, Lawrence R. "When Crisis Strikes Use a Message Action Plan." *Public Relations Journal* 46 (August 1990): 30–31.

Wexler, Jim. "Using Broadcast Television to Control a Crisis." *Communication World* 10 (November 1993): 30ff.

Wilson, James. "Managing Communication in Crises: An Expert's View." *Communication World* (December 1985): 13ff.

# Emergency Public Relations Cases

*Media coverage of CARE's emergency efforts to save lives in So-malia helped the organization raise needed funds for disaster re-lief in that stricken country. Exhibits 11-1a, 11-1b, and 11-1c are news releases about CARE's Somalia relief efforts. Exhibit 11-1d is one of CARE's disaster relief photographs.*

### CASE 11-1 Power of the Media Helps CARE Save Lives

CARE, Atlanta, GA

### Situation Analysis

In mid-1992, Somalia was caught up in civil war and drought, put-ting hundreds of thousands of innocent civilians at risk of starvation. By July, the desperate situation of the Somali people had been covered by only a handful of media. The public relations team for CARE, the worldwide relief and development organization, set out to gain maxi-mum media exposure of the crisis to move the American public and the U.S. government to act through donations and humanitarian aid to save lives.

### Research

Updates from the field office in Somalia and the staff working with So-mali refugees in Kenya revealed that the condition of the Somali people was deteriorating quickly. CARE's chief executive officer and president, along with the head of communications, were sent to Somalia on a fact-finding mission for firsthand knowledge of the crisis. A photographer was hired to capture some of the first images of Somali devastation. An informal survey of media coverage of the burgeoning emergency re-vealed that there were sporadic reports of the situation and limited knowledge among the press of the roots and the depth of the crisis.

### Planning

CARE devised a national publicity campaign to gain visibility that would move its target audiences to support CARE's relief efforts.

### Objectives

- To gain national media coverage for CARE's Somali emergency ef-forts in prominent national print and broadcast news outlets such as the *New York Times,* the *Washington Post,* the *Los Angeles Times,* all three network nightly news broadcasts, the "MacNeil-Lehrer News Hour," and the Associated Press news wire.

- To generate local media coverage of Somali relief efforts in CARE fund-raising offices in cities nationwide.

### Strategies

- Position CARE as the most informed source on the situation and the major player in relief efforts.
- Promote CARE officials, major donors, and celebrity supporters as witnesses to the organization's efforts by sending them on fact-finding trips to Somalia.
- Advocate U.S. support and intervention to facilitate relief efforts.
- Tell the story, highlighting average Somalis, to interest and educate the American public about the people CARE helps.

## Execution

### August–September 1992

- Provided media, both on the ground in Somalia and in the U.S., with regular updates on relief efforts and the changing political and humanitarian situation.
- Secured deskside media briefings for president of CARE with major news organizations such as the Associated Press and the *New York Times.*
- Offered major news outlets (ABC, CNN, AP) the first opportunities to visit Somalia to witness the situation and CARE's humanitarian efforts.
- Wrote Somali human interest stories and sent them, along with photos, to smaller print dailies around the country.
- Took two prominent CARE board members to Somalia and secured interviews for them in business press and local papers (*Investors Business Daily, Philadelphia Inquirer*) as witnesses to the tragedy.
- Wrote letter to the editor to the *New York Times* under CARE chairman's name, advocating U.S. intervention in Somalia to aid relief efforts.

### September–December 1992

- Undertook major advocacy campaign to promote U.S. involvement in Somalia to improve the movement of relief supplies. Placed president of CARE on major broadcast programs ("MacNeil-Lehrer

News Hour" [two times], "Good Morning America," "CBS Up to the Minute," CNN) and in larger print dailies (*Chicago Sun Times, Kansas City Star*) as eyewitness and UN-appointed head of the international community's relief efforts.

- Took renowned photographer to Somalia and placed him in national media ("Today Show," CNN, "CBS Up to the Minute") upon his return.

- Sent CARE media liaison to Somalia to hold press briefings, to direct reporters to CARE stories, and to set up interviews with CARE field staff.

- Media trained CARE personnel and then offered them as experts in all areas of the emergency from health and nutrition to fundraising. Placements included "Good Morning America," *USA Today,* the *Chicago Sun Times,* Gannett News Service papers, and *New York Newsday.*

- Continued regularly updating press on the fluid situation.

- Focused on Somalia in annual fund-raising campaign, the CARE World Hunger Crusade. Enlisted the help of Dick Cavett as chairman. Also highlighted CARE's Somali relief aid in all holiday publicity efforts.

### January–June 1993

By January, coverage of CARE's humanitarian work in Somalia was enormous (see Evaluation). In an effort to continue the focus on Somalia once the situation stabilized (with U.S. military help), CARE PR focused on strides made due to the American public's overwhelming response and U.S. intervention.

- Took actor Charlton Heston to Somalia as CARE special envoy to view the way the U.S. military and relief groups like CARE worked together. The actor appeared on "E Entertainment Television!" and "Good Morning America." He interviewed with *First for Women,* Liz Smith, the *New York Times* Chronicle column, *Family Circle,* and *Senior World.* An Associated Press wire story on his Somalia trip was picked up by hundreds of local papers.

- Pitched CARE president as expert on Somali rebuilding after he helped draft the UN's rehabilitation plan. He appeared on ABC's "Nightline" (2 times), "CBS Evening News," and Minnesota Public Radio and was the subject of feature articles in *Forbes,* the *Philadelphia Inquirer,* the *Boston Globe,* Denver's *Rocky Mountain News,* the *Minneapolis Star Tribune* and the *Seattle Post Intelligencer.*

- To reach a younger audience, the PR team worked with an independent recording company to produce a rap video on Somalia.

This was featured on "MTV Music News," "CBS Up to the Minute," *Billboard* magazine, and *New York Newsday.*

- Conducted media tours in Somalia of villages that CARE helped to rebuild, which were covered by CNN, the "MacNeil-Lehrer News Hour," and the *Christian Science Monitor.*

## Evaluation

CARE's PR and fund-raising objectives were not only realized but surpassed. CARE appeared in connection with the Somalia story in all major broadcast and print news outlets as well as hundreds of newspapers and TV reports around the country consistently over the seven-month term of the crisis. At the height of the emergency in December 1992, CARE appeared in an unprecedented 8,100 media stories. In December alone, CARE was mentioned 21 times on nightly news programs, representing all three networks and public television, and 28 times on network morning shows. In addition, in December CARE appeared 13 times in the *New York Times,* 6 times in *USA Today,* 11 times in the *Washington Post,* and 21 times in the *Los Angeles Times.* The Associated Press, for instance, wrote a story mentioning CARE every day during December 1992.

Intense coverage of CARE's Somalia efforts continued into 1993, with more than 5,000 articles and broadcast stories mentioning CARE's work from February through June, including ABC's "Nightline" (two times), ABC's "Good Morning America," "CBS Evening News," the "MacNeil-Lehrer News Hour" (two times), the *New York Times* (ten times), the *Chicago Tribune, USA Today* (three times), the *Washington Post* (eight times), the *Wall Street Journal,* and the *Los Angeles Times* (eight times).

Nearly $2 million were raised for the Somalia emergency between August 1992 and June 1993 due to CARE's high visibility during the Somali crisis. This allowed CARE to feed more than one million people a day during the height of the emergency (December through February), significantly reducing the mortality rate. For example, in November in the rural town of Baidoa 250 people were dying a day; by February that number declined to less than 20 deaths a day. In 1993, American donations enabled CARE to help the Somali people recover and rebuild their country. In 1993, CARE distributed seeds and tools to 100,000 Somali farmers, provided basic health care at five clinics in Baidoa, and supported 37 local projects in school construction and well and sanitation rehabilitation.

Exhibit 11-1a    Program News Release   (Courtesy CARE)

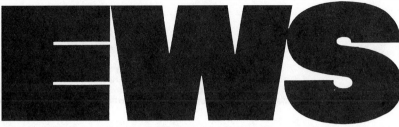

660 First Ave.
New York, NY 10016
(212) 686-3110

CONTACT:   Hope Rosenberg, Ext. 241      (Photo Available on request)
           Carolyn Snyder, Ext. 345
           Christina Horzepa, Ext. 261

### CARE FEEDS ONE MILLION STARVING SOMALIS

Sept. 3, 1992 -- CARE, the world's largest private relief
and development agency, announced today that despite continued
armed conflict, it is providing food to one million hungry
Somalis.  An estimated 4.5 million Somali civilians are without
adequate food and water.  Experts estimate that one thousand
people are dying every day.

"This is a tragedy of enormous proportions," CARE
President, Dr. Philip Johnston reported from Somalia.  "The
suffering of the Somali people cannot be ignored."

Johnston just completed a fact-finding trip to the region.

CARE has delivered more than 35,000 tons of food, including
wheat, sorghum and maize, since May of this year.  The food,
which has been primarily distributed in and around the capital,
Mogadishu, has been donated by the World Food Program, as well
as the Saudi Arabian and French Governments.

The chaotic social situation makes the operation extremely
dangerous, and CARE workers risk their lives every day while
running unarmed food convoys through active war zones.  Relief
trucks are routinely fired on in these areas.

(more)

Exhibit 11-1a
(*continued*)

Program News Release   (Courtesy CARE)

SOMALIA PAGE TWO

In addition to the efforts in Mogadishu, CARE is preparing to receive U.S. airlifts of food to areas west of the capital. The majority of these flights are expected to begin later this month. CARE teams will help truck the food from airports to distribution sites in Baidoa and Bardera.

CARE has been active in Somalia for over a decade. During the first few months of 1992, fighting became so intense that basic services were shut down and supplies such as food, fuel and water were unavailable. During that time relief supplies could not get into the country because of the shelling of Mogadishu port. CARE national staff remained in Mogadishu throughout the crisis and resumed relief activities when supplies again became available.

CARE is currently pursuing funding for the distribution of seeds and tools to 50,000 farmers south of the capital. These farmers were forced to eat their seeds to survive the effects of drought and civil war. The supplies will enable them to plant crops prior to the fall rains.

"Although things seem bleak now, CARE remains committed to its relief efforts in Somalia and looks forward to the day when the civil strife ends and the work of rebuilding can begin," says Johnston.

CARE is accepting donations for its Emergency Fund at 660 First Avenue, New York, NY. Telephone: 1-800-521-CARE

# # #

cnr992

Exhibit 11-1b    Program News Release    (Courtesy CARE)

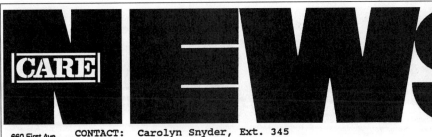

**CARE NEWS**

660 First Ave.
New York, NY 10016
(212) 686-3110

CONTACT:    Carolyn Snyder, Ext. 345
            Hope Rosenberg, Ext. 241

## CARE RESPONDS TO U.S. INITIATIVE FOR SOMALIA

New York, November 30 -- Officials for CARE, the
world's largest private relief and development organization,
today welcomed the United States' offer to send troops to
Somalia to participate in an increased United Nations
military force.  Security continues to be the major obstacle
to providing humanitarian assistance to the Somali people.

The proposed U.S. and other military forces, under the
auspices of the United Nations, would ensure the security
necessary to protect relief workers who are trying to
deliver emergency supplies to Somalia's needy.

Earlier this month, four drivers hired by CARE, which
distributes food to nearly one million starving Somalis
daily, were killed when their relief convoy was attacked.  A
CARE employee was also shot and severely wounded in
Mogadishu port.

CARE officials urge the U.N. Security Council to
utilize the U.S. Government's offer to develop a United
Nations initiative that will protect the international
relief community's efforts to feed desperate Somalis.

# # #

Exhibit 11-1c  Program News Release  (Courtesy CARE)

151 Ellis Street, NE
Atlanta, GA 30303-2426
(404) 681-2552

660 First Ave.
New York, NY 10016
(212) 686-3110

CONTACT:  Hope Rosenberg, Ext. 241

## SOMALI SELF-SUFFICIENCY:  THE DIFFICULT NEXT STEP

Despite Somalia's urgent need for continued emergency food relief and military protection, the international aid community is looking optimistically toward a brighter Somali future.

"The people of Somalia can become self-sufficient," says Dr. Philip Johnston, President of CARE, the relief and development organization,  "but it is going to take a great deal of hard work."

Johnston, currently in Mogadishu, has been coordinating the international relief effort under the umbrella of the United Nations since the fall.  Johnston has helped draft the long-term plan that details how aid organizations in Somalia can work with the people to rebuild their country.

"Many desperate Somalis, who in times of peace would farm, raise livestock or sell goods in the markets, are forced by economic uncertainty to live by the gun," Johnston says.  "We can help these people put down their arms and find a more meaningful way to live by revitalizing the Somali economy."

(more)

CARE plans to stimulate Somalia's ailing economy  through programs that will rehabilitate farms, re-establish the livestock of nomadic pastoralists, rebuild water systems, repair roads and build schools and hospitals.  The organization will also provide training to village health workers to treat minor illnesses and monitor the nutritional status of mothers and young children.

In some areas, CARE has begun to sell food to local merchants to help revitalize commercial markets.  The money from these sales will go to local Somali organizations for rehabilitation programs. In other areas, the organization also expects to purchase locally-produced surplus food.

These approaches are meant to strengthen the normal food production and distribution channels which were destroyed by the famine.  CARE hopes to diminish the scope of emergency food programs once this long-term development is fully underway.

"Food relief is always a double-edged sword.  In the short-term it saves lives; in the long-term it can encourage dependency," says Johnston.  "That's why CARE is immediately beginning development programs that will help the Somalis help themselves."

(more)

Exhibit 11-1c
(continued)

Program News Release   (Courtesy CARE)

PAGE THREE

The final draft of the Somali recovery plan will be completed by the end February.

"Constructing the plan is an important first step to helping the people of Somalia get back on their feet," Johnston says.  "It will take years -- and millions of dollars -- to implement that plan.  We are depending on the generosity of the American public to make it possible."

# # #

cnr193

Exhibit 11-1d

## Saving Somalia: One Meal at a Time

This Somali child was once so malnourished he could barely eat the simplest food without becoming violently ill. One month after reaching a displaced persons camp sponsored by CARE, the world's largest private relief and development organization, he was able to digest three small meals each day. According to CARE relief workers, many Somali children suffer from digestive track ailments that make it difficult for them to eat solid food. To combat this problem, CARE provides life-saving emergency rations in easily digestible form to tens of thousands of poor and hungry Somali children.

(CARE photo by Betty Press; courtesy CARE)

*Tylenol and Pepsi are the two classic product-tampering cases all public relations students should study. Pepsi smoothly executed its crisis response guidelines and saved the company's reputation in the infamous syringe hoax. Exhibit 11-2a is the company's first consumer product advisory following the syringe scare. Exhibits 11-2b and 11-2c are subsequent media releases. Exhibit 11-2d is a follow-up advertisement about the hoax.*

**CASE 11-2**  Pepsi's Crisis Response: The Syringe Scare

Pepsi-Cola Company, Somers, NY, with Robert Chang Productions, New York, NY

## Introduction

On June 10, 1993, a Seattle television station reported that a local couple had discovered a syringe in a can of Diet Pepsi. Soon a second complaint in Seattle surfaced. The pattern prompted the U.S. FDA to issue a regional advisory, urging consumers to empty the contents of their Diet Pepsi cans into a glass before drinking. The warning commanded national media attention, and within 24 hours, reports of syringes in Diet Pepsi cans in disparate locations around the country led every network news broadcast. The intensity of public and regulatory scrutiny, the frightening images of potentially contaminated syringes in Diet Pepsi cans, and the threat to the peak July 4th holiday sales period presented Pepsi-Cola Company with an unprecedented challenge to its trademarks and to its reputation. With no reasonable explanation from a manufacturing standpoint for this bizarre series of events, the FDA recommended a course of no recall. The media, unaccustomed to this course of action for alleged product tampering of this magnitude, persisted in reporting "victims" claims and in looking to the company for answers.

## Research

Pepsi's long-standing crisis response guidelines have been researched and tested for more than ten years. As the company's business and structure have grown and changed, the crisis plan has evolved from a

Courtesy Pepsi-Cola Company

rudimentary, operationally oriented product-recall procedure into a sophisticated communications network. By benchmarking other world-class companies' approaches to crisis situations, including Johnson & Johnson, Pepsi has further refined its crisis management guidelines. Through a process of continuous improvement, actual and simulated use of the plan has shown that effective communication is the key element in successfully resolving a crisis. The crisis plan activated during the 1993 syringe hoax had been successfully applied in managing previous local and regional issues, including plant emergencies, defective packages, and product contaminations. Based on this experience and knowledge, Pepsi's crisis team planned and executed a response to end the scare swiftly and to restore public confidence in its products.

## Planning

The company's crisis response plan was triggered from day one of the week-long scare, when the local Seattle bottler began its investigation to determine what had gone wrong and then to respond to the media and the public. That week, the crisis team worked to assure consumers of the safety of Pepsi products and the manufacturing process, to preserve trust in the 95-year-old Pepsi trademark, and to protect the company's $8 billion business. Public relations assumed the role of coordinating the company's actions with support from the manufacturing, legal, and regulatory experts on the crisis team. The objective was to convince the public that they and the company's products were safe, that planned tampering involving syringes could not logically be occurring, and that a recall would not solve the problem. The strategy was to be open and responsive to the media, to communicate the facts early and often to all audiences, and to work closely with the FDA to investigate the real cause of syringes in Diet Pepsi cans. Centralized communications channels were established to reach all groups affected by the national scare—consumers, the media, regulatory officials, bottlers, shareholders, employees, and customers (retail stores, restaurants, all Pepsi sales outlets)—so that those groups would use logic and reason to see the truth. Because of the accelerated timeframe and unprecedented national scale of the crisis, a budget was not set in advance. The cost of executing the crisis plan was approximately $500,000.

## Execution

The crisis progressed through four distinct stages as new facts were determined and communicated by Pepsi and as the FDA investigation gathered momentum. The crisis team continually assessed media reports and developing events to update communications to all target groups. In the initial stage, the company worked quickly to understand the problem thoroughly and to rule out sabotage in the manufacturing process. The Seattle bottler granted on-site interviews, allowed local news crews into the manufacturing plant to film the high-tech, high-speed canning line, and issued a press release to assure consumers that the company would find the answer. Later, as the local issue became a national news story, it was clear that events were externally driven by what the FDA termed "the vicious cycle of media reports begetting copycat complaints." To counteract this phenomenon, the crisis team created messages and tools—including video news releases, press releases, consumer talking points, bottler advisories, employee bulletins, trade letters, still photos, graphs, and interviews—to reach those groups that could help Pepsi and FDA investigators bring the scare to a swift end. Pepsi relied on television news to reach the broadest consumer audience as quickly as possible. The team engaged Pepsi's longtime video producer and media consultant, Robert Chang Productions, to assemble compelling video footage that would illustrate the company's message. Those images, transmitted nationally via satellite, brought consumers into a Pepsi plant to show them the speed and safety of the manufacturing process and the illogic of so many complaints occurring in so many different locations at the same time. Pepsi CEO Craig Weatherup appeared on every major network news program to declare that the company was "99.99 percent certain" that this wasn't happening in Pepsi's plants. A staff of six media relations managers handled 2,000 calls from print, radio, and television reporters, while 24 consumer specialists, assisted by 40 volunteers, manned the phones to respond to tens of thousands of consumer calls. Advisories were sent twice daily to Pepsi's 400 bottling locations via fax, and six people were assigned to counsel bottlers and field personnel on local issues. The FDA, experienced in product tampering and copycat investigations, served as Pepsi's primary crisis counselor. FDA officials at national and local levels concentrated on finding the cause of the syringe claims, and Pepsi focused on showing that its package and manufacturing were virtually tamper-proof.

## Evaluation

The syringe scare ended barely seven days after it had begun. Although the crisis cost Pepsi $25 million in lost sales, by mid-summer the company had bounced back and ended the season with its highest sales in five years, an increase of 7 percent over the previous summer. Consumers clearly voted their confidence in Pepsi and its products at the check-out counter and in attitude and awareness surveys conducted during and after the crisis. At the peak of the crisis, 94 percent of consumers said that they believed Pepsi was handling the crisis responsibly, and three out of four said they felt better about Pepsi products because of the way the company responded to the problem. Tracking reports from MediaLink, Pepsi's VNR satellite transmission service, showed the highest usage ever for a MediaLink-transmitted VNR with Pepsi's first of four VNRs released during the crisis week. Together, all four VNRs generated viewership of more than 500 million people. Qualitatively, Pepsi's crisis response was deemed a success by the unprecedented cooperation of the FDA and the cooperation among bottlers and customers in resisting demands for a national recall of Pepsi products. In thousands of phone calls to Pepsi's 800 number and in hundreds of letters, consumers expressed their support. And in editorials around the country, the media debated its own role in escalating the scare and subjecting business and consumers to the fear and disruption of unsubstantiated product-tampering claims. The U.S. House of Representatives lauded Pepsi in the *Congressional Record* for its quick and decisive actions to end the national scare.

*PEPSI* **NEWS RELEASE**

*CONTACT:*    Andrew Giangola           Anne Ward
914-767-7495                914-767-7067

## PEPSI-COLA CONSUMER PRODUCT ADVISORY

SOMERS, NY, JUNE 15, 1993 -- In response to news stories of complaints
of syringes or other parts of needles allegedly found in Pepsi-Cola
packaging, the company today announced the following consumer advisory:

- There have been no reports of injuries resulting from these allegations.
  In fact, we have yet to confirm a single report of any foriegn object
  matter found in an *unopened* container.

- Pepsi and FDA's Offices of Criminal Investigation are conducting
  meticulous investigations of each and every complaint. In areas where
  we've received complaints, all production and employee records are being
  checked. We have found no abnormalities.

- While the FDA has announced there is no health risk to consumers,
  they've issued an advisory for concerned consumers to visually inspect
  the cans before drinking.

- Pepsi has no reason to believe there is any manufacturing problem. There
  is no pattern to the incidents in terms of can sourcing, production dates
  or can codes.

- As it appears that this is not a production issue, the FDA warns that
  anyone who willfully tampers with a consumer product or falsely reports
  a product contamination is subject to strict criminal penalities.

- A can is the most difficult of all consumer packaging to tamper with,
  particularly in the constantly monitored, strictly controlled canning
  process. It is highly unlikely for any foreign substance to be
  introduced into a can during the production process, given the
  configuration of our high-speed canning lines, where empty
  cans are inverted upside down, cleaned by air or water, and then inverted
  immediately before they're filled.

PEPSI-COLA COMPANY 1 PEPSI WAY, SOMERS, NEW YORK 10589-2201

# CAN PROCESS FLOW CHART

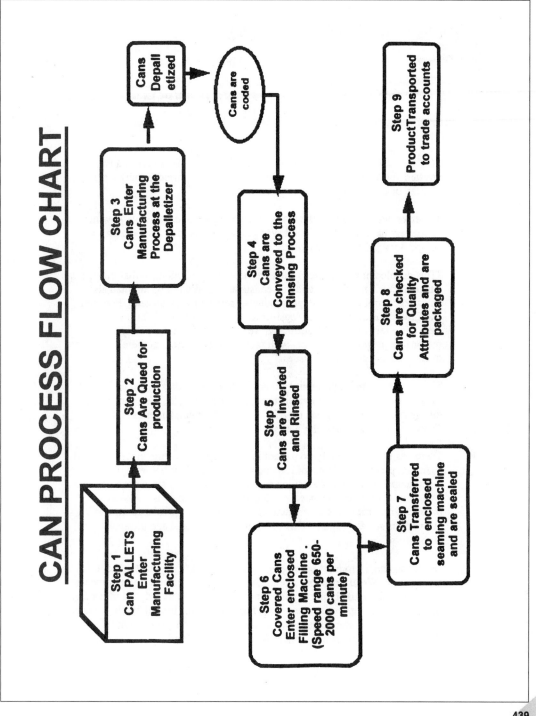

**Step 1**
Can PALLETS Enter Manufacturing Facility

**Step 2**
Cans Are Qued for production

**Step 3**
Cans Enter Manufacturing Process at the Depalletizer

Cans Depalletized

Cans are coded

**Step 4**
Cans are Conveyed to the Rinsing Process

**Step 5**
Cans are Inverted and Rinsed

**Step 6**
Covered Cans Enter enclosed Filling Machine . (Speed range 650-2000 cans per minute)

**Step 7**
Cans Transferred to enclosed seaming machine and are sealed

**Step 8**
Cans are checked for Quality Attributes and are packaged

**Step 9**
ProductTransported to trade accounts

Exhibit 11-2b    News Release    (Courtesy Pepsi-Cola Company)

**PEPSI** *NEWS RELEASE*

CONTACT:    Andrew Giangola   or   Anne Ward
            914-767-7495        914-767-7067

## FIRST SUSPECT ARRESTED IN PEPSI-COLA
## PRODUCT TAMPERING INCIDENT

SOMERS, NY, JUNE 16, 1993 --   A man in Central Pennsylvania was arrested yesterday on charges that he fraudulently reported finding a syringe in a can of Pepsi, the company announced today.

The arrest was the first in the wake of news stories of complaints in which consumers have allegedly found syringes or needles in Pepsi-Cola and competitors' products packaging.

"This development reinforces what we've believed all along -- that this is not a manufacturing problem, and that consumers should not be alarmed about any alleged problem with Pepsi products," said Craig Weatherup, President and Chief Executive Office, Pepsi-Cola, North America.  "While we take each and every claim very seriously, we believe consumers will use reasonable judgement and deal with facts.  The facts are that there's nothing to indicate any production issues."

The spate of complaints about syringes or parts of needles found in Pepsi cans have defied physical evidence and intellectual logic, Weatherup said this morning in appearances on ABC's "Good Morning America," NBC's "Today" and "CBS Morning News."

There has been absolutely no pattern to the alleged incidents in terms of can sourcing, production dates, or can codes, he noted. "Our bottlers manufacture more than 20 million cans a day.  Each one has a code.  Within a 48-hour period, to have needles allegedly show up in cans that were produced in some cases six months apart, in others six weeks apart, and in even others six days apart.  This defies intellectual logic and physical probability."

Of all consumer products packaging, cans are perhaps the most difficult to tamper with, Weatherup continued.  During the high-speed canning process, it is extremely unlikely for any foreign substance to be introduced into a can. In the process, empty cans are inverted upside down, cleaned by air or water, and then inverted immediately before they're filled and closed.  On the filling line, the cans are open and vulnerable for only .9 second.

PEPSI-COLA COMPANY  1 PEPSI WAY, SOMERS, NEW YORK 10589-2201

Exhibit 11-2c    News Release    (Courtesy Pepsi-Cola Company)

# PEPSI NEWS RELEASE

CONTACT:

Andrew Giangola                    Anne Ward
914-767-7495                       914-767-7067

## MORE PEPSI PRODUCT TAMPERING CLAIMS
## CONFIRMED AS HOAXES

**\*\*\*\***

## SECOND SUSPECT ARRESTED
## IN PEPSI PRODUCT TAMPERING INCIDENT

**FOR IMMEDIATE RELEASE: 1:00 AM EST**

**SOMERS, NY, JUNE 17, 1993** -- Two consumers who alleged they found
foreign matter in Pepsi packaging have been arrested, and five more
consumers have retracted their product tampering claims, the company
announced today.

In Branson, MO, a man was arrested after he withdrew his claim of product
tampering in Pepsi packaging after authorities found that a needle which
allegedly entered the Pepsi product was actually from a family member's
insulin syringe supply.

On Wednesday, a man in central Pennsylvania was arrested for falsely
claiming to have found a syringe in Pepsi packaging.

In Herrin, IL, a woman recanted per product tampering claim after she
reported finding a sewing needle in a can of Pepsi purchased from a vending
machine. The needle was taken to the Herrin Police Crime Lab where it was
determined the needle could not have come from the can. After being
interviewed by a Herrin police detective, the woman recanted her story. She
decided the needle was pinned to her clothing and must have fallen off.

Tuesday night in Davis, CA, a 25-year-old woman recanted her allegation of
discovering a needle in a can of Diet Pepsi, one and a half hours after
making the charge.

*PEPSI-COLA COMPANY  1 PEPSI WAY, SOMERS, NEW YORK 10589-2201*

Exhibit 11-2c
(*continued*)

News Release   (Courtesy Pepsi-Cola Company)

The woman had shown Davis Police officers two small pieces of what appeared to be a sewing needle. The woman told the officers she purchased the soft drink that afternoon at a local grocery store. Immediately prior to calling the police, the woman had informed a local television news station of her discovery.

Later, she admitted she had broken a common sewing needle and had inserted it into the open soft drink can, after hearing news reports of needles being found in Diet Pepsi cans.

In Covina, CA, another woman also admitted she had lied about finding foreign matter in Pepsi packaging.

"These developments bring us a day closer to business as usual," said Craig Weatherup, President and CEO, Pepsi-Cola North America. "In spite of numerous allegations, Pepsi and FDA still have not confirmed a single report of any needles or syringes found in an unopened container. There have been no verifiable injuries reported, and the FDA reports that there is no health risk to consumers."

"Product tampering -- or falsely reporting a product contamination -- is a serious federal offense, and the FDA has indicated they will prosecute and all false reports to the full extent of the law," Weatherup said.

Exhibit 11-2d    Follow-up Advertisement    (Courtesy Pepsi-Cola Company)

# Pepsi is pleased
# to announce...

# ...nothing.

As America now knows, those stories about Diet Pepsi were a hoax. Plain and simple, not true. Hundreds of investigators have found no evidence to support a single claim.

As for the many, many thousands of people who work at Pepsi-Cola, we feel great that it's over. And we're ready to get on with making and bringing you what we believe is the best-tasting diet cola in America.

There's not much more we can say. Except that most importantly, we won't let this hoax change our exciting plans for this summer.

We've set up special offers so you can enjoy our great quality products at prices that will save you money all summer long. It all starts on July 4th weekend and we hope you'll stock up with a little extra, just to make up for what you might have missed last week.

That's it. Just one last word of thanks to the millions of you who have stood with us.

### Drink All The Diet Pepsi You Want.
### Uh Huh.

DIET PEPSI and UH-HUH are registered trademarks of PepsiCo, Inc.

# Appendixes

# I

# Questions for Class Discussion and Case Analysis

THE FOLLOWING QUESTIONS CAN BE USED IN CLASS discussions of each of the cases in this textbook. Students can gain valuable experience by leading class discussions.

# RESEARCH

Does the case give adequate background information about the organization itself? What was the major reason for conducting this program? Was the program proactive or reactive? Which audiences were targeted for communication? Should other audiences have also been targeted? How were research data about each audience obtained? Were the data as complete as necessary? Is there anything unusual about the research phase of this case? What are the research strengths and weaknesses of this case?

# OBJECTIVES

Categorize this case's objectives. Which are impact objectives? Specify informational, attitudinal, or behavioral. Which are output objectives? Should they have been more quantitative? Should they have used time frames? Were output objectives used when the ultimate goal was really impact? What is your overall assessment of the objectives used in this case?

# PROGRAMMING

Evaluate the theme (if any) used in this case. Is it short, catchy, memorable, to the point? What major message or messages are communicated in this case? Evaluate the central actions or special events in this case. Are they truly worthwhile and newsworthy? Are they "pseudo-events"? Evaluate the types of uncontrolled and controlled media that were used. Were any forms of communication omitted that should have been used? Was adequate use made of interpersonal communication? Did the communication achieve a sense of "grassroots involvement" through interpersonal communication, or was there overreliance on mass media publicity placement or impersonal forms of controlled media? Discuss the use of such communication principles as source credibility, salient information, effective nonverbal and verbal cues, two-way communication, opinion leaders, group influence, selective exposure, and audience participation. How effectively were these principles used? Explain.

# EVALUATION

Was each of the case's objectives separately evaluated? Describe the evaluative methods used. How appropriate and effective were these methods? Did the program achieve its stated objectives? Was there a real *link* between the case's objectives and its evaluation?

# OVERALL JUDGMENTS

As a whole, how effective was this public relations program? What are its major strengths? major weaknesses? Explain. What are the major PR lessons or principles to be learned from this case? What, if anything, would you do differently if you were assigned a public relations problem like this one?

# II

# Case Problems
and Exercises

# 1. ORAL REPORT

Prepare a 10- to 15-minute oral report on the operations of the Public Relations department of a local organization. The report should include background information on the organization, the definition of its target publics, research methods used, objectives, communication methods, and evaluation procedures. The report will be evaluated using the criteria listed below. Since all PR practitioners should be accomplished public speakers, the report will be graded on both content and delivery.

## Oral Report Evaluation

1. *Organization:* Name of organization, background data, characteristics

2. *Definition of target public(s):* How the organization's PR department segments publics

3. *Research methods:* Discussion of quantitative and nonquantitative methods used by the organization in gathering data

4. *Objectives:* Statement of PR objectives used by the organization

5. *Communication methods:* Explanation of communication activities used to reach public(s) and subsets: (1) action(s) or special event(s); (2) uncontrolled media; (3) controlled media—print, audiovisual, interpersonal; illustration of report with some of the organization's communication materials

6. *Evaluation:* Explanation of evaluation procedures used by the organization to measure PR effectiveness

7. *Presentation of report:*
   a. Organization
      (1) Clear delineation of sections of the report
      (2) Appropriate explanation and details for each section
      (3) Attention-getting introduction
      (4) Appropriate conclusion and summary
   b. Delivery
      (1) Eye contact with class during report
      (2) Conversational quality, avoidance of excessive reading
      (3) Effective use of visual aids—charts, slides, transparencies, chalkboard, and/or other media

# 2. MEDIA RELATIONS

### Chloe's Fashions

In Chicago, Illinois, Chloe's Fashions is preparing to open its doors for the first time. This specialized department store plans to employ and cater to overweight women in an attempt to alter the public perception that heavy individuals are unattractive and care little about the way they look or dress. The print and broadcast media have perpetually reinforced this negative view by presenting the "pencil thin" woman in commercials and magazine ads for clothes and beauty products. In addition, most of today's glamorous movie stars are thin, and those stars who aren't are usually portrayed as comics who can laugh at their weight yet still consider it a problem. Chloe's aim is to present a positive image of overweight women by using overweight models to display their newest clothing lines and to reassure heavy women that they too can look beautiful in the latest fashions. Through a public relations campaign, Chloe's hopes not only to increase public awareness of their opening but to significantly combat views equating style and fashion with thinness. Following the ROPE format, formulate a media relations campaign that would assist Chloe's in accomplishing this.

### Freeze Frame, Inc.

Freeze Frame, Inc., a Boston-based business, has been producing high-quality 35 mm cameras and camera components for 30 years and has marketed them nationwide. The company also specializes in photo developing and emphasizes the speed with which it can process family pictures. For the most part, Freeze Frame has enjoyed high sales levels and respectable profits. During the past seven to eight years, however, the surge of video cameras into the national market has caused a considerable decrease in both the amount of 35 mm cameras sold and the number of customers who bring in their film for developing. Apparently the public is more interested in making home videos than in taking old-fashioned still pictures. Rather than panic over how this new trend will affect business, Freeze Frame, Inc. has decided to expand. Instead of simply making cameras and developing film, it will now offer a new service centered around picture restoration and enhancement. Customers may bring in old family pictures that have deteriorated with age or been ruined by weather and have them completely restored to their original quality. Picture enhancement, a process that alters photo content, will also be offered. Closed eyes may be opened, ex-spouses eliminated, or more suitable backgrounds inserted, depending on the individual preference of the customer. Although Freeze Frame realizes that this new service will not take away from video camera sales, it hopes that it will catch the attention of the public, encourage them to keep taking pictures, and remind them of the high sentimental value that still photos possess. Using the ROPE method, prepare a media relations campaign that will create maximum public awareness of the new service, and provide a positive slant on still photography in general.

## Society for Improving Teaching as a Profession (SITAP)

During the earlier half of the twentieth century and before, teachers were considered intelligent men and women who contributed greatly toward the betterment of society. They were respected throughout the community and held in the highest regard as people and as professionals. The teaching profession today, however—specifically elementary and high school teaching—is not as well respected as it once was. Although the public does not particularly view teaching in a negative light, people no longer possess the deep appreciation and admiration for our teachers that they did years ago. This is true despite the fact that teachers face increasingly difficult obstacles such as lack of student motivation, the hindrance of student drug and alcohol addictions, and the psychological impairment of children who come from broken homes. Teachers are also burdened with the fear of student violence, which has become a frequent occurrence in some districts. Public indifference toward the profession has begun to take its toll on teacher morale. Teachers have become increasingly frustrated with the view that they have an easy job because they only have six-hour work days and because they enjoy long vacations. The Society for Improving Teaching as a Profession (SITAP) is a recently formed, national organization dedicated to renewing the respectability and public appreciation that the teaching profession once commanded. SITAP is planning to hold its first annual conference in Los Angeles. Through the media, it hopes to promote positive public attitudes toward teachers, to reestablish teaching as a prestigious profession, and to encourage young people to consider teaching as a career choice. Using the ROPE format, prepare a media relations campaign that will serve to accomplish these goals.

# 3. EMPLOYEE RELATIONS

## Physical Rehabilitation Corporation (PRC)

Physical Rehabilitation Corporation (PRC) is a company that employs nurses and home health aides who assist patients recovering from accidents, illness, or surgery. Although the nurses and health aides visit the homes of patients, they also have offices in the company headquarters in Portland, Maine, where they spend a good portion of their working week. PRC also employs a number of clerical assistants and supervisors who work both in the main building and in field offices located around

New England. During its 15 years of existence, PRC has always allowed its employees to smoke in the office if they chose. Several of the nurses, supervisors, and health aides tend to have an occasional cigarette in their offices or in the company break room. A good portion of the clerical workers employed by PRC do smoke, and they light up often in their cubicles, the break room, and the cafeteria. In light of America's emphasis on health and fitness during the past ten years, as well as the government's recent proposal for health care reform, the president of PRC (himself a smoker) has decided to enforce a nonsmoking policy in all PRC offices. The president feels that because PRC is in the health care industry, it has an obligation to provide a healthy environment for all employees and should not expose nonsmokers to the dangers of secondhand smoke. He also feels that employees who smoke should be encouraged to quit and that being unable to smoke at work would help in their struggle. The president has not announced the new policy yet, but he is anticipating much employee opposition. Use the ROPE method to propose a suitable internal communications campaign that will announce the new policy and help to maintain it in a positive light.

## The Silver Fox

David Brown is the owner and head manager of a medium-size retail store located in a suburb of Denver. The store, called The Silver Fox, employs five sales managers, fifteen full-time employees and ten part-time employees, and specializes in the sale of fur and leather goods. Profits have been fairly good since the store opened five years ago, and Mr. Brown is even thinking of expanding. Recently, however, a small group of animal rights activists began to picket outside The Silver Fox. These activists have not engaged in any violence, but they carry signs and often taunt and threaten the employees who enter and leave the building each day. Mr. Brown has been told by police that nothing much can be done unless the activists actually physically harm the store or the employees. Silver Fox employees have become quite nervous about the situation. They are afraid to report for work and often avoid going out of the building for lunch. Some employees have even begun to see the activists' point of view. They are now doubtful about their position in the fur and leather industry and feel guilty about the merchandise they handle and sell. Several of the part-time employees have told Mr. Brown that they are seeking other employment. Mr. Brown knows that his other employees and managers can easily find comparable positions in the retail industry if they so desire. As PR director for The Silver Fox, devise a program to deal with the threat of employee defection. Mr. Brown wants his employees to realize that this is a legitimate business, that they have no reason to feel guilty about their positions, and that they need not be intimidated by the activists. Using the ROPE model, outline your strategy.

# 4. MEMBER RELATIONS

## National Organization for Humane Animal Treatment (NOHAT)

The National Organization for Humane Animal Treatment (NOHAT) is a 1,000-member group based in Los Angeles, California. NOHAT represents the interests of all animals, both wild and domestic, and works to prevent animal cruelty as observed in shelters, laboratories, zoos, and even private homes. NOHAT members participate in local demonstrations against animal cruelty and investigate local zoos and shelters to make sure that managers are maintaining certain standards of cleanliness and exercise for the animals kept there. NOHAT members also volunteer to take in abused or abandoned animals and care for them until proper homes can be found. NOHAT would like to promote national legislation to put restrictions on the use of animals in laboratory experiments. The organization is expecting substantial resistance from the medical industry on this issue because many medical professionals believe that animal experimentation is necessary to find cures for cancer and other life-threatening diseases. In order to go forward with such a massive campaign, NOHAT first needs to expand its membership outside of California. It also needs to focus on favorable media coverage to improve its chances of recruiting new members. Using the ROPE format, design a campaign to help NOHAT gain increasing membership across the United States.

## Environmental Society of America (ESOA)

The Environmental Society of America (ESOA) is a national organization that claims about 5,000 members across the United States. Members attend monthly meetings of their local chapters and work on committees to come up with new ways to protect the natural environment. In addition, ESOA lobbies on the local, state, and federal levels to promote or protest legislation on issues concerning the environment. Members of ESOA pay annual dues and participate in fund-raising events such as raffles, bake sales, and community dinners. They rely on the money raised to fund various environmental projects aimed at preserving public parks, beaches, forests, and other natural settings. Although each chapter nominates a leader, ESOA also has a national president who oversees all activities of the society. Every year, one dedicated member is honored by the society for his or her exceptional contributions to the environmental cause. This person receives a special award, which is presented by ESOA's president at a dinner held in Washington, DC.

In recent months, it has been rumored that ESOA's president may have engaged in unethical behavior. Several chapter leaders have reason to suspect that the president used a portion of ESOA's treasury money for a personal vacation and the purchase of a new car. There is no proof yet that the president is guilty, yet many ESOA members are becoming angry at the thought of such behavior, and nearly half have threatened to withdraw from the society and form their own separate organization. Many members have spoken or written to their chapter leaders and expressed concern that those with access may also be siphoning funds for their own personal use. You are a PR director hired by ESOA chapter leaders to improve member relations and to restore trust in the society. Use the ROPE model to outline your strategy.

# 5. COMMUNITY RELATIONS

## Cape Cod Moving Carnival

Laurel Valley is a medium-size, middle-class town located on Cape Cod in the state of Massachusetts. The town contains a church, a grammar school, high school, two small grocery stores, a bank, and several small retail shops and restaurants, which are owned and operated by people in the community. Unlike many other areas of the cape, Laurel Valley is virtually free of tourists. The people who live here are permanent Cape Cod residents and reside in their homes all year long. Some work as fishermen; others make long commutes into larger, neighboring cities to go to work. Laurel Valley has been hit hard by a recent recession. Many residents have been laid off from their jobs, and the fishing industry has also suffered. Town officials regret the fact that they rarely have enough money to fund extracurricular activities such as sports programs and academic clubs. The church building and town sidewalks are also badly in need of repair and renovation. Rather than putting an extra burden on residents by raising taxes, town council officials have made a decision to invite the Cape Cod Moving Carnival to stop over in Laurel Valley on a recurring basis. The carnival follows the format of a circus and includes rides, shows, and animal entertainment. During the spring and summer, it stops at various cities and towns along the cape and stays for about a month in each town. Officials hope that the carnival will generate substantial revenue for Laurel Valley and will relieve the town from some of its financial troubles. Many community members are unsure of the council's decision. They fear their town will be turned into a haven for tourists and may become too commercialized. They also fear vandalism, noise, and traffic problems with the coming of the carnival. They insist that there must be some other way to generate needed funds. Design a PR program that will calm resident fears about the carnival and even generate excitement about the potential tourist industry. Use the ROPE format to outline your strategy.

## Meyers Hall

Northern State College (NSC) is located in Rolling Hills, Massachusetts, a suburb community of Boston. This college offers associate and bachelor degrees in many academic areas to approximately 1,500 undergraduates. NSC has been in existence for 20 years and is drawing more and more students each semester. Because of its small size, NSC offers no on-campus housing of any kind. Most students who come from the immediate area find it convenient to live with their families and commute to school each day. Some, however, must travel daily to Rolling Hills from communities located anywhere from 15 to 20 miles away from the college. Often, these students need to repeat the trip several times on weekends in order to use the college's library facilities. It is difficult to rent an apartment near NSC because the area is surrounded by one-family homes and an elderly retirement facility. In light of this problem, the NSC administration is seriously considering the construction of a new resident dormitory to be named Meyers Hall in honor of Paul Meyers, former president and cofounder of the college. President Meyers has generously donated a large sum of money to help fund the project, and construction is set to begin soon.

Ever since an announcement about the new dorm appeared in a local newspaper, the residents of Rolling Hills have made it known that they are vehemently opposed to the idea. Elderly residents fear the onset of loud noise and student parties. Local families are concerned about student loitering, traffic problems, safety during the construction period, and the aesthetic nature of the building. A group of community representatives stormed into President Meyers' office recently. This confrontation consisted of yelling and frustrated threats on the part of the representatives. The NSC administration is also feeling pressure from the student body not to abandon the project.

You have been hired by NSC to handle community relations concerning Meyers Hall. Use the ROPE format to outline a strategy that will calm the residents of Rolling Hills and elicit their support for the dormitory.

# 6. PUBLIC AFFAIRS

## Committee on Safety Belts (COSB)

Each year thousands of Americans die in car crashes. In fact, motor vehicle accidents are one of the leading causes of death in the United States. These accidents are often due to speeding, drunken driving, and people inadvertently falling asleep at the wheel. Some citizens believe that although a national, mandatory seat belt law might not cut down on the number of accidents, it may significantly reduce fatalities. As of now, mandatory seat belt laws exist in some states but not in others. A group of Americans has formed an organization called the Committee on Safety Belts (COSB). Members of COSB support the passage of a nationwide seat belt law because they feel the belts may save a substantial number of lives. COSB argues that seat belts often prevent accident victims from being thrown from their vehicles on sudden impact. Members contend that death is not necessarily caused by that impact but is more likely the result of trauma to the body when it passes through a windshield or hits a concrete pavement. COSB's main objective is to promote the passage of a nationwide seat belt bill. Assume you are director of public relations for COSB. Using the ROPE model, design a campaign that will bring pressure on appropriate lawmakers.

## Sign Language Education Act

The Hearing Impaired Association (HIA) is a group of Washington, DC, residents who are either completely deaf or suffer from severe hearing loss. Formed ten years ago, HIA now consists of 400 people and continues to welcome additional members. Members meet monthly to discuss the societal barriers they face as a result of their handicap. Of course, one of the biggest obstacles discussed by HIA is the inability of many deaf people to communicate successfully with hearing individuals. This is particularly true in the District of Columbia, which has a large concentration of hearing impaired residents. A few HIA members have suggested that sign language classes be made an integral part of the curriculum in both public and private schools. They hope that, with the integration of sign language, more and more hearing individuals will be able to communicate with the deaf, thus reducing the frustration level for both groups. Although most of the members of HIA are mute, many have hearing friends and associates who would be willing to help them launch a lobbying campaign for a Sign Language Education Act, which would require sign language classes for all schools. Suppose you have been asked by HIA to head up this lobbying campaign. Using the ROPE model, describe your strategy.

# 7. INVESTOR RELATIONS

## Soft Sole, Inc.

Soft Sole, Inc. is a corporation that owns and operates a national chain of women's shoe stores of the same name. Soft Sole shoes are made of the finest quality leather. They are also designed for the high-powered career woman and are therefore fairly expensive. The chain has been in business for five years, yet its success has declined rapidly due to the poor economy and increased competition from more moderately priced shoe stores. President Jim Bailey and the board of directors are concerned because the value of Soft Sole stock is decreasing and investors are not happy.

Recently, Soft Sole was approached by Mayflower, a large, financially sound corporation that has been successful in the men's and women's clothing business for over 40 years. Mayflower is interested in acquiring Soft Sole in an effort to expand its business holdings. Bailey and the board of directors both believe it would benefit Soft Sole to be associated with a larger, well-known corporation such as Mayflower, so they have decided to accept the buyout offer. As a result, investors' shares of Soft Sole stock would be transferred to Mayflower and their value would increase by 10 percent.

You have been hired as the PR director of Soft Sole. Using the ROPE model, explain your campaign strategy to inform investors of the merger. While there will be an initial 10 percent stock increase, investors will have a smaller share of a larger corporation and will have less control over its management.

## Deloney, Inc.

Deloney, Inc. is a newly formed, Massachusetts-based company specializing in the sale of computer equipment and office supplies to local businesses and school systems. The company owners, Jim Deluca, Tom O'Malley, and John Varney, formed Deloney in 1990 after all three were laid off from their former positions.

Start-up financing for Deloney, Inc. came primarily from the personal savings of the owners. The men also offered private stock options to their friends and relatives and used the capital from these investments to cover ongoing expenses. Private shares sold for $1 each, and all investors realized that they were taking a risk.

After three years in business, Deloney, Inc. is doing amazingly well on the local level. The company has become widely recognized throughout the surrounding communities and is known for the excellent quality of its products and service. During the past year, sales have tripled, and Deloney, Inc. has received numerous requests to supply bigger businesses in neighboring states.

Deluca, O'Malley, and Varney are seriously considering these requests and plan to expand their business to service the entire New England area. Based on current profits and favorable customer response, they feel confident that such an expansion would be beneficial. The owners are also planning a public stock offering. Deloney, Inc. has been able to return a profit to its investors each year, and it appears that a public offering would be successful.

You are hired by Deloney, Inc. to inform private investors that the company will go public. Using the ROPE model, devise a strategy for informing them. You need to persuade these initial investors that Deloney, Inc. is in a position to expand throughout New England. Remember that the public stock offering means a smaller interest in the company for all investors.

# 8. CONSUMER RELATIONS

## Snowbusters, Inc.

Snowbusters, Inc. is a large company that has been in business for 20 years. The company has an established reputation for producing fine-quality snowblowers and electric shovels that make snow removal fast and easy. Snowbusters, Inc. has its headquarters in Boston, Massachusetts, and distributes a great many of its products to retailers throughout the New England area.

The company's newest snowblower model, the SX2000, is designed to pick up unusually large amounts of heavy snow, something that previous models were unable to do. During a recent blizzard, the Northeast region of the country was buried in almost two feet of snow. Snowbuster products, especially the SX2000, sold quickly to frantic consumers, who were anxious to clear their driveways and get to work on time. Unfortunately for consumers, a great many of these SX2000s did not work properly, due to a defect in their engines.

Company officials ordered a recall on all SX2000 models sold within the past six months. Of course, customers who returned the defective snowblowers were given a full refund. Even still, consumers remain angry and frustrated because they were left without a powerful snow removal device during the biggest blizzard of the season. Many have written letters to company headquarters expressing their intention never to purchase a Snowbusters product again.

You have been hired by Snowbusters, Inc. as PR counsel in this case. Using the ROPE model, how would you deal with the problems Snowbusters, Inc. has already experienced? Executives know that consumer trust in the company and its products has been severely damaged. They are anxious to rebuild that trust and to boost future snowblower sales in the process.

## Bean Chairs, Inc.

Bean Chairs, Inc. is a company that produces and markets beanbag chairs for preschool children. The chairs are made in the shape of farm animals and are filled with small balls of Styrofoam-like stuffing. Bean Chairs, Inc. has been in existence for five years, and its products have always been considered safe and of high quality.

In order to reduce costs, the company recently began using a cheaper type of plastic covering on their beanbag chairs. In December of this year, a three-year-old child from Milwaukee, Wisconsin, choked to death when he was able to rip through the covering and ingest stuffing pulled from the inside of the chair. Soon after, three other children from Boston, Chicago, and Charlotte, North Carolina, were rushed to area hospitals to have their stomachs pumped after they also tried to eat the Styrofoam stuffing.

Company President Bill Maron ordered all beanbag chairs to be pulled from the market immediately. Bean Chairs' management has decided to design a new series of beanbag chairs made with a more durable covering. They believe that this stronger covering will prevent children from gaining access to the chair stuffing.

You are hired as PR counsel for Bean Chairs, Inc. and are asked to promote the new and improved beanbag chairs. Using the ROPE model, how would you deal with the problems Bean Chairs, Inc. has already experienced? Company management wants to assure the public that the new chairs are absolutely safe for children. The company is very concerned that consumer trust in their products may be in jeopardy.

# 9. INTERNATIONAL PUBLIC RELATIONS

### The Utopian Embassy

Utopia is a Middle Eastern country that was established ten years ago. The country gained independence by overthrowing the ruling Communist party. Although it is located at a geopolitically significant part of the Middle East, Utopia is poor in natural resources. It relies heavily on financial aid from the United States in developing its economy. The U.S.A. has been granting financial aid to the country for the past two years. This year the decision to give aid to the country will be reconsidered. The Utopian embassy is worried about the outcome of the vote because of the media coverage about Utopia. Lately there have been some cases of human rights abuses in the country. These have led to extensive negative media coverage about the country. The Utopian embassy's main objective is to ensure the continuation of the financial aid to the country. Assume that you are the director of public relations for the Utopian embassy. Using the ROPE model, design a campaign to ensure the continuation of that financial aid.

### Sunistan

Sunistan is a country on the southern coast of the Mediterranean. It is a small country flanked with beaches and covered with mountains. Due to its geographic qualities, the country is not developed in agriculture; its main source of income is the tourism industry. Most of the tourists in Sunistan come from its southern neighbors, who are rich in oil but do not border the Mediterranean. Sunistan has a long history of providing high-quality and low-cost holidays; the country also depends on the income of the artifacts it sells to visiting tourists. However, there has lately been a significant decrease in its income from tourism due to clashes between its two eastern neighbors. There have been two instances where the clashes spread over the Sunistani border, and the hotels in the area had to be evacuated for safety reasons. These incidents were covered in depth by the mass media in the neighboring countries and had a negative impact on the country's image. The Sunistani government wants to start a campaign to promote Sunistan as a tourism spot and to persuade past and potential tourists that the country is safe. Using the ROPE model, prepare a campaign to accomplish these objectives.

# 10. SPECIAL PUBLICS

## Jefferson Abused Women's Center

Over the past 10 to 15 years, there has been a significant increase in domestic violence in the United States. The city of Jefferson, Massachusetts, located about an hour south of Boston, has had a particularly high incidence of this type of violence. In response, the city recently constructed a new abused women's shelter. This shelter is designed to serve the women of Jefferson and surrounding communities. Wives and girlfriends of abusive mates are provided with a temporary place to stay, access to psychological counseling, and medical assistance for their injuries.

Ann Walsh, who heads up the new center, was a battered wife for almost 20 years before she finally sought help. For much of her married life, she was unaware that help existed or that anyone cared about her plight. Walsh is anxious to convince battered women in the area that there is a safe place for them to go and that they do not have to remain in an endless cycle of abuse.

You have been hired by Ann Walsh to design a public relations campaign that will encourage battered women to seek aid at the Jefferson Center. The campaign should include innovative ways to convey information about the center's services and should convince women that their choice to visit the shelter may save their lives. Keep in mind that individuals of the target audience may be afraid to break away from their abusive partners. At this time, the shelter has a limited budget and must find inexpensive ways to get the attention of women in the area who may be abused. Use the ROPE model to devise your proposal.

## Pets for Elders

The town of North Adams, just outside of Portland, Maine, has a particularly large concentration of elderly residents. Some have lived there all their lives; others have settled in the area more recently. Many of these elderly residents are able to live and function quite well on their own.

It seems that a majority of them have lost their spouses and have moved to North Adams in an effort to get away from painful memories. The suicide rate is especially high among these older residents. Apparently, many of them suffer from loneliness and the physical deterioration that comes with old age.

An organization called Pets for Elders was formed just a year ago by a young couple who live in the area. The purpose of this organization is to offer elderly persons the chance to adopt a pet to provide them with companionship and love. There are many animals in North Adams in need of good homes and loving owners. Pets for Elders feels that its program may help to solve two problems: (1) elderly residents suffering from severe bouts of depression and loneliness and (2) the vast number of animals that need to be put to sleep because no one can be found to take care of them.

Many elderly people in North Adams are skeptical about the program. Some feel they may be unable to take on the responsibilities of a pet. Others have had no previous experience with animals and are not sure a pet would be a positive addition to their lives. Pets for Elders is anxious to promote the program. The founders would like to expand the organization to other states, yet they must first see if the program can be successful here in North Adams.

Using the ROPE method, devise a PR strategy for promoting the Pets for Elders program.

# 11. EMERGENCY PUBLIC RELATIONS

### Turkish Twist

Cannon Point Amusement Park is located in the town of Concord, New Hampshire. The park has been in existence for 25 years and offers a wide variety of rides and games for children and adults throughout New England. Cannon Point boasts many of the most daring rides in the country, including the largest Ferris wheel and the third-largest roller coaster.

Recently, the park introduced a new ride named the Turkish Twist. Cannon Point promoted the Twist as "a thrilling and exciting ride not meant for the faint of heart." The Twist is modeled in a circular fashion, and passengers are strapped to the sides in an upright position. The ride spins around slowly at first. Eventually, the rate of speed increases and the circular frame of the Twist tilts into a vertical position much like a Ferris wheel. Centrifugal force helps push passengers toward the side walls.

Unfortunately, the Turkish Twist was the site of a terrible tragedy last week. The safety straps designed to hold passengers in place suddenly gave way. As a result, passengers fell into the machinery located at the center of the Twist. No one was killed in the accident, but 15 of the 25 people aboard the ride were seriously injured. Although Cannon Point has remained open since the accident, many of its patrons are now in a panic. They fear there may be other rides at the park that are not safe. This is the first serious accident Cannon Point has experienced in all 25 years of its existence.

You have been hired as the PR director for Cannon Point. Using the ROPE model, design a plan of action that will minimize negative publicity and rebuild the confidence of park visitors.

## United Bus Lines

United Bus Lines (UBL) has its headquarters in Boston, Massachusetts, and has been in operation for 25 years. The company is involved in the tourism business, offering bus tours across the United States to interested travelers. UBL is a well-known and highly respected company throughout the tourism industry and is recommended by many travel agencies as the best way to see the U.S.

Early yesterday evening, a United bus en route to Williamsburg, Virginia, unexpectedly jumped the guardrail of a major highway and collided head on with an 18-wheeler oil truck. Unfortunately, the United bus caught fire upon impact and 34 of the 40 passengers as well as the driver and tour guide were killed instantly. The six passengers who did survive remain in the intensive care unit of a nearby hospital. Only two of these passengers are conscious. The driver of the oil truck was able to escape the accident unharmed.

There is now speculation that the driver of the United bus may have been intoxicated or on drugs. Eyewitnesses have stated that they observed the bus weaving from side to side shortly before the accident. The two passengers who are now conscious have stated that their bus driver was "acting funny" immediately following an hour-long stop for dinner the night of the accident.

You are the PR director for United Bus Lines. Your job is to control the flow of press information concerning the accident as much as possible. You want to avoid any damage to UBL's reputation. You want to do this without minimizing the loss of life sustained in the accident. Using the ROPE model, how would you control press information about the incident? Keep in mind that a loss of confidence in the bus line or its drivers may lead to a drastic decline in business.

# III

# PRSA Code of Professional Standards for the Practice of Public Relations

THIS CODE WAS ADOPTED BY THE PRSA ASSEMBLY IN 1988. It replaces a Code of Ethics in force since 1950 and revised in 1954, 1959, 1963, 1977, and 1983. For information on the Code and enforcement procedures, please call the chair of the Board of Ethics through PRSA Headquarters.

# DECLARATION OF PRINCIPLES

Members of the Public Relations Society of America base their professional principles on the fundamental value and dignity of the individual, holding that the free exercise of human rights, especially freedom of speech, freedom of assembly, and freedom of the press, is essential to the practice of public relations.

In serving the interests of clients and employers, we dedicate ourselves to the goals of better communication, understanding, and cooperation among the diverse individuals, groups, and institutions of society, and of equal opportunity of employment in the public relations profession.

## We Pledge:

To conduct ourselves professionally, with truth, accuracy, fairness, and responsibility to the public;

To improve our individual competence and advance the knowledge and proficiency of the profession through continuing research and education;

And to adhere to the articles of the Code of Professional Standards for the Practice of Public Relations as adopted by the governing Assembly of the Society.

# CODE OF PROFESSIONAL STANDARDS FOR THE PRACTICE OF PUBLIC RELATIONS

These articles have been adopted by the Public Relations Society of America to promote and maintain high standards of public service and ethical conduct among its members.

1. A member shall conduct his or her professional life in accord with the public interest.

2. A member shall exemplify high standards of honesty and integrity while carrying out dual obligations to a client or employer and to the democratic process.

3. A member shall deal fairly with the public, with past or present clients or employers, and with fellow practitioners, giving due respect to the ideal of free inquiry and to the opinions of others.

4. A member shall adhere to the highest standards of accuracy and truth, avoiding extravagant claims or unfair comparisons and giving credit for ideas and words borrowed from others.

5. A member shall not knowingly disseminate false or misleading information and shall act promptly to correct erroneous communications for which he or she is responsible.

6. A member shall not engage in any practice which has the purpose of corrupting the integrity of channels of communications or the processes of government.

7. A member shall be prepared to identify publicly the name of the client or employer on whose behalf any public communication is made.

8. A member shall not use any individual or organization professing to serve or represent an announced cause, or professing to be independent or unbiased, but actually serving another or undisclosed interest.

9. A member shall not guarantee the achievement of specified results beyond the member's direct control.

10. A member shall not represent conflicting or competing interests without the express consent of those concerned, given after a full disclosure of the facts.

11. A member shall not place himself or herself in a position where the member's personal interest is or may be in conflict with an obligation to an employer or client, or others, without full disclosure of such interests to all involved.

12. A member shall not accept fees, commissions, gifts or any other consideration from anyone except clients or employers for whom services are performed without their express consent, given after full disclosure of the facts.

13. A member shall scrupulously safeguard the confidences and privacy rights of present, former, and prospective clients or employers.

14. A member shall not intentionally damage the professional reputation or practice of another practitioner.

15. If a member has evidence that another member has been guilty of unethical, illegal, or unfair practices, including those in violation of this Code, the member is obligated to present the information promptly to the proper authorities of the Society for action in accordance with the procedure set forth in Article XII of the Bylaws.

16. A member called as a witness in a proceeding for enforcement of this Code is obligated to appear, unless excused for sufficient reason by the judicial panel.

17. A member shall, as soon as possible, sever relations with any organization or individual if such relationship requires conduct contrary to the articles of this Code.

# OFFICIAL INTERPRETATIONS
# OF THE CODE

Interpretation of Code Paragraph 1, which reads, "A member shall conduct his or her professional life in accord with the public interest."

The public interest is here defined primarily as comprising respect for and enforcement of the rights guaranteed by the Constitution of the United States of America.

Interpretation of Code Paragraph 6, which reads, "A member shall not engage in any practice which has the purpose of corrupting the integrity of channels or communication or the processes of government."

1. Among the practices prohibited by this paragraph are those that tend to place representatives of media or government under any obligation to the member, or the member's employer or client, which is in conflict with their obligations to media or government, such as:

   a. the giving of gifts of more than nominal value;

   b. any form of payment or compensation to a member of the media in order to obtain preferential or guaranteed news or editorial coverage in the medium;

   c. any retainer or fee to a media employee or use of such employee if retained by a client or employer, where the circumstances are not fully disclosed to and accepted by the media employer;

   d. providing trips, for media representatives, that are unrelated to legitimate news interest;

   e. the use by a member of an investment or loan or advertising commitment made by the member; or the member's client or employer, to obtain preferential or guaranteed coverage in the medium.

2. This Code paragraph does not prohibit hosting media or government representatives at meals, cocktails, or news functions and special events that are occasions for the exchange of news information or views, or the furtherance of understanding, which is part of the public relations function. Nor does it prohibit the bona fide press event or tour when media or government representatives are given the opportunity for an on-the-spot viewing of a newsworthy product, process, or event in which the media or government representatives have a legitimate interest. What is customary or reasonable hospitality has to be a matter of particular judgment in specific situations. In all of these cases, however, it is, or should be, understood that no preferential treatment or guarantees are expected or

implied and that complete independence always is left to the media or government representative.

3. This paragraph does not prohibit the reasonable giving or lending of sample products or services to media representatives who have a legitimate interest in the products or services.

4. It is permissible, under Article 6 of the Code, to offer complimentary or discount rates to the media (travel writers, for example) if the rate is for business use and is made available to all writers. Considerable question exists as to the propriety of extending such rates for personal use.

Interpretation of Code Paragraph 9, which reads, "A member shall not guarantee the achievement of specified results beyond the member's direct control."

This Code paragraph, in effect, prohibits misleading a client or employer as to what professional public relations can accomplish. It does not prohibit guarantees of quality or service. But it does prohibit guaranteeing specific results which, by their very nature, cannot be guaranteed because they are not subject to the member's control. As an example, a guarantee that a news release will appear specifically in a particular publication would be prohibited. This paragraph should not be interpreted as prohibiting contingent fees.

Interpretation of Code Paragraph 13, which reads, "A member shall scrupulously safeguard the confidences and privacy rights of present, former, and prospective clients or employers."

1. This article does not prohibit a member who has knowledge of client or employer activities that are illegal from making such disclosures to the proper authorities as he or she believes are legally required.

2. Communications between a practitioner and client/employer are deemed to be confidential under Article 13 of the Code of Professional Standards. However, although practitioner/client/employer communications are considered confidential between the parties, such communications are not privileged against disclosure in a court of law.

3. Under the copyright laws of the United States, the copyright in a work is generally owned initially by the author or authors. In the case of a "work made for hire" by an employee acting within the scope of his or her employment, the employer is considered to be the author and owns the copyright in the absence of an express, signed written agreement to the contrary. A freelancer who is the author of the work and is not an employee may be the owner of the copyright. A member should consult legal counsel for detailed advice concerning the scope and application of the copyright laws.

Interpretation of Code Paragraph 14, which reads, "A member shall not intentionally damage the professional reputation or practice of another practitioner."

1. Blind solicitation, on its face, is not prohibited by the Code. However, if the customer list were improperly obtained, or if the solicitation contained references reflecting adversely on the quality of current services, a complaint might be justified.

2. This article applies to statements, true or false, or acts, made or undertaken with malice and with the specific purpose of harming the reputation or practice of another member. This article does not prohibit honest employee evaluations or similar reviews, made without malice and as part of ordinary business practice, even though this activity may have a harmful effect.

# AN OFFICIAL INTERPRETATION OF THE CODE AS IT APPLIES TO POLITICAL PUBLIC RELATIONS

## Preamble

In the practice of political public relations, a PRSA member must have professional capabilities to offer an employer or client quite apart from any political relationships of value, and members may serve their employer or client without necessarily having attributed to them the character, reputation, or beliefs of those they serve. It is understood that members may choose to serve only those interests with whose political philosophy they are personally comfortable.

## Definition

"Political Public Relations" is defined as those areas of public relations that relate to:

a. the counseling of political organizations, committees, candidates, or potential candidates for public office; and groups constituted for the purpose of influencing the vote on any ballot issue;

b. the counseling of holders of public office;

c. the management, or direction, of a political campaign for or against a candidate for political office; or for or against a ballot issue to be determined by voter approval or rejection;

d. the practice of public relations on behalf of a client or an employer in connection with that client's or employer's relationships with any candidates or holders of public office, with the purpose of influencing legislation or government regulation or treatment of a client or employer, regardless of whether the PRSA member is a recognized lobbyist;

e. the counseling of government bodies, or segments thereof, either domestic or foreign.

## Precepts

1. It is the responsibility of PRSA members practicing political public relations, as defined above, to be conversant with the various statutes, local, state, and federal, governing such activities and to adhere to them strictly. This includes, but is not limited to, the various local, state, and federal laws, court decisions, and official interpretations governing lobbying, political contributions, disclosure, elections, libel, slander, and the like. In carrying out this responsibility, members shall seek appropriate counseling whenever necessary.

2. It is also the responsibility of the members to abide by PRSA's Code of Professional Standards.

3. Members shall represent clients or employers in good faith, and while partisan advocacy on behalf of a candidate or public issue may be expected, members shall act in accord with the public interest and adhere to truth and accuracy and to generally accepted standards of good taste.

4. Members shall not issue descriptive material or any advertising or publicity information or participate in the preparation or use thereof that is not signed by responsible persons or is false, misleading, or unlabeled as to its source, and are obligated to use care to avoid dissemination of any such material.

5. Members have an obligation to clients to disclose what remuneration beyond their fees they expect to receive as a result of their relationship, such as commissions for media advertising, printing, and the like, and should not accept such extra payment without their client's consent.

6. Members shall not improperly use their positions to encourage additional future employment or compensation. It is understood that successful campaign directors or managers, because of the performance of their duties and the working relationship that develops, may well continue to assist and counsel, for pay, the successful candidate.

7. Members shall voluntarily disclose to employers or clients the identity of other employers or clients with whom they are currently associated, and whose interests might be affected favorably or unfavorably by their political representation.

8. Members shall respect the confidentiality of information pertaining to employers or clients past, present, and potential, even after the relationships cease, avoiding future associations wherein insider information is sought that would give a desired advantage over a member's previous clients.

9. In avoiding practices that might tend to corrupt the processes of government, members shall not make undisclosed gifts of cash or other valuable considerations that are designed to influence specific decisions of voters, legislators, or public officials on public matters. A business lunch or dinner, or other comparable expenditure made in the course of communicating a point of view or public position, would not constitute such a violation. Nor, for example, would a plant visit designed and financed to provide useful background information to an interested legislator or candidate.

10. Nothing herein should be construed as prohibiting members from making legal, properly disclosed contributions to the candidates, party, or referenda issues of their choice.

11. Members shall not, through use of information known to be false or misleading, conveyed directly or through a third party, intentionally injure the public reputation of an opposing interest.

# AN OFFICIAL INTERPRETATION OF THE CODE AS IT APPLIES TO FINANCIAL PUBLIC RELATIONS

This interpretation of the Society Code as it applies to financial public relations was originally adopted in 1963 and amended in 1972, 1977, 1983 and 1988 by action of the PRSA Board of Directors. "Financial public relations" is defined as "that area of public relations which relates to the dissemination of information that affects the understanding of stockholders and investors generally concerning the financial position and prospects of a company, and includes among its objectives the improvement of relations between corporations and their stockholders." The interpretation was prepared in 1963 by the Society's Financial Relations Committee, working with the Securities and Exchange Commission and with the advice of the Society's legal counsel. It is rooted directly in the Code with the full force of the Code behind it, and a violation of any of the following paragraphs is subject to the same procedures and penalties as violation of the Code.

1. It is the responsibility of PRSA members who practice financial public relations to be thoroughly familiar with and understand the rules and regulations of the SEC and the laws it administers, as well

as other laws, rules, and regulations affecting financial public relations, and to act in accordance with their letter and spirit. In carrying out this responsibility, members shall also seek legal counsel, when appropriate, on matters concerning financial public relations.

2. Members shall adhere to the general policy of making full and timely disclosure of corporate information on behalf of clients or employers. The information disclosed shall be accurate, clear, and understandable. The purpose of such disclosure is to provide the investing public with all material information affecting security values or influencing investment decisions. In complying with the duty of full and timely disclosure, members shall present all material facts, including those adverse to the company. They shall exercise care to ascertain the facts and to disseminate only information they believe to be accurate. They shall not knowingly omit information, the omission of which might make a release false or misleading. Under no circumstances shall members participate in any activity designed to mislead or manipulate the price of a company's securities.

3. Members shall publicly disclose or release information promptly so as to avoid the possibility of any use of the information by any insider or third party. To that end, members shall make every effort to comply with the spirit and intent of the timely-disclosure policies of the stock exchanges, NASD, and the SEC. Material information shall be made available on an equal basis.

4. Members shall not disclose confidential information the disclosure of which might be adverse to a valid corporate purpose or interest and whose disclosure is not required by the timely-disclosure provisions of the law. During any such period of nondisclosure members shall not directly or indirectly (a) communicate the confidential information to any other person or (b) buy or sell or in any other way deal in the company's securities where the confidential information may materially affect the market for the security when disclosed. Material information shall be disclosed publicly as soon as its confidential status has terminated or the requirement of timely disclosure takes effect.

5. During the registration period, members shall not engage in practices designed to precondition the market for such securities. During registration, the issuance of forecasts, projections, predictions about sales and earnings, or opinions concerning security values or other aspects of the future performance of the company, shall be in accordance with current SEC regulations and statements of policy. In the case of companies whose securities are publicly held, the normal flow of factual information to shareholders and the investing public shall continue during the registration period.

6. Where members have any reason to doubt that projections have an adequate basis in fact, they shall satisfy themselves as to the adequacy of the projections prior to disseminating them.

7. Acting in concert with clients or employers, members shall act promptly to correct false or misleading information or rumors concerning clients' or employers' securities or business whenever they have reason to believe such information or rumors are materially affecting investor attitudes.

8. Members shall not issue descriptive materials designed or written in such a fashion as to appear to be, contrary to fact, an independent third-party endorsement or recommendation of a company or a security. Whenever members issue material for clients or employers, either in their own names or in the names of someone other than the clients or employers, they shall disclose in large type and in a prominent position on the face of the material the source of such material and the existence of the issuer's client or employer relationship.

9. Members shall not use inside information for personal gain. However, this is not intended to prohibit members from making bona fide investments in their company's or client's securities insofar as they can make such investments without the benefit of material inside information.

10. Members shall not accept compensation that would place them in a position of conflict with their duty to a client, employer, or the investing public. Members shall not accept stock options from clients or employers nor accept securities as compensation at a price below market price except as part of an overall plan for corporate employees.

11. Members shall act so as to maintain the integrity of channels of public communication. They shall not pay or permit to be paid to any publication or other communications medium any consideration in exchange for publicizing a company, except through clearly recognizable paid advertising.

12. Members shall in general be guided by the PRSA Declaration of Principles and the Code of Professional Standards for the Practice of Public Relations of which this is an official interpretation.

# INDEX